BARBARA K. JA

CHASING

BIN LADEN

My Hunt for the World's Most Notorious Terrorist

COPYRIGHT

Library of Congress Control Number: 2020907837
ISBN 9781734978902

DEDICATION

For all victims of terrorism, living and deceased, especially those who have suffered at the hands of Osama bin Laden. We have not forgotten.

TABLE OF CONTENTS

—————

DEDICATION   04
PREFACE   09
RESOURCES   11
PROLOGUE   13

CHAPTER 1: AN UNUSUAL CELEBRATION   15
CHAPTER 2: THE MONSTER TRIP   25
CHAPTER 3: BACK TO NORMALCY?   49
CHAPTER 4: DIAL M FOR MURDER   61
CHAPTER 5: BETWEEN A ROCK AND A HARD PLACE   67
CHAPTER 6: THE FAMILY PARTY   77
CHAPTER 7: THE ACRES HOMES KILLER   95
CHAPTER 8: OTHER EARLY CASES   109
CHAPTER 9: MY HAPPY PLACE   127
CHAPTER 10: RELAX, IT'S JUST PIRATES!   137
CHAPTER 11: THE RAINBOW   147
CHAPTER 12: JOINING THE WAR ON TERROR   153
CHAPTER 13: THE DOCTOR   171
CHAPTER 14: LITTLE RED CORVETTE   179
CHAPTER 15: THE PLAN   189
CHAPTER 16: EVERYONE LIVES!   195
CHAPTER 17: ONWARD!   203
CHAPTER 18: MAKING THE CALL   215
CHAPTER 19: NO DISTRACTIONS   223
CHAPTER 20: THE EYE OF THE HURRICANE   239
CHAPTER 21: THE TRANSATLANTIC AIRCRAFT PLOT   263
CHAPTER 22: THE AMERICAN DREAM   271
CHAPTER 23: THE DIRECTOR   289
CHAPTER 24: THE SEAHORSE   299
CHAPTER 25: WALMART   311
CHAPTER 26: BAHRAIN   319
CHAPTER 27: THE DIRECTOR-Y   329
CHAPTER 28: STARVING FOR ATTENTION   337
CHAPTER 29: INSPIRATION POINT   347
CHAPTER 30: EYE OF THE TIGER   359
CHAPTER 31: CALLING IT IN   365

CHAPTER 32: THE RACE   373
CHAPTER 33: NEW YORK   383
CHAPTER 34: FULL CIRCLE   389
CHAPTER 35: HOUSTON, WE HAVE A PROBLEM!   393
CHAPTER 36: PROVE IT!   401
CHAPTER 37: TEXAS CITY   407
CHAPTER 38: ON THE RUN!   415
CHAPTER 39: CAVE TIME   429
CHAPTER 40: HAMMER OUT WARNING   435
CHAPTER 41: A BRIEF ENCOUNTER WITH CNN   449
CHAPTER 42: PHONE A FRIEND   459
CHAPTER 43: THE STORY OF MY LIFE   475
CHAPTER 44: WAPO   481
CHAPTER 45: NO EXIT   487
CHAPTER 46: MEN IN SUITS   491
CHAPTER 47: MYSPACE   509
CHAPTER 48: ABOVE TOP SECRET   519
CHAPTER 49: REGRETS   537
CHAPTER 50: THE BROOKLYN CONNECTION   549
CHAPTER 51: WHATEVER HAPPENED TO OSAMA BIN LADEN?   561
           TIMELINE   574
CHAPTER 52: A GREAT STORY   577
CHAPTER 53: A TALE OF TWO THERAPISTS   581
CHAPTER 54: OUT OF THE BIN LADEN CLOSET   591
CHAPTER 55: SHIT HAPPENS   603
CHAPTER 56: A NEW BEGINNING   615

EPILOGUE   621
ACKNOWLEDGMENTS   627
NOTES   629
ABOUT THE AUTHOR   657

PREFACE

To say writing this book was hard would be a gross understatement. It took an emotional toll that lasted throughout my entire six-year process. I would often spend weeks at a time avoiding the work because reliving the events from 2006 and beyond was so incredibly painful. And when I'd finally make myself write, it would sometimes cause so much mental anguish that I'd find myself figuratively crying on my editor's shoulder during critique sessions. But over the years, with great effort, I managed to muddle through my anxiety and sorrow and complete this memoir.

I would like to add that because of the unusual nature of my story, many people have criticized it, calling it a work of fiction or an urban myth. But thanks to some clever planning and a little bit of luck, I have retained copies of all the phone and email records of my frequent communications with the Federal Bureau of Investigation (FBI). These documents establish a timeline of my exchanges with the Houston, New York, Texas City, Washington, DC, and other branches.

Anticipating my book launch, I have uploaded these files to my website for public scrutiny. Also on my site is the transcript of a thread from an online forum.[1] It was created fourteen years ago, a few months after Osama bin Laden's arrest. Using the pseudonym Leslie Powers, I shared my experiences with strangers, answering questions and defending my position. The thread still exists on AboveTopSecret.com for anyone who prefers to read it in its original format. You will find that my statements in the thread are consistent with my current narrative.

RESOURCES

Please visit ChasingbinLaden.com/research[2] to download or view copies of phone, email, and message board records. These chronicle my communications with the FBI and my early efforts to share my story. Links to most articles and resources cited in this book can also be found there.

PROLOGUE

I was up most of the night again, with little to comfort me but a large chocolate milkshake from Whataburger. I was starting to see double as I strained to focus on my flickering, tube-type monitor. I had to keep going. People's lives were at stake. I was beyond exhausted, but I was the only one who could do the work—the only one who could follow my system for finding terrorists.

Finally, when my eyes were burning and the words began to jump around on the screen, I had no choice but to stop. I couldn't read any longer. I couldn't focus. The room was dark and cool, and bed sounded nice.

But could I sleep?

I took two sleeping pills and collapsed, fully clothed, on my side of the double bed. As I lay flat on my back, my body sank heavily into the mattress.

Curling a pillow behind my head and under my neck, I felt some sweet relief from my mounting headache. Then, as I pulled a light cover over my body, my heart began to pound quickly, and my breathing became rapid. Instead of decompressing, I began to worry. What if the sleeping pills wouldn't help? They *had* to help this time. I desperately needed rest.

Without rest, I couldn't complete my work. Without rest, I wouldn't be able to think straight or maintain my pace. More importantly, I was terrified that without sleep, I would lose my mind.

I had to sleep. I *had* to.

Slowly my thoughts changed direction, and for what felt like an eternity, my mind mulled over the latest case. I was still working, even as my body began to shut down.

Eventually, my breath began to slow, and my head was filled with splashes of colorful geometrical shapes.

Finally...

Sleep was coming.

Thank goodness...

About an hour into my slumber, at around 4:15 a.m., I spontaneously woke up and for the first time in my life, experienced what could only be described as a moment of clairvoyance.

Feeling ecstatic, I leaned over my partner, Nicki, who was sleeping on her back. I kissed her passionately on her soft, warm lips, then fervently uttered, *"You know we got Osama bin Laden, right?"* A split second later, I rolled back over, glanced at the clock, and immediately fell back asleep.

01

—— ▸ ——

AN UNUSUAL CELEBRATION

Several hours later, the kiss forgotten, my daily routine started over again. I woke up, bleary-eyed, and began working one of my cases by making a barrage of phone calls. I was too entranced to even bother with breakfast. Nearly two hours later, my thoughts returned to RewardsForJustice.net, the government website that listed all of the FBI's most wanted terrorists. I stared at the screen, scouring a short list, uncertain of whom to go after next. This time I'd ask for an opinion.

I flung open my black Nokia flip phone and called the New York FBI. I got through on the third try.

As usual, I introduced myself to the screener as the person who was calling in the Brooklyn tips and asked to speak with the Terrorism Task Force. My call was transferred at 10:34 a.m., on August 16, 2006.

The agent who answered the phone had a mid-ranged, boisterous New York accent. After introducing myself, I confidently stated, "I just want to ask you which terrorist I should go after next."

But instead of advising me, he greeted me with a

playful tone.

My stomach sank as a flood of anxiety washed over me. My mind began to spin. Why did he sound playful? This was odd. FBI agents were usually so humorless.

Did something happen?

Did he *know* something?

I hesitated, stammering, unsure what to say next. But before I could shift into a full panic, a different agent with a deeper voice and thicker New York accent hollered exuberantly from the background.

"Is that the Green Lady?"

My mind started racing. What was that supposed to mean? Why did I have a nickname? It was clear by his tone that it was a term of endearment, but—

Before I had a chance to really process my new nickname, the duty agent on the phone replied loudly and with gusto, "Yeah!" (It's the Green Lady.)

Then the noise in the background was suddenly amplified as I was placed on speakerphone. At that moment, I could hear what sounded like at least a half-dozen male agents cheering and applauding.

The second agent hollered gleefully, this time addressing me directly. "Ya got the lotto picks?"

Confused by the question, I answered in a humorless tone, "No. Why would you think I—?"

For a few minutes, I struggled to continue my friendly banter with the energetic group of federal agents. I was clueless about how to react. I was utterly dumbfounded by the situation and couldn't quite wrap my brain around what was happening.

My responses were no doubt more serious than they should have been, yet my dazed demeanor didn't diminish their enthusiasm. Needless to say, this level of excitement was unprecedented for the normally composed, businesslike FBI agents.

After a few minutes, we said our goodbyes, and I flipped my phone closed, stunned. I stopped and thought for a moment. Why were they excited? So happy, playful? What were they celebrating? Slowly, I began drawing a precursory conclusion.

What tip had I called in a few days prior?

Of course...

Bin Laden... I had called in the location of Osama bin Laden!

A wave of adrenaline washed over me as it sunk in. The New York FBI Terrorism Task Force must have arrested Osama bin Laden that morning because of my tip. An image popped into my mind of federal agents kicking in the door of his Brooklyn apartment at 4 a.m., and taking him in cuffs before he could even remove the sleep from his eyes.

What I didn't know was that my suspicion would be verified over the next twenty-four hours. Just like so many times before, my hunch had been correct.

***

I was still processing what had happened when I heard a loud, mid-toned Californian accent coming from behind me. My body convulsed at the sound.

I wheeled around in my chair. It was Nicki. "What was that about?" I had been unaware that she'd been lying on the bed behind me and had heard everything on my end of the conversation.

I replied in an elated tone, "I think they got him!"

Nicki was a muscular thirty-five-year-old with

straight, long light-brown hair, vivid green eyes, and a quirky sense of humor. She stood in contrast to my robust body, brown eyes, and short, curly, dark hair. Despite her mostly butch demeanor, of the two of us, she was the softer and more feminine.

Nicki often said she admired my tenacity. She would say that when I was working on a goal or project, I was like a pit bull with my jaws clamped tightly to her end of a rope. Once I got started, it was almost impossible to pull the rope away from me. If I latched on to a task, I didn't give up until it was complete. There was no stopping me. I would just snarl and keep tugging. The rope was *mine!* Because of this stubborn quality, Nicki believed that I could accomplish almost anything—even finding Osama bin Laden.

Nicki listened carefully as I laid out the details of my conversation with the FBI. I told her about the commotion on the other end of the line and exactly what the New York agents had said to me. We were both astonished by what had just happened, so we repeatedly went over every minute detail of the phone call as well as the events of the past several days. We needed to know for sure that the celebration meant I had found Osama bin Laden. But no matter what angle we took, the endpoint was always the same: Bin Laden had been arrested that morning.

As we discussed my conversation with the FBI, we analyzed the nickname first. Why would they call me the Green Lady? What did it mean?

After about a half-hour of brainstorming, we drew what seemed like the most likely conclusion: The agents were calling me that because they thought I was going to be "seeing green" by collecting the $25 million reward.

Years later, I would Google "Green Lady" and discover that it's also a colloquial name for the Statue of Liberty. I wondered vaguely if my nickname was meant to be a play on words for "seeing green" and standing strong for America.

But on that day, I hadn't yet made this connection. Satisfied with the "seeing green" explanation, Nicki and I moved on to the next mystery: Why would the second agent ask me if I "got the lotto picks?"

After thinking about it for a few minutes, we remembered the words of a Houston agent. A few days earlier, he had asked me how I found the "Big Guy" (bin Laden). During the conversation, he had also asked me a serious, point-blank question: "Are you psychic?" So, what if the "lotto picks" agent also thought I could be psychic? After all, wouldn't that be the first question a lot of people would ask a true psychic if they met one? "Ya got the lotto picks?" About a week after the arrest, I would be asked once again if I was psychic—this time by CNN.

To the Houston agents, the celebrating New Yorkers, and later, the CNN journalist, there was probably little else to explain how a middle-aged woman living in rural Texas could find the most wanted man on Earth—a feat that had eluded the best minds in the intelligence community for five years.

After our discussion, I rushed to tell Peter and Daun—our kids—the news. They were thrilled. We spent some time fantasizing about the future and the money before they shifted their short attention spans and rushed back to Peter's room to play *Mario Party 7* on his GameCube—their latest obsession.

Meanwhile, Nicki ran to White's Liquor and bought

some cheap champagne. As soon as they made the announcement, we were going to celebrate—celebrate our victory and our new life. After all, I had helped find the world's most notorious terrorist and simultaneously earned $25 million. Our lives would be changed forever, for the better. *So we thought...*

When Nicki got back, I took a moment to shove the pile of "important" papers off the top of the entertainment center, clearing the view for the small tube television we kept in the bedroom. It had been a while since we'd watched back there, so I used an old, white sock to brush a thick layer of dust off the screen. When I finished, I scowled briefly at the sheer amount of filth clinging to the fabric. *Ugh...*

With everything set up, I waded through the mound of dirty laundry on the floor and plopped down on the bed next to Nicki and Midnight, our short-haired black cat. We would spend much of the day excitedly spending the $25 million in our minds and obsessively watching the news for any signs of an announcement. Unlike our kitty, who was calm and on his best behavior, I was full of energy and having trouble waiting. After several hours, I began to grow impatient. *When were they going to make an announcement? When was news of the arrest going to be on CNN? What was taking so long?* My eyes kept wandering from the TV. Occasionally, I'd glance at the blue, pharmaceutical-themed clock on the wall. Time seemed like it was standing still. But mostly, my eyes kept darting nervously toward my monitor. I was like a junkie who needed her fix. I wasn't used to being away from my computer for so long. I pined for the touch of the keyboard, the click of the mouse, the thrill of the hunt, and the mental rush that came from completing my queries.

Of course, anyone who walked into the room could tell how much time I'd spent at that desk. A half-dozen empty Diet Mountain Dew cans were strewn around the workspace, mingling with Snickers wrappers, empty Shipley boxes, crumpled printer paper, piles of plastic cups, and several souvenir coffee mugs. I never bothered to pick up the trash or dishes, or even acknowledge their existence. Only one thing had mattered: the work.

But I couldn't work any more. I couldn't go back to my obsession. Bin Laden had been my ultimate target, so there was no one else left who was worth looking for. I felt like I had completed my mission.

Thank God ...

Honestly, I was glad the work was over. I had been mentally and physically exhausted for weeks. It was time to rest and watch the news. Besides, this was the most time I had spent with Nicki in months. She and I were glued to the set, scrutinizing the news stories and monitoring them for any signs of bin Laden's capture. Several hours into watching, there was nothing relevant in the news.

But wait... What was this? My head shot up as I heard his name for the first time all day: Osama bin Laden.

CNN had announced that in about a week, it was going to air a documentary titled *In the Footsteps of bin Laden*.[3] It would outline his path to 9/11 and beyond.

The timing of the documentary struck me as more than coincidental. Osama bin Laden had been out of the news for years. Yet here he was, his face plastered on the small screen in a movie trailer. On that particular day, the video clip was the only definitive clue I had that something was going on in bin Laden land.

Did CNN know something about bin Laden's arrest? Had they heard rumors? Did they have access to a Washington insider? Maybe they were preparing for a presidential announcement and the excitement that would inevitably surround bin Laden's arrest. Perhaps they were even trying to get the jump on competing networks.

After watching the news for hours and seeing nothing more substantial about bin Laden than the ad for the documentary, I could no longer wait.

I flipped open my phone at 9:47 p.m., and called the FBI in New York for the second time that day. I needed information. But this time, when the screener picked up, I didn't ask to speak to an agent in the Terrorism Task Force. I had a short, simple question, and I didn't want to bother the duty agent.

I knew from experience that asking a direct question to get answers about classified information would be futile. So, on the evening of bin Laden's arrest, I used a tactic I had been taught a few days earlier by a friendly Houston agent. I made my question slightly vague by politely asking, "Can I be optimistic that there will be an announcement from the president?" I expected a normal FBI response such as, "Yes, you can." That way, the agent wouldn't be breaking his oath of secrecy by giving an affirmative answer to a direct question. Instead, the response would tell the truth less explicitly.

This tactic had usually worked for me before. But this time was different. When I asked if I could be optimistic, the agent shocked me by giving a direct answer to my question: "Definitely. Once our report is sent to Washington, the announcement will be made either tonight or early tomorrow morning."

I could almost hear a twinkle in his eyes as he conveyed the information.

I thanked him and quickly ended the conversation. I was anxious to get back to watching CNN.

Wow...the news...the story...*my story* was going to be broadcast either tonight or tomorrow morning! It was confirmed. Before even stopping to tell Nicki or the kids, I started frantically calling everyone in my family. It was late, but I knew they wouldn't mind. I was bursting at the seams. I had *to*...*had to* tell them to watch the news. I made a mad stream of calls and sent an email to my little brother, who was traveling. I had a large family. I told them—anyone who had time to listen—that there was going to be a huge story in the news that involved me. I didn't elaborate. I wasn't ready to tell them. *No*... I would wait. Once they found out about the arrest, I would explain my part in it.

About forty-five minutes later, still invigorated, I rushed to go find Nicki and tell her about the pending announcement. We put the champagne on ice and sat up all night watching CNN.

The ice melted, the champagne grew warm, and the announcement never came.

02

THE MONSTER TRIP

The Road to Hell is Paved with Good Intentions.

Two-and-a-half months earlier, I had just bought a black Hyundai Santa Fe. I decided to celebrate the only new car I'd ever owned by taking Nicki and our children—Peter and Daun (twelve and ten)—on the longest, most extravagant vacation we'd ever been on.

My cousin Nancy was getting married in Yosemite, my favorite place in the world. Growing up, my family and I took annual trips to the National Park, and they had always been sentimental to me. They were full of giant sequoia groves, vibrant waterfalls, spectacular mountains, and long adventures on the park's steep, winding trails. At home base, there were campfires, complete with s'mores, Grandpa's stories, and games of Spite and Malice with Grandma (her favorite card game.) I wanted to relive those experiences with my own kids and partner.

But in 2006, Nicki, the kids, and I would travel beyond Yosemite. As we journeyed throughout California and other western states, we landed in numerous fantastic places, including Lake Tahoe, San Francisco,

Phoenix, Carlsbad, and Roswell. But despite the more exotic stops, one of the most important destinations was the Los Angeles area, where Grandpa and a lot of my favorite kin were still living. For me, our journey was all about family and memories.

We left without planning how long we would be gone or how many stops we'd be making. When it was all over, we would affectionately call our vacation "The Monster Trip" because it was so epic it had taken on a life of its own. In the end, The Monster Trip lasted six weeks, brought us to dozens of locations throughout five states, and cost me around $8,000, effectively maxing out my remaining credit cards.

Grandma had passed away two years earlier, so returning to California was bittersweet. She'd been one of my favorite people, and I missed her. She always had this way of making me feel unique and loved, like I was her favorite. But in reality, all her grandkids were her favorites.

I'll never forget the crisp afternoon when Grandma sat me down and taught me how to play solitaire.

I was seven years old and bored. We were at Yosemite, and we kids and some of the adults had just returned from our trek to Mirror Lake. But it was too soon for dinner or even a campfire. So I knocked on the door of the little, yellow trailer where Grandma was hanging out. The paper-thin metal rattled a bit as I knocked. From behind it, I could hear Grandma's muffled, slightly shaky voice. "Come in."

I swung open the door and stepped up into the cabin. This was no ordinary camper. It was special, a family heirloom. Grandma had bought it back in the '50s using babysitting money. She and Grandpa would keep it and continue to use it until they passed on. Even then, my cousin Clyde—who was as sentimental as the rest of us—took it and renovated it, keeping the beloved trailer in the family.

Inside the miniature dining area, Grandma already had the tiny table folded down. She greeted me and sat me at the bench seat across from her, my feet dangling over the edge.

I started whining, "Gramma, I'm *bored*."

Grandma thought for a moment. "I'll tell ya what. Want me to teach you how to play solitaire?" Her voice had a hint of a Florida accent, though it'd been eons since she lived there.

I looked up at Grandma, curious. "What's that?"

When she explained that it was a game I could play all by myself, I was intrigued. "Sure. Yeah. Teach me!"

Moments later, I watched Grandma as she reached into a nearby drawer and pulled out a bent-up old deck of blue Bicycle cards.

Grandma was a heavyset middle-aged woman with auburn hair and curls that she had professionally set during weekly trips to the beauty parlor. I loved her so much. She was always laughing and smiling and playing games with us kids. She was my favorite person in the whole world.

After she finished shuffling the cards, she looked at me and smiled. "Okay, Barbara, the first thing you do is count them out like this..."

Grandma then demonstrated how to deal the deck, carefully placing the cards in rows. We must have sat there for two hours, just she and I, as she taught me how to play and helped me through my first several moves.

When I finished my first game of solitaire, I looked

up at her with a smile. Then she said words I'll never forget: "Now you don't ever have to be bored. If you get bored, all you need is a deck of cards. You can just play solitaire." With a crooked grin, she added, "My mother used to sit up all night playing, trying to win back all the pretend money she'd lost!"

I had an image of Great-Grandma Virginia, who passed on before I was born, hunched over her own cards, playing into the night by a dimly-lit lamp. Now I knew where Grandma got her love of games. I hoped one day I'd pass that on to my own kids.

My first memory of Grandma was when I was four. She'd collapsed to the ground in pain. I remember how much I cried when the ambulance took her away. I was so worried, it made my stomach hurt. What if she didn't make it back? What if she *died*?

When Grandma returned, I was so happy and relieved that I volunteered to bring her water and other things she needed. After all, she'd been ordered to rest and wasn't supposed to leave her bed. Grandma would call me by clanging a spoon in a glass, and I'd come running. From that moment on, she always called me her "little buddy" and would frequently remind me of how I'd helped her.

That wasn't the only time I stuck by Grandma's side. At Yosemite, her struggles climbing the mountain paths started when I was about ten years old. Grandma never went on any hikes, save one: the hike to the base of Vernal Falls, which was an easy, short one for a girl my age. But that year, Grandma was wearing out. She had back problems and was out of shape, so she kept falling behind. Breathless, she took frequent breaks. I was the only one who would stay behind with her, stopping to sit on rocks next to her as she caught her breath.

Many times, when Grandma would stop, her face would drop. "Honey, I'm gonna turn back. My back hurts. I'm too old for this." She looked sad.

I didn't want her to be sad. Hiking was my favorite thing to do at Yosemite, and I didn't want her to miss out. Besides, I knew she could do it. She *always* made it. I begged her, "No, Gramma. You can do it! It's not too much further. You'll see. And I'm gonna stay with you the whole time."

I was relentless.

With my prodding, she kept going until we eventually made it to the gorgeous bridge at the base of the falls.

I never appreciated how hard it was for Grandma to climb that mountain until I returned at age forty-eight. Like her, I was heavy and having back problems. But every time I thought about quitting, I would remind myself how Grandma pushed herself and made it up that steep incline. I took breaks every few feet, so the going was slow. But eventually, I made it. I had learned from and followed Grandma's perseverance—only this time, I wasn't pushing Grandma. I was pushing myself. And making it to the top felt *amazing.*

Those times with Grandma were the best moments of my life. But there was more to Grandma than her perseverance. She was also a woman of faith—a devout Catholic, always quick to whip out her rosary beads in a moment of peril. Grandma was one of the most anxious people I knew—a worrier. I think it was because she cared deeply for everyone in our family and was constantly terrified that something terrible was going to happen to one of us. Often, prayer was her only solace.

And Grandma passed down her love of the Rosary to me. One time, when I was in second grade, I disclosed to her that I was having trouble sleeping. She told me to pray the Rosary in bed to help me relax—a tip I would use frequently throughout the years.

I remember asking her, "What happens if I fall asleep praying it?"

Grandma replied wisely, "The Virgin Mary will appear at your bedside and finish it for you."

This idea excited me. I wanted Mary to appear at my bedside because it sounded awesome. So I'd sometimes intentionally try to fall asleep while praying the Rosary.

Years later, when I was fifteen and suffering from severe depression, it was Grandma's influence that helped me find hope through faith. I had stopped praying months before and seriously doubted God's existence. I couldn't sleep at night, and I was spending hours listening to depressing music, like Simon and Garfunkel's "I am a Rock:"

> *And a rock feels no pain*
> *And an island never cries*

Life seemed pointless. I began to believe I was going to live a miserable life and eventually die—and then what? Maybe nothing. I felt hopeless.

That summer, Grandma and I watched a movie together one afternoon when we were bored. It was *The Miracle of Our Lady of Fatima*. I picked it because I had seen it as a child and loved it. Plus, I had always been fascinated by the story it was based on.

According to the Church, in 1917, the Virgin Mary had repeatedly appeared to three children in Fatima,

Portugal, and given them messages to pass to the world. These included prophecies and calls for people to pray and repent. On one visit, Mary promised that on October 13, she would give a sign that would make people believe.

It was a drab, rainy day and 70,000 people were gathered in a muddy field watching the children pray while waiting for the promised sign. They were wet, tired, and growing impatient when suddenly the clouds split and the sun appeared in the sky. People were terrified and fell to their knees, into the mud, as they saw the sun change colors and dance around in the sky for a full ten minutes. Some even saw it spin around and plummet towards Earth. They also discovered they could stare directly into it and not be blinded. When it was over, all the people and the Earth itself had inexplicably become completely dry. At the same time, a wave of renewed faith flooded the crowd.[4]

After watching the movie, like the people in the story, I experienced a renewed sense of faith. All of these people—these witnesses—couldn't be lying. I wanted to believe. I wanted to be like those people, like the children, and have *that* sort of unwavering belief in God. My life would be easier if I no longer doubted his existence and could find a reason to live.

Because of the movie and Grandma's influence, I started to pray regularly. And every time I did, I felt a little better, a little less depressed. Although the sadness was still there, I began to feel well enough to want to live. Grandma didn't know it, but her faith and caring may have saved me from suicide.

So in 2006, with my thoughts fixed on Grandma and the rest of my mother's side of the family, Nicki, the kids, and I headed to the happiest place from my past: California. I wanted them to experience the pure joy I had felt there. I wanted to give them that gift.

I was willing to spare no expense. The trip meant that much to me. What I didn't realize at the time was that it would signal the end of my credit and the beginning of a bold, desperate effort to salvage my finances.

***

The first stop—the excuse for our long excursion—was Nancy's wedding in Yosemite. Nicki, the kids, and I were lucky and managed to land a tent site on the valley floor, where we would spend an entire week.

The park brought back countless memories.

One summer, when I was about six, my family and I were sitting around the firepit late at night when I heard people walking in the woods, hollering a name as if they were looking for someone. I was scared for them. Had their child wandered off? My stomach tightened into a knot as I began to worry.

Finally, with a sad little whine to my voice, I asked Grandpa, "Can you tell what they're yelling? I think a kid might be lost."

Grandpa was a muscular, hyper-active man who had a pot-belly, despite working out at Jack LaLanne's gym every day. He was prematurely gray but sometimes let Grandma dye it darker. He often laughed so hard he'd give himself asthma attacks. Despite having near-genius-level intelligence, he had been forced to leave college early and get a job to support his mother and siblings after his father abandoned them. Eventually, Grandpa went to work for the United States Postal

Service, helping man their train cars. On one stop-off in Florida, he met Grandma and immediately fell in love. The rest is history.

Above all, Grandpa was a father and grandfather. He loved to play with and tease us children, often giving us annoying nicknames. Mine was "Mulie" because I was *as stubborn as a mule*. I hated it when he called me that.

Regardless, that night in Yosemite, when I was a kid, Grandpa seemed amused when I asked him about the people hollering in the distance. "No. There's no one lost. They're just looking for Elmer." And then he told me the long-since forgotten tale of Yosemite's favorite bear.

In 2006, with this story still on my mind, I looked across the roaring flames toward my children. My son had already stopped roasting marshmallows. He'd had his fill.

Peter had always been a cute, smart, funny, sentimental little boy. And even though, unlike me, he had blond hair and blue eyes, he looked more like me and almost nothing like his father—so much so that his dad and I used to joke that he was really the "milkman's son." I was constantly bragging about him and how brilliant he was, emphasizing how he'd been reading since he was barely three—not even out of diapers. In preschool, his teacher would sit him in front of the class and give him a book he'd never seen before and have him read it to the group. He also had an amazing singing voice, with perfect pitch, and had been accepted into the Houston Boychoir when he was eight.

But right now, in camp, Peter was busy standing by the pit, catching a stick on fire and swirling the ember end around, forming loops, as if it was one of the sparklers we played with every Fourth of July. I had taught him that trick. I also had shown him how you could write on the rocks with the charred end. I explained that Abraham Lincoln had taught himself to write using that technique. I loved that Peter was playing with the glowing stick. It made me happy because it had been one of my favorite things to do by the fire when I was his age. I was also glad to see him doing something other than sitting at home playing video games. *Yes...* This trip was good for him.

As for the fiery stick, as a mom, I felt obligated to shoot out a warning: "Can you stand back a little? I'm afraid you're gonna accidentally burn Daun."

Peter moved a few steps away from his sister. "Don't worry, Mom. It's fine."

"I'm not worried," I lied. "I just want you to be careful." I imagined the hot coal on the stick poking Daun in the eye.

Peter looked at me with annoyance written across his face. "I'll be careful, I promise... You worry too much."

"I know. It's my job. I'm your Mom."

He smiled a bit and put the stick back into the fire to relight the ember.

I looked toward Daun. Her third set of marshmallows was dangling over the fire on the end of a coat hanger.

Daun looked a lot like a smaller, girlier version of me. She had the family's signature dark, curly hair and brown eyes. She also shared a lot of my personality traits, especially stubbornness and intelligence. Daun was as smart as Peter, but in different ways.

While he was more mathematical and book-smart, she was creative. She was a sketch artist, a sculptor, and a thinker—quick to analyze a situation and come up with solutions. She was also more energetic and devious than Peter. I always had to keep a close eye on her.

I watched as Daun intentionally caught her marshmallows on fire, pulled them away from the pit, and watched them burn until they were completely black. Eventually, she blew them out, leaving a charred mess.

I looked at her. "Do you do it that way just to watch them burn, or do you *actually* like them that way?" Daun had always had a fascination with fire—so much that I didn't let her cook on the stove until she was a sophomore in high school. I was afraid she'd accidentally burn the house down.

Daun looked up and gave me a devious grin. "Yes, I *actually* like them this way."

"I like them that way too, sometimes." Grinning maniacally, I added, "But I personally think you just like to watch them burn because you're a total firebug."

I shifted my gaze back to the pit for a few seconds, once again entranced by its crackling, orange flames. Then I glanced at Nicki before panning back across the blazing fire toward the kids.

"Did I ever tell you the story of Elmer?"

Peter looked at me blankly, apparently as mesmerized by the fire as I was. "No, I don't think so—"

Daun cut him off. She was curious. "Who's Elmer?"

Then I passed on what was told to me around the campfire all those years ago.

"When I was a kid, Great-Grandpa once told me that back in the day, Yosemite Valley used to have a trash heap. Every day, some of the bears would gather at the dump looking for food. Soon, people began congregating around there at certain times of day, hoping to see the bears and take pictures. Everyone's favorite was Elmer. He was friendly and often appeared to be posing for the camera. But one day, Elmer turned up missing, and everyone was upset. So the campers started wandering around the Valley hollering, 'Elmer! Elmeeeeeer! *Elll-meeeeeer!*' looking for him. This continued for days, and eventually looking for Elmer became a Yosemite tradition. To this day, you can occasionally hear people wandering around, hollering 'Elmer!' at the top of their lungs."

I paused, looking at Nicki and the kids, and made a suggestion: "Let's do it right now." So, we all started hollering *"Elmer!"* in unison, like so many tourists before us. But we couldn't do it too loudly because it was nearly 10 p.m., and many people were in bed. Despite this, it was still fun.

Telling that story, I found myself reminiscing on the way Grandma and Grandpa interacted with each other and us children. One morning, after what felt like an eternity to a hungry little tomboy, Grandma finally came out of the trailer. She put our paper plates on the wooden picnic table, which had been carefully covered by a vinyl, red-and-white checkered tablecloth.

It was a typical breakfast when I was a child camping in Yosemite with Grandma and Grandpa. While the cousins were enjoying bacon, eggs, and pancakes, we would get corned beef hash, eggs, and toast. I always secretly thought my cousins' food was better. But my grandparents had lived through the Great Depression and knew how to save money.

After a few minutes, Grandpa nudged me and

whispered, *"Watch this."*

While Grandma was cleaning up in the trailer, Grandpa cupped his hands on his mouth like a megaphone and hollered loudly toward Grandma.

"You sure open a good can, Heidi!"

Grandma, who was always quick with a reply, poked her head out of the trailer. Using her signature shrill scream, she hollered, "Shut up, Jamie!" Her screams were so loud that he'd joke she was the reason he'd gone deaf in his left ear.

And after Grandma hollered at him to shut up, Grandpa burst out laughing. With a flash of her dentures, a big smile spread over Grandma's face as she dismissed Grandpa's teasing with a small flick of her wrist. Maybe we didn't get the pancakes, but we got the best food because Grandma cooked it.

More than ten years after The Monster Trip, Nicki and I would celebrate what would have been Grandpa's 104th birthday, were he still alive. She served me that same meal of corned beef hash, eggs, and toast in his honor.

Moments after we began to eat, I hollered across the table, "You sure open a good can, Nicki!"

She yelled back, shrilly, "Shut up, Barbara!"

We both giggled. Moments later, I felt tears welling up in my eyes.

***

Regardless, the next stop on The Monster Trip, after Yosemite, was Lake Tahoe. When I was a kid, my favorite part of Tahoe was camping by Fallen Leaf Lake on the California side. But nightly, we'd hit the casinos on the Nevada side. This was my least favorite part of Tahoe, but I did like the buffets. We always stopped at one before the adults would gamble, often the one at Caesar's Tahoe.

I remember one particular visit there. I was barely fourteen, but I could pack away massive quantities of food. At the buffet, I tried every type imaginable until I felt like my stomach was going to burst open. My poor six-year-old little brother, Allen, was miserable. But every time he'd finish his plate, Grandpa would laugh and say, "Are you full yet?"

Allen, who was the only blond-haired, hazel-eyed kid in the family, was always eager to please. So, he would gesture his level of fullness by saying, "I'm full up to here." He would then cock his hand on his forehead, military-style, to indicate how far up his body the food had filled him. All along, he was holding his breath a bit, looking like a stuffed tick.

But Grandpa would push him. "I guess you're not quite full yet. Go back an' get more." Grandpa took great pleasure in watching his grandchildren eat and would laugh hysterically as Allen headed back to the buffet for some more chocolate pudding.

Before leaving, Grandma started to wrap a few pastries in a napkin, preparing them to go in her oversized purse. Mom seemed embarrassed by her mother and whispered loudly while fluttering her eyelids nervously (something she does frequently.) "Mom, I don't think you're supposed to take food with you. It's only 'all you can eat' while you're here."

I looked toward Grandma and smiled. I didn't care if she took some snacks to the slots with her. I thought it was funny that her daughter—my mother—even in her early forties, was still embarrassed by her. Mom was also mortified when Grandma would sing in public or tell strangers her "whole life story" while waiting in line at the grocery store.

But on that day at the buffet, Grandma wasn't singing or talking to strangers. Instead, she was holding her ground regarding her bounty. She matched my mother's tone with a calm, but equally loud whisper, "We paid for it. We might as well take advantage of it."

Her purse was wide open, but she paused before putting anything in. I think Mom was making her feel a little guilty—an emotion that had been passed around by all generations in our family, especially among the women.

Grandpa glared at Mom, who was sitting next to him. Waving his hand dismissively and speaking with his thick Bronx accent, he did something he always excelled at: He expressed his opinion. "There now, Betty, just let your mother take it."

Then, in typical Grandpa fashion, he began a lecture, his voice cracking slightly from old age. "Ya see, the casinos here, they got it all figured out. They give you things like low-cost bus tickets, cheap buffets, and free drinks to draw you in. Then once you're there, they got you."

Flicking his wrist contemptuously, he continued, "*They* don't care if she brings a little food with her, as long as she takes it to the slot machines and starts gambling."

At this point, he sounded slightly annoyed. Grandpa had consistently been very cynical about the system and the way things worked. And in this case, he was right. Offering extravagant buffets was a popular marketing technique.

Mom gave up. Grandpa was always right—so he thought—and he always got the final say. She knew there was never any point in arguing with him because he was the most stubborn man she knew. So Grandma smiled as she continued to meticulously wrap the pastries in napkins and shove them in her purse. I handed her a muffin from off my plate. "Here, Gramma. You want this one too? I haven't even touched it."

Grandma looked at me warmly, gently taking the muffin from my hand. "Thanks, honey."

Finally, we all got up, and my family walked us miserably full, sleepy, but happy youths to the arcade. We would be given a five-dollar roll of quarters each, which we would stretch for a few hours while the adults gambled. At the time, it felt like a lot of money. Besides, the games were only a quarter each back then.

Despite the allure of *Pac-Man, Galaga, Frogger,* and *Dig Dug,* at that point I just wanted a nap. The meal had done me in. I longed for a couch or a room in the hotel, but there was no sleeping at the casinos. Honestly, I just wanted to go back to camp and enjoy a nice fire.

Camping was by far the best part of Tahoe. So, decades later, when I brought Nicki and the kids to the area, we spent most of our time camping. But we did make a casino run one night.

I quickly realized I wasn't having fun. The food didn't taste as good as I remembered, and I hated gambling because I hated losing money. I gave up after losing only five dollars. To make matters worse, the lights and noise caused me to have a severe anxiety attack, and the thick cigarette smoke made me feel like I was going to suffocate. We never went back to the casinos or the

Nevada side of Lake Tahoe.

Later that night, the casino trip behind us, we set up a campfire. But it was late, and we were tired. Unfortunately, Peter tripped over the big rusty grill that was sitting next to the fire and fell in the flames, burning his arm.

My mind immediately flashed back to my childhood adventures at Yosemite. My cousin Andrea was about four when she fell in a firepit and had to be rushed out of the valley to a nearby town. Before leaving, they held her arm in a large chest full of mostly melted ice. I remember being terrified for my little cousin. My stomach was in knots, and I was crying uncontrollably. The adults had to keep reassuring me. "She'll be fine. We're taking her to the doctor so they can take care of her."

I wasn't hearing it. I was afraid of people dying from fire. I thought back on the time the curtains in our house burst into flames from some faulty wiring. I was about five. My older sister, Anne, had appeared at my bedroom window and lifted me out as I hopped off the bed.

I remembered sitting in the back of our "woody" station wagon that was parked in our driveway. I was sobbing loudly as my high-school-aged brother, Jerry, and Daddy were trying to put out the fire with a bucket and a garden hose. I was terrified that they were going to get killed and our house was going to burn to the ground. I prayed really hard to God that they would be okay and nothing like this would ever happen again. Nothing ever did, and I always believed it was because God had heard my prayer.

Remembering little Andrea's burn experience, we

immediately put Peter's arm in the ice chest. Then, we gave him some Tylenol and went to bed. When the burn blistered the next day, we knew it was second-degree, so Nicki drove Peter to Carson City to see a doctor.

But the fire incident didn't slow us down for long. Next, we made brief stops in San Francisco and Pacifica, followed by a long, gorgeous trip along the Pacific Coast Highway. We finally arrived in the Los Angeles area about a week later.

We stayed with Grandpa in his small yellow-green home in Panorama City, the place where he'd lived with Grandma for more than fifty years. The front yard had huge shade trees and both pink and yellow roses. And then there were the gardenias—Grandma's favorite flower. She used to cut a few of the white flowers off the bush and put them in a bowl of water on a shelf. It would fill the entire house with the scent of the sweet blossoms. To this day, I can't see or smell a gardenia without thinking about her.

Sadly, in 2006, the yard wasn't the same. Grandpa had stopped watering the lawn when Grandma died. It was nothing but dirt. He'd hire people to blow around the dust. The roses and gardenias were unkempt but somehow still growing. I suppose he must have been watering *them*, at least.

Inside, along the wall in the living room, was the same lime-green, vinyl, hide-a-bed couch that had been there for as long as I could remember. And catty-corner from it were the ancient rocker recliners where Grandma and Grandpa sat. Grandma's chair, which had an unstable frame from so much use, was still there, even though she'd passed away a couple of years prior.

In many ways, the place seemed more like a

mausoleum than a home. All of Grandma's stuff was still there. Her clothing was still hanging in the closet, including her signature pink polyester pantsuit; family games—like *Scrabble* and *Life*—were stacked on the shelves; the eighteen-inch, blue-robed statue of the Virgin Mary was unmoved; and her glow-in-the-dark rosary was still hanging from the bedpost of her twin bed, which sat a few feet from Grandpa's separate bed.

The bedroom configuration, which remained the same, still reminded me of Bert and Ernie's bedroom on Sesame Street. Grandma and Grandpa had settled on twin beds early on because Grandpa moved around a lot in his sleep, and Grandma was a light sleeper.

And all of Uncle Frank's stuff was still in his room at the end of the hall, although he'd died of AIDS about ten years prior. I'll never forget Grandma's grief at losing her baby boy, who was only in his thirties at the time of his death. He was a very talented musician who always hoped to make it big. The remnants of his impromptu studio were still in his room, untouched: a dusty 1980s-model IBM computer, an old-school synthesizer, an electronic keyboard, and other relics from the past. I remember spending hours with him as he demoed his equipment and showed Allen and me how to play *Zork*—the world's most well-known text adventure—on his computer.

Grandma and Frank's stuff would remain in the house until Grandpa passed away in 2011. When my family was clearing it out so it could be sold, I sat on the beloved ugly couch and heaved heavy tears until I was exhausted and dehydrated.

I never went back, even to look for Grandma's glow-in-the-dark rosary, which was the only thing of hers

I wanted. Fortunately, Aunt Dani, my mother's sister, found it and brought it to me. I was incredibly grateful. To this day, it hangs from my bedpost in Grandma's honor.

But in 2006, not long after we arrived at the house, we went into the backyard. The same beloved travel trailer was still parked on the slab leading to the garage. I smiled, thinking back on Yosemite, Grandma and Grandpa's favorite place. Then, I showed Nicki and the kids the best part of the backyard: a lemon tree and an orange tree, lined up next to each other. Unfortunately, they were shadows of their former glory because they had been so over-trimmed over the years. The orange tree only had a few sad Valencias. But the lemon tree, despite its size, was still bursting full of fruit.

I thought back to when I was a kid. My little brothers, Lee and Allen, and I would pick all the good ones off the ground. Grandma would make us orange juice and lemonade in exchange for our labor. So when we arrived at Grandpa's house, Nicki and I did the same for Peter and Daun. They loved collecting the fruit—especially Daun. Nicki took it from them and happily made fresh lemonade.

The next day, we found ourselves driving around my grandparents' old neighborhood. I quickly realized that something had changed. The area wasn't the place I remembered; it was run-down and impoverished. The shops and stores we used to walk to had long since closed. And sadly, I wasn't comfortable letting my kids walk alone in the area, a freedom I used to enjoy when I was their age. I remember how fascinated I had been that stores were within walking distance of Grandma and Grandpa's place—a luxury that didn't exist in my rural hometown.

Back when I was a kid, their neighborhood was special to me. I remember walking along mostly-shady sidewalks to the shops that existed back then. First, there was Thrifty's, the nickel-and-dime store where we ate tasty, odd-looking ice cream cones with cylindrical scoops of various flavors piled on top of each other. Next to Thrifty's was Vons—a grocery chain that didn't exist in Texas. I was always bored when I was dragged into that store. I'd whine, "Mom, do we have to go in there?"

And she'd say, "Just for a minute." But it was never a minute; it was always an eternity of boredom. I never liked grocery stores, even if I got a treat at the end of the excursion.

I also remembered my favorite local shop, located on that same corner: Winchell's Donuts. We never got donuts at home unless they were homemade. Mom used to shape Pillsbury biscuit dough balls into rings and deep fry them in a pan. Then, she'd put the hot "donuts" in a small paper sack filled with cinnamon-sugar and shake it. They were delicious, and we were always excited when she made them, but we knew that they weren't real donuts.

A ten-minute walk in the opposite direction from Winchell's, Vons, and Thrifty's were a bowling alley, a movie theater, and a small shopping mall. The freedom I felt cruising the neighborhood was unreal. I couldn't believe there was so much to do, even without the luxury of a car.

On The Monster Trip, we would see a lot of close relatives: numerous aunts, uncles, cousins, and cousins' kids. The memories of Yosemite and Southern California weren't only mine, but theirs. We had a wonderful, tightknit, extended family, and I never got tired of spending time with them. Each and every one of them was precious to me. But the main reason I was in Southern California was to see Grandpa. After all, he was in his nineties, and people don't live forever.

Peter and Daun seemed to love him as much as I did. They couldn't believe how energetic and playful he was for a man his age. And they were just as fascinated by his stories as I was. Grandpa had always been a great storyteller.

One time, Daun admonished Peter when Grandpa was telling a story, "*Listen. This is good.*" She didn't want to miss a moment. They both listened intently as he reminisced about the Great Depression—his favorite topic.

Grandpa told us about the time he spent a voucher for a bag of coal and dragged his extremely hefty cargo all the way home, only to find out that he'd been ripped off and given slate instead of coal. He and his single mother and siblings nearly froze to death that winter—a genuine possibility, living in the heart of the Bronx. Without fuel to feed their furnace, they were left searching the streets for packing crates and other scraps of wood, ultimately chopping up their furniture to survive.

With little prodding, Grandpa continued to tell stories. Born in 1911, Grandpa had lived long enough to witness technology evolve tremendously. He remembered when radio was first introduced to the public. He had been sitting with an old woman in her home the first time she heard a broadcast. With a mono sound plug attached to her ear, she had been frightened by the music playing from "nowhere." She started rocking back and forth and in a terrified voice repeated over and over again, "I can't believe it. I can't believe it! *I can't believe it!*"

Regardless of Grandpa's amazing stories, I think the reason Peter and Daun loved him so much was that he was fun. On a different visit, when the kids were younger, he had picked up his newspaper and rolled it, as if to throw it away. But when Daun walked by, he swatted her on the butt with it. Before long, it turned into a game. Peter and Daun took turns running past Grandpa as he tried to get them with the newspaper. He kept laughing loudly, while repeatedly telling them, "If this old man can swat you with the newspaper, you're too slow!" It was hard to believe "this old man" was ninety-three.

Unfortunately, my children never got to know Grandma like they did Grandpa. They met her for the first time in 2002, during their first visit to California. They were six and eight. The kids and I hitched a ride in Mom and Tim's motorhome. They were retired, avid RVers. Unfortunately, the trip came too late for Peter and Daun to see Grandma in her full glory. By that year, she was weak from a series of mini-strokes and couldn't play games. She wasn't as much fun as she used to be, but she was still sweet, and Daun remembers that. Grandma's spirit always managed to shine through.

One day, on the same trip when the kids met Grandma, I was sitting next to her on the couch at the home of my Uncle Allen, after whom my little brother was named. She gently touched my face, giving me sweet words of encouragement. I don't remember all of her words, but it was the most genuine moment I have ever had with her. She told me how special I was and how much she loved me. And one last time, she said the words that always warmed my heart: *"And remember, you'll always be my little buddy."*

But, despite Grandma's absence in 2006, The Monster Trip brought back a plethora of happy memories and allowed me to share those moments with Nicki and our children. Because of this, the trip had been really important for me—more important than I even realized at the time. I didn't know it then, but our vacation was a much-needed respite in the wake of the coming storm.

03

BACK TO NORMALCY?

When we finally returned home from our month-and-a-half-long journey, Midnight, our kitty, greeted us skittishly at the door. He had a look on his face that said, "Where the fuck have y'all been all this time?"

Then, in an atypical move, he slunk under the coffee table and avoided us most of the day. He was pissed. It took him several days to get back to his usual, loving self, and I suppose it took us just as long to start feeling normal. The first thing I did was sleep for nearly three days straight. It was so nice to be back in my own bed, in my own comfort zone.

Within a week, I began trying to return to my ordinary life. I called Adam, who was both a close friend and my boss, to tell him I was ready to get back to work.

I had met Adam about a year prior after calling a random computer repair shop that was listed in the phone book. He'd given me a chance back when the only experience I had was fixing my own personal computer (PC) issues. When he agreed to interview me, he asked me to meet him at, arguably, the crappiest burger joint in Pasadena, the dingy older suburb where Adam operated his business.

The next day when I walked into Brawny Burgers, the place stank heavily of old grease and BO. I panned the room and saw a man sitting alone in a far corner—a stout man of average height, with light-brown, slightly disheveled hair, and square-ish metal-framed glasses. Everything about him screamed, "Geek!" *Yes...* That *had* to be him. I walked up and introduced myself.

We sat across from each other separated by a wobbly table that was haphazardly covered by a traditional red-and-white checkered tablecloth. I noted a cigarette burn on one corner. *Classy...* I would spend the next couple of hours trying to convince Adam I could be of use to his business.

First, I explained my background in computers. My big selling point had been that I was enrolled in an online class to get my A+ Certification, the gold standard for computer repair techs. I assured Adam that I was pretty far along in the course and was progressing well.

I also told him that I had recently dropped out of the software engineering master's program at the University of Houston-Clear Lake (UHCL). Taking a moment, I began thinking back on my history with and love of computers, sharing some of my thoughts sporadically with Adam.

I had started out at UHCL in the Computer Information Systems (CIS) program, seeking a bachelor's degree that would allow me to begin a career as a computer programmer. The school's computer science department had been created to train NASA computer engineers and is located close to the Houston Space Center. UHCL's program is considered one of the better ones of its type in the country, attracting students from all over the world.

Studying programming was a natural choice for me. My sister and brother, Anne and Allen, had both been heavily recruited in the field during the '90s and made good money, although Anne had given up her position a few years back in favor of raising children. Regardless, I found that my first degree, which was in liberal arts, was getting me nowhere. I wanted to follow the money and work in a field I knew I would love.

I'd been infatuated with computers since 1983, the year my mother brought home an Apple IIe. Allen and I spent hours on it, playing games together. And after Anne, who was already working in the computing field, taught us a few tricks, we started writing our own code. In his current home, Allen still proudly displays a large floppy disk that contains a copy of one of our *Apple Basic* collaborations—a text adventure called *Adventures in Invory*—inspired by Uncle Frank's demo of *Zork*. Allen went on to get a master's in computer science and has worked as a coder for more than twenty years. And like him, I excelled in programming.

Some of my professors noticed my propensity for the subject. Dr. Mitchell was a pot-bellied older professor with a bad comb-over. He always left his office door open, signaling that he was readily available for students. So, one day I walked into his office to ask questions about a particularly complex problem on his last data structures exam. After mulling over the topic for a while, Dr. Mitchell said the most complimentary words I could hear from a professor: *"You have a superior brain."*

Nicki and I never got tired of quoting him after that. He quickly became my favorite professor.

I really loved coding, and it challenged me in all

the right ways. Every day, there was a new puzzle to solve. Above all, my favorite programming language was assembly—one of my peers' most-dreaded topics. I think the basic structure and repetition played well with my obsessive nature.

But after a couple of years, I discovered that most coding jobs were being outsourced to India. A teachers' assistant about to graduate from the master's program had shared with me that it could take longer than a year to find work, if ever. I felt sad for her and discouraged about my own prospects. If a person with her talent and a master's degree couldn't get work, what chance did I have with a bachelor's degree? When I looked at the job market online, there were almost no listings for entry-level positions.

Not long after my discovery, Allen and most of his colleagues were laid off from their prestigious positions with a tech giant. Even this software behemoth was moving most of its operations overseas. Information technology jobs in America, like manufacturing, were going the way of the dodos. It was a new world and a global economy, fueled by increased worldwide communications and expanded internet technology. Ironically, the same technology that made Allen's career possible had destroyed it.

Discouraged, I decided to drop out of the CIS program. It seemed like a waste of time. However, I had heard that there was still a high demand for software engineers, so I decided to take my credits and use them as the basic requirements to apply for the university's software engineering master's program. With my record, I was easily admitted.

Once I began the program, I found that software

engineering was way easier than programming, but not as much fun. For me, software engineering was crushingly boring. It didn't even feel like a real science. It felt more like art. In fact, it was often compared to architecture in textbooks and by professors. Minimally, I thought of it as a soft science, like psychology.

And to make matters worse, I found out that, like with programming, my job prospects were grim. Entry-level software engineers were expected to be expert programmers with years of real-world experience. Most of my classmates were already seasoned programmers. Once again, I found myself completely discouraged. Why was I wasting my time getting a degree in a field I thought was boring when I probably wasn't going to be hired at the end of it? I dropped out of that program as well.

After telling Adam some of my lengthy history, I explained to him that I had decided to drop software altogether in favor of hardware, which was more fun for me. I also told him about how I'd spent years repairing my own machines, obsessing on every project until the job was done. So I felt confident I could learn the trade.

***

A few days later, I made the forty-five-minute drive to Pasadena. I'd be joining Adam as his sole employee at Computer Doctors.

When I arrived at work on the first day, Adam showed me around the shop, which was a rather large, dusty warehouse space with white walls and a matching, but dirty, tile floor. In the back of the room were a few tall metal utility shelves full of random electronic clutter. Along the right wall were a couple of long, brown, scratched-up tables that housed three computer stations, each composed of an old-fashioned CRT monitor, a mouse, and a keyboard. There were also a couple of whitish tables with a few random parts and peripherals on them, but not much else. Adam explained that the stations were for hooking up the customers' towers, and the blank tables were for more intense hardware work, such as replacing parts.

Sitting on one of the tables was a serial mouse. I had seen one like it before. I remembered using it on my first IBM-compatible system—a filthy, white, mid-sized Packard Bell that was handed down to me from my father-in-law. It came equipped with tech-nology that was already ancient for 1999: *Windows 3.1*, a 486DX processor, a 1400 baud modem, and a hefty 16 megabytes of random-access memory (RAM). At that point, PS2 mice—the kind with the green plug and tiny prongs—were much newer technology, and even they were already being phased out in favor of USB 1.1. Today, most modern computers don't even have serial ports. They've gone the way of floppy drives and tape back-up systems.

Seeing the mouse in Adam's workshop that day, I couldn't help but think, *My God, serial mice still exist?* But Adam had a reason for keeping it around, explaining that sometimes the serial mouse would work when PS2 or USB technology failed. As outdated as it may have seemed, this handy little serial mouse would get me out of a few sticky situations down the road.

We shifted our attention away from the serial mouse to the center of the floor. There was a huge graveyard where filthy machines from eras spanning a decade had been left to die, in various states of disassembly. Also scattered in the pile were random components: old network adapters, 56k modems, floppy drives, and AGP graphics cards, alongside dozens of random twisted cables and other computer junk.

I immediately felt at home.

Adam explained that most of the machines in the graveyard were for spare parts. And some of them he thought were salvageable and could be fixed at some point and sold. Many of them had all working components, except for the most critical: the motherboard. The early 2000s were the height of the "capacitor plague," when hundreds of thousands of machines died due to defective capacitors that had been produced by certain popular Taiwanese manufacturers. Often, a repair job would end abruptly with the discovery of one of those leaky, bulging little bastards.

After showing me around, Adam looked at me intently and asked me for my opinion of the place.

"I can't wait to start!" It was true. I was thrilled.

Adam then took a slight bow, spreading out his arms and waving them politely as though he were ending a theater performance.

Then he said coyly, "Did you notice?"

I stared at him.

"Don't you get it?" He seemed, exasperated.

I kept staring.

"Look at my outfit!"

I looked at him and let out a loud laugh. "Oh yeah! You're wearing scrubs!"

Sure enough, he had even picked the same shade of blue frequently donned by nurses. Adam then placed his hands on his hips and sassed, "Don't you get it?

Computer Doctors! I'm the doctor for computers!"

At that point, I knew Adam was okay. *What a nerd...*

Needless to say, we hit it off right away.

Not long after the tour, I started my first repair job. The first thing Adam did was ask me to seat a stick of RAM.

"I know how to do this," I told him confidently. "I've done it before."

I placed the pc2100 RAM in the slot, plugged in the machine, and turned it on, only to be greeted by a dark monitor and a series of obnoxious beeps coming from the motherboard. I had failed. A wave of anxiety rushed over me. *What if I had broken something?*

As my anxiety grew, Adam patiently demonstrated that I had to loosen the clips and listen for a loud *snap* as I popped in each side of the stick. And of course, it would help if the RAM was turned in the right direction.

I quickly found that I enjoyed fixing computers more than any previous job. For me, it was fun. Each repair project was a new puzzle to solve, a new challenge. The more difficult, the better. When I returned home every day, I'd give Nicki and the kids blow-by-blows of each problem I had solved.

My rants would go something like this:

"I got stuck on a job today. The pop-ups on this computer were so bad that you couldn't even browse the internet. Plus, the entire system was *crawling*. I ran *Malwarebytes, Adaware, AVG,*"—my list would go on *ad nauseam*—"...but nothing worked. Then, after about six hours of beating my head against the wall, I began hunting around on Google for some other tools and found something called *Combofix*. I couldn't believe it. I ran it, and it fixed all the problems in like ten minutes.

That tool is a frickin' miracle! Then I reran everything, and they found all kinds of crap they'd missed before. Finally, I ran chkdsk and *Disk Defrag*. The computer runs like new now. I'm pretty proud of it. Yes, I'm feeling pretty happy about it. And then there was this other computer. It wouldn't..."

At that point, Nicki's eyes would glaze over, and she'd tune me out. Eventually, I'd stop and say, "Do you know what I mean?"

Her reply was inevitable. "No, not really."

Frustrated, I would admonish her. "Weren't you even listening?"

"Not really. All I hear is 'blah blah blah . . . computers.' I can't follow that stuff. Can we talk about something else, *please*?"

She was begging me to stop, but I found it hard to switch gears, especially at bedtime. At night I'd often lie on my back, obsessing on the latest enigma. Occasionally, I would even dream the solution.

Then, the next day, I'd wake up, eager to try out my new ideas. There was almost never a puzzle I couldn't solve. More importantly, I was having the time of my life.

I learned the trade at a very rapid pace. Adam was great. He taught me everything I know about computer repairs. Before I stopped working with him, I had become an expert PC technician. After leaving his company, I briefly started my own business. It was called Janik's PC Czech Up. The logo, which Nicki designed, was a fruit kolache superimposed with a CD-ROM. We even used Vistaprint to have hats made with the logo, which we proudly wore everywhere. They were silly but effective.

At least twice a week, strangers would approach me

and ask, "Is that a kolache on your hat?" I never missed an opportunity to tell them about my business.

The single most important skill I learned from Adam was the art of "Google-fu." I was usually alone in his shop while he was working on location at a home or business. If I was frustrated and desperate, I'd call him with a problem I had stubbornly been trying to solve for hours. He'd answer his phone, and I'd say something like, "I can't get the internet to work on that eMachines computer. I've tried *everything*. I ran all the scans. I reset the proxies. I manually cleared the hosts file. And I reset Winsock. But nothing. I even tried a different network card. I'm getting really frustrated. Do you have any advice?"

Adam would sound harried. He was almost always working on a time crunch. "Have you tried flushing the DNS?"

I'd reply, frustrated, "How do you flush the DNS?"

"You have to go into the command prompt and type something. I don't remember the exact command. Just Google it."

He never remembered the precise fix, only that one existed. He'd then playfully repeat his mantra: "Remember, *Google is your friend*."

I never forgot that lesson. I became an expert at finding all kinds of obscure information on Google, sometimes for extremely rare problems with *Windows ME* or some other outdated operating system. Like that serial mouse, "Google-fu" would come back to help me later. My ability to track down obscure information via internet searches would become my single most important tool, crucial to helping me solve one of the most challenging, cryptic puzzles of my life.

But only a year after I started working for Adam, I would abandon him and disappear for six weeks. I took off with my family and embarked on one of the longest journeys of my life: The Monster Trip.

When we finally returned home and I called Adam to tell him I was ready to go back to work, he told me, "I wasn't sure if you were coming back."

I was shocked by his response. How could he think I wouldn't want to come back? Apparently, I had neglected to call him for most of the time I had been away, and I hadn't given an estimated time of our return. But despite my lack of communication, I never considered for a moment that I wouldn't return to work. Adam and I trusted each other. By then, I was more than his apprentice. I was his friend.

When Nicki, the kids, and I left, our plans had been open-ended, and Adam had understood this. We would travel until we either ran out of money or got sick of it. But I guess we don't tire easily. Six weeks is a long time. Honestly, Adam was probably too bogged down with work to think to send me a text, and I felt a little guilty about not updating him during our trip.

Luckily, Adam quickly got over his initial doubts about my return to the shop. He was more than eager to have me back because, as I'd suspected, he'd been overloaded with business the entire time I was gone.

In other words, he had missed me.

It was mutual. I really needed his companionship. In the days to come, Adam and work would become a much-needed distraction.

04

DIAL M FOR MURDER

Returning home from work one day, I was obsessing about how to remove a nasty virus called rootkit—one of the most stubborn types in the computing world. They start by giving the hackers administrative privileges, then use them to maim *Windows* and the PC's anti-malware defenses. Because they're so damaging, they can be extremely difficult to remove.

But eventually, my focus was pulled away by the internet, through an obscure but intriguing story that was destined to change the course of my life.

The news reports centered on a family who, according to neighbors, seemed like typical, hard-working immigrants. Demetrios and Marina Kalogeropoulos appeared to be living the American dream. They shared a nice two-story home in a quiet middle-class neighborhood in Peabody, Massachusetts, with their two young-adult children, George and Joanne. The mother even owned her own hair salon.[5]

But beneath the surface, trouble was brewing.

Although it is unclear when or why it began, on

June 23, 2006, George D. Kalogeropoulos was clearly disturbed. On that tragic afternoon, motives unknown, the twenty-five-year-old went on a rampage throughout his house. Wielding a knife and a gun, he lunged for his father, stabbing and shooting him multiple times. Demetrios collapsed on the kitchen floor,[6][7] no doubt lying in a pool of his own blood.

Meanwhile, the young man's twenty-three-year-old sister, Joanne, locked herself in the second-floor bathroom. But this was no deterrent for the determined killer, who broke down the door. Moments later, Joanne struggled for her life (likely, according to authorities)[8] as George, who was still wielding his knife and gun, stabbed and shot her multiple times as she collapsed into the tub.[9][10]

Undoubtedly distraught, George then grabbed his high-caliber silver revolver and headed for the family's scarlet SUV. What was going through his head at the time will never be known, but perhaps he was thinking about making an escape.

Sometime later, he apparently pulled the gun on himself and committed suicide, slumping over the steering wheel, dead.[11] A neighbor recalled that in the afternoon she had heard the gunshot and a brief blast of a horn or car alarm.[12] When George's mother returned home, she was greeted by the gruesome scenes in both the car and house. She quickly called 911.[13]

Very little appears to be known about George, but he was a licensed gun owner with at least four registered firearms and had no criminal record. Thus, at the time of the tragedy, authorities were not able to immediately establish a motive.[14][15]

When news of the tragedy spread, the media,

including *The Boston Globe,* started scrutinizing a MySpace attributed to the young man. They were, no doubt, hoping to get a glimpse into George's personal life. Perhaps they could discover a motive or at least indicators that he had been disturbed. However, they found little to indicate a troubled individual other than some minor depictions of violence and perhaps some lies about his accomplishments. However, later the *Globe* retracted its MySpace analysis when editors realized that the account in question didn't belong to George.[16]

Regardless, the idea of looking for a suspicious MySpace to discover at-risk individuals stuck with me. Perhaps finding such information could be used to preemptively stop a murder or suicide. My mind took the situation a step further: What if MySpace could be used to solve mysteries and crimes that have already been committed?

A month later, I'd put this theory to the test.

***

Ever since I was a teen, I have had a morbid fascination with serial killers, mass murderers, and other examples of people committing inhumane acts. The first such story I remember following was the Jeffrey Dahmer case in the early 1990s. I recall wondering how any human being could torture and kill people in such horrific ways, and then cannibalize their bodies.[17] I simply couldn't understand the mind of a psychopath.

From that point on, any time a notorious killer was mentioned on TV, I was glued to the set. And after I got internet, I'd spend at least a few hours researching the details of their lives. These were killers like John Wayne Gacy, who was the prototype for all evil clowns,[18] and Ed Gein, the necrophiliac who furnished his shack with chairs, lampshades, and other items made from the human skin of his victims.[19]

Even suicide cults, like Jonestown[20] and Heaven's Gate,[21] drew my attention. After watching *Jonestown: The Life and Death of the People's Temple*, a PBS special about the 1978 tragedy, I read *Slavery of Faith* in its entirety. This captivating memoir by Leslie Wagner-Wilson detailed her narrow escape with her son and others through the jungle near the cult's compound, while more than 900 of her friends died—mostly at their own hands—by drinking Flavor Aid (a knock-off brand version of Kool-Aid) laced with cyanide.[22]

But of all the disturbing stories that have grabbed my attention, I invested the most time following the OJ Simpson trial. Along with millions of Americans, I eagerly tuned in every day for the latest development as OJ, the retired, world-famous running back, fought charges that he had brutally murdered his ex-wife, Nicole Brown Simpson, and her friend, Ron Goldman. I spent hours listening to Marcia Clark, the district attorney with the iconic long, dark curls, present what she called a "mountain" of evidence.

I judged Kato Kaelin, the long-haired, blond surfer-looking dude—perhaps the world's most notorious free-loader—who had been living indefinitely at OJ's guest house, rent-free. And I defended Mark Fuhrman, the sharp-jawed, dirty-blond detective accused of lying under oath about using the N-word. During the trial, this term was popularized by the media as a substitution for a word considered so vile that no anchors or pundits dared repeat it. Because of his possible perjury and his use of the word, Fuhrman was put on the trial of public opinion. Meanwhile, Johnny Cochran—OJ's fiery defense attorney—labeled him a racist and accused him of planting evidence to frame his client.[23]

Years after the trial, I could still repeat every argument that proved OJ did it.

On the day the verdict was read, I was in my gynecologist's office. Uncomfortable and shifting my feet because I was in my last couple of months of pregnancy, I joined a group of more than a half-dozen doctors, nurses, and patients, all crowded around a small, staticky old television.

A middle-aged nurse impatiently adjusted the antenna as the television crackled with static. We almost missed the moment we'd all been waiting for. Thankfully, after several minutes of monkeying with the signal, she managed to clear it up enough for us to watch. We stood by, nervously listening for the verdict. The suspense in the air was palpable. Finally, we heard the lead juror read the words:

"...not guilty..."

A collective groan filled the room. For a few minutes, we all bonded over our complaints about how unfair it all was. I turned and faced the slender, young black woman behind me, who I'd been chatting with earlier. *"This proves it.* There's no justice for the rich."

She nodded in agreement. "We all know he did it. Just throw enough money at a problem and it goes away."

No one in the room seemed to doubt that OJ had murdered Ron and Nicole. To me, George D. Kalogeropoulos' slaughter of his family was not unlike the

Simpson murders and other inhumane acts that had drawn my attention. And as with those cases, the details of the story, including the idea of suspicious MySpace pages, stuck in my head.

So when I saw the news about a serial killer leaving bodies in the Acres Homes area of Houston, my memory was jarred. The idea of using the world's most popular social networking site to solve mysteries came flooding back into my consciousness as I watched the news with rapt attention.

05

BETWEEN A ROCK AND A HARD PLACE

But away from television, serial killers, and grisly news, I had bigger problems: The Monster Trip had done me in. Although worth it, I had spent most of my remaining credit on our travels and wasn't sure how I was going to pay my bills.

For the past couple of years, I had been using my credit to maintain our lifestyle. We were living so far beyond our means that it wasn't unusual for us to go to Saltgrass Steakhouse and blow over $100 on meals for four. There were no worries because it was just credit. It didn't even feel like real money.

The main reason my use of credit felt so inconsequential is that after a while, I stopped making any actual cash payments. Instead, I was shuffling my debt around each month, paying one with the other through an elaborate series of balance transfers. I had built our standard of living upon a house of cards. And after The Monster Trip, this flimsy reality collapsed and fell into the abyss.

I had dug myself into a deep hole—a grave, even. I

had several maxed-out cards and only enough available credit to shuffle around for a few more months at most. Normally, I could crawl out of the situation by applying for a new credit card. But the maxed-out cards had made my credit score plummet, causing me to get denials on most fronts.

I began to panic. I was trapped. What had I been thinking? I should have known this would happen. But I had lied to myself and everyone around me, believing that one day I'd catch up and pay back my debt. I had never intended to cheat the system. I honestly thought things would magically work themselves out.

But now, in the wake of The Monster Trip, it became increasingly obvious that my debt wasn't a problem easily solved. As each day passed, I could tell I was spiraling further downward into a nightmarish anxiety state. My heart was often racing, my sleep was poor, and I felt like I was going to suffocate. I was crushed under the weight of my debt.

How was I going to support my family without my credit cards? How was I going to pay my bills? Would I be able to keep food on the table? What were we going to have to sacrifice? What would we have to give up? Once again, we would be encumbered by our poverty.

During this period, I frequently had to remind myself to breathe. It wasn't hopeless. There was always a solution. I'd have to turn to Plan B. The problem was that there was no Plan B—at least not yet. I had to think hard and fast before things got worse. I needed to somehow salvage this desperate situation. I needed a solution, a way out. *But what?*

I thought about it for a moment. I apparently only had two options: file bankruptcy or simply stop paying my creditors. Either would be devastating.

***

On the surface, things didn't look so bad. We were still living our lives as though nothing were wrong. And I hadn't yet disclosed to Nicki how awful things were. I usually kept financial problems to myself. I didn't want to worry her unless it was absolutely necessary.

But despite my silence, I couldn't stop obsessing on my descent into this hellish financial crisis, especially at night when my mind was most active. So it's not surprising that a few weeks later, when Nicki and I were settled down in bed, there was a lot on my mind. We lay in the dim lamplight, on our backs, next to each other. As usual, my pillow was curled under my neck, and I had a light-blue sheet loosely draped over me.

Although my body was resting, my mind was still going. I kept churning over the same thoughts for at least twenty minutes, until it felt like my brain was spinning inside with annoying, large gears dry-heaving bits of rust into my head. I was mentally exhausted, but I couldn't stop worrying.

What was going to happen to me? To our family? What should I do about it? What was next? I was afraid to file bankruptcy. It would probably be thrown out of court if my creditors caught onto the game I was playing. *Or what if the unthinkable happened? What if, instead of getting my debt dismissed, I was referred for prosecution? What if I had been unwittingly committing a crime? What if—*

My body convulsed. My mind hit the brakes as my train of thought came screeching to a halt. I vaguely heard Nicki saying something strange.

"...and aliens landed and took over the town."

Uh oh... I knew what this meant. Sometimes she'd start saying weird stuff as a test to see if I was listening. In that moment, I became fully aware of something that I was only vaguely cognizant of a moment before: Nicki had been talking to me for at least ten minutes.

I replied, annoyed, "You don't have to do that. I was listening."

She snapped back at me, "Okay, then what was I talking about?"

I tried to dig into my subconscious to remember what she'd been saying. Maybe I could fake my way out of the situation.

"You were talking about the class you taught last semester."

Still suspicious, she pressed harder. "Okay. What was I saying about it?"

I dug further into my subconscious. I guess a small part of me *had* been listening, but it was no different than seeing an object in my peripheral vision. I knew something was there, but I couldn't quite make it out.

"*Um...*" I stalled for a second, trying to think. "Something about the student who mouthed off to you, right?"

Nicki snapped, "Yes! But specifically, I was talking about how tired I am of teaching. I *really* don't wanna teach next semester, but I don't want to say 'no' to Ruth Ellen."

Nicki was a PhD candidate in educational psychology at The University of Texas-Austin (UT). Dr. Ruth Ellen Schwartz was both her advisor and a person who Nicki occasionally referred to as her "Jewish mom." Ruth

Ellen had designed the learning skills class that Nicki and other students in her program taught. Nicki was always worried about disappointing her.

I apologized. "I'm sorry, honey. I'll try to listen more carefully. I just have a lot on my mind right now. You have my attention."

I propped myself up with some pillows, stared straight at her, and listened carefully. I could tell that Nicki was extremely upset because when she had strong feelings about a topic, she would perseverate about it, repeating the same stories multiple times while trying to analyze every angle.

As her words became increasingly redundant, my thoughts began to drift again. I was back to worrying about my financial crisis. I tried to imagine the alternative to bankruptcy. I'd heard horror stories about collectors and their devious methods. *No...* I would have to change my number. I would have to figure out a way to ignore them, avoid them. I'd have to—

"*Barbara.*" It was Nicki again. She'd noticed that I had tuned her out.

Although she was calling my name quite loudly, I was too stuck in my head and was only vaguely aware of her presence.

"*Barbie.*"

Another failed attempt to get my attention. I was too far gone.

"*Boobie!*"

No response.

And then, "*Hey, gorgeous!*"

I immediately looked up. This was an old family trick that Grandma had invented. If we can't get someone's attention, we holler, "Hey, gorgeous!" Nine times out of ten, it works. This was one of those times. I guess I'm just gorgeous.

I startled, my body convulsing a bit. "Huh? What? I'm sorry, I just can't concentrate right now. I have too much on my mind."

Nicki looked at me a little concerned. "What're you worried about *now*?"

"I can't stop thinking about the finances. It's really awful."

She replied in a tempered voice, "What specifically?"

I drew in a deep breath, followed by a loud sigh. What I was about to say made me uncomfortable. I never liked to talk about money with Nicki. It usually didn't end well.

"We just...we spent *way* too much on the trip." I continued, letting out a rush of emotion. "I'm freaking out."

Nicki tried to be the voice of reason. "Well, we can scrimp and save and cut corners."

But I knew her idea wouldn't work because *I* was the one responsible for paying all the bills. *I* was the one who dealt with all the credit cards. *I* was the one who took on that stress. Feeling more like a husband than a wife, I had taken on the role of provider. She had no clue how bad things had gotten.

"You don't get it." I found myself getting a bit annoyed. "My credit cards are almost completely maxed out. I don't know what we're gonna do!"

Nicki made an innocent suggestion. "I dunno, maybe make a list of some ideas."

I replied tensely, "You mean like things we can cut out?"

She continued. I think I'd interrupted her thought process. "... and like ways to make more money or ideas of what to do about the debt?"

Nicki was still under the assumption our money problems could be fixed. She had probably read too much Dave Ramsey, the financial guru who gives people advice about how to get out of debt—not that it helped her avoid her 1999 bankruptcy.

Meanwhile, I was beginning to get frustrated with the conversation.

"Look, man, all I'm saying is that I don't have enough available credit to keep paying one card with the other. I'm eventually gonna have to stop paying them. I just can't keep doing what I'm doing. It's not working anymore, and this is really stressing me the fuck out."

Nicki kept pressing for a solution. "Well, it sounds like we need a plan."

Once again, I shot her down. "Like *what?* Bankruptcy? I *can't* file bankruptcy!"

I barely got the last word out when Nicki interrupted me. She didn't like where this was going. "Don't...don't... *don't* file bankruptcy. Just don't pay them."

I went from being nervous back to being annoyed. "I can't not pay them. That'd be a nightmare. Collector calls? *Are you serious?*"

"What other choice do you have?"

I could hear the panic in my own voice. "I dunno. I'm freaking out. I don't know what to do. I'm racking my brain for ideas and nothing's coming up. I just keep going over the same thoughts in my head. I can't stop thinking about it. It's *super* repetitive and awful and just tiring. I can't even stand myself."

She looked at me. "It sounds like you need a distraction."

I had doubts that anything could pull me out of my head right now. Still, I felt it might be worth a try. "Like what?"

She looked at me with bedroom eyes, grinning slightly, then singing, "Bow chicka wow wow!"

And people say only men try to fix problems with sex.

"Man, I can't even do *that* right now. You know, when I'm this stuck, I can't . . . Think of something else, *please*."

She came up with more ideas: "A movie? A TV show?"

Once again, I found myself shooting down all her ideas. "I can't do that either. I'm telling you... It's all I can do to carry on a conversation."

Occasionally, when I was anxious and lost in thought, it became impossible for me to concentrate on shows. And realizing how bad off I was would make me even more anxious. Then, I would start worrying about worrying until my emotions reached a head. That's when I'd run out of the room with tears streaming down my face. Exasperated, I would curl up in a ball in bed, wailing, until the feelings passed. Sometimes it took several hours.

But as I was dreading the situation coming to that, Nicki finally made a suggestion I felt was reasonable: "Maybe we can go somewhere and get out of the house."

I gave in out of desperation. "*Uh*... I guess that could work. Where do you wanna go?"

We spent several minutes negotiating. Our options were limited because we lived in a small town, and it was 2 a.m. First, Nicki suggested Busy Bee Café, a local twenty-four-hour country kitchen with the biggest cinnamon rolls I'd ever seen. Even half of one was too much for a typical non-binge eater. But I shot that idea down as too expensive. I mean, compared to most sit-down restaurants, they were actually very reasonable. But eating out was a luxury we couldn't really afford at that point in our lives.

After a few minutes, we decided to go to Kroger and buy groceries. It was open twenty-four hours and was less stressful than Walmart because it was way smaller and less crowded. Almost every time I stepped into Walmart, I'd have a massive anxiety attack. So, Kroger was the path of least resistance, albeit expensive. But even when we were trying to save cash, we could always justify a trip to the store. After all, we had to eat.

Finally, we had a plan. Even if it didn't solve our financial crisis, it would offer me an emotional break. Help was on the way.

06

THE FAMILY PARTY

Despite its mundane nature, the Kroger trip gave me some much-needed stress relief. Still, I felt like I needed a more substantial distraction—a day with no real responsibilities.

That day would come sooner than I'd anticipated.

The next afternoon, I woke up to an unexpected group text from my older sister, Brandy. On Sunday, we were going to be celebrating Dad's birthday at my brother Jerry's house. The parties were almost always held there. As usual, there hadn't been much warning. Sunday was only two days away.

The text was more of a memo than an invitation. Invitations to parties ordinarily imply that it's okay to politely refuse without provocation. In this case, everyone who physically could attend was expected to be there. There was always the conventional yet desperate question—*"Can you make it?"*—followed quickly by, *"What are you bringing?"*

Although the sentiment was never spoken aloud, not coming to a family party was considered a rejection of the family and our traditions, of which there were many—each with exaggerated importance. The quiet fear was that without the parties, the family would fall apart. They were the glue that held us together, and we were all determined to stay close. Needless to say, I usually went.

For more than ten years, all my closest relatives— Mom, Dad, most of my five siblings, and Clyde, who was technically a cousin but felt more like a brother because he lived with us when he was in high school—had gotten together for every important occasion. These included major holidays and birthdays for everyone, even in-laws, nieces, and nephews. Everyone was special. Everyone had their day. These celebrations were so frequent that we often had to combine them, sometimes even mixing one or more birthdays with major holidays. One year, we ridiculously combined Thanksgiving with three birthdays.

But this particular party was just for Dad. Regardless, I was still lying in bed at 2:30 p.m., paralyzed, only vaguely aware that we were already a half-hour late. I was drained from stress and lack of sleep. Plus, the sheer number of parties was overwhelming for me. With nearly 100 percent of my being, I didn't want to go, and I couldn't even *drag* myself out of bed.

But soon, the guilt texts began. It was Jerry, the oldest of my siblings. He was relentless.

Where are you?

Everyone's here but you.

We're going to eat without you.

I knew these were all lies because Jerry liked to tease, and I knew damned well Brandy wasn't there yet. Plus, we never ate until after 5 p.m. Still, the texts worked, and I reluctantly dragged myself out of bed—late. I grabbed Nicki and the kids, and we headed to H-E-B, where we picked up some Barq's Root Beer, Diet Mountain Dew, and other drinks. We were typically the "drink people," with Jerry providing cups and ice. We had taken over the duty a few years earlier after getting tired of Jerry's generic colas, which tasted disgusting and were loaded with sugar. Jerry, who had made his career as a grocery store manager, found this option cheap and easy. He liked to brag about his thriftiness. "I got these three-liters for a dollar fifty each, and they're just as good as name brand!"

We arrived at my brother's place an hour-and-a-half later, "cokes" (Texan for soda) in hand. The driveway was almost always too crowded at parties, and this time was no exception. So we parked in our usual spot on the pristine St. Augustine grass in the shade between a couple of large tallow trees. Grabbing the drinks and gifts, Nicki, the kids, and I passed through the open two-car garage, walking by Jerry's old brown Bronco and the generic-looking white washer and dryer set. We then let ourselves in through the door in the back of the garage. We never had to knock. We knew we were always welcome.

Entering, I looked to the left of the kitchen area at a small, empty table that was supposed to be loaded with chips and dip. Brandy usually brought them to snack on while the food was being prepared. I felt a wave of relief wash over me. *Maybe I beat her here.* It was always a competition.

As we moved farther into the house, Peter and Daun quickly greeted a few people and then took off running to the back bedroom to play with Robbie and

Thomas' new Xbox 360. They were Jerry's boys and were teenagers at the time. They always had the latest systems and all the violent games, like *Dead Rising*, which had just been released that month.

I never bought my son violent video games, and ordinarily we stuck to child-friendly systems made by Sega or Nintendo. Anne took restrictions a step further by refusing to buy her sons, Aaron and Nolan, a system. Eventually, she would reluctantly get them a Wii—the hottest item of Christmas 2006. And even then, they were only allowed to play *Wii Sports* and *Mario* games. I'm still not sure how she got her hands on a Wii. They were in such high demand that they were almost impossible to find in stores for the first couple of years after their release.

Nearly oblivious to what Peter and Daun were doing, I turned toward the kitchen to drop off the sodas. That's when I noticed Mom standing on the pale yellow, 1950s-style floor, facing the counter and making a salad. She looked up, stopped what she was doing, and greeted me.

"I'm so glad you made it!"

Although Mom, who was a city girl at heart, had married Dad and moved to Texas at seventeen, she still had a mostly Californian accent—well maybe more like a Texas/California hybrid after forty years of living in the Houston area.

In her mid-sixties, Mom was finally beginning to show her age. But her hair was always dyed with blonde highlights, and her makeup, which was attractive but subtle, helped mask some of her wrinkles. All in all, she was a gorgeous, well-dressed older woman whose favorite color was green, to match her stunning eyes.

That day, she was wearing a green-and-white striped blouse and a nice pair of jeans.

I looked back at Mom and smiled as we reached out to each other for a hug. She gave great hugs, like everyone else in the family. But Mom's were special.

A few moments later, Dad briefly paused from cutting brisket with his electric knife and greeted me with an equally warm hug.

Although my parents had divorced when I was thirteen, they were both at the party. The past was the past and Mom and Dad got along.

Dad was a lean, olive-complected man, who had a dark tan because he spent most of his time outdoors. He especially enjoyed working in his yard or chasing his cattle around. He had curly hair that was darker than it should have been for someone in his late sixties. A redneck to the core, he was one of the toughest men I knew. He could get kicked in the leg by a bull without hardly letting out a holler. Of course, there would usually be a typical, "Goddamn, son of a bitch!" But that was it. No crying or complaining.

And Dad's barbecue was a favorite at parties. He loved making it, even for his own birthday. Plus, he often brought his own special brand of deer sausage, created from his hunting bounty. And I never dared to skip his beans. Every party he'd ask me for my opinion of them.

Walking past the kitchen, Nicki and I entered the large gaming area and stood next to the pool table. Jerry was leaning over its red velvet surface, setting up his next shot. He and Lee, our younger brother, were playing a very competitive game of 8-ball. I was vaguely aware of The Beatles' "Come Together" playing in the background. *My favorite group...*

Anne and her husband, Mark, were sitting at the bar on the other side of the room. Mark was talking loudly as Anne listened. A fan of all things sports, he was making observations about the pool game.

I took a hard look at my sister sitting next to him. Like me, she looked like a typical Janik, but with wavy rather than curly hair. She also shared Dad's olive complexion, albeit less tanned. Anne had always been beautiful. I used to envy her hair when I was a kid because it was so dark—darker than mine and all of us siblings.

There had always been some level of competition between Anne and I as far as parenting, with each of us quietly judging the other. But "quiet" is the operative term. Our judgments were mostly expressed in looks. We rarely spoke these criticisms to each other's faces. And if we did, it was in the form of unwanted "advice." If we had discussed it more regularly, I'm sure she'd have some words about my housekeeping skills, as well.

But Anne was just one of many people at the party that day. Family gatherings were always noisy, especially when my children and their cousins were younger. I was grateful that we were between generations, and there were no screaming toddlers today. Anne's younger son, Nolan, had been colicky.

All these thoughts passed after a couple of seconds, when I decided it was time to announce my presence. No one in the living room had noticed me yet. As Jerry pulled back the stick and tapped the cue ball, I faced the crowd and hollered jovially, "I'm here! The party can start!"

Jerry peered up at me from the table and flashed a big smile. He looked like his usual self—stocky and muscular. Like Grandpa, he had a pot-belly, despite working out at the gym every day. Jerry's brown eyes were beaming at me under his dark, curly hair. We shared similar features—typical Janiks.

I asked him cheerfully, "Has Brandy made it yet?"

"No. You're not the last one here. It's a *miracle*." Of course, he was teasing. We both knew that Brandy was almost always last.

Nicki and I began chanting loudly, *"We're not the last! We're not the last! We're not the last!"* This was a variation of a great moment from Season 4 of *Roseanne*, when Dan's bowling team, after coming in ninth, enthusiastically and repeatedly chanted, *"We're not the worst!"*

Nicki and I were always coming up with new takes on pop culture references. Often, as with family tradition, we would start singing loudly when we heard a snippet from a tune we recognized, sometimes changing up the words to meet whatever was happening at the moment. We owed this phenomenon to Grandma, who, much to my mother's chagrin, took every familiar phrase as an excuse to burst into song. Every day with Grandma was like stepping into an old-style Hollywood musical. My favorite was *The Court Jester* with Danny Kaye, mostly because the comedian was a family favorite. Mom even gave me the middle name "Kaye" (exact spelling) in his honor.

Making my way through the house, I meticulously sought out every family member and greeted them with hugs. Finally, we returned to the kitchen and cracked open the two-liter bottle of Barq's.

Then Nicki and I headed past the set of burgundy suede-leather couches in the game room, cut through the cramped dining room, and landed in the small, dimly-lit living room. Nicki and I affectionately called it "The Cave" because it was a cool, dark place for us to hide like bats, away from the bustle and noise of the party. It was *our* area—our comfort zone. Everyone knew better than to sit there. Everyone knew it was our spot.

Despite growing up in a crowded, noisy home, I didn't like noise or crowds—something that everyone else seemed to relish. But I wasn't antisocial. We would hide out in our corner and talk to family members, one at a time, as they stopped by or were moving past to the nearby bathroom—the only one in the house.

My half of The Cave was the large couch that sat against the wall. Nicki always sat catty-corner on the matching loveseat. Occasionally, people would seek me out, sit next to me, and engage me in conversation. But a lot of times I was unavailable because I had laid down and passed out from sleep deprivation. During those moments, when they caught me sleeping, sometimes they—mostly Jerry and Anne—would mock me or beg me to get up and "join the living." But I wasn't offended. I knew they were teasing because they wanted to spend time with me. Besides, they were used to me and my idiosyncrasies.

When I got to this particular party, I stretched out on my sofa in The Cave, lying back in my usual position, and drifted off into a half-sleep. After about thirty minutes, I heard a door abruptly close in the distance. I groggily opened my eyes, listening. Several seconds later, I heard Jerry's typical sing-song chant, *"Who's always late for the party? Brandeeeeeeee!"*

Like I said, Brandy was almost always last to arrive. And Jerry never missed an opportunity to tease almost anyone in the family at any time—so much so that early on, mom had affectionately nicknamed him the family "agitator." None of us were spared from his constant teasing—not even young children. He often chased them around the house while annoying them with nicknames like "Critter" and "Squirrel." And they loved him for it. In that same spirit, If I were the last to arrive to the party, I'd get a different variation of the same treatment he had given Brandy: *"Who's always late for the party? Barb-randeeeeeeee!"*

When Brandy arrived with Stella, her five-year-old daughter, in tow, I felt a rush of happiness. Over the past few years, I'd spent countless hours talking to Brandy on the phone, mostly because she was the only one who always answered. She never seemed to get tired of me. This made her an ideal person to call when I was bored, which was often.

Anne, on the other hand, had stopped answering my calls a long time ago because she found my constant, repetitive calling annoying. She had even blocked me on AOL Instant Messenger back in 1999. Like Brandy, Mom would almost always answer. But I used to call her the "Five-Minute Mom" behind her back because after about five minutes on the phone, she'd run out of things to talk about and end the conversation.

After hastily setting up the chips and dip, Brandy started working her way through the house, giving out hugs. I've never understood why the person who was usually last to arrive was given chip duty. The entire point of snacks was to stave off hunger while dinner was being prepared.

And when Brandy made the rounds, her daughter didn't stick with her. Instead she started darting around the house, asking everyone if they'd seen Daun. Stella looked up to Daun and never missed an opportunity to play with her. Daun secretly found Stella annoying, but never let on. She remembered what it was like to be five. And even though Daun would never admit it, I suspect she liked the attention.

When Brandy made it to the dining room that was adjacent to The Cave, I hollered loudly from across the room to try to get her attention. I was too lazy to get up. She was talking to Anne, who had followed her from the game room.

I hollered louder, vying for her attention. *"Brandy!"* I didn't care that I was interrupting her conversation. Amongst my siblings, it wasn't even considered rude. We were fiercely competitive and all sort of took turns speaking over each other. It was survival in a family with six kids.

But despite my best efforts to get her attention, Brandy didn't seem to hear me. My volume was increasing exponentially. This time I punctuated my words. *"Hey, gorgeous!"* When even *that* traditional family tactic failed, I dragged myself off the couch and walked over to greet her, but not before catching the tail end of a heated conversation. Brandy and Anne appeared to be bickering.

As usual, Brandy's long, medium-brown curly hair looked pristine. She liked to brag that all she did to get it ready every morning was wet it in the sink, shake it, and let it dry. Brandy also had an amazingly clear complexion, which made her look like she was in her mid-thirties rather than forty-three. Although she struggled with her weight, she was considerably smaller than I was, and was a very curvy, attractive woman with childbearing hips. Today, Brandy was wearing jeans and a delicate button-up blouse with tiny pink-and-blue flowers.

I started listening in on the conversation between Brandy and Anne. Apparently, Anne was upset because the only meat at the party was beef.

Brandy was exasperated. "I just don't get why you don't eat beef! You're out of your mind!"

Anne replied angrily, "I'm sorry, but I'm just not willing to risk it."

"Risk what?" Brandy retorted. "You *know* there has never been a single case of mad cow disease in this country."

Anne, looking pained and anxious, rationalized, "That we *know* of. The condition of the cattle industry in this country isn't much different from England's. It could happen at any time. I'd rather starve than eat that stuff."

"Fine, then *starve*! But can't you at least let your kids and husband eat it? Nolan is already skinny enough."

Anne's face dropped. At this point, Brandy stopped, seeming to realize that she'd gone too far. Nolan, Anne's ten-year-old younger son, had struggled with weight issues since he was a toddler, and it was a super sensitive topic.

Brandy tried to calm things down. "Oh my God, I'm really sorry. We should just drop it." The regret of her previous comment was written all over her face.

Anne shrugged her shoulders. "It's okay. I'll just run to H-E-B and pick up some turkey franks." Sighing loudly, she headed back toward the game room, sad. From that point on, Dad was sure to bring a pork roast along with the brisket so everyone could enjoy his barbecue. He rarely judged. He just wanted everyone to be happy.

As quickly as the fight started, it was over. This was how it was. Bickering was just part of the family dynamic. No one minded. It was expected.

In fact, Anne often said she *liked* to bicker, which made sense because she had the hottest temper in the family. This also made her the most fun for Jerry to tease because he could always get a rise out of her. Anne, who almost never missed a party, made them fun. Although she had a lot of negative reactions to the family banter, she also laughed the hardest and teased almost as much as Jerry.

Despite her aggravation with Anne's anxiety, Brandy used to catastrophize just as much, if not more, than her sister. Over twenty years of working in the news industry had left Brandy jaded. She'd followed every calamity—every hurricane, rape, murder, and three-car pile-up—since the 1990s. She usually planned for the worst-case scenario and had no problem planting those fears in everyone around her. She could take the happiest moment and twist it into the apocalypse.

One time, when Daun and Peter were six and eight, I enthusiastically shared with Brandy that I was going to get them a trampoline for Christmas. I had somehow scraped together the money and was extremely excited. I was finally going to give my children an excuse to go outside and play—especially Peter, who I could never easily drag away from his technology. And Daun, who'd always been pretty hyper, would finally have an outlet to burn off her excess energy. My thinking was that the trampoline would be a better option than making her run laps around the house until she wore out. Although she really enjoyed the laps, a trampoline sounded more fun. Plus, I had also wanted one badly when I was a kid. I mean, what kid doesn't want a trampoline?

Brandy's reaction to my idea caught me off-guard.

"I don't think that's a good idea."

I was baffled. "What do you mean?"

"I hear of children all the time, jumping on those things and doing tricks. They turn a flip, land on their heads, and break their necks."

I bristled. "But it'd have a net."

She was becoming more emphatic and anxious by the minute. "It doesn't matter if there's a net. You don't get it. They can land wrong on the trampoline itself. Children have been permanently paralyzed or even died from trampolines!"

When I continued to resist her "logic," she panicked.

"Barbara, you cannot, not, *not* get a trampoline! I don't want Peter or Daun to get paralyzed!"

When I continued to defend my position by calling her paranoid, she tried to reason with me from a different angle.

"They will cancel your homeowner's insurance!"

This was shocking. But sometime after our conversation, I discovered Brandy was right. I called Travelers Insurance. Sure enough, according to the representative, having a trampoline on my property was considered a liability and could lead to the cancellation of my policy. Not only that, but Brandy had scared the living hell out of me. What if I got a trampoline and one of them did break their neck? I wouldn't be able to live with myself. After a few days of weighing my options, I was unable to deal with the extreme anxiety the concept was causing me and decided not to get the trampoline.

In an epic display of hypocrisy, guess who bought

her daughter a trampoline for her fourth birthday? I tried to tease Brandy about her reversal years later, but she didn't even remember chiding me for wanting to buy my kids a trampoline.

But that day at the party, when Brandy and Anne calmed down from their fight about mad cow disease, Brandy paused for a moment, looked over at me, and calmly acknowledged my existence. Finally, she walked over toward me.

I gave Brandy a huge smile. "Hey... You made it!"

I lurched forward to give her a hug. We squeezed each other tightly for several seconds, ending with the family's signature warm pat on the back. Her hugs were particularly good. Out of all of my siblings, Brandy was the most caring and nurturing—always the first one to arrive during a family or medical crisis, often rushing out early from her job.

Speaking to Brandy only briefly during the hug, I whispered gently, *"I love you."*

She replied passionately, *"I love you, too."* After a short interaction, she headed off to the bathroom. We would probably talk more later.

I headed back to the couch and lay down as the party proceded around me. An hour later, we gathered in the kitchen for food and brought it back to our prospective spots throughout the house. Some sat in the dining room, while others sat on the sofas in the TV room and the game room. Nicki, the kids, and I ate in The Cave. As always, Dad's barbecue and beans were the best.

When everyone was finished, time passed as I continued to lounge on the couch. Soon, we gathered again—this time around the dining room table to sing "Happy Birthday" and watch my Dad blow out his candles. Then there were the presents. First presents, then cake. Always in that order. It was a tradition.

Finally, I sat down at the couch with a large piece of chocolate cake and a generous scoop of Bluebell Homemade Vanilla—Dad's favorite. Moments later, Mom sat down next to me, holding a tiny piece of cake on a small paper plate. She nodded toward it and repeated her latest dieting mantra, *"It's all about portion control."*

Mom had spent most of her life following every fad diet known to man. The most amusing and worst one was the "cabbage diet." She had pressured me into trying it with her when I was a junior in high school. I lasted one day, after having eaten two full cups of cabbage in a single sitting. *Yuck!* ... It was weeks before I could even *look* at a cabbage again. Sadly, no matter how good Mom looked, she always thought she was fat. And for years, she sacrificed her taste buds in a quest to shed more pounds.

Despite Mom's annoying cake-eating habits, I was grateful she'd come by The Cave. I wanted...no...*needed* her advice on a horrible decision: whether or not to file bankruptcy. Even at the party, my financial dilemma was weighing heavily on my mind.

Although sometimes annoying, Mom was always sweet and nurturing, one of the kindest women I knew. Most importantly, she was always there for her children, a truly great mother. And she had always been there for me, quick to pass me a hundred bucks when I was broke or lend a listening ear, even though I usually rejected her advice. This time I was desperate. This time I would listen. And hopefully, this time I wouldn't be given any guilt trips.

A typical Catholic mother, Mom was once affectionately known as "The Guilt Queen." However, the guilt attempts had become subtler and less frequent over the years, something she was proud of. Occasionally, she would even repeat the untrue statement, *"I don't do that anymore."*

And true to her word, this time when I confided in her, there was no guilt, only sympathy.

I shared my dilemma, and instead of judging, she looked at me and gave me a suggestion: "You should talk to Tim. He did something after his divorce instead of filing bankruptcy."

Then, nervously fluttering her eyelids, Mom continued, "I don't remember what he did, but it fixed his problem. You should just go ask *him*."

Grateful, I thanked her and left to find Tim. Tim was my stepdad—the man who was so smart that he overcame dyslexia to become a mechanical engineer. He also liked to build full-sized, luxury boats from scratch. He was one of the cleverest, most resourceful men I knew. *Yes...* Tim would be a great source for financial advice.

After carefully sifting through the crowd, I found him hovering over the kitchen table. Nearly seventy, Tim was an average-looking man, balding with white hair and a slight paunch. On this day, he was sporting khaki pants and a lime green polo. Although he'd been retired for years, he always looked sharp and professional.

I got up and approached Tim at the dining room table, just as he was sneaking a huge piece of cake along with a massive scoop of Bluebell. The quantity was a luxury Mom would chastise him for—if she caught him.

I could almost hear her saying, *"Tim, you're already pre-diabetic."* Mom had been pushing her portion-control philosophy on him for years. But with Mom safely in the other room, Tim was shoveling large bites of cake into his mouth when I approached him. Maybe if he ate it fast enough, Mom wouldn't catch him.

Regardless of his eating habits, I knew that whatever advice Tim gave me about my finances would be level-headed. He was an engineer by trade and, stereotypical of men and women in his field, almost always came across calm and rational.

Tim listened intently as I explained my dilemma. When I finished, he looked at me with kind eyes and explained to me what he'd done to get out of debt. He called it "poor man's bankruptcy." Tim then calmly and meticulously laid out the facts. But his detailed description was lost as soon as I heard the words, "You'll have to deal with a lot of collector calls, and after seven years all the bad marks will drop off your credit."

"Years of collector calls" was all I needed to hear. I'd heard the horror stories about the aggressive nature of these individuals. People online claimed they were hounded with constant calls, lied to, threatened with lawsuits and wage garnishments, and even told they could be sent to prison. No... No. *No!* Tim's advice, no matter how nicely it was presented, sounded almost as risky as bankruptcy.

My gears started turning as I weighed the alternatives repeatedly in my head. I felt paralyzed. I was terrified that filing bankruptcy could lead my creditors to seek prosecution, yet the outcome of Tim's advice also sounded horrible.

Out of options, my mind began frantically searching

for a way out. Eventually, fate would bring me an idea that I thought would solve my problems—but at a cost.

07

THE ACRES HOMES KILLER

Weeks later, I saw something that immediately reminded me of the murder-suicide case I'd read about more than a month prior. It was a news story about the serial killer in the Acres Homes area.

On July 19, 2006, children were playing hide-and-seek when a boy, hiding in the weeds in an overgrown lot behind Parlay's Café, smelled something foul—rotting flesh. When he first spotted the badly decomposed body of a woman, he thought it was a horse. Calling his friends over, they all looked at the woman's body. She was completely naked except for her white socks.

The killer had claimed his sixth of seven known victims—most of them black.[24][25][26]

They had each been brutally raped and murdered and their bodies were discovered in wooded or otherwise obscured sections of the Acres Homes area—a rundown, old, traditionally black neighborhood. Like the sixth victim, they were all found nude or partially clothed.[27]

Aside from how they died, all the murdered women had something else in common. They all had a history of streetwalking.[28] It is well known that this population is frequently subjected to violent crimes. In this case, the dead prostitutes ranged in age from eighteen to fifty.[29]

Not long after the stories of the killer started hitting the news, there was a public outcry for action. Rep. Sheila Jackson Lee (D-Houston), Quanell X, and other activists quickly got involved.[30] Vigils were held for the victims.[31] There was a fervent call for community action. Speaking to the press, Rep. Lee addressed how to solve the crisis: "Frankly, I believe this will be solved through community involvement and through individual citizen activity."[32]

Families of the victims were understandably vocal. These women were their children, their nieces, their mothers, their sisters. Four days after the sixth victim's body was discovered, the community held a vigil for her. During it, her mother cried out with a message to the deadly assailant. "I want to say to the serial killer, whoever you are, you're a coward. You're not a man who took my baby. And if anyone anywhere knows where you are, I wish they would punch you out. You took my baby away from me, and I need closure."[33]

A couple of days after the vigil, Shauna Dunlap, an FBI spokeswoman, announced that federal investigators and DNA labs would join forces with the Houston Police Department (HPD) to solve the case. She stated empathetically, "We work with HPD all the time. When the locals need assistance, we're here to help."[34] Tips from the public were encouraged and routed through Crime Stoppers and the FBI.

The community pooled its money and doubled the reward of $10,000 to $20,000 for any information leading to the killer's apprehension.[35] I thought about it.

This kind of money could go a long way toward solving my financial crisis. At first, I shrugged it off. There was no way I would be able to help find the killer. I would never have a shot at that money. But...

Of course! ...

My mind rushed back to the story of George Kalogeropoulos, the young man who'd murdered his family. My gears began to turn. The media had been scouring what they thought was his MySpace, looking for warning signs—warnings that he had been in trouble and possibly up to no good. Then I had another idea. *What if this serial killer had a suspicious page? What if I could find that page and use it to track him down?*

What we knew about the features of the killer came from a few prostitutes who had narrowly escaped with their lives. He was believed to be a stocky, African-American man in his twenties or thirties with short hair and a Libra scales of justice tattooed on his arm. He had been last seen wearing a Celtics jersey. Some of the descriptions had him with dreadlocks. Others recalled a long series of tattoos on both arms. Investigators had a theory about the cause of the discrepancies. Many of the women were addicted to crack and other street drugs, and would see ten or more johns on a typical night.[36][37]

In 2006, it seemed as though everyone, even older people, had a MySpace—everyone, that is, except for me. I had always been a bit of a hipster. If it was popular, I didn't want to get involved. One time, I overheard a couple of long-haired, thin young women laughing about MySpace. One of them giggled, "It's like, *so* addictive." That was enough for me to not want any part of it.

Honestly, I didn't like social interaction online, even to play games like *World of Warcraft*. This was despite my love of *Dungeons and Dragons* and fantasy books like Terry Goodkind's *Sword of Truth* series. Plus, I was afraid I'd get lost in the online world and its "addictive" nature. Once I started something, I was all in. There was no middle ground. Sometimes an obsession of mine would last for months or even years.

I knew myself. I wanted nothing to do with MySpace, until this new use for it landed on my radar.

Reluctantly, I created an account for the sole purpose of finding the killer. Not bothering to design an attractive profile or invite friends, I took a couple of days to familiarize myself with the site's powerful search engine. What I found out was shocking. Although searches were intended to bring people together, they had an unintended effect: a complete lack of privacy.

People today, who are used to modern social media, might not realize that MySpace was way different than Facebook, YouTube, or Twitter. It operated more like a dating site. And like with dating sites, people would often use it to hook up or, minimally, find like-minded people—even local ones, if desired. To this end, users could conduct searches narrowed by gender, sexual orientation, location (using zip code radius), approximate weight and height, age range, and even smoking or drinking status, among other things. In other words, by 2006, through MySpace, you could learn almost anything about anyone. This made the site, along with its ginormous database and intricate search engine, perfect for profiling. And that's exactly what I was doing: profiling the serial killer.

I did an advanced search and plugged in everything I knew about the killer: his alleged race, gender, sexual orientation, age range, height range, body type, and zip code. This derived hundreds of hits for men fitting my criteria, all of whom lived within a five-mile radius of Acres Homes.

I spent a couple of days sifting through them, looking for any suspicious pages. On the third day, I found one that made my hair stand on end. The owner's MySpace was filled with pictures of scantily clad, "thick" black women. Splashed at an angle, in red, across the screen was the phrase, *"Texas Boys, We Killa!"*

His profile showcased him as a smiling, heavyset black man whose site stated that he was twenty-five. He had a medium-length afro with hair sticking up from a blue headband and was wearing a flashy royal-blue button up shirt. A photo of one of his real-life friends showed the shirtless back of a muscular black man with tattoos. This, at the very least, established that some of his acquaintances had tattoos.

When I clicked on the link to his photo page, I found a markedly different picture of the suspect. He was wearing a nice, long-sleeved white shirt and a fancy white vest, this time with short hair, just like the description of the killer. The caption read, "About to get my grown man on before the hair pimpin'." Because of the significant differences between this photo and his profile pic, I thought perhaps the afro on his main page had been a wig. In other words, maybe he had been wearing a disguise. I speculated that the long sleeves in the second picture might have been hiding tattoos.

Upon further digging, I found other comments on his page that seemed suspicious. He said he "looked forward to the weekends," so he could "run the streets." One of his favorite types of movies was "horror flicks." But by far, the most chilling piece of evidence was the comment, "I like to watch CSI. It keeps me from killing people." I guessed there was a good chance this man could be the killer, so I decided to try to find his address.

As the night progressed, I became increasingly consumed by the idea of gaining more details about the man. My imagination was running wild. I thought hard, pulling ideas from my memory.

Not long after graduating with my BA in liberal arts from the University of St. Thomas (UST), a prestigious Catholic school in Houston, I had taken on an internship with IDS Financial Services (now Ameriprise). I had joined a group of eager young people who were making minimum wage while being trained to become financial planners for the company.

One of our most difficult tasks was making cold calls to generate leads for the certified financial planners. We would use the Cole Directory, which was composed of thick books that had been purchased by the company for thousands of dollars. Their pages contained all the street addresses in the Houston area, arranged alphabetically by zip code. We then targeted wealthy neighborhoods such as Memorial, Bellaire, and The Woodlands.

Thinking back on the street directory I'd used, I scoured the internet, found a similar online version, and signed up for a free trial. Then I began the tedious process of plugging all the street names within the Acres Homes area into the MySpace search engine, along with the suspect's other data. If during a query all the specs along with the street name made his MySpace pop up, then I would know what street he lived on.

Countless hours later, the user's main page popped up. It was a match.

Nice! ... I had the page-owner's street and zip code.

I felt a rush of adrenalin course thorough my body. I couldn't believe I'd gotten this far.

I needed to burn off some of this energy. I headed to the kitchen. It had a lot of floor space, and I found myself pacing around. I'd hardly noticed Nicki sitting at the kitchen table. She looked over at me. "Cut that out. Stop pacing. You're making me nervous!"

"Leave me alone. I have a lot of pent-up energy right now." I turned away from her and grabbed a Diet Mountain Dew out of the fridge. It was the most caffeinated soda on the market—the reason it was my favorite. What did I ever do before caffeine? All I knew was that I was addicted to it.

Next I looked back toward Nicki and excitedly started blurting out the progress I'd made on the serial killer case. Minutes later, the drink was gone, and I was still pacing. Nicki listened, but was frustrated. I was clearly annoying her. Finally, I told her I had to go, and rushed back to my computer. I couldn't take it anymore. I had to get back to work.

I sat down at my desk in the bedroom and poised myself in the position. *Where was I?* ... Oh yeah... I looked back at the online directory. Every single address on the suspect's street was listed. This was going to take a while. I started meticulously plugging every one of them into the MySpace engine to see if I could get his page to pop up again. Several hours later, I had a full address and a list of names of people who lived there. *Wow...* I was so close. I knew where the page owner lived!

I stared at the monitor. There was a short list of names of people living at that address. I worked my way down the list. Minutes later, I had his name. It was a weird one. *Perfect!* ... This would be easy. His unusual name would make getting more info on him fairly simple.

Stretching, I glanced around the room. Midnight was sleeping on my pillow. *What a sweetie...* I felt a rush of joy. I was so excited about my accomplishments that I wanted to pick up my kitty and hug and kiss him. But I resisted. I was sure he wouldn't want to be disturbed. Besides, I was anxious to continue my hunt. The computer was calling. Maybe I could get my suspect's phone number.

I felt my heart pumping hard as I went to AnyWho. com, my favorite online white-page directory. I had used it before and knew it had a fairly extensive, relatively-accurate database. I plugged in his unusual name and here it was: a phone number and...*interesting...*a second address. This was unexpected.

I turned to PeopleLookup.com, a website that granted access to a thorough fee-based search engine. It was essentially a people finder that allowed me to find out extensive information about anyone in their database—almost everyone in the US. I would use a paid search to get more information about the residents of my suspect's Acres Homes address. There were older adults and younger adults, all with the same last name. *A family!* ... This must have been his parent's home. I rushed back to PeopleLookup and did another quick search. He was the only person listed at the Galveston address. This was probably his current residence.

But I needed to know for sure. This would cost me. I needed to pay PeopleLookup even more for an address verification check. According to the website, the company had access to utility records and could use them to verify if your quarry was still living there.

So I ran the check on my suspect. Moments later, red letters appeared under the Galveston location: *"Confirmed Current Address."* Under his phone number was, *"Confirmed Current Phone." Yes...* He was definitely living in Galveston.

But I needed more. Maybe I could use this information to find out more about him. I would use some sneaky detective work to find out if he had a tattoo.

I called a few tattoo parlors in Galveston, pretending to be the man's friend. With each number I called, I became increasingly nervous. I hated the charade. I mean, what if the artists told the guy someone was asking about him? But that didn't stop me. I had to...*had to* know if my suspect had tattoos. And if so, what were they?

I hit pay dirt on about the third try.

Heart pounding, I used the skills I'd acquired when taking acting classes at UST. The man on the other end answered with the name of the business. I calmly opened the conversation.

"Hey, a friend of mine got some tattoos done in the area. I'm looking to get a tattoo, and I was wondering if he got his in your shop. The artwork is *amazing.*"

The man answered quickly in a mild Texas accent, "Yeah? What's his name?"

I answered and gave the suspect's name. The artist replied in a matter-of-fact voice, "Sure, I know 'em."

I started fishing for more information. "Which ones did you do? I want to make sure I have the right shop."

"I don't remember. It was a really long time ago and I've done thousands of jobs." *Weird...* He remembered his client's name, but not the job. But I guess my suspect *did* have an unusual name. I decided to let it go.

"I guess I'll just have to ask him which tattoo you

did. Thanks."

The conversation had gone smoothly. But as soon as I put down the phone, I began trembling and breathing rapidly. However, the anxiety the call had caused me was worth it. I now knew for sure that the guy had tattoos. For me, this sealed the deal. I had him. I was 99 percent certain I had found the killer. It never even occurred to me that the artist could have been lying to get my business.

***

I soon developed a theory about how the suspect could have gotten away with the crimes: If he was the killer, on any given night he could have visited his parents in Acres Homes, left their house to commit the crimes, and then fled back to Galveston to hide. Eventually, he'd return to Houston and the process would repeat itself.

On August 1, about a week after I began my hunt for the killer, I flipped open my phone and called the FBI. I didn't know what to expect. I had always heard such awful things about them. But with the theory about the killer's identity fresh on my mind, I nervously spoke to a person I assumed was a screener. When I said I was calling with a tip about the serial killer, I was immediately transferred to a duty agent.

Had this been 2020, I would have never gotten past the screener. Nowadays, when you call the FBI to give a tip, they refer you to a special tip line where you talk to a civilian rather than an agent. The civilian, who is a low-paid government employee, takes down the information and promises that you will get a follow-up call from an agent. These overworked individuals are not intelligence officers, but merely customer service representatives who are evaluated based on their ability to quickly dispose of tips, few of which ever make it to agents. Most are placed in a massive database where they remain indefinitely. It is like calling 911 and being told, *"Let me take a message. Someone will get back to you. But don't call us. We'll call you."*[38]

I believe this new system is how the Parkland, Florida, shooter slipped through the cracks. On February 14, 2018, Nikolas Cruz, a former student, walked into Marjory Stoneman Douglas High School with an AR-15 rifle and massacred seventeen people. But this tragedy could have been prevented. At some point prior to the massacre, the tip line was called twice by concerned citizens who were warning about Cruz's potential to become a school shooter. But their words fell on deaf ears. The tips were placed in the database and left to die.[39]

But this was 2006, so when I called the FBI, I was taken seriously and immediately patched through to an *actual* agent, not an uninformed civilian. The person I was speaking with was calm—a gentleman with a professional-sounding tenor voice.

After some rather formal salutations, I tried to hide my anxiety, and stated assertively, "I have a tip about the serial killer."

"Sure, what is it?"

I explained my MySpace theory and shared the URL for the suspect's page. I added confidently, "I also figured out his address. It's actually his parents' home, and it's in the same zip code where the bodies were found."

The agent seemed amazed. "How'd you figure out his address?"

I told him that I narrowed it down using the MySpace search engine, but I skipped most of the details. I didn't want to give away my secrets. I might need them for future cases. Instead, I described the suspect's MySpace and gave the agent my theory about how the man kept escaping justice. I also threw in my ideas about the tattoos, including my thought that the long sleeves in the photos could be covering them. I even mentioned my conversation with the tattoo artist.

The agent seemed intrigued by my process and seemed to think my idea had merit. "Thanks, you've been very helpful. We'll check it out. Is there anything else I can help you with?"

Not sure what was supposed to happen next, I asked a simple question: "Is it okay if I check back in a few days to see how it went?"

"Yes, of course." I was amazed at how accommodating the agent had been. His attitude was so different than the jaded one I had expected from the FBI.

Then, with a brief, courteous salutation, the call ended, and I flipped my phone closed. But despite how nice the man had been, I was shaking slightly after the conversation. Talking to the FBI was stressful.

About three days later, I called back to check on the case. When the screener answered the phone, I introduced myself as the person who called in the tip about a MySpace that might belong to the killer. I was immediately patched through to the duty agent.

A woman with a mid-toned, subtle Texas accent answered the phone. When I gave her a brief recap of my tip, she seemed really engaged in what I had to say.

She immediately replied that yes, she had heard of my tip. Out of the hundreds of community informants, she remembered *me*.

I politely asked, "Is he a suspect?"

Then, in a rather animated voice, she replied, "Oh yes. He's *definitely* a suspect."

Wow... My idea must have been good. I mean, I still couldn't be 100 percent certain I'd found the killer, but based on her response, my 99 percent confidence level did not wane.

However, my opinion would change three years later when a more likely candidate surfaced. In 2009, LaMarques Devon McWilliams made a move he'd undoubtedly live to regret. With a victim locked in the trunk of his car, he drove into a muddy area and got stuck. Instead of abandoning the vehicle and the woman, he pulled her out of the trunk and put her behind the steering wheel.

Then, McWilliams pushed the car from behind while she pressed the gas. The vehicle spun free from the wet earth, and the woman took off in the car, leaving her kidnapper behind, no doubt covered in a pile of mud.

A few minutes down the road, the victim called the cops. Shortly afterward, police arrested McWilliams, who fit well with descriptions of the killer: He was a thirty-three-year-old, heavyset black man with dreads.

The hunt for the serial killer came to a screeching halt after DNA tests run by the FBI linked McWilliams to several sexual assaults in the Acres Homes area, and one of the murders.[40] The authorities believed they had found their man. Two years later, he was sentenced to life in prison for one of the rapes, and all other charges were dropped.[41] [42] To this day, he maintains his innocence.

After hearing about McWilliams and his rape conviction, I became convinced that he was the killer and that I had turned in the wrong man. But although I had failed, I had gained invaluable investigative skills. While looking for the killer, I'd learned how to filter results on MySpace and had discovered methods to figure out the whereabouts of people on the site. This opened my eyes; anyone with internet access and enough persistence could find out almost anything about anyone. *Frightening...*

Regardless, I had discovered my talent for research went beyond finding solutions to computer programs—something that would come in handy throughout my life and especially during my hunt for bin Laden. Plus, successes with the serial killer project gave me the confidence I needed to proceed with other cases.

I also learned a lot about myself. I had enjoyed chasing this man down. I also loved the puzzle-solving aspect of the case. In other words, this type of work offered a mental and emotional payoff. Plus, I felt like my work could lead to something worthwhile. I could pay off my debts and help people in the process.

I had no idea at the time, but soon my work *would* make a difference. It would change the world for the better.

08

OTHER EARLY CASES

Over the next several weeks, I continued my detective work, expanding to missing persons. I was casting a wide net. Maybe one of my projects would be a success. Maybe I could make some money. Maybe I could rescue my finances.

One case I worked on involved a well-liked high school history teacher from Ocilla, Georgia. Tara Grinstead, a former beauty queen, was an attractive thirty-year-old with long, straight black hair and classic features. She was also a beauty contestant coach. In fact, the night before her disappearance, she'd attended a pageant barbecue. The next day, she never showed up for work.[43]

The police went to her home to investigate. Her car was parked in the driveway, unlocked with $100 in the console. In her home, her cell phone was charging and her dog, Dolly Madison, was alone. Her purse and keys were missing.[44] The Georgia Bureau of Investigation was called in almost immediately to aid local police and the sheriff's department with the investigation.[45]

My search began in July 2006, nearly a year after Tara turned up missing. At that point, there were still no new breaks in the case, even though a $200,000 reward had been offered for her recovery.[46] This would be enough money to pay off all my debts, including my mortgage, and still have money left over. So I eagerly took on the project. As usual, I started on MySpace.

I conducted a quick search to see if she was a member. Perhaps I could get some clues from her MySpace, if it existed. Maybe I'd find a suspicious acquaintance or an indicator that she had made prior plans to run away from her life.

Moments later, I got a surprising hit: There was a woman living in Florida with the same name and similar features. She had the same straight dark hair and stunning beauty. She also appeared to be about the same age as the missing woman. The pictures of the woman in Florida made it look like she was partying and having a good time. She had visited her MySpace only one day ago.

Could this be her? Perhaps she'd run away and was living in Florida. I tried to think for a moment why a woman living a seemingly charmed life would make such a drastic change. Maybe she was secretly unhappy. Maybe she'd had a breakdown. There was no way of knowing. I shrugged it off. You never know what is going on with people beneath the surface.

The next day, I called the Georgian authorities and spoke with an investigator. I offered to send him copies of the MySpace woman's profile pic and other uploaded photos so he could tell me if they looked like images of the missing person.

The officer listened with great interest. He agreed

that my theory had promise and asked me to email the photos to him. I got off the phone, sent him the pictures, and called him back a few minutes later. He also noticed the resemblance between the missing woman and the MySpace woman. I suggested to him that we get a forensic artist to look at the images and compare the two MySpace photos to those of Tara. He agreed to show them to a professional, and sounded hopeful that they could be a match.

I anxiously waited for a few days, filling the time by trying to figure out the Florida woman's address. My skills at using the full force of MySpace were getting better. I looked up the address of the person in Florida and found a match. It wasn't too difficult because there were so few people with that name. If this were the same woman, the Georgia Bureau would easily be able to pick her up.

I felt enthusiastic. This could be the one—the case that solved all my financial problems. And maybe I could help someone–help the missing woman's family.

A couple of days later, I received a phone call.

A man with a mild voice was on the other end. I recognized him as the same person I'd spoken with a few days earlier. "So, I forwarded the photos to a forensic artist."

I replied, hopeful, "*Really*? How'd it go?"

"Well, it's a negative. She said the bridge of the nose was too wide and the cheekbones were a little too high."

I could hear the dismay in my own voice. "Well, that's surprising. They sure did look alike."

He replied in a slightly sad tone. "Yes, I know. I really thought we could've had her."

I responded flatly, agreeing. "Yeah. I know. Too bad."

Like him, I was disappointed, so I decided to move on. The search was over. She was the wrong Tara.

Years later, in February 2017, thirty-three-year-old Ryan Alexander Duke, who was a former student at Grinstead's place of employment, would be arrested for her murder. Duke, who confessed to the crime, was still in jail awaiting trial as of July 2020.[47][48][49]

Regardless, for me, in 2006, the Grinstead case was another failed investigation.

Still, I had learned valuable skills that would eventually lead me into the future. I just didn't realize at the time what a huge success was ahead of me.

***

Although I had made no money, my confidence was continuing to grow, especially after the serial killer case. I felt that I could figure out the full name and address of just about anyone on MySpace, given enough time and effort. I would soon put this to the test.

One of my other cases would prove to be more difficult because the woman had a very common name. This would make her relatively anonymous, with thousands of MySpace pages belonging to people sharing the same identifiers. But I was undeterred. I loved a challenge and selected the case partially for that reason. This case would prove to be one of my longest, hardest-fought efforts.

The FBI was offering a $20,000 reward for information leading to the whereabouts of a woman from Hillsboro, Missouri. The missing woman was only twenty-six, and she was eight-and-a-half months pregnant with her second child when she disappeared. I have omitted her name as per her family's wishes.

Although this case had a smaller reward than the Tara Grinstead case, I felt a gush of empathy for her and her family. As a human being, I wanted to help them. I wanted to...*needed to* find her. Of course, I wouldn't turn down the money. I was desperate.

I began to examine the facts of the case.

After going to church, the woman went to the Hillsboro Civic Center to meet with the alleged father of her unborn child. About fifteen minutes into the discourse, she received a call from her former sister-in-law. Later that evening, her family became concerned when they couldn't reach her on her cell phone. Panicked, they began searching for her and called the authorities.

That night, friends of the family found her blue 1997 Pontiac Sunfire, abandoned and unlocked in the Center's parking lot. Her purse, cell phone, and keys were not in the car. She'd vanished. Failing to locate her, the family offered a reward for anyone who could help them figure out where she was or what had happened to her. The sheriff's department suspected foul play.

Maybe if she had a MySpace account, I could find it and look for clues. Perhaps there were communications with a potential perpetrator or comments that could lead to her whereabouts.

I initiated a query, plugging in her age, features, and the zip code of her hometown. Then I slowly expanded the distance in small increments from the area.

But despite hundreds of hits, I couldn't seem to find any MySpace users with the missing woman's name who looked like her. Because of this, the search was taking me an inordinate amount of time. Finally, after what felt like an eternity, I fixed my sights on a page of a woman with similar features to the missing woman. Also, they shared the same first name, middle initial, last name, and birth year.

But by then, I had expanded the search radius to 200 miles from Hillsboro—the missing woman's hometown. If this MySpace user was her, she had moved between 150 and 200 miles from home. With so many towns and cities in that range, finding her location would prove difficult. But at least I had a suspect.

The woman in the photograph was considerably larger than that of my quarry, but it was plausible that she had gained weight, especially since she'd been pregnant. They also both had blonde hair with lighter highlights. Although the MySpace woman's hair was longer, this wasn't a deal-breaker. It had been a year, and the missing woman could have grown out her hair. After all, the woman in the photo was starting show darker roots. They also both had stunning blue eyes and similar smiles.

Then, I noticed something even more interesting...a red Cardinal's T-shirt... Huh? ... *Yes!* ... *She was wearing a Cardinal's T-shirt.* That's a clue! It could be a clue to where she's living. I never watched baseball, so I Googled it. The team was from St. Louis, Missouri, only a 44-minute drive from Hillsboro. This was exciting stuff! It made me feel a lot more certain that I had the right woman.

Like the Tara suspect, the MySpace woman was very much alive and logging on to the platform regularly. I know it was odd to think that a woman who was about to have a baby would run, especially when she seemed to have so much family support. But I thought for a moment how I felt the weeks before having a baby—hormones raging, so ready to get it over with. And then there was the utter devastation of postpartum depression. Who knows? Maybe something happened with the baby. Maybe she panicked. Maybe she wanted out, to start over. But I had to stop—stop trying guess what could be going on inside her head. It was pointless. There were at least a million reasons a person would run.

So I decided to try to find the missing person based on the premise that the MySpace woman was her. But first things first: I had to be certain I had the right woman. The good news was that if it was her, she was alive. I had to...*had to* explore this avenue.

I picked up my phone and called the Jefferson County Sheriff's Department, the entity handling the case. My thought was that, as with my Tara Grinstead investigation, a forensic artist could look at the photos.

I spoke to the lead investigator. He sounded elderly and had a thick Missouri drawl. As I had hoped, he agreed to show the pics to a forensic artist for examination. "Send me th' photo and ah'll pass it on."

I thought back on some of the movies I'd seen with missing persons investigations. The movie version of Stephen King's *Misery* came to mind. In the story, Sheriff Buster, a kind, elderly small-town cop, investigated such a case, alone with only his wits. Of course, his efforts didn't end well for him as he, himself, became Annie Wilke's next victim. Hopefully, my work would have a better outcome.

Regardless, I was grateful that the real live detective in charge of the missing pregnant woman's case had agreed to help me. I didn't tell him where I got the photo because I was protective of my system, but a few minutes later I saved the pics to my desktop and sent them to the investigator via email.

However, the response I got after a two-day wait was disheartening. "Sorry, our artist couldn't make heads nor tails of it. The resolution was just too small."

But even though the photos were a bust, I wasn't ready to give up. There was another way that I could get a positive ID: The missing woman had a dolphin tattoo on her left breast. And the MySpace woman admitted to having a tattoo, in her profile, though she didn't give any details. By my thinking, if the MySpace woman and the missing woman had the same tattoo, that would be a positive identity match. I decided to investigate further.

Unfortunately, her settings only allowed friends to send her instant messages. So I nervously sent the MySpace woman a friend request. It was common for people to friend strangers on MySpace, especially if they both shared similar interests. In this case, the page owner was bisexual. So, we were both gender non-conforming.

A day later, she accepted my request.

I nervously sent her an instant message. *"Hey, don't you have a tattoo? I was thinking about getting one. Any recommendations?"*

She replied about a half-hour later with generic advice, *"Just pick something that's meaningful to you. You're going to have it your whole life."*

We engaged for a bit off and on over a few hours, bouncing around ideas for my "tattoo." The messages were sporadic and never in real time. Eventually, I asked her what kind she had. She confided that she had a fish on her foot. Unfortunately, this was not a match.

However, fish and dolphins share similarities. She could have been changing her story slightly. After all, the missing woman might have been trying to hide her identity.

I thought about it for a moment... A non-matching tattoo was only a negative ID if the MySpace woman was telling the whole truth.

I never messaged the MySpace woman again. It had been a short-lived, awkward ordeal and way too personal. I really didn't want to know any more about her, and I certainly didn't want to be her friend. *No...* It had merely been a fishing expedition, and I got what I wanted: the fish on her foot.

Despite inconclusive evidence, I continued to quietly look for the MySpace woman's address. If I couldn't ID her, maybe the authorities could. If I gave an address, they could go there and check her out in person.

As my focus quickly turned to finding the MySpace woman's location, the work in front of me seemed impossible. Like I said, she was living somewhere in a 200-mile radius from the missing woman's home.

But first, I had to figure out which state she was living in. I entered the MySpace woman's specs and checked to see if she was living in Missouri. Maybe the missing woman never left the state.

I spent the next hour sifting through the hits. But, *no dice...* The familiar page was not in the results. *No...* If this was the missing woman, she had definitely left Missouri.

I Googled a map of the US and examined it carefully. *Eight states...* There were eight states surrounding Missouri, and Indiana was also nearby. I also noticed that

Hillsboro was close to the Illinois border, so I would try there first. I plugged the same data from earlier into the MySpace search engine, this time substituting Illinois for Missouri. I took my time sifting through the listings. A half-hour later, the familiar page popped up...

Illinois...the MySpace woman was living in Illinois! She was close...*so close*...just one state over—a state near the border of the missing woman's hometown. *Amazing!* ... This made it seem even more likely that I had the right woman. A burst of adrenalin rushed over me. This was happening. I was going to *make* it happen!

I looked intently at the screen. *What was next?* ... The task at hand was daunting. I had discovered that the MySpace woman was in Illinois. But I looked it up: There were nearly 1300 cities, towns, and villages in that state. Figuring out which ones were within a 150 to 200-mile range of Hillsboro sounded like a nightmare.

I let out a long sigh. Maybe I was overthinking it. Maybe it would be easy. Maybe she had moved to a major city. I pushed forward... What's the biggest city in Illinois? *Chicago!* Could it be that easy? I checked the distance. *Ugh... Too far.* So I tried Springfield... *Too close...* Bloomington... *Too far...* I kept going, *ad nauseam. This was taking too long.*

A vague thought crept into the back of my mind. *This would be so much easier if I had a map and ruler.* But that would mean going to the store or maybe AAA, hoping to find a detailed map that included both Missouri and Illinois. I would also have to pick up a ruler. I couldn't remember the last time I'd seen one in the house. But this all sounded like effort. Surely there was a way to do this online. I mean, I had the entire internet at my disposal. And then...

Boom! ... Something struck me. *Google Earth...* Of course! ... I could use *Google Earth!*

I patiently downloaded the desktop version onto my computer. It felt like it was taking forever. *Curse my internet.* But still, at least it wasn't dial-up. My crappy Verizon DSL was making all of this possible. If only I hadn't uninstalled the software... I had hastily removed it from my computer a while back, in an effort to clear up resources. But I regretted it. *Google Earth* was so incredibly awesome. You could virtually travel the globe to anywhere on the planet and zone in on minute details— satellite images. It was the coolest thing. I could even see my own house from space, albeit blurry.

It would take me hours to completely master the software, but after only a few minutes of struggling with buttons and features, I managed to home in on Hillsboro, Missouri. I watched as the globe spun and quickly flew me to the town, giving me a bird's eye view of its streets and buildings. As I learned how to control *Google Earth*, I felt a thrill rushing through me. I loved to learn, and I was having fun playing with the electronic planet.

It would take several days and countless hours of work. I drew lines between municipalities, both big and small, carefully measuring distances. And every time I felt like I was close, I would plug their names into the MySpace search engine along with the woman's other specs, hoping for a match. In the end, I found her in the small town of Tuscola, Illinois, just 196-miles from the missing woman's home. From the time that I first took on the case, it had taken two weeks of intense effort to get to this point.

Tuscola... This was *huge!* I finally had a town. The rest would be easy.

I was electric with energy. I felt like I had accomplished the impossible. With no more than a very common name, I had figured out the hometown of a random person on MySpace. I had challenged my mind and solved a really difficult puzzle. Now, I just needed more details: a street address, a phone number—anything that could lead authorities to her.

I got up from my chair and sprinted to the living room. It was time to celebrate. I grabbed Nicki and the kids, and we went to Jade Garden, our favorite Chinese restaurant. We hadn't eaten out in weeks, and devil-may-care about the cost. I needed a break.

We spent the next hour sitting in a comfortable green booth eating, as I excitedly give everyone the blow-by-blow of the past several days. I did most of the talking, and I'm pretty sure Nicki tuned me out halfway through. But still, this was the most I'd eaten in days, and I was enjoying a much-needed energy release.

Finally, we headed home. I shoved Daun's leftover shrimp and broccoli into our cluttered fridge and headed back to work. Stretching, I sat down in the chair and positioned my fingers over the keyboard. *Where was I? ... Oh yes...* I needed to find out where the MySpace woman was living in the small town of Tuscola. There were only about 4500 people in the town and there was only one zip code. This would be easy. I could just look her up in the white pages.

I started with a simple AnyWho lookup. But there was no one in that town with her name; zero luck. I turned to PeopleLookup once again. However, it didn't yield any better results.

I had another look at the woman's site, thinking that maybe there was a clue somewhere in the comments.

There was nothing obvious. I decided to look even closer, scrutinizing every square inch of it. I had to be missing something.

I racked my brain. Normal white pages and even paid people searches had proven useless. *No...* If the woman lived in the town, her residence wasn't listed under her name. She was either using an alias or living under someone else's lease or homeownership. So, I wouldn't be able to locate the page owner using her name. I needed a more sophisticated way to search.

I thought back to the Cole-like street directory I had utilized in the serial killer case—the one that listed all the streets and addresses in a neighborhood. I went through the tedious process of plugging each street into the MySpace search engine, hoping her photo would pop up. I ignored the residents' names because, according to PeopleLookup, there was no one with the missing woman's name living in that town.

After about two days of intermittent queries and miles of frustration, I finally got a hit on a street name. Now for the hard part. I still needed a street address. I would have to input every address on that street.

I feverishly worked my way through them: copy, paste, search, check for a hit. No results. Browser back button and repeat. Copy, paste, search, check for a hit. No results. Back button.

Copy, paste, search, check for a hit. No results. Back—

Wait, what was that? I thought I missed something. I'd been moving too fast. Forward button. And then, the realization.

Oh, my God...

There she was, smiling at me—the MySpace woman.

I'd found her. I'd found her! *I'd found her!* I had her address!

I rushed into the living room to find Nicki. I had to tell someone. I *had to* tell her.

But she wasn't in the common area... I wandered around the house calling her name. *Nickieee...* I looked in the kitchen... Nope. *Nickieee.* Where could she be? I checked the garage. Occasionally she like to go out there and organize her stuff. *No...*not in the garage. Back in the living room, I glanced at the clock: 9 p.m. Too early for bed. *Nickieee!* I began to panic, my heart racing. Why wasn't she answering? This wasn't normal. This wasn't like her. She *always* answered. Images of the missing pregnant woman flashed before my eyes. Her blondish hair...her smile... What if Nicki wandered off and was kidnapped? *Murdered?* What if I never saw her again? I frantically rushed down the hall toward our bedroom, screaming at the top of my lungs. *Nickieee!!!*

But before I reached our room, Daun's door swung open. "*Mom.* Calm down! She just went to the store!"

I stopped cold. I took a deep breath and burst into tears. *I couldn't believe it!* ... Tears turned to rage. I was furious...furious at Nicki. How could she do this to me? Why didn't she tell me where she was going?

I took a deep breath. *Calm down, Barbara. Calm down.* Your daughter doesn't need to see you like this.

"Sorry, Daun." Despite my efforts, I couldn't stop my hot, angry tears. I took another deep breath. "Thanks for telling me. I wish she would have said something."

Daun looked a little worried. "She did... She went around the house asking if anyone needed anything. You must not have been listening."

Wow! ... All this panic... This was *my* fault? I was still mad, but this time at myself. Why did I always do this? Why did I always imagine the worst-case scenario? In that moment, I hated being me.

I managed to calm down a little and looked back at Daun. "Wow, okay. I feel really stupid. I think I'm just gonna go get some water. Besides, I need to blow my nose."

As Daun watched me slink off into the kitchen, she shouted in my direction. "Alright, well, I'm going back to my game."

I sat at the kitchen table, drinking water and sulking. It took me a half-hour to start feeling better. Nicki finally returned home with a few groceries. But by then, I was back at my desk, working.

I frowned at the screen. Sure, I had an address, but whose address had I found? The missing woman's name was not listed at that location even though the address was a match with the MySpace I'd been hunting for.

The name was strange and unfamiliar. Was she using an alias? Or maybe the name belonged to someone she was living with. I had to find out more, so I conducted an PeopleLookup search, hoping for a birthdate or relatives' names. There was neither, which was strange because typically results from the site listed both. Next, I checked MySpace... *Nothing*... Then I looked for birth certificates, marriage licenses, ancestry websites. She didn't appear to be anywhere online, which was odd, even back in 2006. And like I said, the name was unusual. After a thorough investigation, I could find no record of her existence.

Regardless, the name itself seemed like a joke, some kind of a play on the words "marijuana" and "wine." I went back to the posts on the MySpace woman's wall and the comments on her photos. There was an interesting reference to living in wine country. But the state she was in wasn't known for growing wine... *Suspicious*... Maybe the name listed at the Tuscola address was an alias. Maybe the missing woman was hiding there, using a fake name.

So, here's what I had: a possible alias, a verified address, a T-shirt of a team near the missing woman's home, similar hair and features, and a non-matching, but similar, tattoo. *Close enough*... At that point, I felt like I had enough to contact authorities. I was ready to give it a shot. Hopefully, they could go to the MySpace woman's home and have a look at her in person.

One final time, I called the Jefferson County Sheriff's Department. Minutes later, I sent the lead investigator an email with my results. But I never called back to check the outcome because I didn't want to know if I was wrong. The idea of it made me anxious. Instead, I occasionally read the news to see if the missing woman had been found.

Eventually, I lost patience and decided to get a second opinion on the photographs. I went back to the MySpace woman's page to look for more pics. I clicked on the images I had downloaded previously. *Is that...a higher resolution?* I compared the images to my earlier copies. *Yes!* ... The image was larger, clearer. Finally, I had an acquaintance analyze them, and he verified what I feared: The MySpace photos were not of the missing woman, but of someone with the same name. At that point I was 100 percent certain I had the wrong woman. To date, the missing pregnant woman still hasn't been found.

But despite the negative outcome, I was proud of what I'd accomplished. At this point, the most important thing was the process, not finding the missing person nor the killer. I moved on to the next case, and the next, and the next. I tried to follow the path of a convicted killer who had escaped from prison until authorities found him dead by his own hand. Also, I researched the case of a Houston college student who'd been burned to death in her own bed. There were several others, more than I can recall.

None of the cases were fruitful. But none of them were futile. Each one helped me grow increasingly confident that I could locate the residence of nearly any stranger on MySpace. Each new case, each new skill, each new adventure brought me that much closer to finding Osama bin Laden.

09

MY HAPPY PLACE

At first, the investigations were exhilarating. Every case was a puzzle to solve. Sherlock Holmes himself, the famous fictional Victorian detective, saw these types of mysteries as entertainment, once crying out, "Come, Watson, come! The game's afoot!"

Above all, I've always enjoyed intellectual challenges because I find them invigorating. During the missing pregnant woman investigation especially, I felt like my brain was crackling with electricity and my synapses were firing at a rapid rate, particularly when I was drawing the lines on Google maps. Locating the addresses that corresponded with the MySpace accounts was thrilling beyond belief. Even more exciting was the promise of lucrative rewards for my efforts.

But expending so much brain power caused an unintentional consequence: exhaustion. Somehow, through all the excitement, I'd forgotten to take breaks. From the start, I was burning the candle at both ends by pulling a lot of all-nighters. And when I did sleep, I would often grab only two or three sporadic hours. On good days, I'd get five or six. Day and night was irrelevant.

So, not far into my early operations, I reached a tipping point. I felt like my mind and body were going to overload if they were pushed any further. I wasn't sure how long I could keep up the pace and remain rational. In short, I was becoming delirious. What had been fun was now causing me extreme anxiety and tension. My neck and shoulders were so tight that I thought someone could probably bust bricks on them. I knew I needed to let myself take a break.

That night, I had a thought: I could call Adam and see if he had any more computers for me to fix. It had been a couple of days since I'd worked. Maybe focusing on PC problems for a while would give my mind a break from the detective efforts. Besides, even if it was only forty bucks per repair, I needed the money.

During a typical workday, I'd spend several hours running multiple virus scans, Googling solutions, hand-editing registry settings, tinkering with hardware, and completing a myriad of other tasks, each with varying levels of challenge—most of them, fun and interesting. This was my happy place.

Maybe I could go there...

Maybe tomorrow.

***

The next morning at 8:30, I flipped open my phone and gave Adam a call. After several rings, he answered the phone.

"Computer Doctors."

His voice caught me off guard because I was expecting his voicemail. Most of the time, he was too busy to pick up.

"Hey, Adam. How's it going?"

As usual, Adam sounded glad to hear my voice. "Fine. Did you get my message?"

"Nope. You left me a voicemail?" I had just woken up and hadn't checked my inbox yet. Usually, I turned my sound off at night. I didn't like to be unexpectedly woken up.

I continued. "Okay. What do you need?"

Adam filled me in. "Well, I've got three computers for you and maybe a couple more coming later today."

"Awesome!" I loved PC repair work, and I loved money. It was a win-win.

"Well, two of them are really 'virused up.' It should just be some routine scanning."

I knew what that meant: *boring*. It meant loading a long, pre-determined list of anti-malware software and running a million tedious scans. It would take hours, and waiting for the scans to complete was torture because I couldn't tear myself away from the screen. I'd catch myself staring at it, in a trance. I couldn't stop watching as the progress bar slowly inched its way to the end. *No...* I was *compelled* to watch, as if from some unseen force. *There was no choice.* So I would be stuck there, for as long as an hour at a time, pointlessly gawking at the display. Eventually, I'd reluctantly look away, so I could work on another project or go to the bathroom, but it wasn't long before I was sucked back in. The funny thing is, I wasn't even sure why I was doing it. I guess I was just hoping something interesting would happen, that I'd catch the scan in action as it found something.

And when Nicki was around, and caught me glued to the monitor, she would laugh at me and say, "Don't you ever get tired of staring at the screen? What, are you expecting it to do a trick?" I would just shrug her off and keep staring, mesmerized, caught in the circular movement of my mind.

But sometimes, I would get lucky. Sometimes virus issues weren't boring at all. They could make for fun enigmas if the bug was particularly challenging, or *Windows* was really jacked up. And occasionally, the viruses had to be removed manually or by trying multiple tools until I finally found one that worked. Often, yanking the viruses wasn't enough. After removal, the machine would be left so crippled that it had to be rehabilitated through professional tweaking. I almost hoped this machine presented that level of challenge, so I could become absorbed in it. I needed the distraction.

Adam kept going. "The other one won't boot up. It probably just needs a power supply. I just picked up a couple of new ones at Microcenter. They're sitting on the right side of the table next to that old Dell tower."

I knew exactly which tower he was talking about; it had been there a while. It was an older unit, and it needed a proprietary Dell power supply, which we were waiting to come in from eBay. *What a pain in the ass.*

I replied enthusiastically, "Okay, just let me make some coffee and I'll be right over."

Twenty minutes later, I was on the road with my *ginormous* blue travel mug in hand, its lid slapped tightly on. It was the one with the signature Buc-ee's beaver on it. I had picked it up at the large Texas-based convenience store's Bastrop location during a road trip to Austin. When I wasn't holding it, the mug sat shotgun on the passenger side because it was too big for my cup holder. Regardless, Nicki and the kids were still asleep. When Nicki woke up, she'd know I was at work. It was expected.

Thirty minutes into my trip, I was getting closer to Adam's office when I noticed I was having trouble keeping my eyes open. This was a real problem in traffic. I slapped myself on the cheeks multiple times and cranked the a/c on high so it would blow cold air on my face.

But it wasn't enough, so I reached in the center console and grabbed my bottle of ephedra, a natural stimulant that had been popular for weight loss during the late 1990s and early 2000s. Although it had been banned for sale—but not consumption—in the US since 2003, I had purchased several bottles of Metabolife 356, a once-popular diet pill, on eBay while they were still available.

I popped two of the tablets in my mouth and carefully swallowed them with some coffee. I had to be careful not to burn my throat. The trick was to swish the hot beverage around in my mouth until it cooled down. Having taken the pills, I felt a little better knowing that help was on the way. Maybe I'd survive the trip.

Finally, forty-five minutes after leaving home, I arrived at Adam's shop. After getting out of the car, I reached into my pocket and pulled out my keys. Finally, I walked up to the glass door and unlocked it. But as I entered, I stopped dead and convulsed.

"*Hey.*"

It was Adam.

I was practically screaming. "*God...* You scared the *shit* out of me!"

Adam was smirking. "Yes. I hear I can have that

effect on people."

Taking a deep breath, I calmed down a bit. After all, it was just Adam.

"I wasn't expecting you to be here. I thought you'd be out on a job."

Adam was sitting at the far end of the room, using a large Philips head screwdriver to remove the side off an ancient, cream-colored tower. He looked up as I walked in the door.

As I entered, cool air and the smell of dust and electronic components wafted toward me. The environment was friendly and familiar. More importantly, it made me happy. I couldn't wait to get to work.

Unfortunately, Adam couldn't stay, but I didn't really mind being left alone. After all, it was one of my favorite places. He explained, "I'm just here for a few minutes. I needed to drop off a couple of computers and pick up some RAM."

The deal Adam and I had negotiated was that I would work in the office on machines that needed more intensive care. Customers would pay a flat rate for these items no matter how much time I spent on them. Adam would go to homes and businesses and work on-site, charging by the hour. Having me in the office made it possible for him to do more outside work and make more money.

I shook my Buc-ee's mug—the best way to check the fullness level with the lid on...

Empty...

I glanced toward Adam. "Alright. Can I start some coffee before you show me what we have?"

Adam looked back at me. "Sure, but make it quick. I can't stay for long. I've gotta be somewhere in a half-hour." Adam was always busy. Despite being in his forties, he had more energy than most people I knew. But regardless of his packed scheduled, he still managed to make time for me.

A few minutes later, the coffee was brewing. I sat down next to Adam, who was carefully pulling RAM out of the tower he'd just finished cracking open. He sometimes raided his graveyard when he needed older-type RAM or some other random part.

I watched him as he pulled out the RAM, and I commented, "Is that PC100?"

"Yep." This meant that Adam was stealing it to fix a computer that was probably running *Windows 98* or *Windows 2000*. That type of RAM had been outdated years ago.

"Is it 128 megabytes?"

"Yes." Adam was frowning a little. "Are you okay?"

I must have been wearing my heart on my sleeve. "I'm fine."

Adam was persistent. "Are you sure? You seem really worn out to me."

I didn't fight it any more. "Well, I haven't gotten much sleep lately. I'm running on caffeine and fumes. I actually had to take a couple of ephedra just to make it here."

Adam took a moment to chastise me. "Hey, be careful with that stuff. I used to take it years ago, and it really elevated my blood pressure."

I was curious about his experience. "Did you lose any weight?"

"Yes, but it wasn't worth it. It was affecting my health."

I tried to reassure him. "It's fine. I don't have any

heart issues. I've just been thoroughly checked out." It was true. I'd had a stress test and a bunch of blood work a while back. Zero issues.

"Well, that's good. Just be careful."

I nodded. "Yes, I know."

But Adam kept quizzing me. "Is there anything else going on?"

I decided to confide in him. "I'm actually really obsessing on something right now."

"What is it this time?"

"I think I've found a way to pay off my credit card debt."

Adam knew about my money problems. I had turned to him for advice weeks prior, and I knew that he could take my honesty.

"What're you gonna win the lottery?"

I briefly explained what I'd been up to. "I'm actually trying to collect reward money for finding missing people and criminals. Some are worth as much as $200,000."

Adam was supportive, albeit tentatively.

"Wow... That's a lot of money. But how are you going about it?"

I grappled to explain my process in a few sentences: "Mostly MySpace. It's a long story. But my point is that it's really stressing me out, and I'm losing a lot of sleep."

His brow furrowed with concern. "Then why are you still doing it?"

"I can't stop. The obsession is too strong. Besides, the idea of making all that money is exciting."

Still concerned, he shot me a warning: "Okay. Just watch yourself."

"Yes. I am. I'm probably gonna go see a movie or

something. I need a break. I was actually hoping that coming to work today would pull me away from it for a while."

Adam nodded in agreement. "Yes, when I'm overwhelmed, sometimes it helps me to keep busy." He waved his hand toward the coffee maker. "I think it's ready."

I glanced over at him as I headed over to get some of the dark brew. "You want a cup?"

"Sure. Two creams and three or four packets of sugar."

I already knew how to fix his coffee, but he still always felt the need to tell me how he wanted it.

As I went to get the coffee, Adam addressed me once again. "Hey, I've gotta get going. Let me just show you what I have, and then I've gotta bolt."

I walked toward him and handed him the coffee. Adam, who was always polite, gently took the cup and said, "Thanks."

I went into work mode. "Alright, what've you got?"

Adam spent a few minutes explaining the jobs he'd laid out for me. He basically repeated the same things he'd told me over the phone, but with much more detail. I had my work cut out for me.

Then, Adam started to move toward the door, coffee and RAM in hand. "Alright, I'm gonna take off."

But before I could say, "See ya later," he turned around and faced me.

"Hey, you look like you could use a hug. Do you want a hug?"

I didn't hesitate. Adam was a great hugger. "Sure."

He set down all the stuff in his hands and wrapped his arms around me, squeezing tightly. I squeezed back.

We held each other for several seconds.
Adam was a good friend.

10

RELAX, IT'S JUST PIRATES!

I am my own worst enemy.

Despite work's allure, it hadn't been quite the panacea I'd been hoping for. I needed to rest my mind. I needed to not think for a while. What had I told Adam? *Yeah*... Maybe a movie...

I thought for a moment. *Tomorrow!* ... Tomorrow was Sunday, and we had agreed to take the kids to see their father. *Yes*... Jimmy... It was his weekend to see the kids. I always made sure they got to see him every other week. We'd have to make the forty-five-minute drive to his home. Maybe we could incorporate a trip to the movies.

Jimmy was an unrepentant hippie with long salt-and-pepper hair and a scraggly beard and mustache. He lived with his wife, Mandy, in a dilapidated old wooden house with chipping white paint, in a particularly seedy part of the Third Ward in Houston. His home also didn't have adequate air conditioning for the heat of the Southeast Texas summer. So even though he wasn't drinking at the time, leaving the kids there for the weekend would have been inappropriate. To top it off, Jimmy didn't have a car.

Regardless of the situation, I wanted the kids, who were two and four when we were divorced, to be able to spend time with their dad. So, once every other week, we would make the long drive to Houston and bring him to our place to visit. At first, Jimmy and Mandy would often sleep on our old hide-a-bed. But interpersonal conflicts eventually ended that arrangement.

So when Jimmy's weekend rolled around, if we could, we'd pick him and Mandy up and all go to dinner and the movies. This time we decided to see *Pirates of the Caribbean: Deadman's Chest*, the second movie in the franchise.

The Santa Fe was so crammed that Daun had to ride in the hatchback area—an honor she'd volunteered for. We headed for AMC Gulf Pointe 30. Although it was expensive, it was the closest theater still showing the movie we'd chosen. It had already been out for a few weeks.

But despite the allure of Captain Jack Sparrow and the stunning special effects, I couldn't concentrate on the show. My mind kept mulling over the cases and the conversations I'd undertaken with law enforcement, thinking of new ways to solve problems.

I sat there with my family for about twenty minutes, trying desperately to follow the dialogue. When I noticed I couldn't distract myself or rest my mind enough to watch the movie, I began to worry...

If I couldn't take a break, how was I going to continue this effort? I needed to pull out of credit-card debt. My family's financial security—our way of life—depended on it. The constant worrying made it impossible to concentrate. As the movie played on the big screen in front of me, my anxiety got so bad that I started worrying about worrying. It was growing exponentially.

After about thirty minutes, I had no idea what was going on with the plot and hadn't managed to decipher a single syllable of dialogue. Finally, I burst into tears. Trying to control myself, I nudged Nicki and asked for the keys. Confused, she reluctantly handed them to me, and I headed out to the car. I climbed into the passenger seat, took off my shoes, and used my feet to rearrange the clutter of cups and cans in the footwell, creating a brief rattle. Then I turned on the classic rock station, which was playing Kansas' "Carry on Wayward Son." Ripping off my bra using the under-the-sleeve technique and unfastening the button on my Lee jeans, I leaned back in the seat and tried to take slow, deep breaths. *I was shaking...*

But just as I began to calm down a little, the obsessive impulse to work the latest case returned with a vengeance. My mind sped through every detail: My latest quarry had been the prison escapee on the loose. He had a fairly common name, but after plugging in his hometown, I had only found a few MySpace pages that could belong to him. He hadn't been in prison that long, so it was conceivable that he could have created a MySpace prior to his incarceration. According to authorities, he'd been spotted in several adjoining towns. He was on the move. I thought it was possible that he could be posting while on the run.

I tried to remember the details on the various pages. Which one was most likely to have been written by someone hiding from the law? Even if I found his page, how would I track him down to an address? The best I could do was to try to figure out which town he was staying in based on his posts and his known trajectory.

I began to think this case was futile, but I needed to look back over the clues to be sure. I mean, should I give up on looking for him? Should I move on? ... I became frustrated as I struggled to remember details on the MySpace pages. But it was useless. I had to get home. I had to get back to my computer and the internet.

Before long, I noticed our group approaching the car. The movie was over. *Good...* I could finally go home. As they opened the doors, I quickly buttoned my pants and sat upright. The bra was inconsequential.

Nicki hopped into the driver's seat. Peter squeezed between Jimmy and Mandy in the back seat, and Daun, once again, opened the hatchback and crawled into the rear compartment. Peter leaned over behind him toward Daun as they started excitedly discussing the kraken attack. Peter was arguing that the scene was unrealistic because the creature couldn't possibly wrap its tentacles around the ship and tear it to pieces. But Daun was like, "*No!* If krakens were real and that big, they could definitely take out a ship that size." Peter continued to argue. "*No way!* They're basically giant squids. They wouldn't be strong enough..."

But then their voices trailed off. *Sudden silence...* They knew something was wrong. Like the rest of the group, I think my kids were worried about me.

Nicki looked at me, puzzled. "What happened? I was really surprised when you asked for the keys. Why'd you leave?"

She came across as irritated. And I was still a little shaken.

"I was having an anxiety attack."

Then Jimmy piped in. I felt like they were ganging

up on me. *"Why? It's just a movie."*

Jimmy seemed worried. I stalled for a moment. I didn't like his tone. When Jimmy got worried, his tone would switch to a "man-whine." This was a grumpy, adult-male, version of a classic whine—way worse than anything most women and children could produce. Even worse, when he was concerned, his annoying, Oakie accent would ramp up. And there was hint of something else—he sounded incredulous. He was often dismissive of my feelings and probably didn't think I had anything to be anxious about. We were supposed to be having a good time. In that moment, I hated the sound of his voice.

So instead of feeling cared for, I bristled at his tone and was annoyed and defensive. "I'm just too stuck in my head. I couldn't concentrate on the movie. I had to leave. I was freaking out."

Jimmy wasn't surprised. He'd seen this before when we were married. *"Are you okay?"*

Trying unsuccessfully to hold back my mounting aggravation, I replied, *"I'm fine!* I think I just need some sleep. I'm exhausted."

Although this response overly simplified my situation, it wasn't a lie. But I wasn't ready to tell Jimmy about why I was so wiped out. The full truth was that the detective work had been wearing at me.

Jimmy kept going, sounding even more concerned and more whiney, *"Why?* Aren't you getting enough sleep?"

I felt myself becoming defensive. I didn't like my ex-husband's tone. "Not really. *No.* I'm not getting enough sleep. But don't worry, Jimmy. I'm taking care of myself. I actually might start taking something to help me sleep. I just have to catch up." But even as the words left my lips, I had little hope that, even with sleep aids, I would catch up—not anytime soon.

At this point, Peter stuck in his earbuds and began playing with his Nintendo DS. He didn't like these types of conversations. He probably didn't want to think about my anxiety. Daun continued to listen from the back seat. She has always been more comfortable with crises than Peter.

Jimmy persisted, the sound of his voice continuing to wear at me. "*Baby*, are you *sure* you're okay? I know how you are when you get like this. I'm worried about you."

I cringed. We had been divorced for nearly eight years, but sometimes he still slipped up and called me "baby." *Ugh...*

At this point I completely lost patience, but I was trying to maintain a cool exterior. I knew Jimmy meant well. "I'll be fine. I don't really wanna get into it. *Just drop it.*" I didn't have the energy to explain what I'd been up to.

Thankfully, Mandy intervened, turning to Jimmy with her dark eyes, chiding him, slowly and meticulously speaking with her palsied voice, punctuating her words, and moving her pointed finger in a circular motion. "Jimmm...my, leave her alone. I *don't*...think... she wants to talk...about it."

Jimmy relented. "Okay. I'm still worried. But I'll drop it."

I was grateful. After a few moments of silence, I returned to my obsession, only vaguely aware that Jimmy and Nicki were talking about me.

***

Later that night, when Nicki and I were lying in bed, far, far away from my ex-husband, I decided to discuss my anxiety attack with her.

Lying on my back with a pillow curled under my head, I turned and looked at Nicki. "Do you get what happened earlier?"

She tore herself away from her book and craned her head around. "Not really."

I was blunt. "I was having an anxiety attack. I just...I just couldn't watch the show. I couldn't concentrate."

Sounding slightly annoyed, Nicki replied, "Yes. I was really surprised when you asked for the keys and got up and left."

I tried to reassure her because I could tell my actions had hurt her feelings. After all, we were supposed to be having a good time.

"I'm really sorry. It's nothing personal. It was really freaking me out. I was sitting there staring at the screen, and I'm seeing lips moving, but I couldn't understand a word they were saying. There was no pulling myself out of my head."

Nicki went from annoyed to slightly concerned. "Yeah. Well, what're you going to do then?"

I let out a loud sigh. "I dunno. This whole thing with the investigations... I'm starting to feel overwhelmed. I'm not really sure, but I kind of feel like maybe I should stop the work. But at the same time, I could make all this money and pay off my debt. Also, I feel like I'm helping people."

Nicki tried to sound logical. "Yes, it's a hard decision. I don't know..."

Her voice trailed off a bit, and she paused for a moment, trying to come up with a solution. "Maybe you can take a break from it?"

My voice dropped to a near whisper. I was about to say something I didn't want to admit to myself or Nicki. "I don't think I can."

I continued, distraught, "You know how I am. I mean, it's like all or nothing with me, you know? If I do manage to take a break, I'll never go back to the work. I'll stop completely, and there's no turning back. But I'm worried that if I keep up at this rate, I'll go out of my mind."

"Is it really worth your mental health, doing this?"

I let out another loud sigh and paused for a second, considering what she'd said. "I dunno. I mean, you're probably right. But it's really hard to stop. I'm just so enthusiastic about it, you know?"

As usual, Nicki was going to support me, whatever my decision. Regardless, she appeared to be on the fence. "Well, maybe you should keep going then. I don't know, it's hard to say what to do."

I kept fishing for definitive advice. "I dunno, you and Jimmy seemed kind of worried about me."

Softening her voice, Nicki spoke in a subtle, loving manner. "Yeah, we definitely are worried. I mean, it was disconcerting how you couldn't even get through the movie without having a major anxiety attack.

I kept fishing. "What's your main concern?"

"What if you actually *did* lose your mind?"

I took a deep breath as her words registered in my head. "Man, you're right. I probably could."

Looking straight at me with intense green eyes, Nicki questioned me. "Well, do you think you can quit?"

I didn't hesitate. "No. I don't think I can. I can't make myself stop. And I'm beyond exhausted. I'm not sleeping well. I'm not sure what to do."

Then Nicki stated the obvious. "It sounds like you need to catch up on your sleep."

"Yeah. I think you're right... I guess I can go see Dr. Chen. Maybe he could give me some sleeping pills or something."

Nicki appeared relieved that we'd made a decision. "Yes, that might work. Like I said, maybe you just need to catch up on your sleep."

"Yeah. Maybe getting some sleep will help me put on the brakes. I need to stop this...this work somehow. I have to take care of myself. I don't want to lose my mind."

Nicki nodded slowly. "Yeah. I'm pretty worried, and it sounds like you are, too."

I let out a sad sigh. Was I ready to let this go? "Alright, well, I guess I'll give him a call tomorrow and see if I can get an appointment."

"Yeah. Sounds like a plan."

With that, we had reached an agreement. I was going to stop my amateur detective work. I headed to bed, determined that it was finally over.

11

THE RAINBOW

The next day passed slowly as I unsuccessfully struggled to avoid all detective work. That night, I was still so obsessed that I didn't sleep at all. Instead, I passed out around 1 p.m. Tuesday afternoon and woke up an hour or so before dusk. I'd gotten maybe six hours of sleep—not nearly enough. Sitting on our sunken, black sofa, I flipped open my laptop, set it on the coffee table, and stared blankly at the screen. I didn't know what to do without my cases.

Moments later, I woke from my fog and checked my email, refreshing the screen a few times to make sure nothing new had arrived. But the inbox was disappointingly empty. I thought about going to MySpace, but I was trying to resist. It was pulling at me, but I wasn't supposed to go there. I wasn't supposed to work.

Unsure what to do with myself, I quickly became bored and my brain grew foggy. Plus, I was still wiped out from the night before. I began to nod off—my head drooping downward briefly and then snapping back up. This repeated several times before I finally drifted to sleep, maintaining my position at the keyboard.

The next thing I knew, I felt something tapping my shoulder. *Wh...What? ...* Oh... It was Nicki, leaning over at me from her easy chair. She was saying something unintelligible.

Startled, I struggled to respond. "Wh...what? Did you say something?"

"I said, did you get the mail yet?"

I looked up at her. "No... Sorry. I must have nodded off. Gimme a minute to wake up, and I'll go check it."

I looked down at the coffee table and noticed a cup of coffee. Nicki must have set there when I was asleep. I took a quick sip, then set it back down. *Ugh...*lukewarm. But at least it wasn't cold. It was drinkable. I picked it back up and chugged the rest of it. I guess lukewarm coffee had its advantages. Moments later, I pushed myself up with my arms, slowly heaved myself off the couch, and stood up, stopping to catch my balance. *Why was this damned couch always so hard to get up from?* Damn its sunken-in cushions. Oh well, at least it was better than that awful hide-a-bed we had when the kids were little.

After getting up, I worked my way around the coffee table and headed toward the front door. Nicki hollered toward me, "You might want to take your socks off. The ground is *super* wet. It's been raining all day."

I leaned down and pulled off my yellowed, non-matching ankle socks. One of them had the word "USA" stitched in red, white, and blue. It was a pair I'd stolen from Mom when I was fourteen years old, during the 1984 LA Olympics. She bought them because there had been a temporary wave of patriotism when the US hockey team beat Russia for the first time, attaining the gold. Although I had lost its mate years ago, I kept the sock because it was sentimental. I chucked the socks on the ground, grabbed the doorknob and swung open the door.

A moment later, I stepped down over the threshold to the concrete entryway, closing the door behind me so I wouldn't accidentally let out Midnight, who was strictly an indoor kitty. As I moved away from the entrance, I braced myself on the brick column to my left and looked up.

Wow!... Stunned, I let out an audible gasp.

A bright, perfect full rainbow stretched above the lush green field in front of me, ending behind the brick duplexes to the right of the clearing.

I had seen dozens of rainbows in my life, and they were all nice. But normally, they were simply a colorful arc coming out of the sky with no obvious start or finish. Unfortunately, I often didn't even discover them until after they were beginning to fade. And only one end would be touching the ground, if any. When I was a little kid, I used to imagine literally searching for the pot of gold at the end of the rainbow. I always wondered how I could find it if it ended in a cloud.

But this one was different. Both ends were distinct, and touching the skyline on opposite sides of the pasture. And there were no breaks in its brilliant multi-colored arc. Even better, I had spotted it at the height of its spectacular glory. The colors hadn't even begun to fade. They were perfect and bright. It was as if the heavens themselves had opened up in front of me.

Behind the fence on the far left side of the field, a horse leaned his head down, quietly eating grass. The sky sparkled with a reddish haze, indicating the end of rain and the soon-to-be setting sun. It was all so perfect, pristine.

And there it was—not arcing over a broad, powerful waterfall at Yosemite, not in a clearing surrounded by the dense pine forests of Washington State, not over the deep chasms of the Grand Canyon or shimmering over the Rocky Mountains. *No...* The most gorgeous thing I had ever seen was in the field across from our home. None of the neighbors were out gawking at it. No people in cars were stopping to take pictures. It seemed like the rainbow had been sent especially for me, a personal gift from God. I felt so loved that tears begin to well up in my eyes.

Suddenly, I snapped out of my trance and realized I wanted to share the view with Nicki, Peter, and Daun. I swung open the door and hollered into the living room.

"Y'all've gotta come see this rainbow. It's *amazing!*"

No doubt hearing the excitement in my voice, they all came rushing out.

Nicki and the kids were thrilled. After a few moments, Nicki rushed back inside to grab the digital camera. The arc was so wide that it took four shots to capture the entire thing. Later, someone would piece them all together using Photoshop.

After several minutes of basking in the rainbow's glory and cheerfully bantering about its magnificence, we headed back into the house. Peter meandered over to the kitchen to grab a bag of spicy Doritos, while Daun went to her room to play *Pokémon Leaf Green* on her DS. Lucky for her, the system was backwards compatible. Meanwhile, Nicki and I plopped down on the couch and looked at each other, stunned.

I turned to Nicki. "So, what did you think of that?"

Nicki's face lit up. "That was *awesome.*"

"*I know.* That was the best rainbow I've ever seen. Like, a once-in-a-lifetime thing."

Nicki nodded, "I know, *right*?"

I couldn't stop gushing over the experience. "You've never seen anything like *that* before, have you? It's really unusual to see something like that. I mean, right across from our house."

"Yeah. That's why I got the camera."

I hoped she'd caught it all. I wanted to remember this moment. It was special.

Once again, sentimental tears began welling in my eyes. "*My God...* It makes me want to cry. It was so perfect. What do *you* think? It just seems so miraculous."

I began sobbing softly, but Nicki pulled me out of it. "Maybe it's a message."

"Yes, I kind of think so, too. It's kind of like God is telling me, '*You know, Barbara, it's going to be alright. You know, it's going to be alright, no matter what.*' "

Nicki was smiling gently. "Remember Noah? The rainbow is God's promise. I think you're right."

I considered her words for a moment. "Yeah. I mean, maybe I'm supposed to keep going with my work. Maybe I'm meant to help somebody. Maybe something really great is going to happen. *I can feel it.*"

Nicki went with it. "Yeah, well it seems that way—"

I kept going, blowing past her response. "I know it's weird, but it just seems so obvious to me. I think it's going to be okay. I think I need to do this."

Usually when I interrupted her, Nicki got upset. But she didn't seem to mind this time. She kept listening.

"I mean, I'm not going to lose my mind. I think God's telling me that he's watching out for me." Then I fixed my gaze on her, adding, "Do you agree? Should I keep going with this?"

Nicki paused for a second, carefully considering my words. "Well, I think you might be right. Like, it's a message. I mean, how do you feel about it?"

I lowered my voice a bit. "It seems pretty clear to me. But I need you to agree because we're going to go through this together."

"Well, I mean, yeah, I think you should keep going."

Finally, I added, "And there's one more thing: I think I'm still going call Dr. Chen and ask for those sleeping pills."

Nicki agreed. "Yeah, that might be a good idea."

The thought of the sleep aids gave me a glimmer of hope. Maybe I'd finally get some rest.

12

JOINING THE WAR ON TERROR

Sleep not withstanding, the rainbow made me realize that my work was important. Still, I didn't know yet just how important it would become. I was on the brink of bringing down the most notorious terrorist in the world, the kingpin behind 9/11: Osama bin Laden himself.

In reality, I had been no different from every other American during the days and weeks after September 11, 2001. I wanted to do something about the suffering. I gave $15 to a fund for the victims—more than I could afford. I wished I could do more. I *wanted* to do more. But I was thousands of miles away from Ground Zero with little money, and I was too old to join the service, even if I didn't have two young children. There was only one thing, other than displaying flags, that I could do. Out of options, I decided to pray.

For me, prayer was typically an act of desperation. I would turn to God when I was stuck and couldn't come up with any answers, or when there was no easy way out. Maybe it was something dumb, like losing my car keys in the house when I was already running late for an appointment. I would imagine being stuck at home indefinitely. During those moments, when I was panicking, I would beg God for help.

Other times, prayers were for a sick friend or relative. But these types of prayers, though common, were very brief. The second I received the request, I would mumble a few words to myself, like, "God, please help them," and then move on with my day. This way, I could tell the person I was praying for them without lying. I mean, I just *had*. In those moments, prayer was a duty. I had to do my part. Perhaps the combined efforts of hundreds of people's brief prayers to God would make a difference. Maybe there would be a miracle...

And sometimes, there was one.

Baby Bryan comes to mind. My cousin Laura's baby was born premature and clung to life in the hospital for over a year before he could go home. I sent him many brief prayers. One day, I decided to go onto 1800Flowers.com and send Bryan and his mother a pastel rainbow teddy bear. Bringing a gift in person wasn't possible because they were located over 300 miles away in Austin. The bear was $45—a price that was a huge sacrifice for me. It meant not going to the movies or eating out with Nicki and the kids for a least a week or two. But it was all okay because *I had a coupon.*

Later, at an extended family Christmas party (Dad's side), Laura approached me, smiling. After I gave her a tight hug and soft words of greeting, she looked at me and said in an impassioned voice, "You must be *psychic.*"

Confused, I asked her what she meant. "You sent me a pastel rainbow bear." She quickly pulled something out of her pocket. "I've been starting a pastel rainbow ribbon campaign to raise awareness for premature babies."

I looked at her, stunned. "What an amazing coincidence. It must be a God thing."

Laura nodded in agreement and placed a few ribbons in my hand. "Please wear this and pass some out to people you know."

As it turned out, Baby Bryan grew up and became a special little angel who lights up the lives of everyone around him. He would be completely blind and extremely physically and intellectually disabled, needing a lot of extra attention. But he was alive, and Laura and her family were grateful. Little Bryan brought smiles and warm feelings to everyone near him, and he was surrounded by loving parents and a large, supportive family. I believe that the desperate prayers of so many people, and the tireless efforts of dozens of doctors and nurses, made this happen.

What I'm saying is, I have faith in the power of prayer. This is why I was so willing to see the rainbow as a sign to continue my amateur detective work. And it's also why, during the days after 9/11, I meant it when I prayed for the victims. My words were vehement and emphatic. Unlike the brief, dutiful moments of prayer I gave for sick relatives, I poured my heart into it. I beseeched God to help the victims of 9/11, to comfort them, heal them, and provide them with peace. And more importantly, I clenched my fists, squeezed my eyes tightly, and begged that somehow, somewhere, I could make a difference.

Five years later, I would get my chance.

***

In August 2006, only a few weeks after we witnessed the spectacular rainbow in the field across from our house, I joined the War on Terror. My part in it—my efforts—would eventually lead to the location of the world's most notorious terrorist: Osama bin Laden.

There was no good reason why I chose that month to start hunting for terrorists; after all, it had been nearly five years since the Twin Towers fell. My best explanation is that I saw an opportunity and seized it. The weeks I'd spent looking for missing people and criminals had bolstered my self-confidence—so much so that I believed I could do anything I put my mind to if I worked hard enough. Plus, I was convinced that I was on the right track in my detective work, especially with my use of MySpace. So, I plowed forward, becoming increasingly enthusiastic about my efforts, while trying to stave off extreme mental and physical exhaustion.

Around August 3, I was trying to find yet another new case, a new challenge. I was Googling, considering which lucrative quarry to go after next. That's when I stumbled onto RewardsForJustice.net for the first time. Not only did this government website list America's most wanted terrorists, but it gave detailed information about them along with dollar values for information leading to their whereabouts. Most of them were worth $5 million. One success could solve all my problems. *Maybe I could do this.*

I excitedly clicked the link and waited for the site to load...

After a brief scan of the page, the link to the "Most Wanted Terrorists" caught my eye, and I quickly clicked it. Moments later on the screen in front of me was a rather large group of photos with names under them, listed in neat rows. On the top line, near the center, a stern-looking bin Laden stared back at me, wearing his signature beard and white turban. I didn't even consider going after *him... Not him... Not possible.*

But where would I start? My choice could determine the outcome. But there was no logical way to decide, so I chose to leave it to God and chance. I would apply the technique I'd used to get random inspiration back during my religious days (long story). I used to hold the Bible, close my eyes, and pray for guidance. I would then flip through the pages and point to a random passage. Often the result was odd and meaningless, perhaps one of the "begats" from Genesis. But other times, the result was pure genius, a genuine message from God that was well suited for whatever was going on in my life at that moment.

With this in mind, I employed that same system to pick a terrorist to hunt for. I closed my eyes, spun my index finger around, and pointed to a random spot on my computer screen. I opened my eyes and looked at where my finger was touching the monitor. *Him! ...*

In front of me was the smiling face of a young man. Under the photo was a name: *Faker Ben Abdelaziz Boussora.* Wow... That was quite a name! But what was he worth? I eagerly looked under his pic: *$5 million. Perfect...*

Next, I carefully scrutinized his profile page. Boussora was a Canadian citizen born on March 22, 1964. He was forty-two, which was five years older than me, and had a youthful appearance and a smiling, innocent-looking baby face that some people might find attractive. It was probably an old picture, but when it was taken, he was average weight, clean-shaven, had relatively short dark hair, and a dark-tan complexion. If I saw him walking around in Houston, I could have easily mistaken him for Hispanic. But beneath his nice smile was the heart of a killer. He was a senior member of Al Qaeda and wanted in connection with terrorist activity within the US. Whatever he did, it must have been bad, based on the size of his bounty. And because he was Canadian, it seemed reasonable that he could still be on the North American continent and might have a MySpace. As usual, I would begin there.

What people today might not understand is the enormous size and scope of MySpace in 2006, when it was at its height. In July of that year, Mashable.com cited a Hitwise evaluation that MySpace had surpassed Google and Yahoo Mail as America's most visited website.[50] A month later, on August 9, a few days before I found Osama bin Laden, Mashable reported that MySpace hit over a 100 million users and was signing up about 500,000 new users a week.[51]

And in 2006 most people didn't know that Al Qaeda was a very well-structured, modern organization that had been using the internet for recruitment and communications since the mid-1990s.[52] Instead, most imagined the terrorists living in the caves of Afghanistan or hanging out in dusty training camps with no internet or other amenities. However, this was a distorted vision of the terror organization. Yes, there were tens of thousands of operatives in those areas. But by 2006, nearly ten thousand were also living in western states.[53] And bin Laden himself was a billionaire who no doubt appreciated the finer things in life. Plus, Al Qaeda would need a modern global network to recruit operatives and funnel the millions required to run the organization.

Today, most people are aware that terrorist groups recruit and communicate through social networking. Yet back then, I was one of the few people who knew this. The idea was off most people's radar. I was breaking new ground, utilizing a resource that few had considered. In other words, I had learned to think outside the box.

***

Ready to get started, I grabbed a cup of coffee and sat at my desk, trying to relax.

I didn't know it, but the search for Boussora would take about seventy-two hours. Days and nights would blend together, broken up only by occasional pauses to be with family or to sleep. Regardless, moving forward I was extremely familiar with the process of finding people on MySpace. But this new project, hunting for a major Al Qaeda operative was intimidating. I leaned back in my duct-taped, gray rolling chair. Like the chair, I felt like I was barely holding myself together. But I knew I could do this. I *had* to do this.

But first, I took a moment to stretch. I extended my arms forward and arched my back, popping my elbows while feeling a series of satisfying crunches down my spine. Then, I rolled my shoulders several times and rounded my head for a few neck pops. Next, I laced my fingers together and popped my knuckles, which gave out a loud, sequential rip. Finally, I took a deep breath and tensed my neck and shoulders as hard as I could, and let it out slowly to relieve the tension.

This final step was a technique I'd learned in my seventh grade gifted math class. Ms. Crenshaw had spent a couple of weeks teaching us "stress management" techniques. She was acting on the presumption that gifted students lived with more stress than most others. I remember exchanging glances with a particularly snarky girl. We snickered softly and exchanged annoyed, disgusted looks and eye rolls as Ms. Crenshaw taught us the exercises. I scanned the room, and many of the other students were doing the same. *Why did we have to do this?* It was silly and stupid. Did gifted kids *really* have more stress than other kids? Still, we did the exercises, and now, nearly twenty-five years later, I was continuing to draw from what we had learned. Thank you, ma'am, wherever you are. I'm sorry we thought you were so weird.

Having completed my ritual, I was ready to work. After pulling up MySpace and logging in, I picked up my disappearing/reappearing TARDIS (Time And Relative Dimensions In Space) coffee cup, sniffed the dark ambrosia, then blew on it. The mug made me smile. It was special—and not just because it featured the time/space machine from the British science fiction series *Doctor Who.* When you put a hot beverage in it, the heat would cause the image of the TARDIS—a blue police call box from 1960s Britain—to fade from its spot on an iconic London street. It would then "reappear" on the opposite side of the mug, having seemingly launched into the swirling depths of outer space. It seemed unique, and I was pretty proud of it.

Carefully lifting the edge of the cup to my nose, I felt a rush of warm, damp air as I took a big whiff of coffee. *Folgers*—my favorite. Its smell reminded me of home. It's what my mom and dad always drank. It took me back to the days before Starbucks, before the complexity and speed of modern times. Despite the caffeine, I found coffee relaxing. I took a tiny sip. *Piping hot*—too hot to drink. I'd have to wait...

Setting down my drink, I didn't notice as I sloshed a little coffee on the desk. It joined maybe a half-dozen other specks that had dried in the area over the past few weeks. I never bothered to clean them and usually wasn't observant enough to notice them. I also rarely noticed the empty Diet Mountain Dew cans, crumpled printouts, and Snickers wrappers that were crammed next to my mouse and keyboard. If I could use only one word to sum up my work environment, it would have been "cluster-fuck."

But to me, all that mattered were the images on the screen—the pictures, the words, the data. I opened a new browser. Despite the advice of my boss, Adam, and every computer geek I had ever spoken to, I was still using *Internet Explorer (IE)* rather than *Firefox*. The latter was considered to be faster and more efficient, with better security. I guess I was just old-fashioned and didn't want to change. More importantly, I knew how to fix *IE* if it broke. I just wasn't willing to learn the ins and outs of a new browser any more than I was willing to switch to a Mac. *No...* I took comfort from the familiarity of *IE*.

I clicked the blue "e" on my taskbar, and *Internet Explorer* was up in several seconds. My homepage was set to Google, the page I used most often. Clicking the web bar, I typed in *"http://www.myspace.com."* I had never gotten out of the habit of including the hypertext protocol command in the address, even though adding it and *"WWW"* to the web address hadn't been necessary for many years. I guess I was just a creature of habit. My kids probably didn't even know that *"WWW"* stood for

"World Wide Web."

When the login page appeared, I absently typed in my username and password and signed in. I took a fresh look at my MySpace. *Boring...* Recall, a couple of months ago, I had created it for only one purpose: I wanted access to the website's massive database so I could use it as a profiling resource. Because this had been my sole focus, unlike most people on the site, I had never bothered to add many details to my page.

The best way to describe MySpace in the mid-2000s was "bling." Most active profiles were the opposite of mine. They were *extremely* decorative and elaborate. They were usually crammed full of images and often had streaming music and/or videos playing in the background. And there were sparkles, lots of sparkles. For many people, creating flashy pages wasn't just a hobby, it was an obsession. Sometimes less tech-savvy users, who couldn't figure out how to fix up their pages, were so desperate for glam that they would hire people or buy specialized software to "pimp" their MySpace. I personally found most of the MySpace profile pages annoying. They were visually and auditorily gaudy, and notoriously slow to load. And if you were unfortunate enough to still be on dial-up, forget about it. No MySpace for you.

But, as I said, my MySpace was simple. There were no extravagant background tunes, sparkly borders, nor cutesy pics of Hello Kitty. There weren't even any photos of my children. For my purposes, making my page look pretty felt like a complete waste of time.

However, I *had* taken a moment to upload a single lonesome photograph—my profile pic. There, on my main page, was a smiling picture of me sitting at a table at my cousin Nancy's wedding reception during The Monster Trip. I had put a few table decorations on my hat, including a couple of jingle bells. I had also taken a small gold-colored plastic loop and stuck it loosely in my nostrils to pretend like I had a nose ring. I looked like I was having a great time and in high spirits. I think I might have even been a little drunk. It was one of the few pictures I actually liked of myself and was willing to put on my page.

Other than the photo, there were about four or five messages from family members and other people I knew in real life. There were only about a dozen people on my friends list. The only one I didn't know personally was Tom Anderson. Tom had co-founded MySpace with Chris DeWolfe back in 2003.[54] When people signed up to use their site, Tom was automatically placed as their first friend. And most people never bothered to delete him. So, like most new users, Tom's young, smiling face was displayed prominently on my page next to my real-life friends and family.

Once my page finished loading, I briefly checked for any new messages or friend requests. There weren't any; there seldom were. Like I said, I had never really used MySpace for socialization.

Then I clicked on the little blue "e" one more time and a second browser-window eventually popped up. Clicking the star in the upper right-hand corner, I opened my favorites, scrolled down a few dozen saved links, and clicked the one at the bottom: RewardsForJustice.net. The site came up and, once again, I selected the "Most Wanted Terrorist" link. After spotting Boussora, I clicked his profile and was greeted by a list of several aliases and other pertinent information.

Of all the information on the site, the aliases were the most important. There were six in total listed for Boussora, if you included his birth name. I would plug them in the MySpace search engine to see if any suspicious-looking pages popped up. My hope was that the alias being used on MySpace was the alias being used for his current residence. I recalled my guess that he could be living in the US or Canada because he was a Canadian citizen.

Determined, I tried his full birth name first, copying and pasting it into the MySpace query. Even though it seemed unlikely that he would use his real name rather than an alias, I had to rule out the obvious. After all, maybe he wasn't very smart.

But when I pasted in Boussora's complete given name, nothing came up, so I tried a simplified version: "Faker Boussora." Finally, just "Boussora." Although there were a few hits on my latest try, there was no "Faker" or "F" listed as any of the first names. *Okay...* I was finally satisfied that *if* he was on MySpace, he was using a fake name.

I moved on to his next alias and ran it through the MySpace search engine. The singular name, "Abdulaziz," generated several-hundred hits. *Not good enough...* I needed to narrow my parameters more. I went back to Boussora's RewardsForJustice profile and found some new elements to add to my query: age, height, and weight.

After adding Boussora's specs to the search, I placed him within 2,000 miles of Lebanon, Kansas—the geographical center of the US. But even after narrowing the results, there were several dozen hits. I had my work cut out for me.

I slowly started sifting through all the MySpaces of people going by the name "Abdulaziz," hoping to discover a suspicious-looking page. The problem was, I didn't know what a fishy Al Qaeda profile would look like. I doubted that it would have *"Death to America!"* splashed across the page, but that would certainly be a red flag. However, I *did* know what a normal MySpace looked like. So I would try to find a page that didn't look like *that*.

Like I said, most people's MySpaces were extremely decorative. But regardless of glitz level, there was always some standardized formatting. On each profile page was a section at the bottom that showed their Top Friends list. Users could even place them in priority order, with the first ten listed prominently on their homepage. So, people always knew where they ranked in their friends' lives—how important they were to them.

In the upper right-hand corner of their main page, you could see the date of the user's last login. Also, on most profile pages, lined up on the right side of the screen, was a string of messages, often in the form of extravagant videos and graphics. Plus, there were links to members' recent blogs as well as their photo collections.

I began meticulously opening every single entry for people going by Boussora's alias, Abdulaziz, and examining them closely. Most had ordinary profile pics—attractive images of themselves or their children. These pages were fairly typical, full of glitz and glamour. Others had a few friends and recent activity but were relatively unadorned. Still others featured generic place-holding avatars for their profile pic—the default for new users. The generic ones usually didn't have any comments, pictures, or blogs. There were no recent logins and the users were clearly inactive. But every single one of them had at least one friend: Tom.

I worked my way through the pages as quickly as possible, giving each page a cursory glance. Nothing stood out as strange until... *Wait...* That's interesting. In place of a typical profile pic was an avatar, but not a generic one. It was a sketch of a Corvette. It was bright red with crisp edges. It appeared to be an older, classic model. It struck me as suspicious, anonymous. It would be perfect for a man trying to hide—a man like Boussora. I eagerly clicked on the sports car icon and opened the page, but it was mostly blank, another unused account. *Blah...* I moved on.

I spent another twenty minutes carefully working my way down the list of hits and thoroughly examining each new page. *Then...* I caught a glimmer of something in the corner of my eye: my TARDIS mug. Oh, wait... *Coffee!* For the first time in a while, I noticed how tired and thirsty I was. I happily picked up the mug. Coffee sounded awesome. I pulled it to my lips and took a big swig. *Ewww! ...* I nearly spit it out. It was cold—a full cup of cold coffee. *What a waste.* I had completely forgotten about it. But wait. Why was it cold? How long had I been working? It must have been at least a couple of hours. It had just flown by.

I got up and walked into the kitchen with my mug, dumping the disappointing brew into the sink. I looked at the pot. There was still some left. *Thank God!*

I poured myself another cup and added some creamer, which landed on the top in a white clump. I tried to stir it using a plastic spoon. No luck. Even the coffee in the pot was cold, ancient. *No choice...* I would brew some more. I would try to do better this time. I hated cold coffee. Disgusted, I sloshed what was left of the old stuff into the sink and started a new pot.

A few minutes later, after stopping by the bathroom and asking Nicki to tell me when the coffee was done, I returned to my desk, ready to get back to work.

After several hours of examining hundreds of listings for all five aliases, I had found nothing that stuck out as odd. But all along, I kept thinking back to the image of the little red Corvette. It had been the most atypical profile pic I'd seen to date. However, I kept telling myself that it was nothing, and going back to it would be pointless. But something about it kept gnawing at me: If the account was unused, why would he bother to choose an avatar? ... Maybe I had been too quick to dismiss it. Maybe I had missed something.

Finally, options nearly exhausted, I threw up my hands and gave in to my instincts. I *had to* locate the sports car and take a closer look. But I was scared I wouldn't be able to find it again. My heart began racing as I felt myself panicking. It was that same familiar feeling of losing my car keys when I needed to be somewhere. What if the Corvette profile *had* been Boussora's, and I'd messed up my only chance of catching him by closing the browser?

In fact, I'd been working so long I couldn't even remember which alias had brought up the Corvette. I would be forced to start over from scratch. Skipping Boussora's birth name, I once again typed "Abdulaziz" into the MySpace search engine and began scrolling through numerous pages, skimming the profile images. The red sports car had to be there somewhere. It just *had* to be.

I was really worried. What if the page was lost forever? After about a half hour of skimming, I had gone through all the hits. However, the sports car icon had not appeared. I tried moving on to the next alias, but my heart started pounding hard as I began to catastrophize. What if the profile *had* been Boussora's, but he had somehow figured out that someone was poking around on his page? What if he'd gotten scared and deleted his account? What if it wasn't there anymore? It could be lost forever, and I might never find him.

I tried to calm myself. Was it even possible for Boussora to know someone was examining his profile? Could hackers detect online activity with that level of detail? I had no clue, but I tried to assure myself that such technology wasn't likely to even exist. It was more likely that I had overlooked the page in my rush. Yes. Sometimes panic makes me blind to objects that are right in front of my nose. Once again, I thought back on so many lost car keys: They could be missing for hours only to magically pop up later when I calmed down. I would often find them in one of the places I had already checked earlier. Yes, that's probably why I couldn't find the sports car page. The fear of not finding it had put me in a blind frenzy. I was too rushed, too full of adrenaline. I had to slow down and try again.

But I knew I didn't want to tediously repeat the same process. I had already tried that. There had to be a better way. I decided to say a desperate prayer to Saint Anthony, the patron saint of lost things. He was the saint I found myself praying to the most because I was constantly losing stuff to the vortex of clutter in our disheveled home. My prayers to him were borderline superstitious, but they almost always worked *eventually*.

I fervently mumbled under my breath. I needed help—help finding the Corvette.

"Dear Saint Anthony, please help me find it."

After a brief pause, my gears began to turn. *Wait ...* I had an idea. My *Internet Explorer* history. *Of course! ...* I went to "Internet Options" and then "History." After typing "Abdulaziz" in the search box, I clicked the tiny, but familiar icon of a magnifying glass. A few moments later, nearly a hundred links popped up. I started to click them, one at a time, with each link opening a new browser window. The sports car had to be here somewhere. It *had* to be.

The process was slow and tedious, and our garbage internet was making my life difficult. But I was hopeful. Even if it took an eternity to target, one of those links had to lead to the sports car. It couldn't have just disappeared. The process was not dissimilar to meticulously pulling every item out of my bag so I could find my keys.

Two hours later, I clicked yet another one of the numerous links. I wasn't expecting much. But in a few seconds, when the page finally popped up, I raised a clenched fist and thrust it downward in a chugging motion. "Yes. Yes! *Yes!*" Staring at me on the page was the little red Corvette. I had finally found it again!

I took a few moments to take in my victory, but soon a sickening energy began to course through my body. The adrenaline was too much for me. I needed to calm down, to shake it off. *Breathe...* I had to breathe. Drawing air deeply into my lungs, I repeated a mantra: *In through my nose...one...two...three...* I continued to ten. *Out through my mouth...one...two...three...* Again, I ended at ten. *In through my nose...* I repeated the process as long as I could. I had learned this technique from a therapist who had tried to teach me biofeedback as a means of controlling panic attacks. But it usually only worked while I was doing the exercise. The anxiety would come back full force as soon as I stopped counting my breath.

So I had no faith in biofeedback, but I had to try something, *anything*. I needed to relax enough to get back to work. But there was no time for breaks.

Tightening my neck and shoulders and slowly releasing them while breathing out, I tried one final time to blow off the stress. I was close to locating Boussora. I could sense it. I took a hard look at the site, my hands shaking a bit on the mouse and keyboard as I scoured the page. I had to find out if I'd missed something out of the ordinary.

Feeling the thrill of the race, I began planning my next move. A figurative gun had fired in my head, and I was off and running, heading forward with full steam. Now the real work could finally start. I just had to...

13

THE DOCTOR

Suddenly, my head bolted upward as I was jarred from my trance. There was a loud noise. *What was it?* It sounded like...like screaming. What *was* that? Was someone...trying to...to get my attention? *Now?*

"Mom!"

It was Daun. She was screaming. Snapped back into reality, I looked up at my daughter, startled. "What... what was that?" She was tugging at my arm and her face was only about a foot from mine.

"*Mom!*"

This was bad. I could tell. I felt guilty. "I'm sorry. How long have you been there?"

She was angry. "*Forever!* You *never* listen. I called your name a million times. I was like, 'Mom. Momma! *Mommy!*' I even tried, 'Hey, gorgeous,' and it didn't work."

I was not happy with myself. I had been so stuck in my head that I hadn't even noticed my own daughter when she was hollering my name, right in front of me.

Ugh! ... My body tightened and released as I let out

a loud sigh. I wished they understood. By now, Daun, Peter, and Nicki should have been used to me tuning them out. I had struggled to respond to my name most of my life and was often teased for it.

One time in 1985, I attended a high school band banquet. The event was held annually to honor individual and group achievements of band students. This time the band-booster moms had decided to try something different. In addition to the normal accolades, the band director was giving out joke awards, and unfortunately, I was one of the recipients. Mr. Van Buren stood at a podium holding a lavender wooden block with a miniature of the creature from *ET the Extra-Terrestrial* glued on the top of it. Written neatly in silver paint pen on the front of the wood were the words, *"Out of this World."*

The moment I heard the words "ET Award," my heart sank. I knew what it meant; it was not new information. They all thought I was weird—a "space cadet."

Then, in front of maybe 150 band students and parents, Mr. Van Buren told everyone how he always had to repeat my name multiple times to get my attention, even though I was sitting right on from him in the front row. Sometimes, he had to resort to tapping his baton on my music stand. He went on to say nice things about me to counter the criticism, but it didn't matter. All I heard was. *"Barbara... Barbara Janik is a freak."* In that moment, I shuddered at the sound of my own name.

And I knew he was right. I was a freak. I mean, what he said was true. I couldn't easily be roused during band class. The funny thing is that, until Mr. Van Buren mentioned it at the banquet, I wasn't even aware of the problem. Despite how many times he called my name,

I literally only heard it once—the last time he called it.

I tried not to show my hurt, but I don't think it got past Linda, who looked at me compassionately. She was a senior I admired, who was valedictorian and first chair clarinet—the only one who could beat me at competitions. Linda seemed worried, like she was wondering how I was taking it. She knew I was sensitive. She would pull me aside later and ask me how I took receiving the "award." But I lied and said I didn't mind. In fact, when I had picked up the small "trophy," I had smiled, pretending to take it all in stride, mostly because I was embarrassed.

But as an adult, I would learn to embrace my differentness. I knew I would never be normal, so I accepted it and even liked it. In my mind, "normal" was boring. So, when my kids were growing up, I encouraged them to take a similar attitude toward their own oddities, and it eventually worked.

As a young adult, Daun would be the quirky person walking around her college campus wearing an odd assortment of lacey, colorful clothing and donning blue or green wigs. I wish I had been more like her as an adolescent—unashamed.

But back in 2006, when Daun was only ten, and I was searching for terrorists, she still was an innocent little girl whose favorite color was pink and who wanted nothing more than to be like everyone else.

I looked at my daughter. "I guess I tuned you out." I stared back at my computer screen. It was pulling me back in. I shot her a distracted glance. "I'm in the middle of something," This translated to *"Go away. I don't have time for you."*

"But you've been on the computer all day. I wanna

watch *Doctor Who*."

She seemed desperate, but so was I. I didn't want to stop what I was doing. Not now, not when I was in the middle of a major breakthrough. Still, I knew how important *Doctor Who* was to her—and to me, to our family.

I gave her a direct gaze. "Not now. I can't. This is too important. I'm fixin' to find a major terrorist."

Daun believed in what I was doing. She knew it was important and that it could solve our financial problems. But right now, all that mattered was having a bit of my attention. She wanted her mom back, at least for a little while. So she pleaded with me, "Mom, please. Please! *Please!*"

My heart was wrenched with guilt, which was my go-to emotion in these types of situations. Should I stop and watch the show with Daun? Could I even concentrate on it right now? I was flustered. I loved that show. For me, *Doctor Who* was much more than a series. It was a legacy, an integral part of my geek heritage.

Doctor Who is basically about a renegade Time Lord from Gallifrey, a planet whose ancient alien civilization is known for traveling through time and space. The rebellious Gallefreyan, known simply as "the Doctor," does this in his 1960s-style blue police box, the TARDIS— the same one depicted on my favorite coffee mug. The Doctor and his companions use this blue box, which is bigger on the inside and loaded with cool gadgets, to travel to vast worlds and from the beginnings and endings of time. During their adventures, the Doctor and his companions solve mysteries and help people, sometimes saving entire planets, and occasionally, the whole universe.

I had been watching the series on PBS since junior high, so it had always been important to me. When, sometime in the early '90s, they stopped showing the reruns on PBS, I felt like there was a hole missing in my soul. I missed *Doctor Who* so much. Finally, a few years later, I discovered Suncoast Videos in Baybrook Mall. I bought every episode I could afford, and Peter and Daun and I would sit down and watch each one repeatedly. We'd pull out a proper teapot and teacups—none matching—and sit and watch, drink tea, and pretend we were British.

I started the tradition when I used to watch *Doctor Who* alone during my college years, sitting on my foam fold-out love seat in front of the small television in my efficiency apartment. My Irish neighbor, Ciara, who often joined me for tea, had inspired me to start collecting teapots and cups. We would use them and religiously drink Tetley with milk and sugar.

And in 2006, my favorite pot was the large white one with the big blue flowers, because it could accommodate a lot of people and was manufactured in England, the country of honor. Daun's favorite tea was Bigelow's Plantation Mint, so we made it often, but without the milk. I didn't like milk in fruity teas. That would be *weird*.

So when Daun asked me to watch *Doctor Who* with her, I was torn. I considered dropping everything. But I was so close to finding a major terrorist that I couldn't stop. *I just couldn't.* I was too close. My adrenaline was pumping. Hitting the brakes at such high speeds seemed reckless, if not impossible.

Yet Daun looked at me, begging. "Please!"

I was a little more forceful this time and perhaps a

bit agitated. "I'm sorry. *I can't!*"

She persisted. *"Please!!!"*

"I can't stop right now. I just can't. We'll watch later, I promise."

There was a brief pause. I could tell that Daun's gears were turning. "Pinky promise?"

She knew that it was the only way she could force me to do anything.

I never broke a pinky promise, and she knew it. One time, when Daun was around eight years old, I was suffering from severe depression and lacked the energy to drag myself off the couch and go to Kroger. As a result, we were almost out of groceries, with no yogurt or frozen foods and almost no fruit. There were only ramen noodles and a myriad of canned goods in the pantry. The situation was so grave that I had to cut bad spots off the few remaining apples before giving them to my children—not that they minded. Apples were their favorite food.

But eight-year-old Daun had been so desperate for fresh groceries that she made me pinky promise her we would go to the store. I mean, no one ever starved, but Jack in the Box for dinner was getting old. I reluctantly promised Daun we'd go, mostly to get her off my back. Daun could be extremely persistent.

When nighttime rolled around, Daun approached me. As usual, I was sleeping on the sofa. She woke me up.

"Mom, we *have* to go to the store!"

I looked at her groggily. "Not now."

"But *Mom!* It's ten o'clock at night, and you *pinky* promised!"

I reluctantly slogged off of the couch, sauntered

into the kitchen, and started going through the pantry, scrounging for food. I pulled out a large can of Dinty Moore Stew. "Go grab the can opener. We can have this for dinner. I'll make some boil-in-bag rice." I rarely cooked, and when I did, it was in the laziest way possible. Anyone could boil a bag of rice, even depressed people. Daun would open and microwave the stew.

But not this time.

Daun was tugging at my arm. "*No.* We have to go now! You *pinky* promised!"

She had me. I finally gave up. I knew she was right. I had no choice. I couldn't break a pinky promise, *ever.* I knew if I did, Daun would never believe my word again. Besides, she'd have the perfect right to break my pinky.

Because of the vow—and despite my complete lack of energy—the kids and I got dressed, and I dragged myself and them to the store, first stopping at McDonald's for McDoubles. They were only a dollar each, and I knew better than to go to the store hungry. I would see all the food, buy up the entire store, and waste the rest of our food stamps.

So, in 2006, when eleven-year-old Daun asked me to drag myself away from hunting terrorists and pinky promise I'd watch *Doctor Who* with her, I knew that taking the oath was the only way I could get her off my back. We hooked pinkies tightly, and I promised, adding, "...and you can totally break my pinky if I don't do it."

She gripped my pinky even tighter and assured me, "Don't think I won't do it."

Daun looked at me as our pinkies were crossed. "Tonight. You have to promise. *Tonight!*"

I gazed back at her, dead in the eye, and gave her a

little smile. *"Tonight.* I promise."

It was on. Sometime soon, I would have to stop working. I would have to force myself to watch *Doctor Who* with my daughter.

14

LITTLE RED CORVETTE

Moments later, I frowned at the MySpace homepage that was demarcated by the little red Corvette. Having satisfied my daughter for the moment, I could finally get back to work. At least she'd distracted me for a bit, and I felt a little calmer.

I crossed my fingers, hoping this would be the moment when I found something intriguing and relevant. Maybe there was more to this page than just a boring, blank profile. Perhaps something would stand out that I had missed when I had glanced at the page before. Pausing for a moment, I stared nervously at the screen.

I noticed the sports car page had an open profile. That meant that all of its details were viewable by the general public. I thought this was an odd setting for someone who hadn't even bothered to decorate his page or upload any photos.

But there was another, more important advantage to having an open profile: Anyone on MySpace could send him an instant message. This seemed like it could be useful. It struck me that maybe the primary purpose of this nearly blank profile was for recruitment and anonymous communications within the Al Qaeda network. After all, back then, as far as I was aware, very few people were monitoring these types of exchanges. They would have been completely secret and confidential, without the worry of potential wiretapping or government interference. Encryption could be added in the privacy options.

Still, all in all, what was noteworthy about this page was how *not* noteworthy it was, at least on the surface. There was no fancy background, no posts from friends, no blogs, and no music. However, despite the blank appearance of his MySpace, the member was active. According to his homepage, he had joined more than a year ago and was logging in regularly. As with all open profiles, the most recent login date was posted in the upper right-hand corner of the screen. His last sign-in was only a couple of days prior.

I continued to scour the page. First, I looked at Abdulaziz's friends list. It was wiped blank, intentionally. This was obvious because he had taken the time to delete Tom—I mean, *Tom*—the most popular guy on MySpace, everyone's first friend, the guy on nearly everyone's homepage. Normally, only extremely active users who had thousands of friends bothered to delete him. But this page—the sports car page—didn't list *any* friends. Zero. Zip. Nada.

Fine... His prerogative. But why would there be no *Tom*—harmless, friendly, inviting, Tom? This seemed consistent with my theory that the member was Boussora. The lack of friends made it look like the user didn't want to be watched or followed, like he was hiding.

Then, I noticed that at the bottom of his profile page, he had left a single, brief comment. I don't remember his exact words, but as I recall, they were really sexist and had something to do with having multiple women. The promise of seventy-two virgins, which jihadists were told they'd receive in the afterlife, came to mind.

Summing up my observations in my mind, I carefully went back over everything I knew about the sports car page—everything I found suspicious: The member had taken the time to change the generic place-holding avatar to a sports car icon, delete Tom, and add a brief, sexist comment at the bottom of the screen. These, coupled with his recent logins and open profile, made it clear that he was active, but perhaps incognito. He might have been trying to hide out by creating what, on the surface, looked like a blank page—a page that could be easily overlooked. *But why?* ... Perhaps he wanted to use MySpace's secure messaging system but, for the sake of anonymity, didn't want anyone friending him permanently.

Yes... This page was my best guess. It was suspicious because it appeared as though someone had taken way too much effort to make the page look as generic as possible. It was like he had meticulously "undecorated" it—unlike most active users, who seemed to go out of their way to make their sites increasingly gaudy.

No... This was weird. The page had been stripped... *naked*!

***

A chill ran down my spine as I imagined the nude

dead body of a black woman, perhaps a victim of the Acres Homes serial killer. I thought about it. Of all the pages I'd seen that matched one of Boussora's aliases, this was the strangest. If he had an account, this was probably it.

Now my work would go from hard to harder. I knew the sports car page owner's first name was Abdulaziz. On MySpace, by default, when a listing popped up in a search, only the first name was displayed. So getting the last name would prove more difficult.

I decided to start the name search in US-based directories, mostly because they were thorough and easy to access. The first site I visited was Anywho.com. I placed "Abdulaziz" in the first box and left the surname blank. *Damn!* ... A nasty red error appeared: "Last name required." What was I supposed to do? I didn't have a last name! *Ugh...* Then I thought for a second. I knew from experience that with some online directories, I could use an asterisk as a wild card. I quickly put "Abdulaziz" in the first box and "*" in the second box, then clicked "Find." There were about fifty hits, so I start scrolling through them. But... *What?* ... They all had Abdulaziz as a last name! I tried again several times. Apparently, the asterisk caused the first name to move into the last name slot. *Pointless...* Finally, I put "Abdulaziz" in both boxes, and got hits for several people named Abdulaziz Abdulaziz. *Hmmm...* I hadn't thought of that. Maybe his first and last names were the same. Man, Arabic was weird. I tried plugging it into MySpace, but the Corvette didn't pop up. *No...* I needed a different last name. AnyWho was useless. I would have to move on.

Undeterred, I decided to try Whitepages.com. Fortunately, this site only had one slot, so a full name was not required. I plugged in "Abdulaziz" and got more than 500 hits for people with Abdulaziz as part of their name—either first, middle, or last. I cracked my knuckles and took a deep breath... This was going to take a while.

I started scrolling through all the listings, copying only those with Abdulaziz as a first name and pasting them into the MySpace engine. If the Corvette popped up, I'd have his full name.

I moved through them at a maddeningly fast pace. I wanted to get through this tedious process as quickly as possible. As I continued, I would occasionally grimace, clench my fists, or sigh. I was incredibly frustrated but, at the same time, so driven I couldn't make myself take a break. There had to be a match for Abdulaziz and the sports car...there just *had to* be. It was too important.

Exhausted, I examined the screen for what felt like the millionth time. I jumped in my seat a little as my eyes focused on the results...

Yes! ... It was the same little red Corvette! It had finally popped up. I had finally placed the correct full name into the MySpace search engine. I knew the page owner's identity. I stared down at the results: Abdulaziz Abdulla. I had a name. I had a name! *I had a name!*

I immediately went to PeopleLookup.com and retrieved a list of potential addresses. Then, I took several minutes to copy and paste each of them into the MySpace query, hoping they would make his profile—the one with the little red Corvette—pop up again.

A half-hour later, I was looking at the little red car again.

Wow...a match. I had found a match. *I had an address!*

I carefully examined the result, stunned. Abdulla was

in Brooklyn, a mere half-hour drive from Ground Zero.

I could hardly believe my eyes. I continued to stare at the screen for longer than was comfortable. *I had him!* If I was correct, and the page belonged to the notorious terrorist, Boussora was definitely in Brooklyn. The match was 100 percent positive. It was definitely his address—the address of the man going by Abdulaziz Abdulla—the one he had given MySpace when he signed up. In that moment, I was convinced that I had accomplished something that had eluded US intelligence for the past five years: I had found Boussora, a known terrorist worth $5 million!

But I couldn't stop there. I had to be sure. I had to double-check before calling in the tip. After all, the suspect could have moved from his registered address after joining MySpace. I needed to make sure he was still living there. Once again, I turned to PeopleLookup, but this time for address verification. Before my amateur detective career ended, I would spend several hundred dollars—most of my remaining available credit—on these types of searches.

Yet to me, the expense was worth it. I had to know. I had to be certain. Besides, I was hoping for a big payoff. I was gambling with the last of my resources—a gamble that was doomed to fail. Ironically, my quest to fix my money problems would ultimately make them worse.

A few minutes later, I reviewed the list of addresses. Under the suspect's residence was the fortuitous phrase, written in red letters: *"Confirmed Current Address."* Under his phone number was *"Confirmed Current Phone."*

Then I looked a little further down the page, and a chill ran down my spine: *"Owner of the Property: INTER-*

DENOMINATIONAL BROTHERHOOD INC." My mind flashed to the Muslim Brotherhood, the controversial radical Islamic group. I wondered if they were connected to the property owners.

Yes! ... This this had to be the right address. I was 100 percent certain this was where Abdulaziz Abdulla was living. And I was 100 percent certain that Abdulla was Faker Ben Abdelaziz Boussora. I had found him. *Yes* ... I was the one who did this—Barbara Kaye Janik. I had found one of the United States'—no, the *world's*—most wanted men, a terrorist capable of killing thousands who had perhaps already killed many. And he was worth $5 million.

I felt euphoric. My financial problems were over, and I had probably saved lives.

Or so I thought...

But then, I began to worry. How would I inform the FBI and still get my money? I had to do this right. If they arrested him, I needed to be able to prove that I had given the tip. But how would I go about this? I needed some time to think about it. I couldn't just pick up the phone like I did with the other cases. *No...* This time I had to be careful.

I quickly glanced at the clock. It was only 6:20 p.m. Too early for dinner. We usually ate late, which meant Nicki wasn't likely to be busy cooking.

Of course! ... I'd ask Nicki. I had to tell Nicki, Peter, and Daun. I had to share the great news. They needed to know that we were going to start a new life, that our problems were solved.

I slammed my laptop shut and rushed to the bedroom, where I suspected Nicki was taking a nap. Fortunately, she was awake and busy on her laptop.

"Nicki!" Exhilarated, I pounced toward her, landing on my side of the bed. "Hey, I've got great news. Stop what you're doing. You *have* to hear this!"

Nicki kept staring at her laptop. Digital music was coming from it, and her eyes were darting quickly back and forth. I knew she was playing a game. She gave me a micro-glance. "In a minute."

I was desperate. "Come on. *This is important.*"

This time, she didn't bother to look over. "After I finish this round."

I knew I couldn't pull her away right at that moment, but that didn't stop me from trying. My heart was beating fast. I needed to tell someone. I was desperate.

But Nicki could not be deterred. She had been so bored while I was working that she'd spend hours playing the *Real Arcade* games I'd bought her. She was absolutely obsessed with them.

I pleaded with her. "Come on. This is really important!"

No go.

"It'll just be a minute... I'm about to get stuck."

She was playing *Chuzzle*. I knew this meant that her colorful little googly-eyed, fluffy creatures would soon be locked in the grid, unable to move. But I was still aggravated. It felt like her stupid game was more important than my accomplishment.

I sat there, waiting, sighing, cringing. I had to tell someone...I *had to*. This was taking too long. I thought about it for a moment. Maybe I should go tell Daun. *Yes...* Daun. *She'd* be happy for me.

I rolled toward the side of the bed and heaved myself upward. Pushing my fists against the bed for leverage, I slowly stood up and headed toward the door. But before

I made it out the exit, Nicki stopped me. "See, I told you it was almost over. Now, what? What do you want?"

She sounded annoyed. How dare I try to make her stop her game. But as I plopped back down on the bed, I knew my pleading had been justified. We had a lot to talk about.

15

THE PLAN

Nicki looked up at me, exasperated. Her game was finally over. "*What?!* What do you want? I'm done. I *told* you it wouldn't take long!"

But to me, it had felt like an eternity.

I beamed at her, verbalizing my discovery for the first time. "I just found a major terrorist."

She had a look of surprise. "Really?"

There was undeniable excitement in my voice. "*Yes.* I've got his name and address."

"Are you sure it's him?"

There was a huge smile on my face, and I was shaking a bit as my excitement continued to build. "I'm 99 percent certain. It was a known alias on a suspicious MySpace account. Who else could it be?"

"So, what're you going to do?"

I responded matter-of-factly, "Well, I'm gonna turn him in, but I'm not sure how to do it and still make sure I collect the $5 million. I mean, what's next?"

Nicki's gears were turning. "I don't know. What are you thinking?"

"I was thinking maybe a contract. Do you think I should send the FBI an email? Or do you think I should call?"

Nicki glanced at me, a look of uncertainty on her face. "I don't know. Maybe call?"

I had this way of contradicting her ideas, something that annoyed her to no end. "But if I call and give them the information, how do I collect the money? They'll already have what they need. They'll have no obligation to pay me."

Nicki kept throwing out ideas. "Maybe email them and ask for a contract?"

That sounded easier than calling. *Brilliant...* I'd send an email. "Okay, I'll take care of it. Give me a few."

First, I wrote an elaborate message to the contact email on RewardsForJustice.com. But then, about a half-hour later, I thought about it and decided it was smarter to write the FBI directly.

I flipped open my cell phone, called the Houston FBI, and asked for their email address. Afterward, I pulled up Word and spent a few minutes carefully crafting a message. Then I took it to Nicki. I wanted her to look it over. What I didn't know at the time was that she would literally wave on anything I wrote, no matter how obnoxious. Perhaps partners aren't the best editors. After all, she was still my biggest supporter, and not exactly objective when it came to my writing.

I sat next to the bed, in front of my desktop computer, and clicked on the *Outlook Express* icon. I preferred it over using *Internet Explorer* for viewing my emails because I like the added security of downloading file copies of all my correspondences. I didn't fully trust MSN and Gmail to keep them on their servers forever.

It hadn't even occur to me that my emails could still be lost if my hard drive failed. As fate would have it, the Cloud would turn out to be more reliable than my machine's aging hardware. Regardless, my records were safe, and using *Outlook Express* made me feel like I'd added an extra layer of protection, albeit short-lived.

Once the email manager popped up, I pasted my newly composed message, addressed it to the Houston FBI, and clicked "send." But... *Oops!* The email quickly bounced. Panic began to set in. *Were they blocking me?* But why would they do that? *Oh...* There was a typo in the address.

After quickly fixing the issue, I wheeled around in my chair to face Nicki. I felt pretty good about what I had just done. "Do you know what this *means?*"

"What?"

"It means we're gonna be rich! That guy was worth five million."

Nicki's face lit up. "Oh, wow!"

In my mind, I started spending the money right away. "Well, the first thing I'm gonna do is pay off my credit card debt. I'll also pay off our student loans."

Now, *Nicki* was excited. "*Yes!*"

"And maybe I'll buy you a car. I don't need one, obviously, but your truck is very impractical."

Nicki thought about it. "Yeah, it's a stick shift. You can't even drive it. But you could learn..."

I considered her words for a moment. "But I'm not a good enough driver to learn stick. I don't need anything else to concentrate on. I get in enough wrecks as it is."

"Good point."

I kept spending the money in my mind. "Do you think we should buy a new house?"

"Can we move to Seattle?"

I shrugged. I loved the mountains, but I didn't want to leave my family. Besides, I liked our little house. "Perhaps a summer home."

Pausing, I pulled back a bit, reining in my mental shopping spree. "But we have to be careful. We don't want to waste the money."

Nicki agreed. "True. We could totally retire on it."

I continued her line of thinking. "Yeah. We have to invest—make it last. I heard that most people who win the lottery waste it within a year or two and wind up broke again, or even worse off than before."

Nicki kept nodding. We were on the same page. "Yeah. I've heard a lot of stories like that, too. Did you hear about the lottery winner who is living in a dumpy, old—?"

But before she could finish her thought, I interrupted her. "Yeah... I heard about that guy. I don't want to be one of *those* people. If we spend the money wisely and invest, we can make the five million last the rest of our lives. Like you said, we can retire. We'll only work if we want to—like, if we get bored."

I started contemplating all the winners on CBS' *Survivor*. There's a reason why the winners return to try to win another million. I mean, the money goes fast for people who have spent years deprived of it. It's like a starving person who suddenly has access to food. The tendency is to binge and overeat. Some people even end up obese and develop health complications, especially if they have an eating disorder.

As we continued talking, my mind kept drifting back to the email. How long would it take the FBI to respond? Would I get a contract?

Nicki tried to continue the conversation, but I spun around in my chair and faced my computer while she was mid-sentence. I wanted to...*needed to* check my email. This was the first of probably a hundred times that I would check it over the next couple of days. I knew myself. Waiting would drive me crazy. I need to occupy myself, keep busy. Besides, I could hardly contain my excitement. In a flash, I knew what to do. I'd prepare an email to send to the FBI after I signed the contract. It would contain all the info on the suspect. *Yes...* I'd write it and email it to myself for safekeeping.

Without looking up from the monitor, I addressed my partner. "Nicki, I'm going to—"

Nicki stopped me, speaking through clenched teeth. "I was *talking* to you."

I had done it again. I had tuned her out. Even worse, I had become lost in thought and completely left the conversation in favor of my computer. I knew I was in trouble.

"I'm sorry. What were you saying?"

Nicki took a short breath. "I don't remember."

"*Come on!* What were you trying to say before I so rudely interrupted you?"

She had resigned herself to the fact that she'd never finish her thought. "I don't know. It's too late. I don't remember."

Still, I wasn't giving up. I took a wild guess. Weren't we talking about how we were going to spend the money?"

Nicki decided to join in and fish for her lost thought. "No... It was after that."

Suddenly, I had an *aha* moment. "*I know...* It was about—"

But before I could complete my sentence, we were interrupted by the sound of someone lightly tapping on the door.

16

EVERYONE LIVES!

I heard a soft, sweet little voice coming from behind the entrance to our room. *"Can I come in?"* It was Daun. She knew better than to barge in. Nicki had trained her years ago. Our daughter knew that walking in uninvited would invoke Nicki's ire.

Daun opened the door and stepped in. "Can we watch *Doctor Who?*"

I glanced at my watch. It was 7:40 p.m.

"Not now... I have exciting news!"

I explained my find to Daun, careful to highlight the prospect of receiving $5 million.

She was genuinely happy about the money but didn't ask for anything. She didn't care very much about that stuff—fantasizing about the future. She just wanted us to get the reward so I could pay my bills and feel less stressed out. Despite our poverty, she'd almost never felt poor. I had given her a good life. Besides, she wasn't selfish. She only rarely requested things she didn't need. Peter and Daun were the opposite of spoiled, probably because they'd learned a long time ago that asking me for material objects was pointless. The answer was almost always, "No. We can't afford that." Yet they never seemed to mind.

That night, Daun's mind was somewhere else—the reason she had come in. "Awesome news! I'm really happy for you. Now can we watch *Doctor Who*?"

"I can't right now. I have too much on my mind."

She pleaded with me. "But you have to. *You pinky promised!*"

I shrugged. I couldn't argue with that. I *had* to stop. I *had* to watch. Besides, for the most part, I had nothing better to do but wait.

"Sure, but I have to write an email first. And what are we doing about dinner?"

That's when Daun started whining. "I want to watch *now*. Besides, I'm not even *hungry*."

"Yeah. I'm not really hungry either. I'm too excited. Maybe just a snack. A banana and a yogurt. We could just do a scrounge night. Nicki? Is that okay?"

Nicki let out a sigh. She was probably a little hungry, but hiding it. "It's fine. I just had a PBJ."

"What about Peter? Has he eaten anything?"

Daun piped in. "Yeah. He just had pizza rolls."

"Okay cool. Just give me a couple of minutes to write my email."

But Daun wasn't having it. "*Mom!* You *always* say that."

"Just five minutes... I promise."

She finally gave up, and I sat down to write. Well, it took more like ten minutes, but this time I didn't forget my promise. Skipping my snack, I started gathering everyone together.

I addressed Daun first. "Okay, I'm going to get

Doctor Who set up."

Then I turned to my partner. "Nicki, do you want to watch, too?"

"Yeah. Why not? Should I pop some popcorn?" She wasn't as enthusiastic about *Doctor Who* as we were, but she'd watch pretty much anything we put in front of her. I think she just liked to spend time with us.

I responded eagerly. "Popcorn sounds great. And make *two* bags. Peter will probably want a bag all to himself."

We all knew that Peter was a popcorn fiend and had been all his life. I remember when he was nearly three, his father and I would try to sneak some popcorn when we thought he was asleep. Inevitably, little Petie would smell it and come out of bed, rubbing his tiny fists on his eyes. Then, he'd look up at me with a sad little face. "You got popcorn . . . *without me?* I want some popcorn." With our son close to crying because he felt left out, I suddenly felt like a bad mom for not sharing. Inevitably, we would give in. Honestly, I'm not sure why we hesitated. After all, Peter was a toddler. He didn't eat much.

But in 2006, he no longer had a two-year-old's appetite. He could eat an entire bag of popcorn on his own.

I spoke to Daun in a commanding voice. "Daun, go get Peter. I'm sure he'll want to watch too." Back then, when we were still limiting Peter's video game playing, he liked to watch shows with us. This would come to a halt when he turned eighteen and officially became an "adult." I stopped placing as many limits on him, so his playing was unfettered. In other words, he didn't want to stop playing his games long enough to watch a show with us. But twelve-year-old Peter usually joined us for *Doctor Who,* and this time was no exception.

I had attained digital copies of the show a few weeks earlier via BitTorrent, a popular file-sharing protocol. I tried hard not to feel guilty about "stealing" the episodes. Although they had been recently released on the Science Fiction Channel (SyFy), I couldn't afford to upgrade Dish to add it. And DVDs were expensive and difficult to find. Regardless, because the episodes were in digital format, we had no means of playing them on our TV. So we had to watch on the computer in the bedroom.

Nicki and I lay next to each other. Daun curled up by Midnight, at the far end of the mattress, while Peter put blankets on the floor, at the foot of the bed. We watched intently as the storyline unfolded. We were halfway through Series 1, which was the first season released after *Doctor Who* had been picked back up by BBC after a fourteen-year hiatus. Chris Eccleston was playing the ninth regeneration of the Doctor, and he played the role differently from the previous actors. Unlike the others, he had a buzz cut. Also, he was younger and more energetic than most of his predecessors. But the thing that stood out the most was his frequent and enthusiastic use of the expression, *"Fantastic!"* In this episode, World War I-era children were somehow becoming genetically altered to look like they had gas masks infused on their faces. Plus, they were going around continually asking everyone, *"Are you my mummy?"* in creepy voices. They couldn't seem to say anything else. Plus, their condition was *contagious.*

The Doctor kept telling his companions, "Whatever you do, don't let them touch you." The infected children kept up their mantra for the entire episode. "Are you my mummy? Mummy. Mummy! *Mummmmy!*"

Soon, nearly an hour had passed, and there was no wrap-up. *Ugh!* ... A cliff-hanger. That meant a second episode.

After the closing credits, Peter, who was grinning from ear to ear, looked over at me and started repeating, "Mummy. Mummmmy! *Are you my mummy?*"

Daun repeated the same words. "Mummmmy! *Mummmmy!*"

Then, I joined the chorus and the kids and I continued repeating the words in increasingly creepy little-kid British accents.

Finally, Nicki gave me a harrowing stare and, cocking her head sideways, joined in. *"Are you my Mummy?"*

I snapped back. *"Ewww...* No!"

The next thing I knew, Peter and Daun were begging me to watch the next episode. But the terrorist case and the FBI—everything that had been monopolizing my life lately—was drawing me back in. How could I stand to sit through Part 2? I had so many other things I could be doing.

I closed *Media Player* and checked my email. *Nothing...* I stopped myself. *Later...* I needed to wait... I needed to be patient.

I reluctantly gave in to my children. Besides, despite my hesitation, I was having fun. "Okay, let's watch Part 2. But this time, let's make tea. I'll put the kettle on."

Although the British had been using electric kettles for years, we hadn't yet discovered them. Besides, a stove-top kettle that whistled was nostalgic.

"Daun, grab the big pot. It's on the corner shelf. Do you want Plantation Mint?"

Daun looked up. "Yes!"

Peter chimed in, "*And Oreos!*" (His favorite cookies.)

I turned on the faucet and dumped water into our old, blue kettle—the one with the chipped-up ceramic lining—and glanced over at my son. "Sure, Oreos sound great."

When the episode was nearly over, the Doctor had re-programmed the nanogenes that had been causing the transformations so that they would quickly reproduce and reverse the mutation process. The epidemic had been threatening to transform all of humankind into gas-masked, "Mummy!"-shouting children.

The Doctor was going to save the world. He seemed excited. He looked at Rose—his blonde female companion—as the nanogenes flew around in a cloud of sparkling dust, beginning their magic. "*Everybody lives, Rose! Just this once, everybody lives!*"

This was unusual. *Doctor Who* was known for having at least a few deaths in every episode, despite being categorized as a children's show by the BBC. This exemplified how different American and British attitudes were toward death. In the UK and all of Europe, death was considered normal, a natural conclusion to life. In the US, death was feared, and the topic was avoided. It would *never* be featured on a children's show.

All that aside, the Doctor's words had jarred me. "*Everybody lives!*" ... He'd saved the world and all those children. Maybe for me, stopping this terrorist meant everybody would live. Maybe I could help people. Maybe I could save lives. Maybe I could be the hero.

My thoughts returned to the email. The popcorn, tea, and cookies were gone, the episode was over, and the children and Nicki were moving back to more mundane tasks.

It was time to get back to work. *Yes...* It was time.

17

ONWARD!

There are no guarantees in life.

After everyone cleared the room, I moved back to my desk. More than four hours had passed since I first wrote asking for a contract, but the FBI still hadn't written back. I had no recourse but to start working on my other cases to help pass the time. But I couldn't resist stopping every few minutes to obsessively check my inbox.

At nearly 1 a.m., I gave in and wrote the FBI again. Maybe if I worded the email differently, I'd get their attention. Then I went back to work and tried to kill some more time.

Finally, a little after 4 a.m., I couldn't take anymore.

I had to find out what I was doing wrong. I knew agents worked around the clock. Why weren't they responding? *No...* I was tired of waiting, So I picked up my landline and called the Houston office. There was no other way. I had so many questions.

When the screener picked up the phone, I explained that I was the one who turned in what I thought was the serial killer's MySpace. Then I added that I had a tip about a major terrorist. He put me through to a very nice agent with a mild, professional-sounding Texas accent. If I could only use one word to describe this man, it would be "polite."

After cordial introductions, I explained who I was, once again using the serial killer example. I think the FBI must have liked that tip because mentioning it appeared to grab their attention. This time was no exception.

"But that's not the reason I'm calling," I continued, pivoting to the matter at hand.

"Well then, how can I help you?"

I told him that I had information about a terror suspect, but I added a caveat, summoning my best, most assertive voice. "Before I give out the information, I would like a contract. I need assurance that I'll receive the reward money."

He was unimpressed but responded calmly and matter-of-factly. "The FBI doesn't make contracts with the general public."

Looking back, I probably came across a little desperate. But at the time, I could barely contain myself. "What do you mean, there are no contracts? How am I supposed to know I'll get the money?"

He gave me an answer, again in a calm, soothing voice. "You'll just have to give us the information and file a claim later."

I didn't like this answer, so I continued to press. "Are you sure? How do I know if you're going to pay?"

Another polite response followed. "Yes, I'm sure. You just have to follow standard procedures."

I didn't know what he meant by standard procedures, so I asked.

He explained FBI policy to me. "You have to go to

your local office and file a claim."

At this point, I was a little frustrated. "But without a contract, how do I know you'll pay?"

The agent repeated himself. "You just have to go file a claim."

"But how do I know I'll get the money?"

He gave a canned response. "If your tip leads to his arrest, you'll be compensated."

This was frustrating. We went around in circles for several minutes. But after spending what felt like an eternity, I finally gave up and decided to end the conversation.

"Thank you so much. You've been really helpful," I lied.

Yet I thought about it later. Maybe I hadn't been lying. Even though he didn't tell me what I wanted to hear, he had answered all my questions. He'd made his point abundantly clear. There would be no contract. I now knew what to expect.

However, there had been so many vague answers. I still wasn't sure how I was supposed to even know if they got Boussora. I began to worry. My thought was that giving me the reward was not on their priority list. I mean, how was I supposed to prove that I was the one who called in the tip, much less get paid for it? I was beginning to conclude that if I was going to call it in, I would have to trust the FBI. But this concept seemed impossible to me. I recalled Deep Throat's dying words during the finale of *The X-Files'* first season: *"Trust no one."*

And then, another common phrase from *The X-Files* came to mind: *"The truth is out there."* If I was going to disclose the whereabouts of Boussora, I would have to take a leap of faith and reveal the truth. I would have to give out the information, not knowing whether there would be any reward in it for me. To take that step, I needed to devise a plan—something I didn't want to do. So, I decided to push it all away for a couple of hours and work on my other cases. I 100 percent did not want to deal with this.

Somehow, I managed to pass out before the sun rose...

***

After sleeping several hours, I got up sluggishly. I had a sick feeling. I didn't want to think about giving the FBI the tip without a contract. Yet what was my recourse? I was being eaten away with guilt for not calling them right away with this vital information.

But instead of facing the Boussora situation head on, I tried to push it away by continuing to bury myself deep in my other cases. For the next 24 hours, Boussora would simmer on the backburner while I struggled with my conscience. The day passed slowly until, once again, I passed out in in the dark hours of early morning, with nothing resolved.

I woke up a little past noon, August 7, sat up slowly, ambled to the bathroom, and tried to shake off the fog in my head. *Nope!* ... I crawled back into bed. It was nice to be horizontal again. For a few seconds, I felt the pillow dragging me downward toward sleep. It would be great if I could get some more rest. If only—

Argh! ... As I lay there, I could no longer escape my thoughts. I immediately began obsessing on the Boussora dilemma. It had been nearly two days. I needed to deal with this. I began to worry. How could I be sure I'd get the money if I didn't have a contract? How could I even *prove* I was the reason they caught him? I was utterly unfamiliar with the proper protocol. Telling them without a deal could cost me $5 million, but not sharing the intel could mean a lost chance to catch one of the most wanted terrorists in the world— one who might even be partially responsible for 9/11.

I squeezed my eyes tight and tried to push the thoughts out of my mind. *No!* ... I wasn't ready to face this. Not yet. I had to...*had to* stop this. It was too hard. I needed a distraction.

I reluctantly got up and started working my other cases. But as the day drug on, like the day before, I couldn't stop the gnawing feeling that I was doing something wrong. I had found this guy. How could I hold onto this? Even as I worked, I was wracked with increasing guilt. Finally, at around 5:30 p.m., I reached a breaking point. I had to confront this. I had to figure out this out. My gears began turning.

I had a few ideas, but I wanted to run them by Nicki first. The results of my actions would affect her, too. The $5 million would be just as much hers as mine. Our future could be dependent on this decision, and I didn't want to make a wrong choice.

Suddenly, I started panicking. What if I waited too long and Boussora moved? What if he figured out through some hacking voodoo that I'd found him? This information could save lives. Was the money worth the risk of waiting? I knew that, regardless, I had to tell them eventually. It was my duty as a human being. It had to happen.

Energized by my angst, I leapt out of bed and walked

briskly into the living room and plopped down on the couch next to Nicki.

I took a deep breath. I would have to ease into this conversation. "Hey, how's it going?"

Nicki looked up. I glanced over toward her laptop. She was reading the news on CNN.com. "I'm doing okay. But did you know that oil is going up by another seventy cents per barrel?"

I leaned toward her and took a harder peek at her article. "*Wow...* I can't believe it. When are gas prices going stop going up? The national average is over three dollars a gallon. I'm sick of this!"

"I don't know, but it's pretty crazy."

But despite my initial response, I wasn't all that concerned. "At least it's a little lower here because we're near all the refineries."

"Yeah. That's true. I'm glad we're not in California right now." Being from there, she often thought about how things used to be when she was living in Cypress.

I thought back to The Monster Trip. "I agree. Gas prices have always been nuts out there. Remember that gas station before we got into Yosemite Valley?"

"Yeah. I remember that. Over five dollars a gallon! And you have no choice. There's no other gas station for miles around. It's your last chance to gas up. I mean, they've got you by the black and curlies, and they know it."

I winced. I didn't like the imagery. I decided to shift the topic a little. "Well, at least it's always cheaper in the Houston area than other places in the country. I mean, like I said, we're right next to the refineries. Remember, my dad used to work for Carbide."

Nicki thought about it. "That's true."

I kept going. "And you know, the price of oil going up will be good for Houston and Texas. It'll probably mean jobs."

"True."

"And remember, Jimmy is a metallurgical tech. They test the metal used for drilling oil. Maybe he'll find a job. This could be really good. It could mean more child support..."

But then my mind spun off. I was getting impatient with myself. We had more pressing matters to discuss. What was a little child support compared to $5 million?

And Nicki was starting to give me one- and two-word responses, which meant she'd probably stopped listening. I looked back toward her. I was right... She'd already gone back to reading. I had to try harder to get her attention.

"Hey!"

She was a little exasperated. "*What?* ... I'm trying to read!"

"I have something important to talk to you about."

Not bothering to look up or even to stop reading, she replied flatly, "Okay."

"Can you please close your laptop? *This is important.*"

She slammed it shut and snapped her head toward me. "*What?* What is so important?"

Although there was an edge to her tone, I was not deterred.

I softened my voice. "Honey, we need to talk about the tip, the money, how we're going to handle it."

Her voice also softened a bit. "What do you mean?"

I calmly continued, "Well, you remember how I was going to write the FBI and ask for a contract?"

Nicki's demeanor had changed; she was at ease

and no longer annoyed. I had calmed the beast. *Thank goodness...*

Using a gentle tone, she responded, "Yeah. I remember."

"Well, I spoke to an agent last night and asked a lot of questions." It had actually been that morning, but she understood what I meant.

Nicki knew, after all these years, that "last night" could actually mean "this morning." The concept was simple: It was "night" until I went to bed, even if it was 8 a.m. And "morning" was whenever I woke up, even if it was three in the afternoon. But Nicki was unconcerned with my sleep patterns. We had given up on trying to fix them years ago. Years later, I would learn that I had delayed sleep phase syndrome (aka "night owl syndrome"), a condition that affects people's circadian rhythms. In other words, my days and nights were permanently screwed up.

Regardless of my sleep schedule, Nicki was listening carefully. She was worried about how we were going to get the $5 million for finding Boussora.

"What did the agent say? Are they going to send you a contract?"

I replied frankly, "Actually, no. He clearly stated that the FBI doesn't make contracts with the general public."

"*Damn!* They don't do contracts? What does that mean? What're we supposed to do?"

I kept going. "I dunno. I've been thinking about it, and I want to run some ideas past you."

"Okay. What?"

I continued sharing my thoughts. "Well, I was thinking about it, and I can prove I was the one who called in the tip."

"How?"

I kept going. "Well, I emailed Boussora's name and address to myself a couple of days ago. This will have a timestamp that proves it was sent previous to the arrest. This way, if I don't get the money, I could always sue them."

She seemed perplexed. *"Sue the government?"*

"Yeah, I don't see why not. I mean, people sue the government all the time. Besides, lawyers only take money if you win."

"True..." Nicki trailed off, thinking for a moment. "But is the email enough of a safeguard?"

"I don't know. But what choice do we have?"

Nicki looked at me blankly. "What do you mean?"

I gazed back at her intensely. "I can't sit on my hands for too long. What if he moves? What if they don't get him because I waited too long?"

"Yeah, but what about the money?"

I couldn't believe what she was saying. It seemed so obvious to me. "We're not going to get a guarantee, so we're just gonna have to risk it. This is too important. This guy's gotta go down no matter what. I mean, we'll just have to take a leap of faith and turn him in. What do we have to lose?"

"True."

I kept pleading my case. "I mean, what's the worst thing that can happen? The FBI arrests a major terrorist. *Lives* are saved. *So what* if I don't get the money? In the end, it's just money."

"Money we really need."

Financial security mattered more to her than it did to me, but I knew she'd come around.

"Don't you get it? People are more important than

money. Like I said, lives could be at stake."

Nicki shrugged. "True. I guess you're right."

"I mean, we're not getting a contract. What else am I supposed to do? I'm just going to take action and let the chips fall where they may."

"Alright." That settled it. She had finally agreed to my plan.

After the conversation with Nicki, I had a new resolve. I was going to call in the tip, come what may. Even if I never got a dime, I would have helped serve justice. I would still try to claim the money, but if I didn't get it, it wouldn't be the end of the world. No matter what happened in my life, I knew that I would never become homeless or starve to death. My family wouldn't let that happen.

Besides, I had always put people in front of money. *Always.*

Once, when I was really broke, I gave $20 to a bag lady just because I knew she needed it more than I did. The elderly, hunched woman had been standing in front of my dorm building at St. Thomas. She was a regular on campus, digging through all the rubbish to search for aluminum cans. I had felt a rush of sympathy as she laboriously bent over to reach in the trash to retrieve her bounty.

Looking at her lovingly, I handed her my last $20, followed with a quick "God bless you." I did this knowing that I might not have been able to afford food that weekend. She looked up at me, stunned. But before she could respond, I swung open the door to the dorms and stepped inside.

Years later, on August 6, 2006, I felt compelled to give again—this time risking $5 million. I had to get my tip about Boussora to the FBI... I *had to*. It felt urgent. As a human being, I couldn't wait another moment. Like I told Nicki, lives could be at risk. I needed to call the FBI.

18

MAKING THE CALL

Once the screener transferred the call, I held my breath... Then, gathering all my inner strength, I picked up the landline and called the Houston office. Whether or not I got a reward, I was going to tell the FBI what I found. The money wasn't as important in that moment. What mattered was that they get this crucial information. I quickly got past the screener by telling him I had a tip about a major terrorist and identifying myself as the person who'd called in the MySpace page that could be related to the Acres Homes killer.

Moments later, I was greeted by a kind-sounding woman. I'm not sure why, but for some reason (maybe the timbre of her voice), I imagined her as being an attractive woman with long, blonde, curly hair—a lovely Texas woman, dressed in boring, gray business attire.

I introduced myself by name and told her that I was the one who'd called in the suspicious MySpace account. Then I asked a poignant question. "Do you know about my tip?"

She came across mildly enthusiastic. "Yes."

Then, I briefly reminded her of my ideas about the serial killer case. Finally, I asked her a pointed question: "Do you know anything yet?"

Her voice was matter-of-fact. "We're looking into it. It'll take some time."

That was good enough for me. "Well, there's actually another reason I called."

She seemed curious. "Yes? How can I help you?"

"Well, I think I've found one of the terrorists from the Most Wanted list."

She sounded surprised. "Really? Who is it?"

I looked down at my computer screen. I could never remember these foreign names. *"Faker Ben Abdelaziz Boussora."*

"So, what have you got?"

I replied flatly, "I'm pretty sure I have his current alias and address."

She was down to business. "Okay. What is it?"

I hesitated. I wasn't quite ready to trust. "First, can I have your name?" I thought I might need to know it later down the road to verify that I called in the tip.

"Sure... No problem. I'm Agent Miles."

"Thanks. Hang on a second." I quickly opened Notepad, typed in her name, and saved it to my desktop as a text file. "Okay, ready?"

"Yes. You can go any time."

I took a deep breath and started relaying the information. "Okay... I'm going to spell out his first and last name to make sure you get it right. That's Faker Boussora. Ready? ... That's F-A-K-E-R-B-O-U-S-S-O-R-A. And he's going by 'Abdulaziz Abdulla.'" Then, I spelled out his alias and recounted his address and phone number. "Did you get all that?"

"Yes. I got it."

But I wanted to be sure. "Do you mind reading it back to me?"

She read it back, then asked me a logical question: "I got it... But how did you get that information?"

I recalled the adage, *A magician never reveals his secrets.* But it was too cliché. Instead, I took a serious tone. "I don't really want to tell you my methods, but I have a system."

I was pretty sure the idea of looking on social media for criminals had barely been tapped by authorities. So, I wanted to save what I considered an original idea for my own personal use, without fear of competition. My tactics were worth too much money, and I didn't want people stealing my ideas. Besides, I wasn't sure if anyone else could follow my train of thought.

But Agent Miles was skeptical. Her accent came out a little stronger. Perhaps it picked up when she got a little emotional. "Okay. But what on *Earth* makes you think it's him?"

I only hesitated for a moment before giving a quick, confident response. *"Because I'm really smart, and I think I'm onto something."*

I'm not sure why saying I was "really smart" was good enough for Agent Miles, but she suddenly sounded excited. "Well . . . I hope it *is* him! That'd be amazing!"

My voice was a little excited too at this point. "Well, I'm pretty sure it is! Will you look into it?"

Agent Miles then said the words that I wanted desperately to hear. She emphatically said, *"I'll pass it on!"*

I was genuinely grateful. "Thank you!"

"You're welcome!"

"Can I call you back in a couple of days and find out if y'all got him?"

Agent Miles had a smile in her voice. "Sure."

We exchanged salutations and I hung up the phone.

Yes! ... Maybe they'd get this guy. I had high hopes.

A few minutes later, I remembered the email I had sent to myself—the one with the suspect's address and phone number. I forwarded it to agent Miles and called her again to tell her to look for it, reaching her on the second try. This would be my modus over the next few weeks: When I sent an email, I would also call. It was simple. I would have proof that I was the one who gave them the intel, and the body of the email would ensure that the information they received was correct.

My job complete, on the evening of August 7, I had nothing else to do but wait...

***

The next day, I called back on my cell phone, but Agent Miles wasn't available. I decided to talk to the nice young-sounding man who answered the phone. I wanted to know if my tip had been correct. The answer wasn't what I wanted to hear.

The man sounded stoic. "I cannot confirm nor deny that information." This was some of the canned, typical FBI-speak I would eventually become accustomed to. Getting information out of the FBI was an art—an art I was only beginning to learn. I was going to have to learn their language—to talk like them.

But I still didn't know exactly how the FBI worked, so I asked a general question: "Well, how can I find out if he's been caught?"

He cited policy. "You can't. Information is only given out on a need to know basis." In that moment, I could hear nasty, unspoken words echoing through my brain: *And you don't need to know.*

I protested. "Then how am I supposed to collect the reward money?"

He was still blunt. "I don't know. You just file a claim and see what happens."

"But how am I supposed to file a claim if I don't know if they got him?"

Then, he changed the subject for a moment. "You know what? While I have you on the phone, can I get your Social Security number?" I wondered why he wanted it. At the very least, I guess it meant I was a person of interest. At the time, it didn't occur to me that they would need it to identify me if my tip turned out to be correct. In retrospect, maybe he was trying to help me in case of a future claim for a reward.

But instead, my mind went in a different direction.

"I guess you probably want to do a background check." It occurred to me that if I *had* reported the location of an Al Qaeda operative, they might have been concerned that I had some sort of ties to the organization.

I proceeded to tell the agent what he'd find on my record, which wasn't much. I mean, there was a time I was arrested at a pro-life rescue. But this only showed me to have a history of activism, not ties to criminal or terrorist-related activity.

Next, I gave the agent information about my medical history, in case it came up in his search. Honestly, I didn't really know what he was looking for, but I wanted to be as transparent as possible.

The agent didn't confirm nor deny if there would be a background check, or why he needed my Social Security number, but I gladly gave it to him before turning the subject back to how to collect the reward money.

We went around in circles for a while before I finally gave up. I doubted Agent Miles would have given a different response because this new man's answers seemed pretty standard. No. I would just have to wait and watch the news like the rest of the world. Surely, if such an important terrorist had been caught, it would be on CNN. And if that happened, I would try to collect the money.

At first, there was nothing relevant in the news—no news of arrests, nothing huge in the War on Terror. I watched CNN frequently when I wasn't working on one of my other cases or searching for new ones. During the wait, I wasn't even looking for other terrorists. Before I continued my work, I had to know if my tip was any good. If it were incorrect, using the same method to find others would be pointless, a waste of time. As the hours dragged on, I eventually began spending more time in front of the television than my computer. I didn't want to miss anything.

But after a day and a half of obsessing on whether or not I got Boussora and watching the news nonstop, I was exhausted both mentally and physically. I wasn't sure how much I could take. My brain wouldn't power down.

I kept retracing the same steps. I needed to prove they got Boussora. I needed evidence—something concrete to present to the FBI when I tried to claim the money. My thoughts were circular and redundant, annoying. I couldn't think of anything else. I couldn't take breaks from my worrying. I couldn't sleep. I was too fixated...

Then something disrupted my thoughts: It was Nicki, calling from the other room. "Come into the kitchen, Boobie. I've got something for you."

I reluctantly pulled myself away from CNN and dragged myself into the kitchen and joined her at the table. "What?"

She grabbed a yellow shot glass that had the words *"THE THING"* inscribed on it. It was a souvenir from The Monster Trip—from the Bowlen's on I-10 in Arizona that tried to lure people into the truck stop by promising a look at the mysterious "Thing."

She must have noticed how stressed out I was and wanted to calm me down. Nicki carefully opened our bottle of Hot Damn! and poured me some of the cinnamon-flavored fluid. Sliding the shot glass across the table to me, she gave the command,

"Drink this."

It wasn't the first or the last time she'd try to calm me down with alcohol, especially in the weeks to come.

I was grateful for Nicki's help. "Yes... I could use it. Thanks. I just can't shut my brain down."

"I know."

I took a deep breath, held it, and tensed my neck and shoulders. Then I released my breath and relaxed my muscles, letting out a deep sigh. *Here goes nothing.* I took the shot, hopeful that it would help.

But three shots later, I was only slightly more relaxed. I was a large woman, so I had a high tolerance for alcohol. But I'd had enough, and I didn't want any more. I was starting to feel a little queasy. It would have to do.

I looked over at Nicki who was getting ready to pour the next shot. "Thanks, but I think I'm done."

She picked up the shot glass and bottle and put them back on the shelf. "I hope it helps... Why don't you try to get some sleep?"

It sounded like a great idea. I would lie down and see if I could get some rest. I knew I couldn't keep going like this. I needed an "off" switch. But still, even with the alcohol, I only managed to get about four hours of sleep that night. I would have to figure out a different way to unlock my brain. Alcohol was not the key.

19

NO DISTRACTIONS

August 8, 2006, was no better than the day before. All my worrying was making me so miserable that I couldn't even concentrate on my cases. Instead, I was glued to CNN, watching, hoping for a break in the Boussora case.

But despite my obsession with the news, my cases were calling. *Yes...cases*—plural. Even while hunting for Boussora, I hadn't given up on my efforts to find other wanted and missing people. It was true, I got no breaks. I never stopped. Not even after concluding my first terrorism case. I blew right through it and feverishly kept up my detective work, working all the normal cases. I wouldn't even look at another terror suspect until I knew if I was right about Boussora. I didn't want to waste my time.

On that day, I was lying on the couch with my eyes fixed on CNN. I had been there for hours, unwavering, once again hoping for news about Boussora. *If only they would—*

What? ...

My thoughts were interrupted. Something was tugging at my shirt.

"Mom!" It was Daun. She seemed absolutely exasperated.

I was pulled out of my trance for a moment. "Wh... what?" I was annoyed.

"I wanna watch Animal Planet!" It was her favorite channel. At that age, she wanted to be a veterinarian. She would eventually abandon that dream when she found out how hard it was to get into vet school. Instead, as a young adult, she became a pescatarian.

But this was 2006, and I wasn't ready to give up the TV so she could watch Animal Planet. I quickly dismissed her. "Not right now, honey. This is important."

I was watching an analysis of Bush's recent statement about a crisis in the Middle East that was responsible for the price of oil going up. I was very interested in anything having to do with the president. Maybe somewhere in the story—however unlikely—they would drop a clue about Boussora's arrest. I was desperate, but there was nothing so far—

Suddenly, I felt something tugging on me again.

"Mom!"

"Wh...what?" She had startled me. "I told you... This is important!" I started staring at the screen again, watching, hoping. I couldn't pull away.

"We've been watching the news *all day!* I wanna watch something else!"

"Umm, sorry. Can you repeat that?"

I had tuned her out, sucked back in by the allure of CNN.

Daun quickly repeated herself. She didn't mind because she was used to it. I tuned her out so often that my requests for repetition had become routine. Fortunately, this time around I heard her. The story about the president had just finished.

It was at that point that I realized how bad things had gotten. I couldn't even break away from my obsession long enough to properly address my daughter's concerns. I felt like my life was this colossal Category 4 hurricane. I couldn't "unhear" the wind blowing down the exhaust vent in our kitchen and the sideways rain pelting my windows. And if I tried to venture outside, I was at risk of the wind blowing me over.

In other words, I was barely holding it together.

No... It had become crystal clear that I needed to try to ease up on my obsession a bit. First, to that end, I knew I needed to force myself to stop watching the news.

I reached for the remote. It wasn't where I saw it last. I dug in the couch cushions for a moment. No luck. I looked at Daun. "Watch whatever you want, but I can't find the remote."

"Yay!" Daun had won.

While she scrambled around the living room searching for the remote, I got up and pushed the power button on the TV harder than necessary. I was sick of CNN, but I couldn't stop. I was addicted.

But what would I do now? If I couldn't watch the news, I couldn't get on my computer. After all, the internet was the world's largest source of news and information. And if I couldn't get on my PC, I couldn't work on my cases. *Whatever...* I needed a break from them, too. Regardless, there was nothing new to report to the FBI, so I didn't know what to do with myself. I felt trapped, panicked.

I know... Conversation! That was something I could do that wasn't off-limits. I'd have to go get Nicki. Hopefully, I could pull out of my thoughts enough to talk to her.

Nicki was in the bedroom frantically digging through her dresser drawers. I could tell she'd lost something. I wasn't sure if I could pull her away from her quest. She kind of freaks out when she can't find something that belongs to her, no matter how inconsequential it seems.

"What're you looking for?"

"I can't find that lesbian ring you got me." When we first started dating, I had given her a pink-and-silver ring that displayed images of two curvy women with their naked bodies intertwined.

"I thought you didn't like that ring?"

"I like it. I just don't like to wear it in public."

I already knew why. We had been together for seven years. "Too 'out'?" Nicki could be kind of shy around people she didn't know.

"Yeah. Have you seen it anywhere? The last time I saw it, it was on the dresser. And now it's not there. It's just disappeared!"

She was inconsolable, and I knew that if we didn't locate the ring, I wouldn't be able to talk to her about my problems or anything else. She could be very determined when it came to finding lost items. She wouldn't give up easily.

The problem is that the dresser was extremely cluttered with pill bottles, hats, keys chains, handbags, and random jewelry. None of it was trash. It was just a pile of stuff.

I started moving things around slowly and carefully to search for the ring.

Nicki punctuated her words, sounding accusatory. "What are you doing?"

"I'm trying to find your ring. Don't worry. I'm being really careful." I cringed, worrying that I'd just tripped a landmine. She didn't like me touching her stuff.

Nicki looked away. "Okay, just be careful." *Shoo...* Trouble averted.

"I wi—" But before I could get the words out, she stopped me. She was holding something in her hand.

"Found it!"

Thank goodness...

After giving Nicki a moment to catch her breath, I decided to approach her with *my* problem. "Okay...well . . .can you lie down next to me for a minute? There's something we need to talk about."

"Yeah. Sure. Just let me put this away." Slipping the ring on and then off her finger, she placed it in the second drawer of her new jewelry box that had recently been added to the junk on her dresser.

I lay down on my back on my side of the bed with my pillow curled under my neck. Nicki lay on her side next to me. "So, what's up?"

"I...I...can't stop thinking about all this stuff."

Nicki was smart. She knew what I meant, but I'm pretty sure she wanted to hear me say it. "What stuff?"

"The terrorist... How to get the money. How we're going to prove they got 'em. I just keep watching the news, hoping to find some evidence."

"I know you are..." Her voice turned deep and sultry. "Maybe I can distract you. Do you want a massage?"

"No. I..." But I wasn't feeling sexy, and I knew her "massage" wouldn't help. Instead of helping, her offer backfired. I started bawling uncontrollably and gasping for air. "I just feel so overwhelmed. I can't stop thinking about all this shit. I don't know how much more I can take!"

Nicki was compassionate. "Maybe you need to take a break."

"I know. I just don't know how. Nothing is helping."

"What about the alcohol? It didn't help?"

"Maybe a little. But I still only got four hours of sleep. I can't do this without sleep." I was still bawling. Snot was running from my nose. "You got any tissue?"

"Yeah." She pulled a few tissues from her nightstand. She was always prepared. I gratefully took the wad and blew into it.

Then Nicki made a futile attempt to fix the problem.

"Hey. How 'bout if we get out of the house? Go to Walgreens. I need to pick up a prescription."

"Nah. I'm not in the mood. I'm too upset. But maybe later when I'm feeling better."

She pushed the idea a little further before moving on. She was probably tired of being cooped up. She wanted to go somewhere. *Anywhere.*

"Okay. But let's definitely go to Walgreens later. I think it would be good for us to get out and get some fresh air." I knew that instead of "us," she was really talking about herself.

But despite her strong desire to exit the premises, she turned back to trying to help me.

"Okay. How about some booze? Do you want to try the alcohol again?"

I was desperate. Maybe it would work this time. But no alcohol yet... I was too— I suddenly realized that I was parched. Crying made me thirsty.

"Not right now. Can you just pass me some water?"

I need to calm down. She handed me a bottle from on top of her dresser.

I drank half the bottle in one swig, blew my nose again, and tried to slow down my breathing. The water was a relief, and I felt slightly better. Maybe I would try the alcohol after all. I was still sobbing, but more softly.

I decided to try her idea. "Alright, let's go into the kitchen. I guess it wouldn't hurt to try the booze."

Moments later, we were sitting at the kitchen table. And as I took my cinnamon-flavored "medicine," I looked down at the wooden surface, away from Nicki, who was pouring shots for the second day in a row.

Although I was still upset, I wanted to plot the next move. "We need a plan."

"Sure." Nicki got up, came over to my side of the table, and started massaging my shoulders. Her hands were strong, and I wasn't sure whether it felt good or if it hurt like hell. She was going hard.

I was quiet for a moment, soaking in her act of affection until the pain of the rough massage became intolerable.

"*Owww!* ... A little softer." She eased up, but a little too much. I could hardly feel it.

"Go ahead, take another shot." This time, I poured it myself as she continued to massage my shoulders. I could feel myself calming down a bit.

At her prodding, I took a third and then fourth-and-final shot of Hot Damn! Any more and I could have gotten sick. I was already a little nauseous. I wasn't much of a drinker. I was just desperate.

By then, I'd stopped crying. I grabbed a napkin off the table and blew my nose, wadding up the paper and putting it in a paper bowl on the table. "I've had enough, honey."

"Are you sure?" She still seemed worried.

"Yeah. We've gotta talk."

Nicki stopped massaging me, went back to her side of the table, and sat down. "What do you want to talk about?"

I let out a loud sigh, choosing my words carefully. "I don't know what to say. It's like I was telling you... I'm just... I'm exhausted. I can't stop thinking about all this stuff. I need a break. I need to take a couple of days to do nothing, maybe take a few extra sleeping pills."

As Nicki and I had agreed, I had gone to the doctor and gotten a prescription sleep aid. But although it was helping, it didn't always work. I still wasn't getting nearly enough rest. Maybe if I took a couple of extra for a few nights—

Nicki abruptly interrupted my thoughts. "Yes. You definitely need a break. And a few extra sleeping pills couldn't hurt." But Nicki appeared to be overwhelmed and clearly wanted to stop talking. She lurched forward as if to get up, probably to go to the bathroom.

But I stopped her. "No... *Wait...* I'm not done..."

However reluctantly, she acquiesced to further conversation. "What can I do? I've given you alcohol and a massage." She glanced at me coyly. "And you've refused *other* ways of relaxing. What's left?"

Blushing a bit, I tossed out my idea. "I need you to hide my laptop from me, and keep my phone."

"*Why?*" She sounded perplexed.

"I can't stop. I can't control myself. I need to take a break. *Please...* I'm desperate."

Nicki was empathetic. "Sure... I can do that. Anything else?"

"Yeah. Can you watch the news for me?"

Once again, she seemed perplexed. "What do you mean?"

"I mean that I can't watch the news right now. It's too overwhelming. Can you just watch for any news about captured terrorists? Or maybe evidence that they might have gotten him?"

"Sure," she agreed, reluctantly.

"But you've got to watch all day. I mean, at least most of the time. You might miss something."

"*Fine!*" Nicki was obviously annoyed. I mean, she'd do it. But I got that she thought I was being a little ridiculous. Besides, she was getting tired of the conversation and was anxious to get out of the house. "Can we go to Walgreens now?"

"Sure..." But even if Nicki was done talking, I wasn't ready to stop yet. "I wasn't finished... Before you take my stuff, I need to send out a couple of emails. I need to let Adam and Agent Miles know that they shouldn't expect to hear from me."

Her words were sharp and punctuated. "*Fine!* ... But can you do it later, after we get back?"

"Yeah, sure. Just let me get dressed."

Ten minutes later, we were out the door and headed to Walgreens. Fortunately, the kids were old enough to be left at home for an hour or so. Neither of them wanted to go. Daun was happily watching Animal Planet, and Peter was playing *Mega Man X* on his GameCube.

As Nicki and I headed out, I said a silent prayer that our plan would work, and I'd finally get some rest.

***

That night, a little before midnight, I sent two emails. Here is a portion of the one I sent to Agent Miles:

> *I am taking a break for a few days, so if you call, leave a message and someone will get back to you...*
>
> *—Barbara*
>
> *P.S. Keep me posted. Email is the best way to reach me right now.*

If I requested it, the FBI would return my calls. But normally, I would just obsessively keep calling back until I reached the duty agent, preferably Agent Miles. Like I said, emails to the FBI tended to be one-way communications. A couple of minutes later, I wrote Adam. After all, he was both my boss and a concerned friend. Below is a slightly redacted version:

> *I have decided to stay home and take it easy. I am... avoiding TV and computer and telephone.*
>
> *Email me if you want, or call and leave a message, and someone will get back to you.*
>
> *Take care,*
>
> *Barbara*

He gave a two-sentence reply:

> *I understand. Take care and hopefully see you soon.*

Adam knew I was going through a tough time. He was so sweet. It would be nearly a month before I'd go back to work. Even after I took six weeks off for The Monster Trip, he had taken me back. He was a good friend.

But despite my mental exhaustion, I wasn't sleepy yet, and I wasn't ready to stop. My brain was working overtime, thinking about the news. Was there anything in the latest stories about Bush? Were there any hints from Congressional activity? Why wasn't there any news about Boussora? I felt in my gut that I had the right guy. If they never announced it, how would I claim the money? I mean, I really needed the money. After all, I was still swimming in debt. I already knew I couldn't file bankruptcy and that if things didn't change, I'd be forced to stop paying my bills. This reward was supposed to be my way out of my financial crisis—my exit.

I looked at the clock. It was nearly midnight. This was late for most people. I desperately wanted to get on a schedule. I needed to catch up on my sleep, but I worried if I took the sleeping pills too soon, they wouldn't work. My mind was still going a mile a minute. But I had to...*had to* try. Finally, I leaned over toward the nightstand, grabbed the bottle of sleeping pills, and took three of them—one extra. *God, please let them work this time.*

I lay on my back in my usual position, with my pillow curled under my neck and my sheet lying loosely on top of me. I was extremely wound up, and my neck and shoulders were in knots. Lying down caused a similar reaction to submerging myself in a scalding hot tub. My breathing and heart rate sped up so much that I was afraid I would hyperventilate. Then, tears began welling in my eyes and my nose started running. In other words, as with a hot tub, laying down was forcing me to release physical tension. And I knew what was causing my stress: the culmination of over a month of sleep deprivation and too much caffeine.

I eventually calmed down and began to relax. But I still wasn't sleepy. The medicine would need time to take effect. I wasn't even sure if it would work *at all.*

Nicki was lying next to me. Like me, she was having trouble sleeping.

"Hey."

"Hey." Nicki sounded a little groggy.

"There's something bothering me."

"What's that?" Despite the question, she didn't seem too concerned.

"I keep hearing clicking noises on the phone line when I'm on it." Back then I was still sometimes using my landline to avoid depleting my cellular minutes.

"So?" She didn't seem to know what I was getting at.

I could hear the worry in my voice. "Do you think there's any chance they're tapping my phone?"

Nicki's words started sounding mumbly as she fought sleep. "I dunno. Why would they?"

"I mean, they don't know me. What if they think I have terrorist ties? How else would I have this information? Maybe they'd want to know for sure."

She began to get a second wind but seemed slightly annoyed. I was keeping her up. "They're probably not tapping the phone."

"But what about the clicking? It makes me suspicious."

At this point, she gave up all niceties. "*Oh my God.* It could just be static on the line."

"Yes, I thought of that. I agree, but I still worry. I mean, how would I know for sure?" I kept going, hearing the anxiety in my voice grow. "It's not like I have anything to hide. It's just that I'm finding myself being careful about what I say over the phone. The suspicion makes me nervous."

"That's understandable. They *are* the FBI." She had finally joined me in my uneasiness. And for the moment, she seemed wide awake.

I awkwardly tried to lighten the mood. "I feel like I'm ready for a tinfoil hat."

"Hey, if it makes you feel better," she joked back.

But the humor was short-lived as my mind fixated on my anxiety once again. "But seriously," I continued, "How would I know for sure?"

"Why don't you search online and see if there's any way to check whether or not you're being wiretapped?"

"That's a good idea. While I'm online, I could also find out if clicking is any indicator." Looking back, I think I'd gotten that idea from watching *The X-Files*. I seemed to recall a few scenes where Mulder or Scully would hear clicking on the line and either hang up or stop sharing relevant information. I also seemed to remember this being a common occurrence in spy movies.

Regardless, I leaned over to my left and grabbed my laptop off of my chair. I didn't bother to get out of bed. Instead, I lay back down and propped the computer up on my chest. Then, I started scouring the internet for information. It was a race to see if I could get the answers before the sleep aids knocked me out.

I concluded my research a few minutes before 1 a.m. Supposedly, there was a phone number that I could call in Washington, DC, and once I called it, I would be able to tell if I was being wiretapped, based on the noises I heard on the line. The test was simple: You dial this number. If there's static and breakups on the line, you're being tapped. If you get a constant tone, you're not.[55]

I picked up the phone, slowly and nervously punching in the number: *(202) 543-9994*. Then, I strained my ears, listening carefully for any indication either way. I needed results. I needed peace of mind.

There were no clear breakups and no obvious static, but the tone wasn't constant. I also heard a little crackling on the other end of the line. So, to me, the test was inconclusive. And I quickly realized I didn't even really know what I was listening for. I handed the phone to Nicki, but she wasn't sure what she was hearing, either. I ended the call without the reassurance I'd hoped for, wondering if the trick was legitimate.

Another concern, one I'd come across on the internet, popped into my mind. Some of the more paranoid people online feared that the number was a trap. The very act of calling it could be a red flag for the government that you had something to hide. Then, they'd *actually* tap you.

So, if anything, my experiment made me feel worse. I immediately regretted calling the number. Even though there had been a little crackling, the distance to DC could have caused degradation in the line. I decided that this was bullshit, and I needed to just stop. Despite myself, I would try the line again in a couple of days. But at the time, all I could think of was one thing: sleep. I was finally beginning to get sleepy. I set down the phone, pulled the cover over myself, and closed my eyes. After a few seconds, my mind began to drift...

Moments later, I saw a narrow dirt road surrounded by green grass and yellow flowers. I was whizzing down it at a fast pace—just my body, no car.

Suddenly, my body jerked...

Nope! ... I was definitely still awake. Once again, I was painfully aware that I was starting to fall asleep. I attempted to control myself by trying not to worry about whether or not I'd sleep. But it was like the old joke, *"Don't think about white elephants. Whatever you do, don't think about white elephants."* Of course, all you can think about is white elephants.

Moments later, despite myself, I began to drift a bit again, but...

One more time, my body convulsed.

Grandma? ...

Another image had appeared—this time, the kind face of my grandmother. Just for a moment, she was there with me. I could see her wrinkled complexion and the gentle curve of her lips. She was smiling.

But how can it be Grandma? ... Grandma is dead...

A comforting thought came to me: Maybe she was paying me a visit, encouraging me.

Then the specter faded, and I started worrying again about whether or not I'd sleep. *My God, will I ever fall asleep?* What if I do this all night? I needed sleep so desperately.

Finally, I saw swirling colored lights surround me and fade to black.

20

THE EYE OF THE HURRICANE

I awoke abruptly and glanced at the clock. It was 10 a.m. *Eight hours of sleep.* Nice... Much better than the five or six I'd been getting lately.

I got up and found Nicki, who was sitting in her easy chair. I groggily greeted her. "Good morning."

She responded in kind, and we spent a few minutes talking about everything that she had accomplished since she'd gotten up. In the two hours since she'd been awake, she'd done the dishes, taken out the trash, and started the laundry. *Chores...* I couldn't remember the last time I'd done any chores. Just the thought of them was making me sleepy. Finally, I stopped her mid-sentence as she was beginning to tell me about another oil price hike.

"I hate to interrupt you... Sorry... But I think I need to lie back down."

But this time being interrupted didn't seem to bother her. *No...* This time she seemed more annoyed that I wasn't going to stay up with her. She sounded almost whiney. "*Really?* But you just got up!"

I defended my position: "I know, but I'm trying to catch up. Remember, I'm supposed to be resting today. I'm gonna try to force myself to sleep some more by taking a couple more sleeping pills."

"Are you sure that's wise? What if it messes you up for tonight?"

I continued my defense: "It'll be fine. I don't sleep at night half the time anyhow, so what does it matter? I really need to do this. Besides, I'm just gonna be on the couch, so hopefully I won't over-do it."

Nicki relented. "Yeah. I guess you're right. You should try to get some rest."

But I wasn't quite ready to hit the couch. "Yeah, but before I lie down, there's something we need to do."

"What's that?"

I started in on the plan. "Remember what we talked about yesterday?"

"What?"

I reminded her of yesterday's conversation about taking a break from my work.

A few minutes later, I found myself gathering up anything that could be a distraction—anything that could pull me away from sleep. First, I surrendered my cell phone, handing it over to Nicki with a recap of the plan: "Remember, keep this on you in case someone important calls. If it's not pressing, just write it down. Okay?"

"Sure." She didn't seem to mind. I think she was worried about me.

While I was thinking of phone calls, I gathered up all the landline phones in the house. "Here... Hide these somewhere. Just don't forget where you put them."

Then I surrendered my laptop. "I want nothing to

do with this today. Just hide it somewhere safe."

Handing over my computer pulled my attention to the desktop towers in our house—both mine and the kids'. I was capable of sneaking onto theirs if I had to. I wasn't worried about Nicki's PCs because I wouldn't dare touch her stuff. I didn't need that kind of drama in my life.

But to avoid being tempted by all the accessible towers in the house, I would need to disable them.

But how? ...

Of course! ... They wouldn't work without power. I would just have to steal all the power cords.

I crouched next to my tower, shut it down, and yanked out the cord.

Then, I headed for the living room, where Peter was on his PC. We had moved his desktop out there so we could monitor him and keep him from being on it all day and all night. He was playing on Neopets.com, a gaming website designed mostly for children, though people of all ages frequented the site. Players would care for their Neopets (virtual pets), mostly by playing *Flash* games to earn "Neopoints." This currency could then be used to buy food and supplies for their pets. Peter and I used to play *Neopets* together, and he had never really forgiven me for ruining his virtual toy (magical Fire Lupe plushie) by having my pet play with it. This made the plushie morph so that it was no longer magical. It was also no longer worth 500,000 Neopoints.

But the ire I received for ruining Peter's Fire Lupe plushie was no match for the look he shot me when I told him I was going to have to kick him off his computer and steal his power cord.

"*Mom!* I'm playing *Neopets!*"

"Sorry. This is important. I need a break from computers, and I can't have any around right now."

"But *how long?*" He seemed desperate.

"Maybe a day or two."

At that point, he started to whine. "*What? That's forever!*"

But I persisted. "Nope. You can just play on your DS. Besides, I've been trying to get you to do other things."

"I know but—"

I cut him off. "Don't you have a new Michael Crichton book I just bought you?"

He nodded. "Yeah."

"Well, read it."

"Yeah, I do need to read that. I guess I could wait a day or two." In his way, I think he was being supportive. I felt relieved when he calmed down and agreed to read.

Next: Daun. I knocked on her door lightly and opened it. She was lying in bed playing on her DS.

"Hey, I need your computer cord."

Like Peter, she sounded whiney. "*Why?*"

"I'm taking a break, and I don't want to be tempted to get on your computer."

Daun looked at me, puzzled. "What about *your* computer?"

"Yeah. I've already gathered my power cord and Peter's."

Daun furrowed her brow. She seemed concerned. "Okay, but when do I get it back?"

I repeated what I told her Peter. "Maybe a day or two."

Daun didn't put up much of a fight. She wasn't as attached to her machine as Peter was.

"What're you gonna do with yourself?"

"I'll probably just work on my art." Always the

artist, as long as she had a pencil and paper she was never bored.

"Remember, I also bought you a couple of new books." I was always trying to get her to read. She had dyslexia, and she needed practice. I often took her and Peter to Barnes & Noble and let them pick out a few books. And ever since she'd discovered Mary Pope Osborne's *Magic Tree House* series, I noticed her interest in reading had gone way up.

"Yeah. Thanks. I'm looking forward to reading them. But I'm still going to work on art first. Maybe later..." I knew she'd read later. Every night we had "reading time." The kids had two choices once they were in bed: they could sleep or read. They almost always chose the latter, unless they were particularly exhausted.

Moving on from the kids, I began rummaging around the house and meticulously gathering all the extraneous power cords. I'd acquired quite a few since beginning my computer repair tech job. Finally, with every cord we owned (I hoped) in my arms—except Nicki's—I precariously surrendered the pile to my partner. There were close to a dozen.

Nicki sounded exasperated. "What am I supposed to do with all these?" There were so many cords she could barely hold them in her arms.

"I dunno. Just throw them in a box and hide it somewhere... *Come on...* It's going to be fine. We just have to do this. It will only be for a couple of nights."

I continued making a mental list of anything else that might prove to be a distraction. The process felt exactly like hiding all the knives and pills from a suicidal person. I needed to feel safe—safe from myself, safe from my obsession. I needed to stop everything for a while, no matter how long it took. I was afraid that if I didn't get any rest, I would lose control, lose my mind. I could feel it in my bones. Something great was going to result from my work. But if I collapsed from exhaustion or reached the point where I could no longer focus, all would be lost. I wouldn't complete whatever was supposed to happen. It was that important to me.

So, what else was missing? I thought hard. Landlines: check. Cell phone: check. Laptop: check. Towers: check. I pushed myself further. Think, Barbara, *think*. What's left? That's when it hit me:

Television...

How was I supposed to block television? I began to trouble-shoot the situation. Maybe I could surrender the remote... But then I could just get up and use the buttons on the set. I thought about it. The TV in the bedroom was really small. Maybe I could just have Nicki take it out of the room. Then, I thought of something better. I unscrewed the coax cables from the back of the set. While I was back there, I braved the dust and dug around for the extras that had been collecting for years. Finally satisfied that I'd disabled the TV, I headed into the living room and grabbed all the cables in there, as well. There would be no television for *anyone*. Finally, I handed all the cables to Nicki. But her patience was wearing thin. "Don't you think you're going overboard?" She knew I never did anything halfway, but to her, this must have felt more extreme than usual.

"No... I don't trust myself right now. Can you think of anything else?"

Nicki seemed done with me. "It's enough! You're really annoying... You *always* do this. You always take things too far!"

I knew she was right, but I knew I needed to be thorough. I needed to be sure.

"Okay, I think that's everything anyhow."

Nicki mock-glared at me. It had been quite an ordeal gathering everything—for me and everyone else in my family. "Well, this had better help because you're a real pain in the ass."

"Well, you're a real *bitch!*" I retorted with a crooked smile.

The anti-media sweep finally complete, a sense of relief washed over me. There was nothing left to distract me. I hoped I could sleep, or else I would be *really* bored.

I grabbed a glass of ice water and headed for the couch, first stopping to turn off the living room light and switch on the ceiling fan. I took two sleeping pills, stretched out on my back, curled my pillow under my neck, and pulled a light cover over myself. I lay there for forty-five minutes trying to slow down my brain, but I was unable to let go of my detective work. And when I *did* occasionally pause to think about something else, it was always the same: I kept worrying about whether or not I would sleep.

After an hour passed, my muscles began to relax a bit. I knew the medicine was working. I began to drift... I was exhausted...so exhausted...

I think it's coming...

I think sleep is coming...

Next, the swirling lights arrived again.

And then...

***

The next thing I knew, I was half-awake, vaguely

aware that I was still lying on my back on the couch.

But I couldn't move. I was paralyzed, helpless.

I felt heavy. I pushed myself hard, carefully rolled off the couch, and tried to pull myself up.

Argh! ... In an instant, I was back on the couch. In reality, I hadn't moved an inch; I'd dreamt it.

Like before, I shifted my body weight hard and rolled off the couch. This time, I started dragging myself toward the light switch near the front door.

Bump...

Nope. I was still on the couch—still paralyzed.

This scenario played out maybe a half-dozen more times as I repeatedly tried to get up.

"Nicki!"

Nothing.

"Nicki, I need help!"

Zip.

"Nicki. Nicki! *Nicki! Help. Help! Help!"*

The more I yelled and screamed, the more I didn't get a response, the more my terror grew.

Was it possible I would be stuck that way, paralyzed indefinitely? I needed to get up!

I was unaware that my screams were actually whispers.

After what seemed like an eternity of unrelenting terror, I heard a loud crash—like someone had dropped something fragile. My eyes popped open, and I hollered out loud for the first time—hollered toward the crashing sound. *"What was that?!"*

I heard Nicki wailing loudly in the next room—the kitchen. Concerned, I was compelled to drag myself off the couch.

I felt heavy...dizzy...awful...*traumatized.*

But I had to help Nicki. Nothing else mattered in that moment.

By the time I made it to the kitchen, Nicki's wails had settled to sobs. She was meticulously picking something up off the floor, tears flowing from her eyes. I circled around the pile of shards and headed toward her.

"What... What happened?"

"I dropped the Route 66 mug—the one Sammy gave me."

Sammy was her favorite childhood friend and her first contact with a gay person. From a young age, he and Nicki had been inseparable. Sometimes they would play with Barbies, often pairing two Kens together. Despite not having seen him in years, she still talked about him all the time.

The mug was special because Sammy gave it to her. Losing or breaking anything made her sad, especially if it was a gift.

I was sympathetic. I knew what the mug meant to Nicki. "I'm sorry. I wish it'd been one of *my* mugs. It'd be easier." I wasn't as attached to my things. She, on the other hand, was inconsolable and needed a few minutes to compose herself.

I sat at the kitchen table and started sipping at a room-temperature glass of well water, waiting patiently for her to calm down. I hardly noticed the acrid taste of minerals in the hard water. I was still in a fog, and my head was throbbing with a dull ache. My body felt heavy, numb, and tingly. The worst part was that I was still incredibly sleepy. While sitting at the kitchen table, I had to fight a strong urge to go back to the couch.

I had to wake up. I was terrified of falling back asleep and not being able to get back up.

I waited until Nicki finished sweeping up the bits of mug on the floor. Fortunately, it had broken in large chunks. Maybe she could glue it back together. But I knew from experience that rarely worked out. I waited for Nicki to calm down before I told her what happened during my nap.

"Didn't you hear me calling you?"

Nicki was perplexed. "I heard you mumbling something in your sleep."

Apparently, my attempts to scream had been futile.

I gave Nicki a long, sad look and began sobbing loudly. "It happened again..." I could barely get the words out: "*Sleep paralysis...*"

Sleep paralysis is a phenomenon that affects people with sleep disorders. For me, it would only happen occasionally, at times when I slept too much. I had experienced this sensation dozens of times over the past several years.

I explained to her what it was like this time and how horrible I was feeling. My head was still throbbing, and it was taking all my power not to get back on the couch. Just as I was sympathetic about her mug, Nicki was sympathetic about my sleep paralysis.

"Oh man. I'm so sorry. That sounds awful."

"Yeah... I hate it. I just hope I don't fall back asleep." I still felt heavy and groggy as I spoke to her. I was still terrified of falling back asleep—terrified of it happening again.

My tears slowed a little, but my sadness was palpable. I grabbed a napkin off the table, wadded it up, and blew my nose. I got up and walked to the sink and repeatedly splashed water on my face. The shock of the water on my numb cheeks helped me wake up slightly for a moment, but it wasn't enough. I grabbed a rag from a nearby drawer, wet it, and draped it behind my neck.

Sitting back down, I pleaded with Nicki. "Any chance you could make me some coffee?" I always wanted coffee after waking up from sleep paralysis. I needed to stay awake. I was desperate.

Nicki gazed across the table at me. "Actually, I just made some. That's why I was getting the mug—that's when I broke it."

I fumbled for words. "Oh, yeah. Sorry..." I felt sad for her, but it did little to draw me away from my own problems. "I guess since you already made it, do you mind getting me some?"

Nicki got up and went to the cabinet. She picked the solid-black mug—the least sentimental choice. Then she scooped some Great Value non-dairy creamer and plopped it into the bottom of the empty cup. I couldn't understand why she did it that way. It wasn't normal. It was backwards. Most people put the coffee in first and then added the creamer. But she insisted on putting the creamer in first. She always claimed that pouring the coffee in would mix it up, and she could save a spoon. We were always taking shortcuts to create fewer dirty dishes. Finally, she poured the coffee, which turned a lighter color as the dark fluid swirled into the cup. The creamer was mixing in *somewhat*. Then, she set the mug down in front of me. I sniffed the coffee and picked up a dirty spoon that was sitting on the table and quickly stirred my drink with the handle—the clean side. *Better...*

Nicki smirked at me. "Why do you always do that? It's gross! And you *know* it was already mixed."

I protested. "It doesn't matter. I used the clean end. Besides, when you do it that way—put the cream in first—it never mixes good enough."

But after that brief moment of distraction, my physical sluggishness began to drag me back down. I leaned forward and buried my head in my hands. Sleep was pulling at me, trying to drag me down... But I couldn't give in. I shook my head, trying once again to wake myself. I couldn't risk it. I couldn't risk going back to sleep. I was still terrified the paralysis would come back. I couldn't shake it.

I was miserable...

Then I glanced up at Nicki, bitter. "You see what happens? If I don't get enough sleep, I'm miserable. If I get too much, I'm miserable. Either way, I'm miserable. I can't win!"

Finally, after a brief pause, Nicki shifted the topic a bit. "Well, do you think the sleep helped *at all?*"

I was grumpy, and I felt myself begin to cry again, but I sucked it up. I needed to stop this. It wasn't helping. "I dunno if the sleep helped. I just feel so wrecked. I can hardly keep my eyes open, and I have a bit of a headache. I hate sleep paralysis. I hate when this happens."

"Okay," she replied blankly.

In "Nicki-speak," this meant that she was done with the conversation.

***

It took nearly two hours, but after forcing myself to stay awake and consuming copious amounts of coffee and Diet Mountain Dew, my mind slowly began to pull out of its fog. And that's when the boredom set in. I was antsy and didn't know what to do with myself. The cases were calling, but I was still supposed to be resting.

I approached Nicki, who was in the living room watching TV. "Anything in the news? Have you been watching?"

"Yes, I've been watching all day. I only stopped to wash the dishes. I'm getting tired of the news, but it's still going in the background. I don't think I missed anything important."

I was annoyed. "You were supposed to watch the whole time! Why did you stop to do the dishes?"

Nicki was annoyed back. "Oh my God. I did my best. I'm not like you. I can't just watch it constantly."

I was frustrated. "Well, if it ever comes up again, try harder."

Nicki was exasperated. "Look. I did my best. What do you want from me?"

I decided to back off. "I don't know. I'm sorry. Thanks for watching. At least I got some rest."

"Well... Are you feeling any better?"

I wasn't really sure how much the extra rest was helping. I mostly just felt anxious—anxious to get back to work. "I dunno. I still can't stop thinking about all this stuff."

"So, what're you going to do?"

"I don't know. I gave up all my distractions. Now I don't know what to do with myself."

Nicki tried to help. "Can I make a suggestion?"

"Sure."

"Do you wanna watch a movie? I got some new DVDs from Netflix." Nicki had been receiving Netflix movies—three at a time—for months. Most of the time we never got around to watching them, so joining was kind of a waste of money. The streaming service didn't exist yet.

Without hesitating, I shot her idea down. "I don't think I can concentrate on a movie right now." I recalled the *Pirates of the Caribbean* fiasco that happened weeks ago, when I couldn't stop obsessing long enough to watch the movie. I had beelined out of the theater in tears, scared of my own brain.

Nicki seemed a little frustrated. "I'm running out of ideas. What're you going to do?"

My options were limited as I faced a dilemma that had become commonplace. "All I can handle right now is conversation."

"Okay."

However, even words had their drawbacks. "But I'm afraid if I do, I'll just start talking about my work again. I can't stop."

Nicki was puzzled. "But maybe you can at least try it. You can talk to me if you want."

But that's not what I wanted. "Honestly, I just think I need some outside support."

"What do you mean?"

Often, when I was really bored or distraught, I would call everyone in the family until I got a response. Although, under my current circumstances, I didn't think I could tell them what was going on with me, I felt like hearing their voices would make me feel better. Besides, sometimes their problems and experiences could be a good distraction. *Yes...* I needed to call them.

Then, I gave Nicki my real agenda. "I want to call my family, but I don't have my phone."

She wasn't sure what to do. "But you *told* me to keep your phone."

I thought briefly about the scene in *Young Frankenstein* when Dr. Frankenstein locked himself in a cell with his monster. He was going to try to soothe the beast by showing him he was loved. Before going in, Frankenstein ordered Inga and Igor not to let him out:

> *No matter what you hear in there, no matter how cruelly I beg you, no matter how terribly I may scream, do not open this door, or you will undo everything I have worked for.*

Moments later, after the monster started growling menacingly, Dr. Frankenstein began screaming, begging for his life:

> *Let me out. Let me out of here. Get me the hell out of here. What's the matter with you people? I was joking! Don't you know a joke when you hear one? HA-HA-HA-HA. Jesus Christ, get me out of here! Open this goddamn door or I'll kick your rotten heads in! Mommy!*

Asking Nicki for my cell phone felt a lot like that moment. What would she do? Would she leave the cage door securely locked and hope I could work things out with the monster? I mean, would she keep my cell phone? Or would she give in and hand it back to me? In Dr. Frankenstein's case, his colleagues refused to let him out.

Trying to keep calm, I started begging Nicki to give me my phone. "I know I told you not to give it back to me, but I'm desperate." Like Dr. Frankenstein, I was panicked and needed a way out. I was so incredibly stuck and so incredibly antsy. I had all this balled up energy and nothing to do with it. I *needed* to call my family. I needed a distraction.

Nicki came across a bit frustrated. Shrugging her shoulders, she held her ground. "Well then, I don't know what to tell you."

But I wasn't giving up without a fight. "What if I pinky promise you that I'll only call family?" As childish as making this kind of bargain with my partner might have felt, it was worth a try. Like Daun, Nicki knew I'd never break a pinky promise. I was too stubborn and superstitious to do so.

"*Fine!*" I could tell she was tired of the conversation. She reached into her pocket and pulled out my Nokia. Then we briefly linked pinkies before she reluctantly handed it to me.

"Did I get any calls or messages?"

"Nope."

"Well, I'm gonna head back to the bedroom and make some calls... *Thank you.*"

I was relieved to have my cell phone back, even if I could only call family. I headed for the bedroom and lay down on my back again, this time with the light on.

I flipped open my phone and called Brandy. She was always the first one I called, and I had her number memorized. Honestly, the main reason I always called her first was that she was the most likely one in the family to answer the phone—and the most likely to give me significant air time.

After about seven rings, her voicemail picked up. I left a message: "*Hey. Just calling to see what you're up to. Call back if you get a chance. Love you.*"

Next was always Mom. I had her phone number memorized, too. Actually, I had all of theirs safely locked in my mind. That's how often I called them.

Mom answered the phone. "Hi, Barbie!"

I cringed. I had fought hard for my name to be changed to Barbara when I was six. I had only recently started tolerating family occasionally calling me by my old nickname. It was annoying, but I understood why they did it. They were being sentimental.

"Hi, Mom, how's it going?"

"I'm doing *great!*" I knew it was true. She and her husband, Tim, were building a new RV park together in Beaumont. They were living there in their motorhome while undergoing the arduous process of building a new park from scratch. This was a massive undertaking, and the only thing she ever talked about. Sometimes, Nicki and I would take the kids there and spend a few nights. Because the park was unfinished, we had the whole place to ourselves. During the day, we would swim and fish in its small lake and ride Mom and Tim's ATV. In the evenings, we would barbecue. Then, we would play *Mexican Train* with the folks until bedtime.

But I didn't care about any of that at the moment. I had bigger problems... But I didn't dare to talk about any of my *real* issues with Mom because she preferred to keep things positive. Plus, she would minimize everything—try to normalize it. No matter what it was, she'd wave her hand dismissively and say "*Oh... I do that all the time.*" If I said, "*Mom, the sky is falling,*" she'd probably say, "*My sky fell yesterday and everything was fine.*"

I especially didn't dare talk about my overwhelming, stressful search for Boussora. Instead, despite my trepidation, I began whining about my finances. But this time, instead of minimizing my problems, Mom changed the subject and shifted the topic to her and Tim's RV park. But I didn't mind the shift, because I didn't really want to talk about my problems, anyhow. After all, I was looking for a distraction. But the relief from my own thoughts didn't last long. Mom only kept up her banter for seven minutes before running out of things to talk about. After exchanging I-love-yous, we hung up.

In that moment, I could hear Dana Carvey's high-pitched Church Lady voice from *SNL* playing in my head: *Wasn't that conversation special?* I mean, *wow...* I had gotten more than the usual five minutes. I had gotten a full *seven* minutes. As my thoughts turned even more sarcastic, there was the Church Lady's voice again: *Who could have inspired that? ... SATAN?!*

I continued to call family members in rapid succession. I was bored, obsessed, and still in need of distraction. Anne was next. She always came after Brandy and Mom, but Anne didn't ordinarily answer the phone, and when she did answer, she was annoying—going on about mad cow disease or whatever her latest obsessions and compulsions happened to be. I'm not sure why I even tried dialing her, except that calling her was part of my ritual. She *had* to be next. She was *always* next.

As usual, Anne didn't answer. I was pretty sure she'd gotten tired of me calling all the time and would ignore the phone if she saw me come up on her caller ID. I guess the feelings of annoyance were mutual.

Next was Lee, who was always after Anne. I liked talking to him because he had a calming effect on me. He was unshakable. He had been drum major in junior high, but never seemed flustered by his position. He would calmly stand on the podium in his cute green, white, and gold uniform and do his salute, which involved some early '80s popping moves. (Back then, he was a really good break dancer.) Then, in high school, he was so good at baritone that he was often given solos during field performances. He once told me that he never got nervous...about anything, *ever*. And it showed in his perfect executions. He went on to get a full music scholarship from Blinn College in Brenham. *No...* I never understood Lee's calm demeanor. Compared to him, I was wreck. I would say, all in all, he was the most normal, easy-going one in the family. And unlike some of the others, he didn't annoy me or make me anxious. Looking back, I'm not really sure why he wasn't the first person I'd call in a crisis. For some reason, I always turned to Brandy. I guess I was just a glutton for punishment.

Like Anne, Lee rarely answered the phone. This time was no exception. I couldn't believe it. Here I was with this large, so-called loving, supportive family, and I couldn't get a hold of anyone when I needed them. I was quickly running out of people to call.

I had one more chance: Jerry. He was easy to reach because he was always at work. He was a grocery store manager with his own store, and I had the direct line to his office. Even if he wasn't at his desk, I could ask someone to go get him. He was always good for a few minutes.

Jerry also was relatively calm and normal, even though, as I alluded to earlier, he often teased people to get a rise out of them. He'd say mean things to us siblings, and when we got mad, he'd laugh hysterically. Jerry was also fiercely competitive, a sore winner. When we were growing up, when he won at *Monopoly*, he gloated, laughed, and did the "Jerry Dance"—a move that involved jumping around and sticking his butt out at us. Of course, he would always cheat by hiding an orange $500 bill under the board and sneaking it out at a crucial point in the game. We had a family tradition: The winner got to sign the board. He held the record for signing it the most often.

Despite being obnoxious, over the years, Jerry stopped teasing me. Or, I should say, he teased me less often than everyone else. He knew I was sensitive.

After years of trying to get a rise out of me, he had given up and said something unexpected: "You're no fun to tease. You never react. You always just look sad." Then, he mostly stopped trying. The fact that I was no longer his victim made him more approachable, which is why I was willing to call him in 2006.

Jerry picked up his office phone after a couple of rings. "Welcome to your friendly neighborhood store. This is Jerome Yah-nik."

He always pronounced "Janik" the Czech way, with the "J" sounding like a "Y." I don't do that. I was raised pronouncing it wrong because it was easier for people who were unfamiliar with Czech culture. But Jerry had switched to the Czech pronunciation a while back. And why Jerome? Jerome was *Dad's* name. Calling him "Jerome Yah-nik" sounded weird, foreign.

Unfortunately, Jerry couldn't stay on the phone this time. *Oh well...* It had been worth a try. Sometimes he had time to talk while at work. Besides, calling him at his store was usually the only way I could reach him. His cell phone always went straight to voicemail, and he was almost never home to answer his landline.

My brother ended the conversation abruptly. "I'm sorry, Barbara, I just can't talk right now. We've got the district manager coming in tomorrow, and we're in the middle of a massive cleanup."

Then, I gave him the customary "I love you" and he did the same.

My final sibling was my youngest brother, Allen. But I never called him. He was living in Austin and was always busy with his programming job. I was extremely proud of him, but he was hard to talk to. As a function of his young age and his distance from home, he seemed a little more emotionally detached from the family lately. Although he still showed up for Thanksgiving and Christmas, it felt like he wanted to be left alone to live his life. Remembering how I felt when I was his age, I had decided a while back to respect that.

Then there was Dad: I couldn't call him because it was after 6 p.m. By then, he had usually had a few too many beers and could be kind of unpleasant.

Finally out of family members to call, I snapped my phone shut. I had promised Nicki I'd only call family, and I had called everyone I could. The distraction had lasted a mere thirteen minutes. *Not good enough...*

A bit disgusted, I clutched my phone tightly, got up, and walked back into the kitchen. Nicki was preparing dinner.

I watched her as she stirred a noodle concoction, no doubt to keep it from sticking to the pan. I noted the open boxes next to the stove. "Tetrazzini?" We made a lot of "Helpers" in our family.

She replied without looking up, "Yeah... I wanted something easy."

"Anything to go with it?"

"Nah. I'm feeling lazy. This should be enough. I'm making two boxes."

Then, I mentioned my true mission. "Hey, can you take this?" I shoved my phone in her direction.

"Okay. Just gimme a sec. I'm trying to cook."

Finally, after what felt like an eternity, Nicki stopped what she was doing, grabbed the phone, and shoved it in her pocket. "How'd it go?"

I gave her a recap of the last thirteen minutes of my life, ending with, "Yes, once again, the 'Five-Minute Mom' didn't disappoint."

Nicki seemed amused. "Really? She only gave you five minutes?"

My eyes rolled into the back of my head. "Yeah... Big surprise." (Okay, it was actually seven minutes, so I guess five was a slight exaggeration.)

At least there was one good thing going for me at that moment: We were about to eat dinner. Nicki set the timer for twenty minutes, the recommended time to simmer the mixture. I started clearing the table. This was a ritual. Every time we shared a meal, someone would have to remove the trash, plates, and food left on the table throughout the day. Most of us were really bad about not cleaning up after ourselves. I was the worst.

After the table was clear, I headed toward the cabinet. "Paper or regular?"

Nicki clenched her teeth. "Paper... I *don't* want any more dishes. I just did them." I didn't blame her. Sometimes the dishes would pile up for two or three days at a time, until they were overflowing out of the sinks and onto the countertops. We could never keep on top of them. It was even worse when Nicki wasn't around to help. During school semesters, she was away in Austin five days a week.

After the meal, I only had a few more hours to kill before bedtime. We pulled out a Netflix DVD: *Chronicles of Narnia*. Now that I was more relaxed, and well-fed, I felt like I could handle a movie. I loved a good fantasy.

Around 2 a.m., I took two more sleeping pills and headed back to bed. *Tomorrow...* I would get my life back tomorrow. My work...my technology. I was ready. I couldn't wait. I was blissfully unaware that while I had been resting, a big story was breaking in the world of terrorism.

21

THE TRANSATLANTIC AIRCRAFT PLOT

Imagine a United Airlines jetliner filled with 300 travelers cramming the aisles, mostly Americans. They're leaving Heathrow Airport on a typically cool, drizzly August morning in London, heading to San Francisco.

A young businessman wearing a gray suit is rushing home to his wife, who had unexpectedly given birth a few days early. He was a new dad. It was a girl!

A balding history professor in jeans and a T-shirt is returning home from sabbatical with months of research on the British Empire stored on his laptop.

An elderly English couple sits near the back, looking at pictures of the twins on their camera phone—a set of rambunctious, blond seven-year-old boys. The proud grandparents are visiting the US for the first time in two years and can't wait to see their grandbabies.

A nun sits quietly reading her Bible while absent-mindedly twirling her fingers on the special medallion that represents her order. She misses her family—the other sisters she hasn't seen in the decade since her transfer.

All these people are minutes from their destination, ready to land in San Francisco.

The nun looks up for a moment as a Middle Eastern gentleman sitting in the front of the plane calmly gets up and pulls down his carry-on suitcase. He gets soda and Vaseline out of his bag and sits back down, setting the items on the tray in front of him. These seem like odd things to pull out of a suitcase, but she guesses he's thirsty and has chapped lips. Then she looks a few seats ahead of her. Another Middle Easterner is pulling down his bag and getting something out—the same items. This was really strange. What were they up to? A wave of anxiety floats over her, but she soon forgets the situation and returns to her reading. The oddness of it slips out of her mind.

A few minutes later, the nun glances up from her Bible again and finds herself staring in disbelief. The same men have stood back up. The first Middle-Eastern man has opened the soda and Vaseline and is shoving some wiring in them.[56] This time, the businessman and the history professor, who were sitting across the aisle from the man, notice him, too. From several seats back, the grandfather points and whispers to his wife, "Look at that man. I think he's making *a bomb!*" But before she can respond, two other men stand up and are doing the same thing. They suddenly start shouting something in Arabic. Most of the people are unfamiliar with the language and can only make out the word *"Allah!!!"*

There's a loud, collective gasp in the cabin as chills run over the spines of shocked travelers. No one knows what to do, what to think. *Is this another 9/11? Are we all going to die?* There is utter chaos as everyone begins screaming and crying. The world flips upside down and everything seems surreal.

A couple of average-looking men get up and try to rush the nearest bomb-maker, but there's no time. It's too late. In the same moment, the nun screams, *"God, help us!"* as the businessman frantically texts his wife, *"Let Jenny know I love her."* The professor locks his hands behind his head and bends forward toward his lap, bracing for impact. The elderly couple holds each other tightly, shaking. They're going to die, but at least they're together. Then, the plane explodes and plummets into the crowded heart of the city, killing all 300 passengers along with the crew and thousands more people on the ground.

Now, imagine similar scenarios occurring as many as ten or eleven times on flights from London headed not only to San Francisco, but Washington, DC; New York City; Chicago; Montreal; and Toronto.[57] [58] The planes explode into their respective cities within minutes of each other. The devastation takes 10,000 lives,[59] both in the aircrafts and on the ground, considerably more than the 2,977 lives lost on September 11th.[60]

Imagine the devastation to their families, their friends, the world. Jenny, the newborn, will never meet her daddy and will grow up with a grieving mother. The twins will never play *Chutes and Ladders* with Grandma and Grandpa again. The history professor's book will never be finished, and his students will have to deal with the shock of losing their favorite professor. The nun will be in heaven too soon. She'll have to wait to see her family—the other sisters—until they join her there.

But something happened. Something changed all that and altered fate.

On the morning of August 10, when I tuned into CNN after a day of completely avoiding the media, I was thrilled to wake up to good news. While I was resting, British police had arrested twenty-one suspected terrorists in London (later updated to twenty-four),[61] [62] the men who had been planning the bombings. *Yes!* ... I was sure the plot had been brought down by my tip about Boussora. If I was right, I'd helped save thousands of lives: fathers, mothers, children—people of all races, ages, and walks of life.

According to authorities, Al Qaeda was behind the plot.[63] And that meant that ultimately, bin Laden was behind it. This made sense, because it had been such a large-scale attack with uncanny similarities to 9/11, but even more lethal. *Yes...* It definitely stank of bin Laden. He was a visionary, always thinking big. This plot was exactly his *modus operandi*. Like previous attacks, he would slowly, meticulously prepare his plan and his forces, waiting for the right moment. And on August 9, 2006, the strike was imminent. According to CNN, intelligence had intercepted an encrypted message that simply said, *"Attack now."*[64] But somehow, in some way, the plot was stopped. Al Qaeda, and Osama bin Laden himself, had been stopped.

For me, the Earth stood still... It had happened... In my mind, I finally had concrete evidence that my tip had led to Boussora.

Then I felt a sudden head rush as my thoughts turned to the money—the $5 million reward. I knew it, I just knew it... *I knew* I was going to get the money! I ran out of the bedroom to join Nicki, who was in the kitchen making grilled cheese and tomato soup for lunch.

"Nicki!" I was ecstatic.

Nicki was in a trance as she carefully pulled up a corner of the sandwich with a spatula. She wanted to see if it was toasted enough on the bottom, ready to flip over. Nope, not even close. Sometimes, she could be impatient when cooking, especially if she was really hungry.

"Hang on." She replied absently, not even bothering to glance up from the stove.

I stood next to her, breathing heavily. "I have great news!"

She still didn't look up. She kept frowning at the sandwich. "Just wait 'til I flip it."

Once she flipped it, she turned and faced me. "Do you want one?"

I replied quickly, "Sure, but there's something I need to tell you."

"This better be quick." I doubt she was prepared for what I was about to say.

"I think they found him!"

"Who?" Nicki seemed perplexed.

"The terrorist!" I still couldn't remember his name.

"What do you mean? What happened?" She sounded more enthusiastic.

My voice sped up. "I just saw it on CNN! They just stopped a major terrorist attack!"

"*Wow!*" She had caught up with my excitement. She sounded thrilled.

I continued, propelled by pure adrenaline. "Well, they must have found out about it because of the terrorist I turned in. That's gotta be it! They must've gotten him!"

Nicki's face had lit up. "Yeah. The timing... It just *can't* be a coincidence." The plot had been brought down just two days after I called in my tip. We were convinced that the two events were connected.

My gaze stayed on Nicki. "I'll bet they tapped his phone before they arrested him. Maybe that's how they found out about the plot."

We kept talking like this for a while before starting to fantasize about the money again.

Then I caught a whiff of something. Was something burning? I looked toward the stove. "Oh my God, Nicki. The grilled cheese!"

The conversation stopped as Nicki lurched toward the stove to hastily remove the sandwich before it set off the smoke alarm. *Trouble averted...*

I volunteered to eat the burnt sandwich rather than the perfect one. I didn't mind because it reminded me of Mom's cooking. She used to burn food a lot because she was so busy chasing around six kids.

After Nicki handed me the plate with the charred grilled cheese, I decided I would scrape off some of the black coating with a butter knife—a technique I'd seen my mom use. I liked to joke that if food is burnt, it was made with extra love. So, despite the blackened bread, I was happy. *We* were happy. Besides, pretty soon we might have a personal chef cooking our meals!

When Nicki was done cooking our sandwiches and microwaving our tomato soup, I recounted the news I'd heard about the transatlantic aircraft plot. I didn't know very many details yet. So, I simply told her that a major terrorist plot involving passenger planes coming out of Britain had been thwarted.

But I wasn't willing to wait until the full story emerged. I had a very important call to make. I picked up the phone and asked for Agent Miles. She wasn't available, so I called back a few minutes later. This time she was free to talk. *Thank God...*

I heard her familiar mild Texas accent as she greeted me.

I told her who I was, and she immediately remembered me. Unable to contain myself, I blurted out my reason for calling: "I heard about the plot that was brought down."

"Yes."

"Well?" I asked.

"Well, what?" She sounded puzzled.

"I think y'all owe me $5 million."

She seemed even more perplexed. "*What?*"

"I think the plot was stopped because y'all got the terrorist I turned in."

Her tone turned slightly irritable. "*What?* ... Barbara, if you think you had anything to do with this—"

"I know I did. The arrests happened just two days after I called in my tip."

But my argument appeared to further aggravate her. "No, this plot was brought down by a huge investigation over several months across multiple intelligence agencies and countries."

This idea echoed the rhetoric in the news at the time.

I bickered with her for a little while before giving up nine minutes later.

Despite her clear annoyance with me, Agent Miles had never told me to stop calling the FBI. However, in that moment, she nudged me toward a slight change in my approach.

"You know, when you call, you don't have to ask for me by name. You can talk to whichever duty agent is on staff."

My stomach sank. Maybe Agent Miles was getting tired of dealing with me.

But then I thought about it for a moment. Talking to whomever happened to be on duty would be more logical than waiting to speak to a specific agent. This way, I would be free to call any time, day or night, rather than waiting for Agent Miles' shift. So maybe she wasn't merely trying to pass me off on her colleagues. Maybe she wanted me to get my tips to their office faster. In that moment, I decided to stop asking for agent Miles when I called the FBI. I would give my tips to whomever happened to be on duty.

Regardless, at this point, it seemed evident that I wasn't going to get any money. But despite Agent Miles' skepticism, I was convinced that Boussora had been arrested based on my tip, and my intel had influenced the takedown of the transatlantic aircraft plot. So I began to plan my next move.

Even with no hope of receiving a reward, there was no question in my mind what I should do. Money or not, I felt it was my duty as a human being to use my newfound MySpace system to track down more terrorists. I went back to RewardsForJustice.net, once again skimming the faces of some of the most wanted men in the world. Then my eyes locked on my next target, the most notorious face on the page.

I stared into the cold, steely eyes of Osama bin Laden.

22

THE AMERICAN DREAM
Making the Impossible Possible

I paused and took a deep breath. Was there even a minute possibility that I could do the very thing that had eluded the federal government for the past five years? Could I *really* find Osama bin Laden?

What made me think I could do this? What made me so special? After all, I was just some thirty-seven-year-old woman living in rural Texas. I was just a normal person (sort of), living a normal life.

Or was I? ...

I thought back on my life for a moment. If I did this— if I actually managed to locate bin Laden, this wouldn't be the first time I'd accomplished the impossible.

***

It was 1999, and I was going through a divorce. I had become a single mother during a time when Daun and Peter were only two and four, barely out of diapers. Most people in my position would resign themselves to living in misery and poverty for a while. But I wanted a change, a new life.

One of the first things I did when Jimmy and I broke up was to try dreaming up a way to get a house. I got on my slow, beat-up old computer and dialed into America Online (AOL) and started looking into Habitat for Humanity.

I also went to a great effort to clean up my credit. I found out it had some blemishes when my bank denied my Christmas loan application. Apparently, I had some bogus late marks from old student loans as well as a small medical collection account. At the time, I was always responsible with money, so I decided to fix these problems so I wouldn't get turned down by future lenders. I filed disputes with the three major credit bureaus to remove all blemishes and asked my mom to pay off the $300 in medical collections.

Next, to solidify child support and custody arrangements with Jimmy, I began searching for a cheap way to establish them. After calling around, I discovered the Gulf Coast Legal Foundation, a local charity that offered free legal services. I made an appointment and went in for an assessment.

On the day of my meeting with the lawyer, I decided to dress myself and my kids up nicely. To me, this was appropriate for meeting with legal counsel.

A half-hour later, I pulled up to the Gulf Coast Legal Foundation in my burgundy 1989 Pontiac Parisienne. The thing was huge, a boat. This made it a real gas guzzler. And to make matters worse, there were huge dents on the side (the result of my terrible driving,) and most of the windows wouldn't roll down. This was particularly disastrous when I drove it during the heat of summer, because the a/c didn't work. And the harshest feature was the cracked radiator. I had to fill it up completely every time I drove it so the engine wouldn't overheat. *Yes...* the Parisienne was a disaster, but it was *my* disaster, and despite everything, it ran. I guess, ultimately, that's all that mattered. And despite my car's obvious flaws, it got us there—to the lawyer's office. Fortunately, it was wintertime, so we didn't arrive sweaty.

The organization was located in a repurposed two-story wooden house. Dragging my two tiny children into the building, I sat down, filled out some paperwork, and waited to speak to the attorney. A few minutes later, I was called upstairs. The receptionist volunteered to entertain Peter and Daun while I met with the lawyer.

When I got to the lawyer's office, the door was slightly ajar. I knocked lightly, and a confident female voice told me to come in.

After I stepped in and closed the door, a middle-aged woman with straight, shoulder-length brown hair stood up to greet me. I stepped forward, introduced myself, and shook her hand firmly. As I sat down, I noticed her jaw visibly drop.

She looked perplexed. "You've *got* to be kidding me!"

This wasn't the reaction I was expecting. "Why? What's wrong?"

Still seeming shocked, she answered my question with her own question. "What are you *doing* here?"

The lawyer's confusion took me off guard. "What do you mean?"

"You aren't like most people who come into my office!"

Stunned by her answer, I repeated the question. "What do you mean?"

"You don't look like them. You don't act like them."

Oh, yeah. I considered the lawyer's words for a moment. *Poor people* come in here. I guess I didn't look like a poor person. I thought about the kind of people I often saw in the food stamp office or waiting in line at the local food pantry. A stereotypical poor person would be disheveled, wearing jeans and a stained T-shirt they'd gotten free at a blood drive. Sometimes they had missing teeth and were heavyset. Some of them smelled bad and looked as if they hadn't showered or done laundry in months. Many of the women would be there with several children. It wasn't uncommon to see a young mother chasing around a toddler who was only wearing a drooping diaper. Diapers were expensive, so the child might only be changed two or three times a day—or maybe only when they pooped.

As I was still processing her comments, she asked me, "What's your story?"

How could I express to her the misery I felt as a human being? I had a college degree and so many hopes and dreams. This wasn't how I had pictured my life turning out. I was extremely depressed. I was so devastated by the loss of my job as a high school theology teacher (long story) that I didn't think I was even capable of working. I felt utterly incompetent. The best I could do was help my children live a comfortable life. We had plenty of food, plenty of diapers, a working car, and good health.

After talking with me for a while, the lawyer started asking me about my aspirations. "What are you planning on doing with your life?"

I didn't hesitate; I already knew the answer. "I'm going to try to get a house."

I had always wanted to own my own home—the hallmark of the American Dream.

I gave her a determined gaze. "I'm actually looking into Habitat for Humanity." But even as I said it, I was worried about this option. I had to put "sweat equity" into our new home by helping others build theirs. Once I earned enough construction time, others would help me with mine. That sounded reasonable in theory, but I was overweight and out of shape. Plus, I was tired all the time and would get out of breath just from walking from our apartment to my car.

The lawyer's tone was matter-of-fact, but kind. "Actually, there's another option that might work better for you."

Then she described a program through the US Department of Agriculture-Rural Development (USDA-RD). They offered low-interest loans to people with low incomes who wanted to live in a rural area. She pointed toward the window. "It's only two streets over in the bank building. You should stop by there."

This woman may not have known it, but in that moment, she changed my life forever. After leaving the office, I drove the short two blocks to the Rural Development office. When I got there, I asked a bunch of questions and left with an information packet and loan application.

Rural Development loans offered several advantages over conventional ones. The most important one was that it was possible for someone who was really poor, like me, to receive a home loan because the interest was subsidized by the federal government. In fact, people considered to have very-low income would only pay 1 percent interest. Plus, closing costs were extremely low.

However, as with traditional loans, the borrower had to have good credit. Fortunately, this wasn't an obstacle because of the effort I'd made to clean up my credit after Jimmy and I broke up.

Excited at the prospect of owning a home, I filled out the paperwork, gathered my proof of income—at that time, less than $1,000 per month—and with great hope, submitted it to the office a few days later. After waiting for about a week, I received a call and was told to come into the office. They had made their decision.

My heart pounding, I put water in my radiator, grabbed my kids, and made the forty-five-minute drive to the office. When I got there, they said I was approved. Then, they handed me a piece of paper. I stared at the page for a moment as its contents slowly sunk in: "*$48,000.*" I looked up, panicked, my eyes tearing.

"I can't buy a home for that amount!"

The crinkly, gray-haired woman was quick to agree. "No, you can't. I'm sorry. You'll just have to try again when you have more income."

But I wasn't ready to give up without a fight. My brain started working overtime as I scrambled for ideas.

"I get help from my family. Can I count the help from family?"

She shook her head slowly. "No. It has to be dependable income. We can't accept that."

I began to argue. "But they *are* dependable. They've never missed a payment."

But she persisted, giving another quick shake of her head, "No. I'm sorry..." Then after a brief pause, "Can you think of anything else?"

Another desperate thought popped into my head. "I get food stamps. Can I count food stamps?"

Unlike my other idea, the answer wasn't an immediate "No."

"Let me go check with my supervisor."

With that, she walked away.

I stood in nervous anticipation. This would add $330 to my income and could *actually* make a difference. I felt my heart leaping in my chest. There was still hope.

A few minutes later, she came back.

"Yes, we can accept food stamps as income. Just bring by your benefits letter sometime."

I thanked her and bounded out.

I dropped off the appropriate documents the next day, and a week later I was back in her office to get the results. The same older woman greeted me. "Hi, Ms. Janik. You're getting to be a familiar face around here. I'll bet you want the results."

I was eager. "Yes. What were you able to find out?"

She reached behind her to get my file. A minute later, she pulled out a single page print-out and handed it to me. The dollar amount will forever be engrained in my head: *$80,650*. Wow! ... I felt a rush of energy. This was enough for a house. *I was going to get a house!*

But little did I know that doing so would require a tireless, vigilant, three-month campaign. As it turned out, finding a home that met Rural Development's strict standards, for that amount of money, would be practically impossible. To make matters worse, I was only given ninety days to find my home before the loan offer expired. It sounded like a long time, but I would find out soon that this, by far, was the most difficult hurdle. And if I didn't make it, I wouldn't' be allowed to try again for another year. I was in a race—a race to get my new home.

Not yet aware of this complication, I was doggedly determined to make my dream of owning a house come true, no matter how much energy I had to expend. I wouldn't rest until it happened, I wouldn't be discouraged, and I never once had any doubt that I would get a new home.

When I arrived at my apartment, I sat on my tattered, blue sofa and scoured the printout that described Rural Development's requirements for our new place: I could buy a used house and pay to have it repaired to meet their specifications. I could also buy a manufactured home that met specs and put it on a permanent slab on my own plot of land with well and septic. Or, I could have a brand-new house built from the ground up by a Rural Development-approved builder. I looked into all my options, with zero doubt in my mind that $80,650 could get me something.

The first thing I did was contact a realtor and explain my situation. The next day, an amicable, middle-aged woman with blonde, bouffant hair took me to a couple of homes in Triple Bar Estates, the complex that I'd lived in with Mom, Lee, and Allen when I was a teenager in the '80s. The development carried fond memories. The homes also featured city water and sewage. This would allow me to avoid the cost of installing well and septic. However, both properties I viewed were electric-only and seemed pretty rundown. And living in Triple Bar would also mean paying for city utilities, an expense I wanted to avoid. Plus, I doubted that with repairs, I could keep the total cost under my approved loan amount. I couldn't go above my spending limit because I only had about three thousand saved up, which I needed for closing costs. I had scraped it together from insurance settlements after a series of car wrecks. My shitty driving skills had paid off.

Abandoning the idea of buying a fixer-upper, I decided to look into manufactured homes. Rural Development recommended that I check out Palmer brand, because they met specs. I went to a lot and viewed some high-quality homes and endured a high-pressure sales pitch. The Palmer homes were nice and looked more like small wooden houses than trailers. I thought perhaps I could get a place for under the amount of my loan. However, when I got a price quote, they were around $50,000. And Rural Development required all homes to have well, septic, and a fixed permanent foundation. Thus, by the time I added the half-acre of land needed to accommodate the septic system into the mix, the total cost wasn't any cheaper than building a new home from scratch.

So that was it. I was going to go big. I would have our home built from the ground up. With only ten weeks left in my three-month time limit, I shifted into high gear. Nearly every waking moment, I obsessed on the house. I visited multiple realtors, called every builder on the list, and started driving around like a madwoman, searching for an acceptable spot for our new property.

The first place I considered was Rosharon. When I got there to look at the lot, I was informed that it was in a flood zone. I called Rural Development to ask about my options. It turned out that they would only approve requests for lots located in Zone X, the least likely to flood in the entire area. This severely limited my options. Galveston and Brazoria counties, which were the only real rural areas nearby, were highly prone to flooding because of the hurricanes and tropical storms that sometimes came in from the Gulf of Mexico.

After several futile attempts at finding land, I finally found a Zone X spot down a dusty road in Manvel. It was a dead-end with no trees. The area was ugly. A small, country-looking boy with jeans and a buzz cut stared up at me from his bike. Could this be our home? At this point, I was willing to take just about anything. Hopeful, I called Rural Development so they could examine the property. However, I called them again a few days later and received terrible news: There was a gas pipeline on the lot, which was not allowed.

Even harder than locating acceptable land was finding a builder. I called every single one on the approved list. Some of them answered the phone only to tell me they were no longer building Rural Development homes. Most of them didn't even bother to return my calls when I left a message. But finally, after many futile attempts, I had a hit. I received a call back from a man with a mid-toned country accent. He said he was building houses in Liverpool, which was Zone X, and might be willing to work with me. I set up an appointment and met the man in a model home in his housing complex. We sat at a large table and discussed our options.

The man across the table appeared to be in his early sixties. He sported a potbelly and straight, slightly-disheveled white hair. He seemed eager to work with me, and handed me a series of blueprints to look through. My main criteria were that he could build within my budget, be a one-story house, and have three bedrooms with the master across a hallway from the kids' rooms. That way, no one could fall down the stairs or be forced to climb up and down them every day. And if Peter and Daun needed me or there was an emergency, I could hear them screaming, "*Mom!*" from across the hallway.

I picked the perfect home. Although it was wooden and not designed to be on a fixed slab, the man assured me that the plan could be altered to meet those parameters. He told me to take the blueprint and think it over. Excited, I went home. My dream was finally going to become a reality.

But when I called the contractor back the next day to follow up, he didn't answer. I left a message, but he didn't return my call. After at least a week of frustration and no responses from him, I concluded that he'd changed his mind. Since he was the only one on the list who'd bothered to even give me the time of day, I was sad and frustrated. Despite this, with only two weeks to go on my time limit, I was still 100 percent positive that I would get a house.

However, I think I was only one who really believed it, other than perhaps my children. My ex-husband, Jimmy, would often look at me scornfully and chastise me in an annoyed voice.

"*Barbara, they're not gonna give you a house!*"

But I didn't listen to him, not for a second. There was no room for doubt.

Rapidly running out of time, I continued my search. *Only one week left...* I only had one week until the loan offer would expire, and I hadn't even locked in a builder. Desperate, I called Rural Development and asked them for an extension. They said they didn't give extensions, but not to worry. I could always apply next year.

I was immediately repulsed. *Screw that! ...* I'm not waiting another year. I didn't think I would have the heart or stamina to go through this exhausting process again. More determined than ever, I decided to meet with one more realtor—this time, in the town where I grew up.

The next day, I sat across a desk from a young, slender woman with straight, shoulder-length blonde hair. *Blonde...* Why were they always blonde? The woman had the slight Texan lilt that was unique to my hometown, so I knew she was a local. After introductions, she folded her hands and looked across her desk.

"How can I help you?"

I explained the Rural Development program, its parameters, and my level of frustration with the process. I had endured three months of it, and this realtor was probably my last hope.

After listening carefully to my story, she gave me an intense gaze. "I know someone who might be able to help you."

I was both shocked and skeptical. "Really? Can you tell me about him?"

She went into action. "Hang on a sec. I'll give him a call and see if he can come by."

She quickly made a phone call and informed me that a contractor would be there in ten minutes. Soon after, a stout, older man with curly gray hair and a thick mustache entered the room. He introduced himself as Mr. Grant. He had a firm handshake and was friendly and very country, wearing denim overalls. He explained, in a thick rural Texas accent, that he was a home-building contractor. Then I told him about my dilemma.

He looked at me with kind eyes. "I'm a builder and I'm constructin' homes in the area right now. I have two lots of land 'round here that should do it for ya, half-acres in Zone X."

This sounded promising, but there was one major problem: "Are you on the approved builders' list?" I'm sure Mr. Grant could hear the worry in my voice.

He replied matter-of-factly, "No, but I can fill out all the paperwork and go through the inspections to get approved."

I felt like this man was a miracle from God.

I hopped into his truck, and he took me around my hometown, showing me some of the houses he'd built. They were amazing mid-sized brick homes. He did beautiful work.

Finally, he turned toward me from the driver's seat. "Do you wanna see the land I've got for ya?"

A few minutes later, we arrived at the spot. Like Mr. Grant had promised, there were two nice lots, both with beautiful trees—something that I desperately wanted. Most of the land I'd looked at didn't have any, so these lots were particularly appealing. And as a bonus, just across the street was a lush pasture with about three or four cows roaming in it. This was the best land I'd seen so far, and the thought of living on it made me happy. I told him that I wanted the corner lot because it had more trees than the other one.

Rural Development examined the land a couple of days later and turned down the corner lot because, like the one in Manvel, it had a pipeline on it. However, they said the one next to it was perfect. Looking back, it had actually been a better choice because, like the spot in Manvel, it was on a dead-end road. So, it would rarely have a lot of traffic, making it much safer for children. Plus, there was a hardy tallow tree in the backyard with long, full branches that could easily provide shade for a swing set.

Next, Mr. Grant had to go through the arduous process of getting approved. With such little time to spare, this seemed impossible. The approval process, like most government red tape, was probably long and complicated. And what if Mr. Grant's work was deemed unacceptable? What if he failed?

Fortunately, Mr. Grant called Rural Development and was able to secure a ninety-day extension. Within that time period, his business was approved as an official Rural Development contractor. Soon after, we started working out the details for my new home, discussing brick color and blueprint alterations, etc.

My dream was going to come true. It was a miracle brought to fruition by pure grit, determination, and perhaps an unrealistic conviction that I could do anything I set my mind to.

When I was in high school, Mom once leaned toward me, her face only about a foot from mine, and placed her hands gently on my cheeks. Her face was flushed as she told me the most sincere, fervent words I had ever heard her utter. *"Barbara, you're really special. You're so smart. You can do anything you put your mind to."*

And I believed her. Because of her encouragement, I've always had unrelenting confidence in myself, despite years of struggle. This characteristic would serve me well in the future.

***

Things continued to improve once we got our new home. The mortgage was cheaper than rent, my dad had bought me a well-maintained 1991 red Crown

Victoria, and I started wrangling the system in a way that improved our lives even further. We weren't rich, but we weren't hurting. Despite our poverty, through my cleverness and resourcefulness, we were living a lower-middle-class lifestyle.

I had always known what it was like to live a good life. I'd come from a middle-income family and was surrounded by siblings who would grow up to be successful. Jerry became the head manager of a grocery store before retiring and opening a successful online business. Brandy became an award-winning journalist living in a nice home in the suburbs. And like I said, Allen and Anne both became both successful computer programmers who held high-paying jobs at prestigious companies, Meanwhile, Lee became a successful entre- preneur with dozens of employees, and would, at one point, buy a Porsche just for fun. And although my parents only had a small part in raising him, my cousin, Clyde—who was like a brother to me—also turned out well. He became a wealthy entrepreneur who once told me he had "more money than he could spend." In other words, none of my siblings, or even my cousin, were hurting for money. All but Clyde had college degrees. They credit their success to their upbringing. Mom and Dad had done their job well and raised happy children who became thriving adults.

So that left me—the least successful one in my family. But still, I had managed to acquire a nice little brick house and fully-functioning car. And my kids and I never went hungry. Plus, by the time Nicki came around, we managed to go on road trips a couple of times a year—sometimes even out of state, like during The Monster Trip. And I always managed to give us spectacular Christmases, with dozens of presents under the tree.

But the most important result of my determination and fastidious ability to get our needs met was that it made my kids feel secure. Like I said, they never really felt poor, even though when they asked for something extra at the store, the answer was usually "No." They never complained. Instead, they seemed proud of my resourcefulness.

When Daun got her first cell phone in junior high, it was a little red flip phone. Most kids got phones in grade school and by 2006, most people had smart phones. But Daun liked her little flip phone. She was proud that it was different and outdated. She used to show off how retro it was. She would show it to her friends, flip it open, and touch the screen. "Look, I have a touch screen!" Obviously, the simple little phone wouldn't respond, but she was literally touching the screen. She never grew tired of that joke.

Then there was prom. I bought Daun's dress on Amazon for $30. But Daun didn't care about the cost. She was proud that I didn't waste hundreds of dollars like every other mom. After all, it was beautiful, puffy, and the perfect shade of violet. No. Instead of being embarrassed by the low price tag, Daun continually bragged to her friends about what a good deal I got.

Then there was Peter. He tended to ask for expensive video game systems, but only for Christmas. I usually managed to scrape up enough money for it and a few games. However, the rest of the year he didn't get any more games. But he never complained. He was just happy for what he got. He knew how we struggled, and he was grateful.

And my resourcefulness also came with an unintended bonus: it gave my kids a sense of security. One time, when Peter was twenty-three and having financial problems, he confided in Daun. He was living in Austin as an independent adult and had just totaled his car. Even worse, Peter worked for Grubhub, so he needed a vehicle for delivering food. He wasn't sure how he was going to replace his car, much less pay rent, so the situation was triggering daily anxiety attacks. Daun had reassured him by reminding him that I was there to help.

"It's going to be alright. You know, Mom's really clever, and she won't let anything bad happen. She always has this way of making things work out."

It makes me feel good that my cleverness with money has made my kids feel safe and secure. But there was a caveat. Peter had responded to Daun's words of consolation. "I know Mom will help me figure it out. That does make me feel a little better. But it also causes me anxiety because she's not going to live forever."

So now I know what to do to assure my kids will trust their future: I can never, ever, die.

23

THE DIRECTOR

But thinking back to 2006 and my boldest scheme to achieve financial stability—the hunt for Osama bin Laden—I realize that the results didn't only affect my family, but all families. No doubt, countless lives were saved, and Al Qaeda was severely crippled. In other words, the world was a safer place.

Unfortunately, most people didn't know about bin Laden's arrest, and they didn't get to feel the sense of relief and security that I felt because he was out of the picture.

Instead, something completely different happened.

***

It was August 2006, days after the news about the transatlantic aircraft plot, and I was at it once again. I had moved on from Boussora to a much bigger target. As I sat at my desk in the bedroom and stared at Osama bin Laden's face on the screen, a surge of adrenaline rushed through me at the thought of finding him. If I could locate Boussora, maybe I could look on MySpace for sites with similar attributes to his that might belong to bin Laden. I could even use the same process. Maybe there was a pattern for all Al Qaeda operatives on MySpace. Maybe, just maybe, I had developed a system for finding terrorists.

Could it possibly be that easy?

I would start by searching for bin Laden's aliases on MySpace. Then, when I found an alias that matched a suspicious page, I would use the name to go online and try to find corresponding addresses. Next, I would plug each result into the MySpace search engine, hoping to find one that would make bin Laden's MySpace pop up. Hey, it worked for Boussora, why not Osama bin Laden? Easy-peasy...

So I thought...

There I was, sitting at the same cluster-fuck desk where I'd had the breakthrough that led to Boussora. I set a cold can of Diet Mountain Dew next to my keyboard. I repeated the same stretching ritual as a few days prior, when I had begun searching for Boussora. Then I took a long slug of soda, set it down, and let out an audible sigh. I was ready to go.

But something had changed in me. I was certain I would never see a dime from finding Boussora. I had no way of proving that I had actually found him and that he'd been arrested. I had no recourse. This might mean that even if I found bin Laden, I would never receive the $25 million reward.

Yet somehow none of that mattered. Missing out on $5 million didn't deter me. I had discovered a system for finding terrorists, and I was going to use it. The money was almost irrelevant. I mean, I wanted it. Who wouldn't? But the money wasn't what was on my mind. *No...* I was determined to locate as many terrorists as I could. I was driven by a strong need to save lives and get justice for 9/11. It was my duty as a caring individual and a US citizen. I had to do what I could to help. There would be no more stalling—no more negotiations about contracts. I was all in, and I was going to do it as quickly as possible.

But why bin Laden? Why then? Why go straight to him after Boussora?

It was simple: I was overconfident. Also, I wanted to test my system. Would it really work on one of the most elusive men in the world? I *had* to try.

However, locating Osama bin Laden was different. It would challenge my system in a way that I could not have predicted. The road to bin Laden wouldn't be straightforward. It would be more like finding my way through a nearly impossible corn maze.

I signed on to MySpace, hopeful as usual. Then, I opened a second browser and surfed to Osama bin Laden's RewardsForJustice profile. I looked at the first alias on his list: his full, real name, "Usama Bin Muhammad bin Laden." Not expecting any relevant results, I typed it in, letter by letter, *"U-S-A-M-A B-I-N L-A-D-E-N."* Unsurprisingly, there were several hits. Celebrities and world figures were often mimicked on MySpace. I brushed past these. Nothing to see here.

Then, I typed as many iterations of his name as I could think of, none of which led to anything interesting. I knew at this point that inputting his real name or any variation of it was pointless. But starting there felt a little bit like a warm-up exercise. I changed "Usama" to "Osama," added and took away middle names, and switched around word orders before moving on to the second alias: "Shaykh Usama bin Laden." Taking the new name through a similar process, I ended with "Shaykh bin Laden."

Having gotten that ritual out of the way without finding anything unusual, I moved on to the next six aliases. Fortunately, these names were shorter and didn't contain as many iterations. I began madly copying and pasting each entry into the MySpace people finder. I copied "The Prince," expecting nothing, and I was right. Next, I tried "The Emir." *Nothing...* I kept working my way down the list. Although I had only been working for about an hour, by the time I reached the eighth alias, the suspense was killing me. I was afraid that I wasn't going to get any good hits. It appeared that bin Laden liked to pick unusual names for his aliases. Not even any normal-looking MySpace pages were coming up. I was getting nothing.

I was beginning to believe he didn't have a MySpace or that he wasn't using a known alias. Either way, my investigation seemed like it was grinding to a screeching halt.

I looked down at the last name on the list: "The Director." I thought about it for a moment. Who would use The Director as a registration name on MySpace? I almost didn't want to bother plugging it in. There was no way this was going to derive a hit. But if I had skipped it, my search would have felt incomplete. *No...* I needed to be thorough. So I reluctantly typed the letters into the MySpace search engine.

I blinked at the screen in disbelief. A page popped up. *What was this?* The profile pic was a crisp drawing of a blue, majestic-looking seahorse. The rest of the page matched Boussora's pattern: It was nearly blank with no friends, not even Tom, who was literally on almost everyone's friends list. *Yes...* Like Boussora, The Director had, weirdly, deleted Tom, which took extra effort. And there was a conspicuous lack of comments—zero—even more barren than Boussora's page. It was like he'd put effort into making his page look blank. But despite this, as with Boussora and his sports car, The Director had taken the time to upload a seahorse sketch for his avatar. Plus, he had logged in just two weeks prior. *Yes...* The page was super suspicious...

This *had to* be him...

But...

What the hell could I do with a name like "The Director?" This wasn't a real name. It didn't fit well with the premise of my system. I was supposed to find an alias that went with a page that fit the near-blank pattern. I would then use that name to try to find an address.

But this alias made my system impossible. Osama bin Laden couldn't rent an apartment with a name like "The Director." *No...* With a name like that, my system was useless.

In that moment, I was stuck. I felt like the trail to bin Laden had grown colder. If I couldn't find him through MySpace, it was all over. There wasn't anything else I could do. It would be the end of my very short search. My detective work always started with MySpace. I had no other ideas or decent resources. I would have no choice but to move on to another terrorist on the list.

I shot up from my chair, disgusted and discouraged. I was done. I wandered into the kitchen for a snack. I needed something sweet.

***

Feeling a bit overwhelmed, I pulled a honey bun out of the half-empty box on top of the microwave. Taking huge bites of the pastry, I headed for the living room. But it was gone before I reached the couch. I looked down at my sticky, empty fingers. *Nooo!* ... I hadn't even tasted it. I was too preoccupied with the hunt... I *had to* go back for another try. But first, *water*... I realized in that moment just how incredibly thirsty I was. I sauntered back into the kitchen, picked up a plastic cup, and got some ice water. *Sweet relief...*

Moments later, I grabbed another honey bun and stood there, eating. Next thing I knew... *What?!* ... My hands were empty and sticky again. I hadn't tasted the second honey bun either. *Jeez...* I licked my fingers and wiped my hands on my jeans. At least the sugar had relaxed me a bit. I sat down in my designated spot at the kitchen table and took a slug of water.

I paused for moment, lost in thought: At that moment, Nicki clumsily settled in the chair across from me. After a brief pause, her eyes lit up. "So, has there been any more news on the terrorist?" She was talking about Boussora. She had no clue that I had moved on to Osama bin Laden.

"No. There's nothing new. I don't think I'm gonna get any money."

"Really? *Why not?*"

I could hear dismay in my tone. "I don't have any way of proving they found him. I'm not sure why, but I don't think they're going public with it."

Nicki was concerned. "Why not?"

"I don't know. Maybe they don't want people to

know he was in Brooklyn."

Nicki thought about it. "Maybe. But what are you going to do?"

Despite my earlier frustration, I actually had no intention of quitting. "What can I do? I'm just gonna keep going."

"What do you mean?"

I laid it out for her. "I mean, my system works, so I'm going to use it. I'm going to keep looking for terrorists."

However, Nicki wasn't satisfied. "But what about the money?"

I shrugged. "I don't know. But this is more important than money. I think I'm supposed to keep going. I mean—the rainbow—I think God wants me to keep going. None of this is a coincidence. Something great's gonna happen. I can feel it."

I thought back on younger me.

After Grandma helped me rediscover God at fourteen, I became very religious for a while. During those years—especially as a young adult—I often prayed to God to tell me what he wanted. Whatever it was, I would do it. No matter what, above everything, I wanted to do his will. The problem was that I could never figure out what he wanted. Despite all my prayers, there was no clear direction, no clear voice. Finally, after years of struggling to figure out God's will, I gave up. I stopped praying. I even stopped going to church.

But now I was in my thirties, and those years were long behind me. *So I thought...* But this hunt for terrorists—bin Laden, even—was a game changer. I felt like God was finally taking me up on my naïve, youthful desire to do his will. He had finally given me a mission.

To me, it seemed obvious: Stopping terrorists was something God would want me to do. *Yes...* I had a system that worked, and he wanted me to use it to find as many terrorists as I could. I believed this to my core.

Nicki interrupted my thoughts. "Hey! I thought we were talking!"

"Yeah. Sorry. I was just stuck in my head for a moment. What were you trying to say?"

"Okay. I was trying to say, it's great that God wants you to do this and stuff. But I still want the money!"

"So do I, but that's not what matters right now. What matters is completing my mission. I'm going to do this. I *have to* do this." I put my foot down. This was happening. It had to happen. It was *meant* to happen.

Nicki moved to the next logical question: "So, what's next?"

I stalled for a moment, wondering how she was going to take what I was about to tell her. "I'm stepping it up. I've actually been searching for Osama bin Laden."

She had been facing downward, but her eyes snapped up to attention. "*What?*"

She looked shocked.

"Yes. I don't really think I'll find him, but I just thought I'd give it a try."

"*Really?*" She still seemed stunned.

"Really. I've already been working on it."

Nicki sounded excited. "Wow?! Any luck?"

I started sputtering a bit. "Actually, yes. I think I found his MySpace."

"What? Really?! *Are you sure?!*"

"I'm pretty sure."

I explained to her what I'd found: bin Laden's alias, the non-name—The Director—and his chosen avatar, the seahorse. Her eyes lit up. "So, what's next?"

"I dunno. I'm actually stuck. I mean, The Director isn't really a name."

"True."

"What am I supposed to do with that? I can't exactly find an address registered to someone calling himself The Director."

"True."

I kept going, formulating my next steps. "I'm just going to have to scrutinize the page and see if there's anything I missed. There's gotta be something there. I'm probably just missing it."

"I hope so. Isn't he worth twenty-five million?"

But in that moment, I wasn't thinking about the money. "Yes, but that's not what's important. I mean, it's Osama bin Laden. *Osama bin Laden*! ... What if I could find him? ... *My God!*"

"Yes... True."

Her voice was flat and measured. She was taking everything in stride. But unlike her, I was growing more animated by the minute. "I mean, I could help bring justice for 9/11. This is so much more important than money. It's just so much more."

"True."

"If this happens, it's because it's supposed to happen. I'm gonna give it my best. I'm gonna try. It's the least I can do. And maybe this could save lives."

Her demeanor picked up. "Maybe it could. *Wow...* That'd be awesome!"

I stood up, grabbed a mug, and absently poured myself a cup of coffee. "I'm going to go work on it some more." Without a second thought, I sped off, absently sloshing a splotch of coffee on my sleeveless "Homo"

Depot Tee-shirt—the one that Nicki had bought me at the Houston Pride Festival the year before. *Damn it! ...* White! It was a *white* shirt. Coffee stains were the worst, and I would never get that spot out. *Why was I so clumsy?* This is why I hated wearing light colors.

As I left the kitchen, Nicki didn't get a chance to say goodbye or discuss plans for the evening. *No...* I was exiting the conversation. As I whipped away, I missed what was, no doubt, a look of dismay on Nicki's face. I would be gone for hours, and she knew it.

24

THE SEAHORSE

I stared at the page for at least a half-hour.

There had to...*had to* be something I was missing. My eyes kept slowly and repeatedly scanning the entire page, starting with The Director's (bin Laden's) seahorse avatar in the upper left-hand corner, then moving tediously to the middle and then the bottom. Like I said, all sections but the avatar were completely blank—no friends, no comments, just the familiar MySpace template. Then, my focus turned to the name on the page. As usual, the profile only showed the first name. It was "The," which seemed really weird. Apparently "The" was his first name and "Director" was his surname. But this information wasn't very helpful. I continued to scrutinize the page. There had to be something else there...*anything*...

As I sat at my chair, I knew I had a mission to accomplish. I was looking for Osama bin Laden and wouldn't stop until I was satisfied that I'd exhausted every channel.

Frowning at the screen, my thoughts briefly

wandered to a little girl who existed a lifetime ago, a girl who had her *own* mission.

I was in second grade—seven years old—and Mass had just ended. I'd taken my First Communion earlier that year, so I had proudly received Christ's body, like the adults. Pretty soon, I would have my First Confession. I heard that most people did it the other way around, but our group was special. We got Communion first.

(*It was the '70s and I didn't realize it at the time, but my First Communion class was part of a Vatican II experiment. The Church had decided to switch things up and introduce the Eucharist prior to Reconciliation. As an adult, I never really understood this change, because you were supposed to be in a state of grace before receiving Communion. We were also were never taught the Act of Contrition. We were supposed to just make something up and ask forgiveness for our sins. Strange times...*)

But when I was a little girl, all I knew was that Mass was over, and Momma was going to light a candle.

I knew what that meant. I'd been taught in CCD (Catholic Sunday school) that if you lit a holy candle and prayed, the smoke would bring your prayers up to heaven, and God would answer them. This sounded wonderful. I wanted the smoke to bring *my* prayers to Heaven. And I thought lighting a candle sounded fun!

I looked up at Momma with hopeful eyes. "Can I light one, too?"

Momma looked at me. I think she was trying to figure out if I was big enough for this.

"Sure."

Then, she folded a dollar into a rectangle and handed it to me. "Here. Push this into the donation slot.

It's supposed to pay for the candle."

I looked over the candles very carefully. "Momma, I want *this one*." I pointed to a little white votive sitting in a red holder. It was prominently displayed at the center of the group.

"Do you want to light it?" She was holding a book of paper matches.

"No, Momma, I'm scared o' matches." I remembered the time I'd played with matches on the front porch. They were paper, like those. I accidentally burnt my pinky. I started crying and hollering. I ran to go get Momma. Moments later, she put my finger in cold water and told me to never play with matches again. She told me I could burn the house down. I felt guilty and I was scared. I would never do *that* again!

Momma looked at me. She had a funny look on her face. "No, silly. You don't have to strike the match. Just light the matchstick with one of the lit candles, like this." She then demonstrated, using the now-burning match to light her candle.

"Oh... I can do *that!*"

She handed me the matches, and I lit my favorite candle, careful not to burn myself with the surrounding flames.

Then, I knelt next to Momma in one of the back pews, not far from the candles.

"I can't think of what to pray for."

Momma tried to help me think of something. "Well, is there anything you need?"

I shook my head. "Uh-uh."

It was true. I had never felt neglected. I was happy, had plenty of toys, and was well fed.

Momma made a suggestion: "I know. You can pray

for peace in the Middle East."

(During the '70s everyone was worried about Israel and Palestine. Plus, Iran was proving to be an enemy of America.)

But I didn't know all this when I was a kid. I just knew that peace sounded nice. And I hated, hated, *hated* war! I just wanted people to be happy and not die.

From that day forward, I would light a candle every week after Mass and pray for peace in the Middle East. Eventually, I switched it up a little and started praying for *world* peace instead of focusing on the Middle East. And when I blew out candles on my birthday cake, I would repeat the same prayer.

The last selfish birthday wish I remember making was when I turned six: I had asked for a *Planet of the Apes* treehouse. I probably just liked the idea of talking monkeys. But my wish turned out to be futile. The structure didn't include any action figures. It became a piece of junk in a pile of forgotten toys. *Meaningless...* I didn't really *need* it.

Regardless, my prayers for world peace lasted until I was thirteen, shortly after my parent's divorce. As I mentioned before, around that age I became severely depressed and started doubting God's existence. To me, a world without God was a world without hope or meaning. We would trudge through a miserable life and then die. *Worm food...*

***

Fortunately, by August 2006, my spiritual crisis had abated and my faith had returned. But in that moment, it was the seahorse that was driving me. It was pushing me to the edge of sanity. It gave me both hope and despair—hope that I would find Osama bin Laden and despair that the task at hand might be impossible.

That morning, the seahorse stared at me from the screen, mocking me. *"You're never going to figure this out!"* He looked stately, like a leader. He was coral blue, a king among seahorses. I couldn't help but wonder why bin Laden picked this figure. What did it mean? *Come on, Barbara, think*. I had to be creative—perhaps more creative than I'd ever been before. I somehow had to lasso and ride this seahorse to bin Laden. *But how?* ...

The only detail that stood out on this page was the seahorse, so I examined it carefully again and compared it to the sports car. The seahorse was a vibrant, medium shade of blue, with purple undertones; its colors evoked a sense of royalty. The crevices and indentions were crisp and concise, although not as much as today's computerized graphics. Comparing it to a photo of a living seahorse, it seemed pretty realistically proportioned. Its head was dipped slightly as though it were neighing. Its icy black eyes stared off to the side of the page. Its tail was coiled loosely under its body, in a way that made it almost look prehensile.

Hmmm... Was it possible that this fish had something in common with primates and marsupials? I knew this was irrelevant, but it captivated me nonetheless. A quick trip to Google gave me the answer: Apparently, seahorses could, in fact, grip and manipulate objects with their tails. *Fascinating...*

Fascinating, yet getting me nowhere.

What bothered me was how different the seahorse was from Boussora's avatar. I mean, there was still a definite pattern. Terror operatives and sympathizers, as far as I knew, never uploaded photos of themselves or any other human being. They only used simple avatars, which were always sketches. But I had assumed that they would stick to pop symbols, like the Corvette. I theorized that this phenomenon was meant as ironic. After all, they were picking things that were dear to Americans—the people whose country they hated most. This could even serve to further throw investigators off their scents. And the pop symbol pick would hold true for everyone I would observe in the network during future cases, except bin Laden.

So I formulated a new theory: Perhaps Al Qaeda MySpace network members normally picked an avatar that was meaningful to them—true to form for idealists. And make no mistake, Al Qaeda sympathizers *were* idealists. They were, essentially, violent activists who idealized their culture and religion, holding it in higher esteem than anything else, including fellow human beings.

As for idealists, I thought about Boussora. Like my theory about bin Laden's seahorse, the Corvette might have meant something to him. *Yes...* A man like him might want and appreciate a sports car, especially since he was youthful and from a developed nation (Canada). Boussora might have seen himself as a powerful, fast-paced high roller, throwing caution to the wind and zooming at 120 miles per hour on a busy highway. Yes, members of the network were clearly risk takers. Like the sports car, he might have seen himself as daring and dangerous. And that particular car would have been associated with a desirable lifestyle. Regardless, the commonalities in the sketches made suspicious sites like his easy to spot, especially since they were attached to known aliases.

But the seahorse stood in stark contrast to the Corvette. It was unironic and humorless—something that might be picked by an older, more methodical person, like bin Laden. *Yes...* Whoever chose this took himself very seriously. This person was probably even more idealistic than the others. He wanted more than danger. He wanted something bigger.

Perhaps, picking a nonhuman living creature could indicate someone who had a higher regard for nature than civilization. But I wondered if the seahorse had an even deeper meaning, even beyond this. Maybe it stood for something.

I cracked my knuckles. I needed to do some research. I started Googling "seahorse meaning." I discovered that seahorses tended to represent the divine, roaming alongside Poseidon in Greek mythology. In the same mythology, seahorses sometimes led drowning sailors through a vortex to safety. The seahorse, as a spirit animal, could represent power and authority. It could also symbolize a father figure.

It made sense that bin Laden would see himself as the right hand of God. If he was nothing else, he was a religious zealot. *Yes...* The seahorse could represent what he considered his divine calling.

But the representation of power and authority and "father" might also fit with how Osama bin Laden would see himself. Could he have picked the seahorse because he liked symbolism? Was he that deep? Bin Laden was most certainly intelligent. This could be it—the reason for the seahorse. Maybe he felt like it was an apt symbol for himself. But *was* this why he picked it? And did it even matter? And there was one more gnawing doubt:

What if The Director wasn't bin Laden at all. What if I was wasting my time?

Pushing away my doubts, I moved on. Theorizing why Osama bin Laden would choose the seahorse was getting me nowhere. *Ugh!* ... I was still no closer to lassoing the horse. After a careful, deliberate twirl and toss, the rope missed the mark and landed flatly on the ground. I was no closer to finding bin Laden.

The Corvette and the seahorse couldn't be further apart symbolically. Certainly, they both represented strength—a muscle car and an armored, regal fish. Beyond that, they shared little in common. But perhaps bin Laden wasn't like the men who served under him. Maybe his motives were different. I doubt that the promise of virgins in heaven was his inspiration. *No...* He was the leader, the one who inspired men to blow up airplanes or strap explosives to themselves and walk into crowded buildings. He himself would never pick the daring, reckless sports car. He valued life—*his own life.*

I started thinking about Charles Manson and his "family." Most people believe he was a mass murderer. But was he? Manson never killed or physically harmed anyone. *No...* He was a magician who could use his powers to get other people—his family—the cult—to kill people.

Yes... Bin Laden was like Manson. He was the cult leader, but would never get his own hands bloody. He wouldn't submit to suicide bombing like his henchmen. This wasn't his place. He was above all that.

And then I took another look at the profile pics. Something was striking about them, something that gave the seahorse and the Corvette a mundane commonality: They were both works of art. I began to examine them side by side. Could they have been drawn by the same artist? ... *Maybe* ...

Not being an artist myself, I was only guessing. But the sports car appeared to be less concise and sharp than the seahorse, more minimalist. *Yes...* It seemed most likely to me that these symbols were downloaded somewhere off the internet with no credit to the source. I doubted Al Qaeda had recruited one of its own to draw up special symbols. There were plenty of graphics everywhere online and even clip art that could be copied from *Microsoft Office* or *Print Shop*.

But none of this information, none of this speculation, could lead me to bin Laden. There had to be more, something I was missing...

I let out an audible sigh. I was too close to this. I needed some time away to regroup. At that moment, I heard some murmuring. Looking up, I noticed someone was trying to talk to me.

"Are you okay?" It was Nicki.

"Yeah. Why?"

Nicki was sitting on the couch next to me, and I had hardly sensed her presence.

"You sighed."

She often called me out when I sighed. During those days, I used to emote loud exhales so often that Nicki had nicknamed me "Sigh Master." And when she said or did something that elicited a sigh, she took pleasure in pointing it out. "*Oooo!* ... I made you sigh!" she'd say with a crooked smile. This tease had become a running gag. I would typically smile back unless I was particularly annoyed. But this time she mentioned the sigh because she'd picked up on my angst. She was worried that something was wrong.

I tried to explain what was happening. "I'm still working on Osama bin Laden. You see here..." I pointed to the screen. "I think this is bin Laden's MySpace."

Nicki sounded puzzled. "Really? Wow! *Are you sure?!*"

I explained about the pattern and the alias—The Director. I continued, telling her what I'd learned about seahorses and had observed about its regal colors and my thoughts on its symbolism.

I asked for some advice. "Any ideas? I'm kind of stuck."

Nicki gave me a look of dull surprise. "I don't know. It's like you said. Maybe it's symbolic."

"Yeah, but it's not helping much." My mind started going. There had to be more; there's just *had* to be. Bin Laden left this clue and it must mean something. It must lead *somewhere*. I was following a trail of breadcrumbs. I just needed the next crumb.

Nicki seemed frustrated. "I don't know. I don't think I can help you."

Ugh... I felt utterly alone in this. Why did everything have to hinge on me and my tired little brain? I thought back to Dr. Miller's words when complimenting my programming work for his class. "You have a superior brain."

But did I? Was it enough?

Nicki noticed I was frustrated, even more than she was. "You need to loosen up. You wanna hang out with me in the bedroom?" She gave me a sultry smile.

"I don't think that will help! I'm too distracted..."

"Are you sure?" She turned around, exaggeratively swinging her hips back and forth, as she sauntered toward the bedroom. I knew what she was doing. She was trying to get me to follow her.

I was remorseful. "It's not going to work! I'm sorry, I just can't. You know how I am."

Nicki turned around and shrugged, her face dropping a little. "Okay..."

It had been a while.

I defused the situation by responding to her in a loud sing-song voice.

"Gandhi! ... Gandhi! ... Gandhi!"

Then we started chanting it in unison. This was an inside joke—a reference to a scene in *Go Fish*, the 1994 lesbian classic.

Go Fish was one of my favorite movies. Watching it on the Independent Film Channel after my divorce helped me with my coming out process. In the film, Kia jokes about her friend, Ely, who is stalling on having sex with her new girlfriend, Max. *"Two or three more dates— what is this, the lesbian Gandhi?"*

Regardless, after I nixed sex as a solution to my problems, Nicki tried another idea: "You want some lunch?"

I looked at the clock: five o'clock. This would be dinnertime for most families, not lunchtime. But not for us. We just sort of ate whenever. Everything worked on *my* schedule.

"Yes, lunch. Any ideas?" My stomach grumbled a little. For the first time, I noticed just how hungry I was.

"I could make us some tuna." This was a go-to for Nicki, perhaps her favorite pick for lunch.

"Sounds great!" Honestly, at that point, dried cardboard sounded pretty good, so yeah, tuna was awesome.

"How many cans?"

"Better make three. I'm sure Peter and Daun will want some. I'll go ask." I was always worried they wouldn't get enough to eat. It was a mom thing.

I headed down the hallway and poked my head in each of their rooms and asked them if they wanted tuna. *Yes*... Tuna was on.

I reported back to Nicki and continued our previous conversation. "Can we go somewhere after we eat? I need to get out of the house. I need a break so I can regroup. I might even need to sleep on this next clue. I'm still stuck."

"Yeah. We could go to Walmart. We're out of apples, bananas, and yogurt."

I'm not sure how other people gauge being out of food, but in our family, if we were out of yogurt, we were out of food. It was one of our favorite snacks, right up there with apples. Like I said, the kids were constantly eating apples. Nicki even gave them the nickname "little apple -biters." It was a reference to when Robin Williams as Mrs. Doubtfire called his children *little ankle-biters.*"

Nicki pulled me out of a slight haze. "Yeah... Let's go to Walmart after lunch."

But then, a feeling of dread washed over me.

The open spaces and crowds in Walmart bothered me. Often, we'd go at 2 a.m. when there were few people around. But, at that moment, it was still early evening, and the store would be packed.

I tried in vain to comfort myself. I tried not to worry about the pending anxiety attack that could be triggered by the vast, crowded store. Maybe I'd be okay this time. Maybe I could power through it. Besides, I *really* needed a break—a change of venue. Maybe walking around would help clear my head.

25

WALMART

Two hours later, we stepped in the doors of Walmart, kids in tow. Everyone had their own agenda. Nicki and I grabbed a basket and began inching toward the back of the grocery section. As always, we'd buy cokes and water first.

But before we could get too far, Peter started begging. "Can I go check out the video game section?"

"Sure. But you have to *promise* you'll stay in that section. I don't want you wandering off."

He sounded exasperated. *"Mom!"*

"What?!"

"It's just Walmart. I know my way around the store!" He was both shouting and whining at the same time.

"I know, but I need to be able to find you when it's time to go." For a brief moment, I wished we had the "electronic leash."

Peter was twelve, and he still didn't have a cell phone. I thought the idea of kids having their own phones was ridiculous. I didn't have one when I was a kid, and I'd survived. Besides, I couldn't afford an expensive family plan. And even if I could, Peter and Daun would probably just lose or drop their phones. It was pointless. Still, they kept telling me that all their classmates had phones. And they would ask for one at times, but thankfully there was only minimal pressure or whining involved. Like I said, they knew we were poor. It would be another three years before I finally gave in.

Ultimately, without cell phones, they were in Walmart with no easy way to communicate with me. I didn't really want to be separated from them, but they were getting older, and I had to trust them to be alone at some point.

Unfortunately, before Peter ran off toward the video game section, Daun also chimed in. "Can I go, too?" Of the two, I worried about Daun more because she was younger, more impulsive, and overly friendly with strangers.

"No... You're staying with us."

Daun was persistent. "Please..."

"I'm sorry, Daun. I just think it's a bad idea."

Then she played the guilt card, which sometimes worked on me. "But you're letting Peter go!"

Still, I held my ground. "Peter's two years older than you."

"I know, but it's not *fair!*"

I looked back at her sternly. "No. It's *not* fair. But you'll get to do more by yourself when you get older."

"But I'll be with *Peter!*"

"Yes, but you don't always stay with him. You wander off, and we can't find you."

But she wasn't giving up without a fight. "*Mom*, it's just Walmart. We come in here all the time!"

The guilt was starting to wear on me. I guess I *was* being a bit overprotective.

She kept pushing me. "Besides, you let Peter go off by himself when *he* was ten!"

This was true, but my kids had developed at different rates. Because of Daun's dyslexia, she had a poor sense of direction. She was also way more impulsive than Peter.

I tried to explain it to her—why I treated her brother differently. "Peter was ready to go on his own at ten. I just don't think you're ready yet. I'm sorry." I hated to admit it, but I think I was also a little more protective of her because she was a girl.

She shot me a look.

My voice softened a bit. "Sorry. Not this time, honey. Maybe next time."

"You *always* say that!"

I paused, considering her words. Daun was right. I couldn't protect her forever. She was getting older every day.

Daun made a final ploy. "What if I pinky promise you that I'll stay with Peter?"

I shrugged. This was the ultimate promise, so I knew Daun wouldn't break it. She'd be fine because I knew in my heart that Peter wouldn't step a foot outside of the video game section. He was too obsessed with them. They had systems set up for kids to try out new games. I would know where they were at all times.

I took a deep breath and finally relented. "Okay... But only if you pinky promise."

We hooked pinkies and shook them. Before she could pull away, I tightened my pinky on hers. "You promise you'll stay with Peter the whole time?"

"I promise!"

I squeezed her pinkie tighter, bending it slightly. "And if you break the promise, I'll totally break your pinky. Don't think I won't do it!"

Daun grinned up at me. "I know..."

In an instant, Peter took off jogging toward the electronics section, and Daun followed close behind him. I hoped they'd have fun... I thought back to when they were little and I would strap them to the multi-kid cart to keep them from touching things along the aisles. Then when they got too big to sit in the multi-kid cart, I'd get a regular one and make them keep at least one hand on it at all times. If I gave them any slack, they'd start running in circles and possibly knock things off the shelf.

But that was a long time ago. No more extreme measures were needed in the grocery store. They were older and better behaved. Still, they usually accompanied Nicki and me so that they could help pick out the groceries and so I could keep an eye on them. But things were different this time. Nicki and I were on our own, and the kids were off in the video game section, left to their own devices.

Nicki and I headed along our usual route, beginning at the back of the store and working our way around. As I'd feared, Walmart was crowded that day. Although my children had always been well-behaved, often others were not. However, today there weren't any screamers driving me crazy. Most of the babies were cute and on their best behaviors. I looked down the aisle. A Latina mother was leaning over her two-year-old, who was sitting in a shopping cart. She scolded him softly, "*Dámelo. No es tuyo.*" I pulled some of my college-level

Spanish out of the cobwebs in the back of my brain. *That isn't his!* ... She scooped a small box of animal crackers from his tiny hands and put them back on the shelf. The child cried for a few seconds but calmed down as soon as she plugged a pacifier in his mouth. I sighed. I remembered those days.

But as we shopped, my mind kept wandering further and further from the task at hand. I couldn't stop obsessing on the seahorse. *What was I missing?* I was still solving the puzzle. I just wanted to go home. It was pulling at me more with every step around the store.

I needed to work. It was important...

I glanced down at the cart. There were cokes in it. Where did *those* come from?

Moments later...

What?!

I startled to the sound of a loud voice: It was Nicki.

"I asked you three times already. *Do we need eggs?*"

Oh, wow... I really needed to pay closer attention... Where were we? *Oh yes...* We were getting margarine and heading in the direction of the eggs.

I finally answered the question. "Uh... I dunno. That's more like Daun's department."

Daun had always been obsessed with eggs. Sometimes, just to be funny, she'd say the word "eggs" at random. It was a little weird, but in her defense, eggs were one of her favorite foods. It still is.

Nicki was frustrated. "Daun should have stayed with us so she could help pick out the food."

"I know."

"Well, should I get some?" I was wandering back into seahorse land.

"Get what?"

"Eggs!" Nicki was near her wits' end.

I managed to snap out of my haze for a second. "Yeah, it never hurts to have eggs. We go through them so fast. If it's too many, we'll just boil some."

Nicki grabbed a dozen off the shelf and handed them to me. "Do these look okay?"

I absently opened the carton, still thinking about the seahorse. *What did it mean?* It had to mean something! It was the only clue I had...

It was difficult, but I reluctantly paused my mind for a moment and carefully spun each egg in its slot. If it was cracked, it would stick to the carton. I watched for that while I was spinning them.

I gave the all-clear. "Looks good."

After about fifteen minutes in my state of confusion, I began to panic, my body trembling slightly, and my mind running in circles as I kept bumping into people.

People... So many people. People everywhere. I needed to get out of there. I felt trapped, claustrophobic, like I couldn't breathe. And I couldn't shake the feeling that everything that could go wrong, would go wrong. What if I stopped sleeping again? What if I couldn't keep up my work? What if things didn't work out? What if I didn't find Osama bin Laden? What if people died because of me? I was terrified. Everything around me seemed surreal. I had to...had to...*had to* get out! And—

Oh my God, *the kids...*

The kids were on their own. They could get lost or snatched up by a pedophile. God, I hated Walmart. I was anxious every time I came in there, but this time was different. It was worse.

Most of the time, under these circumstances, I

would go sit down on one of the benches near the front entrance or flee to the car. But this time, I just wanted to go home. I wanted to feel safe. I wanted to know everything was going to be okay, and the kids were all right. I wanted to bring the whole family together—*now!*

Ever since the kids were little, I'd had recurring nightmares about losing track of them at a carnival, a mall, or some other crowded area. I would stumble around in a panic, searching for them. I would normally locate Peter first, grab his hand, and wander around anxiously looking for Daun, calling her name. I usually wouldn't find her, and it would leave me with a sick feeling. It was a horrible dream and always a relief to wake up from. This fear of losing track of them was awful and deep-rooted, coming from the instinctual momma bear inside of me.

But in that moment, at Walmart, there was nothing natural about my reactions. I felt myself starting to hyperventilate, so I tried to slow my breathing by counting to ten with each inhale and exhale. *In through my nose...out through my mouth.*

I looked at Nicki, panicked.

She looked back, concerned.

"What? ... What's wrong?"

"We have to go!"

Nicki sounded pissed. "What? *Why?* We just got here!"

I pleaded with her. "We just have to. We have to go *now*. I'll take the groceries. You just go get the kids."

Nicki knew what this was. She'd seen it before. I was having a panic attack. This happened a lot at Walmart.

"Why don't you take the keys and go sit in the car? I'll finish the shopping."

Yeah... That was the usual plan. But like I said, this time was different. The car didn't seem safe enough. I needed...*needed to* know everyone was safe—everyone, not just me. I needed the whole family to be together because, in that moment, I felt like everything was falling apart. The hunt for bin Laden... *Everything...* Everything that was happening was adding to my anxiety exponentially.

"No. We just need to go. *All* of us. I'm sorry." I was persistent.

Now Nicki was palpably angry. *"Fine! ...* I'll go get the kids!"

I burst into tears. I hated it when Nicki got mad. She didn't really understand what I was going through. Sometimes, I wished she could step inside my head for just a moment to feel what it was like. It often sucked being me.

About thirty minutes later, we were safe at home, but my anxiety hadn't completely subsided. I beelined back to the bedroom, stripped down to a T-shirt and underwear, turned off the lights, and curled up in the fetal position on my side of the bed, waiting for the anxiety to pass. Nicki knew better than to ask me to help with the groceries.

Within twenty minutes, my breathing started to slow down. About a half hour in, I was out cold from exhaustion.

26

BAHRAIN

My eyes popped open. I tried to focus on the ceiling fan for a second, but I winced and quickly looked away. The fan's lights were on—four 60-watt bulbs stinging my eyes all at once.

Ugh... Blinded!

I had been sleeping hard, but I could feel thoughts still processing in my brain. I had never stopped trying to solve the puzzle of the seahorse.

There is a moment between being asleep and awake, just as I'm becoming conscious, that has given me some of my best ideas and intuitions. This was one of those moments.

In a flash, I had an idea. What if I translated the word "seahorse" into Arabic? *Yes...* This might lead to the next clue. I could hardly wait to get to my computer.

But first... I twisted my body toward the nightstand, and started feeling around for my glasses. When that failed, I turned on the lamp and tried to look with my eyes. *Pointless...* All I could make out was the blurry lamp and a few scattered lumps of nothing. I noticed that the drawer was open. Maybe my glasses had fallen in. I started fumbling clumsily within the drawer, creating loud rattling noises as I shoved around empty pill bottles, broken rosaries, and random crap. I began to panic, knocking shit on the floor. Where were they? Had they fallen on the ground? Why was I so careless? Come on, I had to find them so I could try my seahorse translation idea. I imagined having to order a new pair and wait days, completely blind.

Still searching the drawer, I finally felt a lens from an old broken pair of glasses I had kept in case of emergencies. Plus, I liked the color. Unlike my current pair, they had a cool blue tint.

Holding the lens up to my right eye, I leaned over the edge of the bed and scavenged the floor with my left hand, pushing aside piles of wadded-up pieces of paper and coke cans, making more rattling noises. *Why?* ... Why *now?* Maybe I should ask Nicki to help. She had a way of finding things. It was her superpower. She'd always had a good eye for detail.

"Nicki!" I yelled out for her, incredibly helpless without my glasses and nearly in tears.

But Nicki didn't come. Sometimes, it was hard to hear people in the bedroom if you're on the opposite side of the house.

"*Nicki!*" I yelled again, but louder.

Still no response.

I felt my face flush red as tears welled in my eyes. *Why?*

Ordinarily, at this point, I would stumble into the other room and ask her for help—something that often annoyed her. But I had to be extremely desperate. And I was... I *really* wanted my glasses so I could get up and get back to work.

But before I went stumbling toward Nicki in the other room, I caught a glimpse of something dark and oblong on the nightstand. *God...* Right in front of me... There they were, their black frames blending in with the base of my lamp. If I weren't so nearsighted, I would have seen them sooner. I thought about my ex-husband for a second—the joke he used to make when he lost his glasses. I could hear Jimmy's Okie accent echoing through my head. *"I can't find my glasses without my glasses."* I smiled a little at the irony, even though by now, it was a cliché.

Snatching my spectacles from the base of the lamp, I placed them carefully over my eyes. *Sweet relief...* I was utterly helpless without them. My eye doctor once told me that without corrective lenses, I would be legally blind. I thought briefly about the old days before most people had access to spectacles. Good thing this was modern times. And thank goodness my sight was correctable... After watching the world focus around me, I could finally breathe...

Before moving forward, I glanced at my wrist, scanning the place where a watch was supposed to be. This made me think of my mother. When I would ask her for the time and she wasn't wearing a watch, she'd say, "A hair past a freckle." I eventually understood the joke, but when she first told it, I was only four and found it confusing.

Chuckling to myself for forgetting that I wasn't wearing a watch, I looked up at the clock. It was 10:20 p.m.

I have this ritual that I often perform when I wake up, even from the shortest nap. I try to calculate in my head how much time I had been out. I did some quick math in my head. *Okay... We left Walmart at 8:30 p.m., and we got home at 9 p.m. I lay down and stewed in my brew for about twenty minutes before I passed out. That's 10:20 minus 9:20. So... I was out for about an hour. Not bad for a nap.*

For a moment, I begrudged how exhausted I was. I needed another so-called "crash day"—one of those days when I did nothing but sleep. I needed to catch up, but there was no time. Everything I was doing was too important. I had to...*had to* find him. *I had to find Osama bin Laden.*

I grabbed my laptop and headed to the living room.

Slouching on the couch, I crossed my right leg over my left to hold up the laptop. This would work. Within seconds, I was joined by Midnight, who was trying his best to get me off the computer. His furry little body was making it difficult to type. Well, I say little, but he was kind of big for a cat. For some reason, when people came over, they'd comment about how fat he was. But he didn't seem overweight to me. He just looked healthy. Like Peter, he was high-normal. Now me... I was *fat*. But, not Midnight.

Midnight kept encroaching on my space, purring and walking over my keyboard as I attempted to ignore him. I tried to type as he planted himself on me. His black fur was soft on my hands. It felt nice. But damn it, I had work to do! I was undeterred by his attempts to distract me. Unconsciously, I gently pushed him to my left side and petted him into submission. It was nice to have company.

Finally settled, I anxiously opened *SYSTRAN Translate* and chose the input and output languages.

It was my go-to when I needed high-level accuracy. Although it wasn't as convenient as *Google Translator*, I trusted the results a little more.

Next I typed *"seahorse"* into the interface. The word transmuted into a series of indescribable squiggles. *Perfect!* ... It was Arabic.

I copied and pasted the script into Google. The results were overwhelming. There were hundreds of hits, most with pictures, lovely pictures—so many color varieties... Before then, I had only seen the skeletal remains of black seahorses. But these were different. They spanned a huge spectrum. Many were yellow, red, or even rainbow-colored. Some could even *change* color for camouflage. Where would I begin?

I started clicking on a few links and translating them using *Google Translator* because it was convenient for website translations. Although seahorses were quite fascinating, I became frustrated because I wasn't finding anything helpful.

What was I looking for, anyhow? What was I expecting to see, bin Laden's favorite seahorse? I mean, *really?* ... Where was this going? ... But I kept pushing myself. My energy seemed boundless. Research was my thing, and I was good at it. One day, I would use these skills to obtain a master's degree in history. After graduation, my university would even let me keep most online library privileges. But in that moment, I had no training and limited resources. There were no academic journals, no extensive news databases—just me, Google, and the same grit and determination I'd used to get my house.

Finally, a couple of hours into my quest, I found an interesting article from CNN-Arabic. The Google translation was inferior and hard to follow, but what I got out of it mattered more than the intent of the original article.

Apparently, there were plans to build a seahorse-shaped group of resort islands off the coast of Bahrain. Like the manmade island resorts being constructed in Dubai and Qatar, Bahrain's seahorse-shaped island chain would be dotted with hotels, luxury homes, shops, and promenades.[65]

This would result in the destruction of coral reefs that sustained marine creatures, including seahorses. The developers were killing *seahorses* to build a clump of islands that honored seahorses!

But when I read the article in 2006, the irony was lost on me. Like I said, the translation was poor. All I could get out of it was that the seahorses off the coast of Bahrain were in danger and perhaps even dwindling in population.

Although essential details were obviously lost in translation, I had what I needed to move forward: the clue I was searching for. Maybe bin Laden was worried about the seahorses off the coast of Bahrain. Maybe he'd chosen them as his mascot. The blue color of his seahorse image looked a lot like the color of the sea where the resorts were to be built.

The plight of the seahorses off the coast of Bahrain seemed like a cause a super-idealistic person like Osama bin Laden would care about. I thought about him for a second. *Was* he more idealistic than his followers? *Yes...* Most certainly. He was their leader, the idealist who built more idealists by radicalizing vulnerable individuals. A true cult leader, he led people to his beliefs, his vision of a utopian world where Allah ruled and everyone followed a fundamentalist interpretation of the Koran. Perhaps in this world, he'd hold a high position. Maybe through fighting his holy war, bin Laden could somehow make this happen for all generations and bring down the "evil" Western empire—aka, the US—through his jihad. He believed that somehow this relatively small band of religious zealots could, through violent acts of terror, change the world for the better.[66] If this wasn't extreme idealism, nothing was.

I knew these types of people. Idealists take on causes and become activists. And in this particular case, they became the violent ones I mentioned earlier. Some activists champion a single issue, while others champion many. These types of people sometimes care more about nature than human beings. Perhaps Osama bin Laden was one of those people who carried the mantle for more than one cause. It was even possible that he cared more about seahorses than the people he eagerly sacrificed to his terrorism efforts. Perhaps by picking an image of a seahorse for his profile pic, bin Laden was paying homage to those regal creatures and/ or trying to raise awareness about their plight.

But maybe not... I mean, it was a stretch—a leap of faith. It didn't matter though. The seahorse was my only clue, and I had nowhere else to go. This was my assumption: If bin Laden lived in Bahrain, he'd be more likely to care about the seahorses off its coast. So, that location was a possible starting place. Yet as far as I knew, Bahrain wasn't known as a hotbed of terrorism. *No...* Bahrain was a wealthy, modern nation—a sparkling island surrounded by a turquoise sea that attracted millions of tourists every year.

So once again, I turned to MySpace. I decided to

search for pages that were similar to Boussora's and bin Laden's. I looked for simple, unadorned profile pages with zero friends (even Tom) and few comments, if any. In addition, the profile pic had to be a sketch of a pop-culture item, like the Corvette, or something meaningful, like the seahorse. Finally, the user had to have an open profile, available for public viewing and instant messages.

I scoured MySpace for pages that met these criteria, this time focusing on people from Bahrain. I surmised the features of a typical Al Qaeda operative after skimming several RewardsForJustice profiles. Then, I browsed to the MySpace search engine and plugged in Bahrain as a location, along with an approximate age range, gender, and body type.

I spent the next several hours sifting through thousands of hits, profiles of young or middle-aged men living in the area. Several perfectly matched the pattern I was searching for. This was enough to make me think there could be a group of Al Qaeda operatives hiding in Bahrain. Most importantly, the results of my query were enough to keep me moving forward in my search for Osama bin Laden. If other terrorists were in that country, he could be, too.

Although the evidence was shaky, it was a start. With nothing else to go on, I would try to locate bin Laden in Bahrain. I initiated a search by looking for online white pages. Maybe I could find a listing under one of his known aliases. Then, I would finally have a real, usable name, unlike The Director. Plus, I would have an address. I'd finally know where he lived. I could only hope such a directory existed.

I went back to Google to look for the white pages,

feeling my adrenaline surge, when—

What?!

I felt something rough and wet on my left arm. I looked down. I was being licked. *Oh!* ... Midnight! I had been petting him the whole time I'd been reading the article, without even realizing it. What a sweetie. He was trying to return the favor by grooming me.

I started stroking his fur lovingly, this time aware of what I was doing. I briefly wondered if Midnight could sense my anxiety and exhaustion. Maybe he knew I needed him. Maybe he sensed what was coming.

27

THE DIRECTOR-Y

Despite Midnight's advances, I was desperate to get back to the hunt for Osama bin Laden. But before I could reach for the keyboard, I felt my stomach wrench. Oh my God, *I was starving!* I had no idea how long it had been since I'd eaten.

I took a moment to pet Midnight's head and play with his ears. Then, after giving him a big kiss on his furry face, I got up slowly, which was the signal for him to leap off me. I set my laptop on top of a stack of bills on the coffee table and headed into the kitchen. There was no fruit nor yogurt. There were no honey buns. I had eaten them all. There was nothing I wanted, so I went back to the bedroom to look for Nicki.

She was lounging on the bed, playing *Neopets* on her laptop. I addressed her with a camped-up sweet, syrupy voice, "Hey, sweetie...honey...*baby*..."

Nicki was immediately suspicious. She shrugged, grumbling sardonically, "What do you want?"

"I'm really hungry, and we don't have anything good here."

Nicki agreed. "I know. We need groceries. *Somebody* made us rush out of Walmart without finishing our shopping."

"Yeah, I know."

"So, let me guess... You want me to go to the store." It's true. Sometimes I would guilt her into going alone.

I could hear an annoying whine in my tone. "No. Going to the store would take too long. I'm hungry *now*. I was actually hoping you could go pick something up."

Nicki replied coyly, *"Maybe..."*

The timbre in her voice meant she was interested and would probably do it.

But my hunger was making me impatient. *"Please...* I'm starving!"

Nicki didn't resist. "Yes, what do you want?"

"I was thinking Whataburger."

Nicki grinned at me. "Get out of my brain! I was thinking the same thing."

We both let out loud chuckles.

"Are you coming with?"

"No, I just made a major breakthrough. I can't stop. I was hoping you would go get it."

Nicki seemed disappointed, so she tried to add a caveat. "What do I get out of it?"

"All my lovin'."

Nicki mock-resisted. "Hey. *No fair...* I get that anyhow!"

"Okay, you get a kiss." I leaned over and gave her a peck on the cheek.

Nicki gave in. "Okay, what do you want?"

"The usual."

Nicki knew what I was talking about. "So, an A-1 Thick and Hearty Burger and a large chocolate milkshake?"

"Yeah! Get the meal. I definitely want the fries! And get everything large, including the milkshake. I'm so hungry, I'm about to gnaw my arm off for sustenance."

Nicki grinned. This was something we said a lot. She also used to joke that if we were ever stuck on an icy mountain, starving like the Donner Party,[67] I could eat her.

Regardless, Nicki wasn't surprised that I ordered so much food. She was used to me eating a lot at once, especially when I was stressed out. The burger I was ordering was double meat, the fries were ginormous, and the large chocolate milkshakes were Texas-sized—a whopping forty-four ounces! I couldn't wait, especially for the milkshake. Chocolate and sugar were my heroin. They never failed to relax me.

"What about the kids?"

"I'll go see if they're awake."

I went and peeked inside the kids' doors. Hmmm, they had crashed. After all, it was 2 a.m. Of course, it was summer, and there was no bedtime, so all bets were off. I just hoped they wouldn't wake up and wonder why we were eating Whataburger without them. I went back to Nicki and gave her the news.

"They're asleep, but I feel like you should get them something in case they wake up."

"Are you sure?"

I was insistent. "Yeah... I would feel terrible if they woke up hungry and smelled fries, only to discover we didn't get them any."

Nicki nodded in agreement. In a few seconds, she was out the door.

***

By the time Nicki came back with the food, I was so starved that I was almost willing to eat the can of Hormel chili that had been shoved in the back of the panty for over a year. It was the most disgusting variety I'd ever tried. Texans are super picky about their chili. As far as the canned variety, I'd normally only eat beanless Wolf Brand. Regardless, if I wasn't getting Whataburger, the Hormel crap would have been in my future.

She took off and was back an hour later. *Thank goodness... She was finally home...* I grabbed the food and sat at my usual spot across the table from her. Within ten minutes and with minimal conversation, I had finished all of it.

Better...

I was a bit more relaxed, but I was anxious to get back to my computer. *Where was I?* ... The seahorses in Bahrain...right...*Bahrain...* Yes... I'd been looking for a directory. I told Nicki I was going back to work and frantically headed back to my laptop.

Slumping on the couch with my fingers at the keyboard, I began surfing the web. For a moment, I could hear Adam's words echoing through my brain: "*Remember. Google is your friend.*" Yes... Where there was Google, there was hope. So, of course, I started with Google.

It took a while to find a directory. The search terms were getting progressively more complicated, and I have no idea how much time had passed before I finally discovered it. However, it really didn't matter. The time flew by when I was in the zone.

Finally, I found InfoSpace.com, which provided

content and services, including directories. From there I found Infobel, an international online database in which people's contact information is listed. From there, I found a Bahrain email directory. Of course, this wouldn't lead me to where bin Laden was living, but it would help me pinpoint whether or not he was in Bahrain. And if I found an email address, it could open the door for a reverse email search somewhere.

I stared at the page. Okay... If bin Laden lived in Bahrain, maybe he was using one of his known aliases—hopefully, one that would get me further than The Director.

I slowly went through the aliases. The process was very similar to hunting for bin Laden on MySpace. I worked my way down the list, copying and pasting various names and trying them with different combinations and omissions.

Humming softly as I worked, I was absently aware of a weird mix of "Hey Jude" and "Row, Row, Row Your Boat" playing in my head. Ever since I'd discovered music in junior high, I constantly had an earworm. Sometimes, snippets from a single song like "I'm So Tired" from The Beatles' *White Album* would be stuck in my head for days, drowning out much of the noise around me. Back then, I was aware that there was a tune in my head. But by my thirties, the never-ending music was more subconscious. And I would often hum along without being aware of it, especially when I was concentrating. The humming was even more frequent when I was anxious or under stress. In this case, I was humming because of all of the above. This was a tough time in my life, and I think music was my mind's way of trying to ease the tension.

Continuing to hum, I looked down at the list of aliases once again. I had made it to number seven: "Hajj." *Hmmm...* This name was simple—one word, no iterations... There had to...*had to* be something here. I was desperate. The next and final alias on the list was The Director. I knew that one would get me nowhere.

So, with little recourse, I was eager to give the name, Hajj, a try. It was so short that I didn't bother to copy and paste. I put my fingers on home row and typed the letters manually: *"H-A-J-J."* There were around a half-dozen hits, but none of them were just "Hajj", by itself.

Regardless, I quickly fixated on a single entry— the only one spelled with an "i" at the end. It made me shudder: "Hussain7 Hajji." It seemed suspicious. I mean, Hussain had the number seven after it, which was jarring compared to all the other listings. None of them had numbers, so this one stuck out. *But what was the point?* ... What was it supposed to mean? It wasn't even really a name. How was I supposed to work with *that?*

But there was more: For me, the name "Hussain" conjured up images of a haggard Saddam Hussein after his capture. Could bin Laden have picked this name out of a sense of solidarity with the besieged former dictator of Iraq? I mean, the spellings— Hussain and Hussein— were different. But did that matter? ... I thought about it for a minute. Although bin Laden didn't associate himself with Saddam Hussein, he might have seen the US interference in Iraq and Hussein's subsequent treatment, as a grave injustice.

So Hussain7 Hajji quickly became my prime suspect. *Yes...* If any of the Hajj listings were bin Laden, this would be it.

Then there was the alias, itself. "Hajj" or "Hajji" weren't normally used as a last name. And Hajji was more like a title. I Googled it. The background was quite interesting: "Hajj" is actually the name of the pilgrimage that all good Muslims are supposed to make to Mecca at least once in their lifetimes. After they complete the journey, they're given the title "Hajji" with an "i", which can be added to their first name. So the word had very real spiritual and cultural significance in the Muslim world. I could see why a religious zealot like bin Laden would be drawn to it.

But on the other hand, it was such a common title that including it as part of a name in a directory would seem almost ludicrous. It would be practically equivalent to putting "Sister" or "Brother" in front of the names of all baptized Christians listed in our US white pages. It just wouldn't be done.

Yet here I was, with the name Hussain7 Hajji. What was I supposed to do with this information? Like I said, it wasn't even really a name.

Satisfied that he could be bin Laden, I looked down at the email address. *Damn it!* ... The email address was partially starred out. Maybe Hussain7 didn't want to be found.

Honestly, what was next? I couldn't call the FBI with a name like Hussain7 Hajji and no location other than somewhere in Bahrain. Plus, I wasn't even 100% certain I had the right guy. *Garbage!* ... I needed more... I needed something concrete.

I was frustrated, but undeterred. So I started searching for other directories, maybe something with more relevant information.

Three hours later, my mind was dry-heaving

thoughts. I was so incredibly tired of Google. The process had been tedious and nearly fruitless. More than thirty hours after I had begun my hunt for bin Laden, all I had was some super-shaky evidence, based on a sketch of a blue seahorse and an unsubstantiated guess that he *might* be in Bahrain. I was utterly stuck and exhausted. I had to stop. I couldn't think anymore, and sleep was collecting in my eyes, making it difficult to stay focused on the screen.

I slammed the laptop shut, disgusted.

I looked at the Star Trek Enterprise clock on the wall. It was 5:30 a.m. I had done it again. I'd been up all night. Heaving my body off the couch, I dragged myself to the bedroom. Stopping by the bathroom first, I popped two sleeping pills and plopped down in bed next to Nicki, fully clothed. I was too tired to even take off my bra or jeans. Nicki had been asleep for hours.

28

STARVING FOR ATTENTION

The next morning (well, it was really noon, so *my* version of "morning"), I grabbed my glasses and sat up in bed. I found myself staring at the candelabra my Aunt Elizabeth had given to me three Christmases ago. Half the votives were red and the other half, green. I was only vaguely aware that they were covered in dust.

Three of the candles were burning. Nicki had apparently lit them while I was sleeping. She was lying in bed next to me, listening to music on her iPod Touch. When I tapped her on the shoulder, she unplugged one of her earbuds.

I looked at her and addressed her with a sultry tone. *"You lit candles."*

She replied in kind, *"Yes."*

Lighting them often meant she was in the mood.

I kept going. "Does this mean you're—"

She knew where I was going, so she interrupted me. Her response was anticlimactic. "—No. I just took a big dump. I was trying to spare you the smell."

Ewww... That was *not* what I wanted to hear. I

snapped back at her. *"Not sexy!"*

She gave me a huge grin. "You wanted to know."

Ugh . . . I guess I *had* asked. "Yes, but that's not exactly what I wanted to hear."

Nicki kept going. "Love me, love my poop."

Oh jeez...

I quipped back, *"What* did I marry?" Well, we weren't exactly married. It wasn't legal in Texas yet, but saying it was good enough for us. Besides, we had registered as "domestic partners" in Austin—a privilege that allowed Nicki to get the cheaper, in-state tuition cost at UT.

I was ready to move on from the candles and the smell. "I'm getting up. Do you want me to blow out the candles?"

"No, leave them on. I'll get them later. They're kind of nice." I giggled a little to myself. It was funny how technology had changed our lexicon. I mean, we left candles "on" rather than "lit."

After hitting up the kids' bathroom, (I certainly wasn't risking going in ours), I dashed to the kitchen and got a big bowl of Cheerios. This was one of my least favorite cereals, but I was desperate. I cursed myself for leaving Walmart early the other day: *Man, I wish we had bananas!* When I was feeling energetic, I liked to cut them up and add them to my Cheerios and dump in a pile of sugar. This made the bland circles more palatable. I guess I'd have to settle for sugar without bananas. *Sigh...*

When I finished eating, I still had sugar-infused milk left over. When I was a kid, there was always so much sugar left over in the bottom of the bowl that I would dig it up with my spoon and say I was diamond mining—referring to the sweet crystals. But there were no "diamonds" this time, so I just added some more cereal to the mixture and ate more.

At that moment, Peter walked into the room with a large comforter draped over his head. Even though it was August, I always kept it cold in the house because I was usually hot. Back then, I unapologetically called myself "The Air Conditioner Queen." It didn't bother me even a little that the rest of the people around me were normally cold, even in August.

Peter looked at me a little sad. "Hey, did you eat the rest of those?"

I opened the box and examined its contents, pulling open the plastic lining. "No, there's a little left. See?" I showed him the inside of the box.

"That's nothing! I'm *hungry!* Why'd you eat the rest of it?" In that moment, Peter eerily reminded me of his Dad. He seemed to be emulating a higher-pitched version of Jimmy's man-whine. *Ugh...*

I cringed, but I felt guilty. I was depriving my kid of the last of the cereal. "Oh man, I'm so sorry. Is there anything I can get you?"

I felt like I'd stolen food from my child, something that was a limited resource. For the second time that day, I cursed myself for leaving Walmart early. *Damn it! ... I should have just stuck it out. Why did I always do this? This wasn't cool. We need more food. I needed to do better.*

In a moment of panic, I regretted all the long hours I'd spent looking for Osama bin Laden and others. I was neglecting my children. They needed their mother, and they needed easy access to sustenance. Why was I such a bad mom?

I flashed back to my own mother—remembering

something she had done since I was little. When there wasn't that much to eat in the house, we would whine at her. *"Mom, there's nothing to eat!"* But instead of expressing her internal guilt, she'd get defensive. Agitated, her eyelids would begin fluttering nervously and her face would turn bright red. Then, she would lift her hands and start counting on her fingers while laundry-listing every morsel we had left in the house.

"What do you mean, we don't have food?! We have eggs! We have milk! *We have cereal!"* She would continue her litany *ad nauseam* until we stopped her. And when I grew up and became a teenager, she'd add, *"We have food!* We just don't have any convenience foods, and *you're too lazy to cook anything!"*

I mean, she wasn't wrong. When I was in high school, I never cooked or made any food that took effort. Regardless, after years of hearing Mom's tirade, it became so predictable that as soon as it began, my little brothers and I would start laughing. In the end, I would give in and reluctantly scrounge for something I didn't particularly want—maybe a small Red Delicious, the only type of apple she ever bought. When I was a kid, I thought those were the only type in existence. *Boring...*

So in 2006, when Peter started complaining that there wasn't enough food in the house, I channeled Mom's guilt and frustration. Feeling panicked, I spit out a list of things for him to eat.

But Peter was disgusted that I'd polished off the cereal.

"*Mom!* We need to go to the store! There's no yogurt. No bananas. No *apples!"*

"No. Actually, we bought yogurt when we went to

Walmart"

"You *know* what I mean. We need food."

I kept going, being progressively more defensive. "*I know*. But at least I got your favorite flavor, peach. Sorry, it's not the fruit-on-the-bottom kind. We can only get that at Kroger."

"Yeah. Thanks, I love peach yogurt." He dropped his comforter and went over to our magnet-and-picture-laden refrigerator to grab one.

"And I think there's still a couple of spaghetti bags left in the freezer if you want one." Nicki used to make a big pile of spaghetti and meat sauce and divide it up in single portions. She'd stick them in freezer bags for the kids to thaw out when they wanted a quick meal. It was one of their favorite foods.

"Cool!" Peter reached up and started rummaging through the freezer section. "I don't see them."

"Yes. I think a couple got shoved to the back."

Peter dug deeper. "I still can't find them. I don't think they're there." *Ugh...* He was so helpless!

"Hang on. I'm pretty sure they're still in there. I'll get them. Give me a second." I snapped up from my chair and headed for the freezer. I took out a few things, reached in the back, and pulled out two spaghetti packets. I had found them in like three seconds. *Typical...*

I thrust the packets at Peter. "*Here!* ... God, you're lame! They were right where I said they were. They were in the back, behind the frozen peas.

Peter probably felt kind of stupid. "Thanks, Mom... Sorry."

I softened a bit. "Tell Daun she can have the other one. I promise we'll go to the store soon."

Peter seemed to feel a little better. "Yeah, I know.

Thanks."

He then swung around, opened a cabinet, and pulled out a large blue bowl. My kids were very familiar with how to use a microwave.

A few minutes later, while Peter was waiting for his spaghetti to heat up, I headed toward the living room and my laptop. But first, I stopped by Daun's bedroom, which was only a few feet from the common area, to see if she needed anything to eat.

I swung open her door and looked in. She was lying on her stomach reading a *Magic Tree House* book. "Hey, how's it going?"

"Just reading."

I sighed. Even if I had trouble keeping food in the house, at least my kids loved to read—even Daun with her dyslexia. It made me feel like a good mom. At least I was doing *something* right.

I addressed Daun, who had set her book down. "Which one is it?"

"It's the one with the volcano."

Wow... One I was *actually* familiar with. "Pompeii? Didn't I read that one to you?"

"You started it, but you never finished."

I felt a little guilty, so I quickly changed the subject. "What have you eaten today?"

Daun replied politely, "Not much, but I just woke up an hour ago."

"Okay... Well, there's still a spaghetti packet left if you want it. I found a couple in the back of the freezer. There's also yogurt. But sorry, we're almost out of Cheerios." I wanted to make sure she knew we still had food. It was imperative to me that everyone knew they had access to sustenance, no matter how limited the choices.

"*Awesome!* I'll get some spaghetti when I finish this chapter. I don't like Cheerios that much anyhow." Her favorite had always been Cinnamon Life.

Meanwhile, the sensation of the Cheerios in my stomach didn't last long. It had been a meager meal—a snack, really. But it had to be enough. There were few other choices. And besides, I needed to go back to work.

Time passed quickly as I continued my relentless search for bin Laden.

But several hours later, I felt my stomach lurch and begin to grumble again. I looked at my watch. *Damn!* ... It had been at least eight hours since I'd eaten—since *anyone* had eaten a meal. But who needed food? I needed to lose weight, anyhow. Unfortunately, my stomach wouldn't let me ignore my most basic need any longer. I found myself stumbling into the kitchen and opening up the refrigerator door. I stared in for a few seconds, saw nothing of interest, and closed it in disgust. Once again, I regretted leaving Walmart early.

Man... We needed to go to the grocery store. But I wasn't ready to go back to Walmart or even Kroger. I needed to finish what I started—my search. I was so close to finding bin Laden, and I wasn't ready to stop yet.

I grabbed a Diet Mountain Dew out of the fridge and headed for the living room to look for Nicki. She was sitting in the recliner staring at her laptop.

I decided to get her attention. "Nicki!"

She startled, snapping her head up from her laptop. "*What?*"

"I'm starving and we don't have any good food here."

She slammed her voice at me. "Yes. I've been saying for days that we need to go back to the store!" It seemed the lack of food was getting to her. She was probably, what we call today, "hangry."

I found myself whining at her. Like the other day, when I begged her to pick up Whataburger, I needed a quick fix. "Yes, but I'm hungry *now*. I don't wanna wait for a trip to the store."

"Okay, then what do you suggest? We can't just keep putting it off!"

But I was persistent. "I really don't wanna leave the house. I'm really close to a breakthrough."

"You always say that. You always say you're close to a breakthrough."

"But this time I really am. This is important. I can't stop!"

I didn't want to tell her that I was close to finding bin Laden. I knew how absurd it would sound.

Nicki pushed the subject. "Okay, then what should we do about dinner?"

I made a mundane suggestion. "How about we just order a pizza?"

About that time, Peter came running out of his room and hollered enthusiastically. "Did you say pizza?"

I guess he was hungry, too. He normally didn't get this excited about pizza. We ordered it so much that it had become kind of boring.

Then Daun poked her head out. "Pizza seems good to me too. I'm hungry!"

Once again, I felt the gnaw of guilt. I was still neglecting my family. *For the love of God,* when was I going to make myself stop all this and go to the store?!

I scanned the room, looking at the hungry faces of

Nicki, Peter, and Daun. It was worth the money, even though I was low on credit. We needed to eat.

"Alright, we'll do pizza. What does everyone want?"

We spent a few minutes negotiating toppings, then I picked up the landline and quickly punched in the digits without thinking. I had the Domino's number on mental speed-dial.

Finally, I let out an audible sigh of relief. Help was on the way.

***

When the pizza got there, I gobbled down six slices in about ten minutes, not even stopping to taste the pepperoni or jalapeños. In the end, all that was left was a hint of cheese and spice floating around in my mouth. But my stomach felt better, albeit overly full. Pizza was easy to binge on, especially if I was starving.

But I wasn't starving because of a lack of money. I still had credit, at least for the time being. My mind simply wouldn't let me stop working until my stomach started raging at me. And because of my mounting obsession, this hadn't been a typical dinner. Usually, we'd all sit around and have a conversation during and after the meal. And during most meals, I would sit silently for the first ten minutes while I mindlessly gobbled my food, vaguely listening to everyone else talk and *actually* enjoy their food—food that I had barely tasted. When I was done eating, I would participate in the conversation. Ordinarily, it was fun and often silly. But this time, when I finished eating, I didn't stop to talk to Daun, Peter, or Nicki. I was too busy obsessing. I knew I was close—very close. Stopping to eat was like torture, albeit necessary torture.

After guzzling down the rest of my Diet Mountain Dew, I picked up a crumpled napkin and wiped my mouth one last time. Scanning from Daun to Peter and finally fixing my gaze on Nicki, I made a special request. "Do you mind if I take off? I need to get back to work."

I probably missed a look of exasperation on Nicki's face as she shrugged her shoulders and replied in a flat voice, "I guess..."

Nicki and I had only been together for three years, though we'd known each other for eight. I wouldn't figure out until years later that that "I guess" really meant "Yes, I do mind." So, oblivious of her true feelings, I got up and rushed off to the couch, grabbing another Diet Mountain Dew on the way. I needed caffeine. It was going to be a long night.

29

INSPIRATION POINT

I slumped on the sofa, flipped open my laptop, and opened the fresh can of Mountain Dew I'd brought back with me from the kitchen. As with dinner, I hardly tasted it. I chugged it in a few gulps, crushed the can, and tossed it toward the small trash bin in front of the bookcase. However, this effort was futile, as it bounced off the other empty cans in the overflowing basket and landed with a *plunk* on the floor, joining the rest of the deluge of garbage. I shrugged my shoulders and moved on, glancing at my screen.

Before I got started, I scanned the room, searching for Midnight. Moments later, I spotted him, sleeping contently on his little blue bed under the coffee table. *No companion this time. Just me.*

Settling my hands on the keyboard, I went back to the Bahrain directory and typed in *"Hajji"* once again. There it was: Hussain7 Hajji–that elusive name–with no place of residence, just a partially redacted email address. There would be no reverse email search. What was I supposed to do next?

I scratched my head. *Flakes...* I usually had terrible dandruff, which was no doubt triggered by stress. I had a bad habit of picking at it, especially when I was concentrating.

I stared blankly at the screen. The caffeine wasn't enough. I needed another brain boost. I plugged in a set of cheap earbuds and opened *Media Player*, setting the volume to high. I selected The Beatles' *White Album*—my favorite. I had ordered a special extended version from Russia a while back. *Ugh...* I hated the extra tracks, which were rough studio takes with a lot of annoying snippets of dialogue mixed in. To me, putting the raw crap at the end of the list wrecked the integrity of the album.

So I clicked on the playlist I had created to exclude the "bonus" tracks.

Better...

I waited for the blaring, familiar music to drown out any extraneous thoughts and distractions. I was finally ready to go. Then...

Boom! My intuition kicked in.

Why didn't I see it before? *Hussain7!*

Of course! ...

It was a screen name... *It looked like a screen name!*

I frantically typed *"H-U-S-S-A-I-N-7"* into Google, and...

There it was! ...

"Hussain7" called up a couple of forum websites that were almost entirely in Arabic. I clicked on the first one and used Google to translate the page. As the translation lay bare before my eyes, I entered the hidden world of Al Qaeda.

***

It was not unlike passing through the tunnel that leads to Inspiration Point (Tunnel View) at the entrance of Yosemite Valley. First, there's a long stretch of darkness, then a sudden burst of light... As you emerge from the tunnel, a breeze blows in from the distance, and stretched out before you as far as the eye can see is a fantasyland of mountains and waterfalls—the most breathtaking sight in the world, at least to me. It was akin to Dorothy exiting the wreckage of her crashed house and entering Oz. Everything is black and white, drab. Then she opens the door and music starts playing as she steps over the threshold. Suddenly, everything is alive and in Technicolor.

Seeing the translations for the first time was *that* dramatic, bringing me the same rush—the same flood of emotions. Before my eyes, the website had gone from a dull page, written in a language I had no hope of understanding, to a rich pocket of invaluable information. I was anxious to get started.

The first page—the one I'd just loaded and translated—contained the term *"Hussain7"* in the descriptor text. It was Shabablek.com.[68] I examined the scripts. *Interesting...* It was a profile for a user going by Hussain7. *Aha! ...* I was right. Hussein7 *was* a screen name... *Nice!*

Next, I carefully scrutinized Hussain7's profile for anything relevant. I was hoping to find out more about him, maybe a place to start. Reading the page was a tedious process because I was going slowly so I wouldn't miss anything. Working my way left to right, line by line, down the page, I finally reached the bottom right-hand corner. By that point, I'd almost given up on finding anything useful. Then, there it was, in his personal data, something that gave me hope: a location. Hussain7 was claiming to be from Bahrain! *Wow...* A location! This, I could work with. He was also claiming to be a professional soccer player. *Interesting...* And his birthday was listed as August 1, 1974. Of course, if Hussain7 was Osama bin Laden, most—if not all—of the information on the profile would have been fabricated. But the fact that Hussain7 was claiming to be from Bahrain, convinced me, 100 percent, that this "soccer player" was the same Hussain7 in the Infobel entry. After all, it had been in a Bahraini directory.

This knowledge was enough to propel my search forward. I mean, for God's sake, Hussain7 had basically attached himself to the name Hajj—one of bin Laden's aliases. Between that and the weirdness of using a screen name in a white page listing, Hussain7 became my prime suspect. I believed he might be Osama bin Laden, and the subsequent steps in my investigation relied on that assumption. But I needed proof, so I began digging deeper into Shabablek.com. I was hoping that I could also find more detailed location data.

The first thing I did on Shabablek.com was click the little red button in the upper-right-hand corner of the screen in the *Adobe Flash* banner. It was an icon of a house—the universal symbol for "homepage." After a few seconds, I was staring at a different, glitzier page. It looked professionally put together. On the left side of the banner was an animated *Flash* cartoon silhouette of a smiling man waving a Syrian flag. This created a sense of Syrian pride and nationalism. *So...okay...this was a Syrian website.* And based on the imagery, I was expecting some political discussion. I was right... As

I examined the translations of the topics and posts, it would become evident that many of the threads focused in that direction.

On the surface, Shabablek seemed like an ordinary social site—a place for people to meet and share ideas. In fact, the main feature was message boards with massive amounts of threads covering a large variety of topics. It would be easy for a group like Al Qaeda to hide within its threads and communicate in coded language.

Yes... Message boards. I could work with that. I was very familiar with the format, having participated in several forums in the past. In fact, Nicki and I had met in the late '90s through the AOL "Lesbian Coming Out Forum" and its connected chat room. In other words, I knew my way around these types of sites—sites like Shabablek.com. More importantly, message boards meant human interaction, maybe even communication amongst terrorists and their sympathizers.

It was about 4 p.m., and I was ready to dig deep into the threads. I felt exhilarated. I was finally getting somewhere. This was what it was all about. This was exciting. But was Hussain7 *actually* bin Laden? Could I prove it? More importantly, could I use information off the site to figure out his current location?

But the board was different from any I had ever encountered because it was in Arabic. However, I was undeterred. I guessed it would work the same as the English language ones I'd experienced, and I was right. Despite the awkwardness of the translations, I was easily able to follow the site's mechanics.

I began reading eagerly, struggling at first to follow the results of Google's translation. Reading Google's broken interpretation of Arabic reminded me of how

Mom described reading Chaucer's *Canterbury Tales* for a college class. The professor assigned it in its original form: Middle English. In the beginning, to her, it seemed a lot like word salad—words she felt like she should understand, but couldn't quite grasp. But after reading the *Canterbury Tales* for a while, she started to get a sense for it, and it became easier. She could mostly understand what was happening.

Like Mom reading Chaucer, I was eventually able to understand the bad translation from Arabic to English a little more easily, while extrapolating enough data to keep me going. My initial thought was that I could find some more details about his geographical location. Maybe that would tell me where to search for Hussain7, and I could look for another, more detailed, directory.

I was hopeful and enthusiastic, at least at the beginning. But after spending several hours sifting through the threads, I began to realize that I was looking for a needle in a haystack. Although the contents were fascinating, I had found nothing leading to Hussain7's residence or proof that he was bin Laden.

Maybe later... I would go back to Shabablek.com later. I was certain it would prove useful. But not yet...

So I decided to move on to the other website that came up in a search for Hussain7: QatarFootball.com.[69]

Like Shabablek, the focus was on message boards. The first thing that stood out to me was its aesthetics. Unlike Shabablek, this site was super simple and most likely created by an amateur web designer. There was no fancy *Flash* media, and the pages were completely devoid of glitz or glamour. In other words, it was basic and unadorned—nothing like MySpace.

As with Shabablek.com, the images on QatarFootball.com were steeped with a sense of nationalism. A large drawing of a soccer ball in the upper-left-hand corner featured a maroon, white, and black soccer ball with the shape of the Qatar Peninsula proudly displayed on it. Plus, the entire site was decked out in that same shade of maroon—the dominant color of the country's flag.

Regardless, on the surface, QatarFootball.com seemed like a legitimate soccer site. And it probably was. *Mostly...* But I soon discovered that parts of it were likely being used for nefarious purposes.

I glanced at the topic list. Each section was headed by a sketch of a tiny version of the Qatar flag-themed soccer ball. Interestingly, the board was extremely active, with hundreds of thousands of posts. I would have never expected a Qatari sports site to be this popular. I mean, the entire Qatar peninsula had a population of only 1.01 million in 2006. Hundreds of thousands of posts? *Really?* ... How many soccer players and enthusiasts could there be in this tiny country? Plus, the site had only existed for four years.

Despite this, the sections seemed pretty normal for a soccer message board. There were topics about the World Cup and the Youth Cup, and a section devoted to sports other than soccer.

But there was something weird: The most popular section was under the group heading "Forum Rules." On most message boards, this was a standard section designed for new members and introductions. It was also normally one of the least traversed. So, why was "Forum Rules" so popular? As I thought about this point, something caught my eye: a very popular subtopic under the thread that felt out of place. It was called "Away from

Sports." The description was poorly translated, but I got the gist of it. *"To discuss public issues, local issues, and open dialogue away from sport but with a sporting spirit."* This meant politics! Could Al Qaeda communications be hiding there? *Maybe...* I started skimming through some of the threads, searching for anything suspicious.

But as I struggled through the multitude of political posts, I quickly began to feel overwhelmed. As with Shabablek, trying to find anything relevant seemed nearly impossible. *No...* I had to narrow my query somehow. What I actually needed was more specific information about Hussain7. Although the discussions were fascinating, they were getting me nowhere. I decided to explore the website further and go back to the topics later.

Finally, after about twenty minutes of clicking buttons, I stumbled upon a useful search engine. It allowed me to check for any threads that Hussain7 had participated in. *This was great...* I could try to get into his head and figure out what he was all about. I quickly searched the forum for his screen name and dozens of threads came up, most of them located in "Away from Sports." My thought was that this guy must be really into politics.

And I was right.

Most of discussions Hussain7 had participated in or initiated were about local topics. But there was something that stood out about one of his threads: At least on the surface, it seemed to be about sports, but it was placed in the "Away from Sports" section. *Interesting...* Why would he post about sports in "Away from Sports"? It wasn't logical, which made it suspicious. I would have to dig deeper.

In that particular "Away from Sports" thread, the participants, including Hussain7, wrote about a group of four soccer team members, training in secret. But here's the thing: Why would only *four* of them practice in secret? Why not the whole team? I wondered if the reference to a "training session" was really code for an "*Al Qaeda* training session." I thought about the infamous camps in Afghanistan, other Middle Eastern countries, and Pakistan. That could be it. They could be talking in code to plan Al Qaeda operations.

Interesting...

Another point that stood out was that Hussain7 himself, and others, referred to him as "the commander," which can also be translated to "the leader" or "the captain." It could have meant he was a soccer team captain. But to me, the designation "commander" sounded similar to "The Director." And we all know who the "commander" of Al Qaeda was: bin Laden himself.

Years later, I would consult with a professional Arabic translation expert. Apparently, the words for "director" and "commander" are not an exact match in Arabic, but for my purposes, they were close enough. Besides, like I said earlier, it was suspicious that there was a discussion about sports—a soccer team practice— in a thread that was specifically titled "Away from Sports."

But although I thought it showed compelling evidence that Hussain7 was bin Laden, this information didn't get me any closer to finding his current alias or location. And as I worked, I found myself becoming increasingly frustrated. I had been at this–the hunt for bin Laden–for days, only rarely taking breaks, although I was at least getting some sleep thanks to the magic of sleeping pills. But I had to keep going. I was so close. I could feel it... I clicked yet another link...

Argh! ...

I felt a sudden rush of pain in my gut, like my bladder was going to explode. I realized for the first time that I had been holding my pee for hours. And at that precise moment, the discomfort had become unbearable. I was about to lose control! I clenched hard, grabbed my laptop, got up, and ran to the bathroom.

About an hour later, I was still on the toilet hunched over my computer.

Suddenly, there was a knock on the door.

It was Nicki. "How much longer?"

I was startled. Why was she up? Oh my gosh, the time... I glanced down at my laptop. It was 8 a.m. I'd been up all night. I shrugged it off and addressed my partner.

"Hang on. I'll be out in a minute!"

Five minutes later, she began to lose patience. "Come on! You're taking *forever*. I need to poo!"

"Okay. Hang on. I'll be right out!" Reluctantly, I finished my business, grabbed my laptop, and exited the room.

Nicki glared at me as I brushed past her. *"Jeez!"*

I headed back to the living room and plopped down on the couch. It was more comfortable anyhow. If only I had thought to grab another coke. *Oh well...*

Time to get back to work...

I was back on QatarFootball.com, completely stuck. I had spent hours sifting through the tens of thousands of questions, comments, and tirades. Yet I still didn't feel like I was any closer to finding Hussain7's location or even a usable alias.

I had to keep going...

I went for another few hours, sifting through large quantities of text until my eyes began to burn. Rubbing them, I realized that dried congestion was building up. I dipped my forefinger into the plastic cup full of tap water that was sitting next to me and used it to clean out my eyes.

Better...

Sitting up straight and stretching, I took a deep breath, held it for a few seconds, and released it. There had to be more... I had to think... As usual, this would require caffeine.

Not wanting to stop working, I turned to Nicki, who was in her easy chair. "Hey... Any chance you could get me a coke?"

"Sure. What kind do you want?"

I chuckled inside. Nicki was finally learning to speak Texan. She knew I didn't necessarily mean Coca-Cola. It had taken her years.

"Mountain Dew."

After a brief pause, Nicki got up to get my soda. I took a long swig of water while waiting. I was really thirsty.

About thirty seconds later, she returned with a cold Mountain Dew. *Caffeine for the win!*

She handed it to me. "Here." Wow... It was freezing. *Perfect...* I loved my drinks really cold.

"Thanks." As usual, I was genuinely grateful.

Nicki took a moment to check up on my progress. "How's the research going?"

"I don't want to talk about it."

Based on her response, I must have seemed exasperated. "*Why?* Is there something wrong?"

I practically screamed my reply, sounding frantic. "I

don't know! I've been at this for more than twenty-four hours straight, and I feel like I'm banging my head against the wall!"

Her face dropped a little, settling into a look of concern. "Well...what are you going to do?"

"I'm just gonna keep working for now. I think I'm close, *really* close. But I'm missing something, maybe something simple." I lurched my hands toward the mouse and keyboard, set down my coke, and stopped short of placing my hands in position. I glanced anxiously at my screen and then back at her.

After a short pause, something clicked in Nicki's brain. "Well, you seem to be pretty anxious to get back at it. I'm gonna go back to my book."

I nodded and mumbled under my breath, *"Yeah..."*

Ordinarily, I would ask Nicki what she was reading, but I was too preoccupied, too focused. I needed to get back to work. As my right hand caressed the mouse and my left one hit the keyboard, I forgot for a moment that anything or anyone existed but me and my computer screen.

After our brief interaction, I felt a little better. I grabbed the Mountain Dew on my right, popped it open, guzzled half of it, and immediately let out a loud, satisfying *hiss*—a ritual I'd followed since childhood. It was an imitation of the satisfying noise made by the man in the 1970s Nestea commercials. He'd take a long sip of instant iced tea and let out a long hiss before stretching out his arms and plunging backward into a large swimming pool. In a way, I was about to take the Nestea plunge. The water would be refreshing like the Mountain Dew, but also shockingly frigid.

30

EYE OF THE TIGER

More than twelve hours later, I was still at it, taking only occasional breaks for food or other necessities. I had been searching for Osama bin Laden for about thirty-eight hours straight. I was utterly exhausted, and I was beginning to wonder if I was wasting my time.

I mean, if I wasn't going to succeed, I had to give up at some point. And I was very close to doing just that. I could hear Kenny Roger's voice in my head, belting out his hit, "The Gambler:"

You got to know when to hold 'em
Know when to fold 'em
Know when to walk away
And know when to run

It was that kind of moment... Do I walk away or do I run?

But I knew I couldn't fold. *No*... I was too stubborn. I never ran from a challenge...

My mind flashed back to my mother's words. I was

in fifth grade when I came to her and begged her to let me quit softball because I wasn't any good at it and was constantly being teased. But Mom wouldn't have it. She looked at my tearing eyes and pushed me with her words. "No, Barbara. You're not going to quit because *you're not a quitter!*"

So I was going to do it. Come hell or high water, I was going to find Osama bin Laden. My mind was set.

Two hours later at 3 a.m., my hope, but not my determination, had started to fade. I was tired...*so tired... so exhausted*. But I had to keep going. This was my moment. I could feel it.

Finally, something clicked. Why was I beating my head against the wall? Some say that insanity is doing the same thing over and over again and expecting different results. That was the problem! I needed to break the cycle. Reading the QatarFootball board was clearly getting me nowhere. I was running around in circles, chasing my tail.

The midnight oil was slowly burning away, time was wasting, and I felt stuck. So I did what I always did when I was stuck on a computer repair problem: I turned to Google. Adam's words reverberating in my head for the *n*th time. "*Remember . . . Google is your friend.*"

I returned to the familiar search engine and typed "*Hussain7.*" Maybe I'd missed something. Once again, I saw the first hit on the screen: Hussain7's Shabablek profile. I paused for a moment, drawing a deep breath. What the heck? I thought I'd take another look. Maybe there was something there.

As the page slowly materialized on the screen, I squeezed my eyes together tightly. Under my breath, I groaned a desperate prayer: "*God, please help me find him...*" Then ...

BOOM! ...

My eyes popped open and fell on something I hadn't noticed. Was that a link to Hussain7's ICQ instant messenger profile? Why hadn't I seen that before? But there it was, right in front of my nose. Like with all the keys I'd lost and then found in the past, this final clue–the ICQ address–seemed to have popped up out of nowhere. I clicked the link with anticipation...

Aha! ...

There it was:

A name. A name! *A name!*

Ali Hussain. It wasn't one of bin Laden's normal aliases. If Hussain7 was, in fact, Osama bin Laden, then this was the name he was currently using. Now that I had a name, maybe I could finally find him. Suddenly, the tiny spark of hope I had for locating bin Laden ignited something in my soul, which bursted into a roaring flame.

If I knew then what I know now, I might have been discouraged. In a recent Google search, I discovered something interesting. There is, in fact, a Bahraini soccer player with a similar name: Husain Ali. However, the first and last names are reversed and the birthdates don't match; they are off by seven years and several months. Plus, the spellings were different. I consulted the same Arabic translation expert who had helped me sort out the meaning of "commander." Apparently, although the names, Hussain (double "s") and Husain (one "s") are the exact same in Arabic script, the Romanized versions vary by region. In other words, the differences in spelling indicated that the two men were from completely different areas. Based on this, the name reversal, and the wild variance in birthdates, I came to a conclusion: It seems obvious to me that bin Laden was unconvincingly borrowing from Husain Ali—the soccer player's—name and occupation. This probably gave bin Laden a false sense of security.

But back in 2006, I had never heard of Husain Ali and even if I had, I might have come to the same conclusion. There was no stopping me. The Texas Cyclone roller coaster had made it uphill and was coasting downward quickly. I figuratively raised my arms and let out a scream. I was ready for the ride. *Here I go...*

Now that I had a name, I knew what to do with it. I would use it to uncover bin Laden's location. I turned to a detective site I'd joined—a sleazy one that didn't require a license. They would let *anyone* access their database for a fee. Regardless, after typing *"Ali Hussain"* into its search engine, I got a long list of email addresses. If one were registered under the name Ali Hussain, perhaps I could do a reverse lookup somewhere and find his place of residence. I would make a note of any suspicious-sounding email addresses so I could try that method.

The first suspect used an address with the word *"commander"* embedded in it. Could this be Hussain7? Its original form was in English. In other words, it was not an Arabic translation, so I didn't need to worry about any major conflicts between the meaning of "commander" and "director."

But the owner of the email wasn't located in Bahrain, where I thought bin Laden could be hiding. That didn't rule him out as the correct Ali Hussain, but his location made it seem less likely.

I kept going...

While continuing to sift through several more pages of email addresses, a single entry stopped me cold. *This Ali Hussain was living in Brooklyn... Wow! ... Brooklyn,* where I'd found Boussora. This was it... *I knew it!*

I mean, if I had found one Al Qaeda operative in that area, surely there could be others—even bin Laden himself. Maybe he was hiding in plain sight, in the last place on Earth most people would expect him to be: Brooklyn, New York, minutes from Ground Zero.

This guy *had* to be Osama bin Laden!

I felt it in my bones...

I immediately went to the US section of the detective website and searched for Ali Hussain in Brooklyn. There it was: multiple addresses for the same individual with the same birthday.

Ominously, some of these listings predated September 11, 2001. My stomach turned with a sick feeling as a dark thought crossed my mind: *What if bin Laden was there when it happened—when the Twin Towers fell?*

I remembered a *Washington Post* article that came in the wake of 9/11. Apparently, a few hours after the jetliners crashed into the buildings, the FBI had detained and questioned several Muslims in New Jersey. They had allegedly been holding tailgate-style parties on rooftops in Jersey City while watching the devastation at a safe distance.[70] Maybe bin Laden was celebrating with his followers, from his own rooftop in Brooklyn, as the towers fell.

Disgusted at the image, I decided to move on. These dreary thoughts weren't going to ruin this moment for me. *I was so close...*

I pushed forward, picking up my momentum again.

Eagerly, I navigated to PeopleLookup.com. Now that I knew bin Laden was most likely in Brooklyn, I had to get a verified address, a current one. As before, this would cost me. I once again found myself pulling out one of my last remaining credit cards.

I nervously paid PeopleLookup for an address verification and prayed for confirmation that Ali Hussain (bin Laden) lived in Brooklyn. I crossed my fingers as the page slowly loaded. The "thinking" of the search engine seemed suspended in time. *Damned DSL.* It was taking forever. *Come on! ...*

Finally, I felt a wild rush of adrenaline wash over me like a tsunami. There it was, written in red, below the location of Ali Hussain: *"Confirmed Current Address."* Under a phone number were other words, also in red: *"Confirmed Current Phone."*

With those mundane words, I had just found the world's most wanted terrorist.

31

CALLING IT IN

I pushed the backlight on my digital watch. *Damn!* ... It was after 6 a.m. I had been up all night again, and it had taken me a full forty-two hours of near nonstop effort to get to this point.

I was nervous and excited all at once. But I was also filled with questions: What was I supposed to do, call the FBI and tell them I found Osama bin Laden? They would think I was crazy! Hell, even *I* thought I could be crazy. Was this even possible? Could I really have just found bin Laden on the internet through a series of hunches?

But I could feel it: Somehow, I knew I was right. I was 95 percent certain I had just found Osama bin Laden. Call it intuition. Call it whatever you want. It happened.

But I was scared—scared to pick up the phone. I closed my eyes and breathed in and out slowly. *Ten counts in...ten counts out...* I followed every breath while the moments passed. Slowly, my mind turned back to bin Laden.

I had to...*had to*...force myself to make the call.

I reached for my Nokia and started to key in the familiar digits. As with all other important phone numbers, I had the Houston FBI's memorized. I didn't believe in autodial. It would dull my mind...

A few seconds later, I cleared the digits. My hand was shaking. *Could I do this?* How could I just call an FBI agent and say, "I think I found Osama bin Laden."? I mean, what a thing to say. It sounded nuts...

Another twenty seconds passed... I reached for the phone again and punched in the sequence. This time, I held my breath for a moment and reluctantly hit the "call" button. It rang twice, but before the call could connect, I quickly hung up and cleared the number. This time, I snapped the phone shut and disgustedly slammed it on the coffee table as if it burned to the touch. It took all my power not to chuck it across the room.

I waited about thirty seconds and took another deep breath. *I had to do this...* Lady Macbeth's words flowed into my consciousness. I had played her in my acting class at St. Thomas. Lady Macbeth was trying to convince her husband, the general, to murder King Duncan and take the Scottish throne. In that moment, I uttered her words, *"Screw your courage to the sticking place."* I often thought of that line when I was trying to muster up the courage to complete a difficult task. This was one of those moments. The information about bin Laden was too important to sit on.

I tried to calm myself. I needed to be strong. *Come on, Barbara... You've got this.* You *have* to do this. You *have* to call. What if it *is* bin Laden and you never reported it? ... He needs to go down... I glanced at my watch: 6:10 a.m. Now or never...

To hell with it...

I picked up the phone, punched in the numbers again, and hit the "call" button for a second time.

The phone rang three or four times before a very nice-sounding male agent picked up and greeted me. I introduced myself as the one who turned in the terrorist in Brooklyn, and asked for the duty agent. I was immediately patched through.

A sedate agent with a mild Houston accent answered the phone. As with all the other agents I'd spoken to, he was polite and professional. But, how was I going to tell him about bin Laden?

I tried to focus. *Think, Barbara...think.* Don't blow this.

I introduced myself and tried to be nonchalant. "I'm not sure how to say this."

He tried to reassure me. "It's okay. Just say it."

But I still wasn't ready. Shaking slightly, I let out a shallow sigh. "I'm afraid you might think I'm crazy."

The agent spoke to me with a soothing voice. "It's not my business to judge. I'm in the business of sharing intelligence, wherever it comes from."

Those words made me feel better. My tips were considered *intelligence*. This meant that they—this man—valued my input. I felt like I could do this.

"I think I..." Taking in a long breath, I readied myself to make a leap of faith. "I think I might have found Osama bin Laden."

Despite the unusual nature of what I had just said, the agent remained calm and professional, and seemed unsurprised. "Okay, where do you think he's located?"

He quietly took down the information without questioning where I got it. I told him I would follow up with an email. The conversation went on for a full eight minutes before we gave our salutations and hung up our phones.

The call over, I sat behind my computer and pulled up *Outlook Express*. I would have to word the email carefully. I didn't want to sound foolish or presumptuous. Looking back on that day, I failed at both.

I was definitely overconfident. I began reworking it a bit, trying to get the right wording. *"This is the name and address I found for..."*

No... I deleted the line and started over. I needed to hedge more. I wasn't 100 percent certain that the man I found was him.

"I believe this individual may be Osama bin Laden." I kept writing, and at the end of the email, I copied and pasted the address and phone number from People-Lookup that included the words *"Confirmed Current Address"* and *"Confirmed Current Phone"* for his landline. I nervously clicked "send" and followed up with a call to let the duty agent know to look for the message. I got through on the second try.

There... It was over... I had done my duty.

I sat there for a couple of minutes, worrying, mulling over what had just happened. It seemed surreal. Was this really happening? Had I really found the most wanted man on the planet? Was this even possible? Had I lost my mind? But beyond the self-doubt, I was pretty sure I'd just turned in the location of the monster behind 9/11. More than anything, I was elated, thrilled.

I felt a mad desire to pounce on Nicki, to wake her up and tell her. But it would all be really confusing to a half-asleep Nicki. *No...* I wasn't sure enough that I'd found him. What if I *was* losing my mind? I needed to discuss this with her when she was awake and rational. Besides, Nicki needed her sleep. At least one of us should be rested.

I thought of an old Sucrets commercial. Barbara, a ruffled-looking middle-aged blonde woman, is fast asleep when she begins hearing a repeated plea from her husband, who is next to her in bed. His voice gets a little louder with each repetition of his mantra: "Barbara, you up? Barbara, you up?! *Barbara, you up?!*"

Barbara looked and sounded mildly annoyed.

"I'm up *now!*" She then offers her husband aspirin and Sucrets, adding a plug for the items. She closes the scene playing solitaire in bed, exasperated.

"At least one of us can sleep!"

That was that. I was a little envious of the fact that Nicki could sleep. I longed for rest, but it wasn't forthcoming.

Regardless, an important concept crossed my mind as I considered waking her to tell her the news: *"Let sleeping Nickies lie."* It was my take on the expression, *"Let sleeping dogs lie,"* or like I always said when my kids were infants, *"Let sleeping 'babies' lie."* If I woke her up, she'd only growl at me, like a California black bear. It was pointless.

I vaguely considered going to bed. But I was so keyed-up that I couldn't possibly stop what I was doing. I had *way* too much adrenaline pumping through my veins. *No...* I wasn't done. I kept going over the call in my head, recounting every word of the conversation. Did I do well? Did I miss anything?

But my thoughts quickly turned to the next project. I couldn't stand it. I felt like I was going to explode. Now that I knew some of America's most wanted terrorists were in Brooklyn, I felt like it would be easy to find them. I *had* to try out my new system using the Brooklyn parameter.

I retraced the process I'd used to locate Boussora and went after Jamal Ahmad Mohammad Al Badawi, a co-conspirator responsible for the bombing of the USS Cole, who had escaped from a Yemeni prison earlier that year.[71]

As before, I searched for a matching alias on MySpace for an individual whose nearly-blank profile matched the pattern of bin Laden and Boussora's pages. Once I found a viable name and MySpace, I would try to find that person's address. Any locations in Brooklyn were suspect, even if I couldn't get an exact match with the MySpace profile. I could only assume that most operatives, for the sake of anonymity, wouldn't use their real address when signing up for an account. Boussora was the exception. I guess he hadn't been smart enough to give a fake residence.

Yet even during my search for Al Badawi, something was gnawing at me. I couldn't stop thinking about the PeopleLookup reports from earlier. There was so much information on them. One contained lots of confirmed addresses of other residents in bin Laden's apartment complex. I thought some of these people might be affiliated with him. It could be a hotbed for terrorists. Another report listed Ali Hussain's (bin Laden's) previous residences. If it were the same man, this record was proof that he had been living in Brooklyn a few months *prior* to 9/11. And what if other terrorists had moved into these locales? What if they were Al Qaeda safe houses? The FBI might be able to use this list to catch more terrorists.

After a while, I couldn't stand it. I sent a couple of emails to the FBI that contained copies of some People-Lookup hits. But this time I didn't call Houston to tell them about the emails. I was anxious to get back to the search for Al Badawi. *I was so close.* No... I would just call everything in at once. Finally, having given in to my urges, I was back on the trail. More sifting through directories, a quick address confirmation and...

Nearly twenty minutes later everything was set. I had a confirmed address in Brooklyn that matched with one of Al Badawi's aliases. Compared to finding a bin Laden suspect, finding an Al Badawi lead had seemed almost too easy. I quickly emailed the FBI then made the call.

Satisfied, but exhausted, I glanced at my watch one last time: 7:20 a.m. *Wow!* ... This was late, even for me. Not confident that I could sleep, I popped two sleeping pills and headed for bed. I was excited by the success of my new system and wanted to keep implementing it, but I had to make myself wait. I needed to rest.

There would be more time to work tomorrow.

32

THE RACE

August 12, 2006: I woke up feeling exuberant. I turned on the lamp, grabbed my glasses, looked up, and checked the time. It was nearly 1 p.m. *Six hours of sleep... I'd done worse...* Not enough, but better than most nights... Thank God for the sleeping pills. I bounced out of bed and into the living room. I couldn't wait to tell Nicki what had happened. I scanned the room. She was sitting in her recliner.

I plunked down on the couch next to her.

"Morning!"

"Morning." Nicki replied without hesitation, despite it being afternoon. As usual, she knew what I meant.

Then after a short pause, she added, "You seem pretty chipper." She wasn't used to me waking up in a good mood.

"Yeah. I feel great. I've got some really awesome news!"

"Really?"

Nicki seemed intrigued at first, but instead of listening intently, she got up from her recliner and headed toward the kitchen.

I shouted toward her, "*Hey!* I was trying to tell you something!"

I guess she'd gotten desensitized to all my "important" announcements. I had to laugh at myself. I was literally "the boy who cried 'wolf.'"

"I'll be back in a second. I'm just going to get some coffee. You can still talk. I'm listening."

But I knew she wouldn't be listening, at least not carefully. "I'll just wait until you get back."

"Okay."

Coffee sounded nice. Maybe she'd get me some. "Hey, would you mind getting me a cup, too, while you're in there?"

"I'm already on it."

Nicki came across slightly annoyed that I thought I had to ask. She was usually pretty considerate, especially when it came to food and drink. She loved to surprise me with a cup of coffee, and she knew exactly how much creamer to put in it. It was always perfect. She made the best coffee. Sometimes I would try to get her to make us a pot by appealing to her sense of pride. I would say, "Can you make the coffee? You make it better than I do. Mine always turns out too weak or too strong." This was only half true. But I suppose it always tastes better when someone else makes it.

But this time, the coffee was already brewed. A few moments later, Nicki handed me my favorite mug—the one with the disappearing/reappearing TARDIS.

"Thanks, honey."

Coffee in hand, she sat back in her chair and looked at me. "So, what's new?"

I took a cautious slurp of my coffee, careful not to

burn my mouth. I could feel my heart racing as I told Nicki the news. "I think I found Osama bin Laden!"

"What? Really?! *How?!*"

I recounted my process in detail, laying out every step.

Nicki was thrilled. After listening with rapt attention, she finally replied, "Well, did you call the FBI?"

"Yes. I called last night." It had technically been that morning, but she knew what I meant.

Then I told Nicki about the conversation with the agent. She seemed particularly intrigued when I recounted his words about sharing intelligence wherever it comes from.

Then Nicki asked an obvious question: "Are you going to tell the kids?"

I thought about it for a few seconds. "Not yet. I'm gonna wait until I know for sure. I don't want to get them all excited."

Nicki nodded. "Makes sense."

For about an hour, we went over the events of the last couple of days *ad nauseam.*

The biggest topic of the conversation was about the agent's "sharing intelligence" comment. We kept going over his words and analyzing them. We both felt these words were validating. Clearly, the agent valued my input. Why else would he call it "intelligence?" For that matter, why would the FBI even bother to take my calls if my tips were utter nonsense? No. I was on to something. My system was working. I could feel it.

At some point, Nicki continued talking as my thoughts wandered somewhere else. Something was gnawing at me. I wanted to get back to work. I was confident my system was effective, and I couldn't wait to use it to find more terrorists. The thought of it was thrilling.

At this point, I grew impatient and stopped Nicki mid-sentence.

"Hey."

As usual, she hated being interrupted. "*What?!* I was talking!"

"I'm sorry, honey, I'm really anxious to get to work. But *please*, what were you saying?"

Nicki tried to verbalize her thoughts, only to realize she was drawing a blank. The moment was gone; she gave up. "Never mind. I can't remember..."

I resisted the urge to say, "*Then it must not have been important.*" Nicki hated when people used that as an excuse for someone else's forgotten thought. It was a bad habit I'd picked up during my years with Jimmy. However, with Nicki, even when the words "*it must not be important*" crossed my mind, I never verbalized them. I didn't want to draw her ire.

Moments later, I finally managed to break away from Nicki. I practically ran to my PC tower in the bedroom, where I could be alone. I didn't want any distractions. It was going to be a long, exciting day.

***

I worked feverishly throughout the afternoon and evening, implementing my new system. I fell into a pattern as I worked my way down the RewardsForJustice list: I would use my system to find a suspect, then I would email the FBI, sending the current alias and address. Minutes later, I would follow up with a phone call to make sure they got the information.

I felt like I was running a race with no clear finish line. I didn't think I'd stop until I'd turned in a suspect for every listing on RewardsForJustice.com. Once I got started, I found it nearly impossible to stop. I was too focused on the work. I only took breaks to eat or pee. I was unstoppable, working straight through to the next morning.

However, there was one notable exception. The entire time, a single thought kept creeping into the back of my mind: Did I *really* get bin Laden? I needed to know. I needed to find out somehow. So, a few minutes after calling in my first tip of the day, I started rapidly dialing random FBI field offices in the Houston, New York, and Washington, DC areas. I even called other government centers, including the Department of Homeland Security and the White House. I was desperate and felt compelled to reach out. Thirty-five minutes later, I had called eight different numbers.

Finally, I was satisfied that no one knew anything. I had no recourse but to reenter the race. From that moment on, my work was completely unfettered. I kept up a wild sprint straight through the night and into early morning, calling the Houston office several more times with various terrorist tips.

And no one in the FBI seemed annoyed by my repeated calls. They just kept calmly taking my tips. The very fact that they weren't rejecting them spurred me on. Why would they have a screener if they put calls from just any crackpot through to the duty agent? I could only come to one conclusion: They didn't see me as a crackpot. I was on to something. My tips were helping, and this thought was the impetus for continuing my work.

In fact, I didn't just *think* my tips were helping; I *knew* they were helping. At one point, I called the FBI for the express purpose of asking about this. In a brief conversation, I had asked a mild-mannered agent, point-blank, "Are my tips helping?"

His response sounded well-rehearsed. "I can't confirm nor deny that."

I was a bit exasperated. "Then how am I supposed to know if I should keep going?"

Then, he started spouting off policy. "Information is only given on a need-to-know basis." I cringed. Was he really implying that I didn't need to know? ... *Me?* ... I was the one calling in the tips!

However, before I could protest, the agent kept going. "You can't ask a direct question. You'll never get an answer." Then he gave me the advice that would serve me well during the days to come. "You have to hedge. Say something like, 'Can I be optimistic that my tips are helping?' "

With those sage words, I decided to try it. "Okay, well. Can I be optimistic that my tips are helping?"

His response floored me: "Yes, you can."

I couldn't believe my ears! I had gotten actual feedback from the FBI, and I was doing well. My tips were helping bring terrorists to justice!

Flabbergasted and unable to think of what else to say, I hollered, "Thank you so much!" and quickly got off the phone. I would have to remember this advice!

I didn't know it then, but in a few days, I would use this tactic to find out that there were plans for the president to make an announcement.

Incredibly, by August 13 at 5:39 a.m., I had turned in five suspects, including Osama bin Laden—all within a 24-hour period. Their profile pics were fascinating: a beach ball, a sand castle, a boom box, and, of course, the seahorse—no photos or human beings, all sketches.

And during the final tip—Abu al-Masri—things had really got interesting. At 5:40 a.m., I was patched through to the duty agent. A mid-toned man calmly answered the phone. I carefully laid out the tip, primarily pointing to the email I'd just sent them. I was certain the call would be quick, like most of the others. But this time, something was different. Unlike most of the agents I'd spoken to, this agent wanted to keep the conversation going. He started prodding me and asking a lot of questions, none of them relevant to the current tip.

The entire time, the agent addressed me in the same calm, tempered manner that I frequently heard from his colleagues. But I could also hear something in his tone that I hadn't heard before. *Was it?* ... Yes... It was curiosity.. He was interested in me, my methods, and my motives. There was no other reason for him to ask what I was about to hear.

A few moments into the conversation, the agent asked an earnest question: "So you think you found the 'Big Guy?' "

I stammered for a second while I thought about what he meant. *The Big Guy?* Oh, yes... He must have meant bin Laden. The Big Guy at the head of Al Qaeda—the man worth $25 million. He wanted to know if I thought I had found bin Laden!

"Yes, but I'm not 100 percent certain."

He continued with a string of questions. "So you think he's in Brooklyn?"

"Yes. I think so."

The conversation continued for quite some time.

His voice was serious and professional, with a hint of fascination. As we talked, sometimes his words were cryptic, like when he called Osama bin Laden "The Big Guy," and other times he was clear and direct in his language. In other words, like all the other agents I'd encountered, he often spoke in code to protect his oath of secrecy. This is why he used the name "The Big Guy" instead of "Osama bin Laden." I was certain that finding bin Laden would be Top Secret and that mentioning him by name would be a breach of classified information.

The agent continued his line of questioning, and the next one floored me.

"So, are you psychic?"

Psychic? Wow... Where did *that* come from? ... But he wasn't joking. He was dead serious.

My mind flashed to television shows like *Medium* and *Psychic Detectives* that featured people who used supernatural methods to help law enforcement find missing people, murderers, and serial killers. *Fascinating...* He thought I was one of *those* people? At first, I felt he might be playing with me. But what happened next convinced me that he was not.

"No," I answered flatly. (I wasn't psychic.) My heart started pounding again. Why was the agent asking me that? I scrambled for a reason. Maybe if I had found bin Laden, it was the only explanation he could fathom. What I had accomplished must have seemed unreal, if not impossible.

Then, his next words nearly flattened me to the floor. "So, how did you do it?"

How did I do it? Do what? I must have accomplished something! Did I actually find Osama bin Laden? Was that possible?

Shaking slightly, I answered honestly about my methods. "I just research things on the internet."

"Then I think you're a gifted researcher." The agent was echoing words I had used to describe myself in an email I'd sent before calling in the Boussora tip.

Gifted researcher? If I was a "gifted researcher," that must have meant I found something... Of course! ... *The Big Guy!*

After a little more banter, the agent asked another unexpected question: "So, are you doing it for the money?"

Wow... Not only did he want to know how I did it, he wanted know my motives. In my mind, there was only one reason he would ask that: He thought I could get money—the $25 million. But this wasn't at the heart of what I was doing. The reward was only a vague consideration at that point.

Again, I was frank about my motives. "I was at first, but now it's more about catching terrorists and finding justice for 9/11."

The words he spoke next made me feel proud: "Then I think you're a true patriot."

Did he just say that? This was the biggest compliment that a federal agent could give me.

Altogether, the call lasted a full twenty minutes—the longest exchange I'd ever had with an FBI agent. And it hadn't been a normal conversation. It had been more like an interview with a member of the press. Maybe someday I'd be answering these same questions for CNN.

When I finally hung up the phone, I quickly thought over everything he'd just said: He asked me if I found The Big Guy. I said yes, and after a series of questions, he called me a "gifted researcher" and a "true patriot." My gears turned as it slowly sunk in... *Oh my God...* I think I *actually* found Osama bin Laden!

I wasn't crazy... I had done it. It was clear: I had found Osama bin Laden!

I couldn't wait to tell Nicki!

But, wait... *Damn!* ... She was asleep. I knew better than to wake her up—even for this. As usual, she would be grumpy and incoherent. *No...* This had to wait until morning. I had no recourse but to go to bed.

33

NEW YORK

I woke up several hours later, utterly exhausted. I had gone to bed on August 13, and it was still August 13. The last 24 hours had been wildly productive, but today I needed a break. Instead of working, I would spend the day discussing what happened with Nicki and watching CNN for any news about bin Laden. After all, I knew at that point that I had found him. It was just a matter of time before he was arrested.

But by the next day, August 14, 2006, I was tired of wasting my time watching the news and was ready to get back to my mission. I got up around 12:30 p.m., grabbed some coffee, sat down at my desk, and got back to work. Despite my rapid anti-terrorism efforts, I was still trying to keep up with some of my early cases. So I spent about a half-hour following up on my lead about the missing pregnant woman. I repeatedly called the head investigator, but the call kept going straight to voicemail. After an embarrassing amount of tries, I finally gave up, bored. It was time to return to the war on terror.

I transitioned back into it quickly, continuing my

way down the RewardsForJustice list and calling the FBI occasionally with tips and ideas. Then, a little after 2 p.m., something extraordinary happened: During a six-minute call to the Houston FBI office, the agent said something I wasn't expecting. He calmly made a special request: "From now on, we want you to call the New York office directly." Then he gave me the number to the New York FBI office.

Wow... The *FBI* was giving me *instructions!*

I was flabbergasted but tried to act nonchalant. "Okay. Do I just ask for the duty agent?"

He kept going, speaking in a clear, directive voice. "No. Actually, you need to ask for the Terrorism Task Force and give *them* the information."

Terrorism Task Force? There was only one reason they'd tell me to call that department. They must have been finding terrorists based on my tips.

Some skeptics have said to me that maybe the Houston office was tired of me and wanted to pass the buck. But here's the thing: They didn't just tell me to call *New York*, they told me to specifically ask for the *Terrorism Task Force*. This meant something, and I knew from my dealings with the FBI that it was something huge. They wanted me to get my tips to New York faster. Not only did they want the information, but they must have been following up on my leads rapidly.

Plus, there was something else that stood out. Normally, if I called an FBI office that was not near me, I was referred to Houston. In other words, the Bureau usually tried to route people to its local offices. So, what they told me to do—call New York—broke from that, which made me feel special.

Before getting off the phone with the Houston

agent, I asked one more important question: "Should I also send the tip via email, like I have with your office?"

He replied affirmatively, "Yes. That'd be a good idea."

"So, can you please give me the email address for the New York office?"

My request was granted.

I got off the phone and continued to work at a fevered pace. About an hour later, I stopped and called the New York FBI to verify that I was going to be working with them. I introduced myself as the person calling in the Brooklyn tips. Then, as instructed, I asked for the Terrorism Task Force. I was immediately patched through.

The man who answered spoke with a fast-paced New York accent as he greeted me. But before giving out my information, I had to make sure I had the correct department. "Is this the Terrorism Task Force?"

The agent was matter-of-fact. "Yeah."

I explained who I was and that the Houston office instructed me to call them directly with any new tips.

The agent came across harried and a bit flustered. "We're really busy right now. Can you just call Houston for now?" I thought about it for a moment. Yes, they were probably busy because they were chasing down my leads. It was too much to be a coincidence. *Wow!*

A few minutes later, I called Houston. I explained to their screener that I was the one calling in the Brooklyn tips. The female agent sounded like she was snapping to attention. She punctuated her words with a sense of importance. "I have been briefed!"

Her tone seemed proud—proud to be a part of what was happening and to be in the know. My head spun a bit.

Briefed? Wow… So the screeners were being "briefed" about my calls? I guess they needed to know to put me through to the duty agent. This made what I was doing appear to be of significant value. They didn't want to miss my calls.

The screener promptly put me through. I conveyed to the Houston agent that the Task Force had told me to continue working with them for now. However, he was adamant that I needed to talk to New York directly. And he told me to try them again later. He would make sure they got the message. I guess the New York Task Force agent I'd spoken to earlier had *not* been briefed.

At around eight o'clock that same evening, I called the New York Task Force for the second time. This time, I informed them that I was going to send a link to Osama bin Laden's profile on Shabablek.com. From that moment forward, New York took my calls without question. This would continue for the better part of two days.

When I got off the phone, I excitedly went back to RewardsForJustice.net and picked another operative from the list: Ali Sayyid Muhamed Mustafa al-Bakri.

Determined, I navigated to MySpace and, as with the others, started copying and pasting al-Bakri's aliases into its search engine. The more I used my system, the easier it became. And the more the FBI encouraged me, the more fun I was having. The words of Dean Winchester in *Supernatural* come to mind: *"Saving people, hunting things, the family business."* I suppose there are similarities between the monsters in that show and the monsters who planned and executed 9/11.

Regardless, before I could get very far in my search for al-Bakri, I felt a tap on my shoulder. Spasming, I wheeled around, shaken. "Nicki, you scared the shit out of me!"

Nicki looked at me. "We need to stop and have dinner."

I knew what this meant. Nicki wanted me to help.

"What're we having tonight?"

"We were thinking, chicken. We haven't had it in a while and Peter requested it." Baked chicken thighs over carrots and potatoes was Peter's favorite meal.

"Sure, sounds good to me." I was a bit annoyed that she wanted me to stop everything and help prep dinner, so my next words came out a little snarky. "I guess you want some help with the carrots and potatoes."

Nicki was a bit annoyed, too. "Yes. You've been working all day. You should just come into the kitchen and spend some time with me."

Although her tone had more than just a small trace of annoyance, I knew she was well-meaning. Nicki was just as invested in my work as I was. Over the next several weeks, we would spend hours going over all the minute details of conversations with agents and fantasizing about what we'd do with the $25 million. *Yes...* Nicki was all in, but she knew that I needed rest, food, and family time, so I could maintain the energy to continue my efforts. In other words, she didn't want me to wear myself out. And I knew she was right. I needed to force myself to take breaks.

I finally replied to her question about dinner. "Chicken sounds good, as long as I don't have to wash the potatoes." I couldn't stand the feeling of dirty, dry russets on my hands. The texture was a feeling that, to me, was like nails on a chalkboard. I had the same problem with the sensation of touching peach fuzz or dry velvet. If I accidentally grazed any of those, or similar items, I would repel from it as if from a hot flame. *No...* I never washed the potatoes—and she knew that wasn't about to change.

Nicki gave me a knowing look. *"Of course.* We'll just get Daun to do it. Besides, she's really thorough." Daun knew how to use a vegetable scrubber. She usually got that particular job. Sometimes, she could be pretty meticulous.

Reluctantly, I agreed to comply with Nicki's request to join her in the kitchen. "One sec. Let me save this." Using my normal method, I opened *Notepad,* saved the name of the alias in a text file.

Slowly, I got out of my chair, climbed over a small pile of trash and dirty laundry that was blocking the path in the bedroom, and headed to the kitchen. *I suppose I could use a break...*

However, the break didn't last long. I continued working through the night as if lives depended on it— and maybe they did. I called in two more tips, including al-Bakri by 5 a.m. It felt a bit like I was a firefighter in a mad dash to pull as many people as possible out of a burning building. I was running on that kind of adrenaline and desperation. I had to keep going until I got them all—all terrorists on the list. I went to bed determined to make that happen.

34

FULL CIRCLE

But in just over a day, everything changed. After weeks of tireless detective work, August 16, 2006–the place our story started–finally came around. It was the day the FBI Terrorism Task Force in New York arrested Osama bin Laden. Sometimes I reflect back on the moment I found out about it.

It was around 10:30 a.m. when I called the Bureau to ask which terrorist I should go after next.

The agents had been playful, even *fun*, that morning.

Before their attitude could sink in, an agent in the background had hollered, "Is that the Green Lady?"

I was puzzled by the nickname, but before I could think about it too much, the original agent replied with gusto, "Yeah!"

I was put on speakerphone. A third agent, who sounded like he was going to burst at the seams, addressed me directly. "Ya got the lotto picks?"

I was stunned. Why had the agent asked me that? Did he think I was psychic? Maybe he couldn't fathom any other explanation for how I'd found bin Laden.

Maybe he was of the same mindset as the Houston agent who had asked me point-blank, "Are you psychic?"

In that moment, I maintained a serious, albeit puzzled, composure and told them I couldn't give them the lotto picks.

When the conversation ended a few minutes later, I hung up the phone, confused. It slowly sank in why the New York FBI Terrorism Task Force was so hyped-up: They had found and dealt with Osama bin Laden, and I was the one who'd given them his location.

Then there was Nicki; my excitement was her excitement. So, of course, she had been the first person I told. We spent nearly an hour going over the facts and everything they implied. Then we spent most of the day watching CNN, hoping there would be word from the president.

Around 10 p.m., I got impatient and called the FBI in New York one more time. I asked if I could be optimistic that there would be an announcement from the president.

The agent had answered that there would "definitely" be one as soon as their report was sent to Washington.

I hung up the phone, frantically called everyone in my family, and told anyone who would listen to watch the news. I didn't tell them why, just that the story was going to be huge and that it involved me. Next, I rushed to tell Nicki and the kids about the announcement. We put champagne on ice, determined to watch TV until the president came on the air.

Finally, Nicki and I had snuggled under the covers all night, watching CNN, fantasizing about the $25 million reward and waiting for the promised announcement. The champagne grew warm, the ice melted, and the announcement never came. I didn't bother to put the bottle away.

35

HOUSTON, WE HAVE A PROBLEM!

But even after the ice melted, I wasn't done. I wasn't ready to sleep. I crept out to the living room, careful not to wake up Nicki.

It was 5 a.m., and once again I was on the phone with the Houston FBI. I was immediately patched through to the duty agent. I introduced myself as Barbara Janik and quickly added my usual mantra about being the person calling in the Brooklyn tips. At some point, I had started regularly mentioning my name.

The man on the other end was polite and professional, a typical FBI agent. I wondered briefly if I'd spoken to him before. His voice sounded familiar. But despite this, something was different in his tone.

Before asking me what I needed, he paused briefly and followed with a slow, sincere statement: "Thank you for your tips." He never told me why he was thanking me, but it seemed obvious to me he was talking about yesterday's arrest.

I responded honestly. "I'm just glad I could help."

Then I told him the main reason for my call. "Please

tell Agent Miles to look for an email." It would be my last written communication to her. I was wrapping up some unfinished business before ceasing my detective work. Bin Laden would be my last case.

He promised to pass on my message, and then I threw in a quick question. "Do you know why there hasn't been an announcement?"

"I don't know," he answered frankly.

"Do you have any idea when there will be one?"

He didn't know the answer to either question, so I got off the phone. I needed a better plan. *Someone* had to know something, but I was too exhausted to chart my next steps.

Disappointed, I took my sleeping pills. As I fell asleep, a vague thought was swirling around in my brain: *Maybe tomorrow...* Miss Scarlett's iconic Georgia drawl from *Gone with the Wind* moved into my mind. I could hear her quivering voice as her world fell apart. *"Oh, I can't think about that now. I'll go crazy if I do, I...I'll think about it tomorrow..."* And then there were her desperate, hopeful words as the scene fades. *"After all, tomorrow is another day."*

***

I woke up in a panic after only three hours of sleep. When I realized there still hadn't been an announcement, I felt frantic energy coursing through my veins. Why would the president sit on this? When would there be an announcement? What if it never happened? I took a deep breath and tried to redirect my thinking. *No...* I'm probably just worrying too much. I should give it some time. I mean, he had to prepare a speech. Maybe they were still planning.

After all, I had just spoken to Houston a few hours before, and the agent didn't know anything. *What next?* I didn't want to bother New York. I needed to think harder. But first, I needed to feel better, less anxious.

More importantly, I had a strong desire to tell someone other than Nicki and the kids what had happened. I was bursting with excitement and I wanted to share it. *But with whom?* Which sibling or parent wouldn't freak out or, worse, tell me I was crazy? Who would have a calming effect on me? And who would have time to talk to me? I immediately thought of Lee. Even though I could relate more to my sisters, they usually made me feel worse because of their worrying and worst-case-scenario catastrophizing. *No...* I would call Lee.

I picked up my phone and punched in his number. It was just past 8:30 a.m., and I knew Lee would be awake. After a couple of rings, I was begging him in my head. *Come on, Lee. Answer the phone.*

A few seconds later, he finally picked up.

"Hey, Barbie." I winced but shook it off. *I hated that name.*

As usual, Lee's greeting was friendly and inviting. I could almost see a slight grin on his face as he spoke. He was a nice-looking, chiseled, and well-groomed individual who many considered metrosexual. He was also the spitting image of Dad in his old army photos, but with lighter hair.

"Hey, Lee. Got a few minutes?"

"Sure. Wow, you're up early." My family knew that I was rarely out of bed before noon. What they didn't realize was that this was a special occasion.

A few minutes later, I nervously told Lee what was going on. I told him about finding Osama bin Laden and the promise of an announcement.

He was predictably calm and collected. He never called me crazy. He just appeared to accept what I was saying as fact.

Then I told him how worried I was that there hadn't been an announcement yet.

Lee was so levelheaded that he tried to reassure me, rather than judge me. "You know, they just found out about the arrest. Maybe they've got to prepare speeches and stuff. Sometimes it can take a while to get things going in Washington."

I took comfort in his words. "Yes, you're probably right. But that doesn't stop me from worrying."

Lee kept going. "Just try to be patient. Give it some time."

After nearly twenty minutes on the phone with Lee, I felt slightly better and was determined to wait it out for a bit.

Not!

I put down the phone, but in a matter of minutes, I picked it back up and called Lee one more time. I needed more guidance. Lee tried to convince me to be patient. And after a lengthy push-back, I agreed to try. I'd just kick back and watch the news for a while.

However, my determination to wait only lasted about an hour. I was too worried and stubborn to take Lee's advice for long. *No...* I wanted to...*needed to* get more information somehow. But first, I needed a plan. Houston didn't seem to know anything. Maybe I could ask a source closer to the action: I decided to try the Washington, DC office.

I Googled the number and gave it a quick call. I didn't get past the screener. He acted like they didn't know who I was or what I was talking about. Maybe the Washington branch had not been briefed.

But at the same time, I knew this was BS. I was tired of messing around. I needed to call New York. *Yes...* They would probably know when there would be an announcement. They had been on the front line, so they were likely to be informed first. After all, it was an agent from that particular office who promised me there would be one.

When I reached the screener, I introduced myself. But this time, instead of asking for the Terrorism Task Force, I decided to talk to the screener. There was no need to bother the warriors from August 16.

However, when I got on the phone, the conversation took an unusual turn. I found myself being thanked once again for my efforts, this time by a grateful New Yorker. We had a friendly chat for more than five minutes. His appreciation felt like a warm hug, and I was grateful. Before I got off the phone, I asked him if he knew when there was going to be an announcement. But, like the Houston agent from hours earlier, he didn't know.

A few minutes later, I called Houston, hoping they would be willing to talk to me, to tell me more than New York had. Once again, I introduced myself. But like the call to New York, what came next was different than usual.

The screener didn't patch me through to the duty agent right away. Instead, she took a moment to talk to me. "Thank you *so much* for your tips." She sounded sincere and dewy-eyed, sentimental. I imagined her eyes slightly welling with tears as the words came out of her mouth. I felt touched. They were some of the most heartfelt utterances I'd ever heard. Echoing my earlier words, I told her I was glad I could make a difference.

A few seconds later, she passed my call on to the next person. I spoke at length with the duty agent. He didn't know about the announcement, but he took time to thank me for my tips. Then he passed the phone to another agent, who also thanked me. They were gushing with emotion, and I repeatedly told them how glad I was to help out. By the end of the call, I had spoken to about three or four agents. Although no one had any new information, one thing was crystal clear: I was being treated like a hero.

The call had lasted fourteen minutes—one of the longer ones I'd experienced with the FBI. I was overwhelmed with emotion as I got off the phone. Yet I soon began to worry. Why didn't anyone know about the announcement? What was the hold up? What if there wasn't going to be one?

I quickly tried the DC office again, followed by the Department of Homeland Security. Still unable to find out anything, I called Houston one last time before taking a break. I would just have stall for a bit longer. Like Lee said, maybe I just needed to be patient. Maybe the president needed time to prepare his speech.

I headed for the living room. Maybe I could kill some time watching CNN. Maybe there would be some hints about bin Laden, or maybe the president would make a surprise appearance.

But as I approached the couch, I noticed that someone was in my spot. Daun was stretched out, holding the remote. She was watching Animal Planet again.

Daun paused the show and looked up at me. "Hey! Did they make the announcement?"

I shrugged my shoulders. "No..."

I was feeling a little down.

"Really? Why *not?*"

I shrugged again, this time a little annoyed. "I don't know. But maybe they made the announcement while I was asleep. Mind if I put on CNN?"

I'm not sure why it didn't occur to me that I could simply check the internet for answers, but I guess I was so used to catching my news on Dish that an alternative didn't occur to me.

Normally Daun would fight me. She hated the news. Yet she knew how important this was to me—to us.

"Alright..." She sounded slightly disappointed. But then she said something logical: "I can just record it." *Of course! ... The DVR... I kept forgetting we had a DVR. Duh!*

***

After nearly two futile hours of watching CNN, it became evident that there had been no announcement about Osama bin Laden. If there had been, it would be dominating CNN's coverage. Of all the networks, they were the best at killing a topic.

Frustrated, I decided to pick up the phone again. I would call Houston one more time and ask if they knew when there would be an announcement. As before, there was no need to bother New York. They were probably really busy and might still be celebrating. Besides, like earlier, I wasn't even calling in a tip.

But as soon as the screener answered the phone, I

started feeling anxious. Something was wrong. I could sense it.

I introduced myself as usual, but the agent seemed tense. When I mentioned the Brooklyn tips, he acted like he didn't know who I was.

"I don't know what you're talking about."

My stomach sank. The man was lying. He knew damn well who I was and what the Brooklyn tips were. They all did. I spent a few minutes arguing with him, trying to convince him to patch me through. However, despite this, he got me off the phone quickly.

My mind began to race as panic set in. *What next?* ... Oh, yes... New York. I would call New York! Maybe *they* would still talk to me!

Yet, the scenario was the same. I spent a few minutes arguing with a stubborn New Yorker who refused to acknowledge my existence.

This was awful. I felt nauseous. I had pushed myself beyond my limits, but the reward for all my efforts would likely be nothing at all: No acknowledgment, no money, nothing. This couldn't be happening. This wasn't happening...

But it was.

Still, I was wasn't ready to give up. There had to be something I could do! ... *Anything!*

The landline! ... I decided to pick up the landline. Maybe if the call was coming from a different number I could get through. It was worth a try. I called Houston three more times before giving up. They weren't going to let me past the screener. *Period.*

I decided to make a final last-ditch call to New York. This time I would *demand* answers! This time I would *not* play around!

36

PROVE IT!

I picked up the landline one more time, ready for a fight. A brash man with a thick New York accent answered the phone. I introduced myself in my usual manner, as Barbara Janik, the person who had called in the Brooklyn tips.

I got a response that was similar to before, but it seemed edgier, even more annoyed.

"Never heard of it." The man spoke quickly and sounded like he was anxious to get me off the phone, but I wasn't having it.

"Sure, you have."

But the guy was adamant. "Nope."

This time I pulled out all the stops. "Come on, you *know* you guys arrested Osama."

The words that came next were jarring, angry, and serious. *"Prove it!"*

I scrambled. I knew I couldn't prove it. I had to think fast. He was giving me what I wanted. "You guys were celebrating something really big the other day, and I know that's when y'all got him."

The reply was even angrier. "You got me. Now turn me in. It'll make ya feel better."

I replied calmly and politely, "I don't want to—"

Before I could get the words out, he repeated himself, this time in a voice even louder and angrier. "You got me. Now turn me in. It'll make ya feel better!"

I tried to formulate my words quickly before he could interrupt me again. "I don't want—" My voice was tempered and solemn.

He repeated himself a third time, still not letting me speak. "You got me. Now turn me in. It'll make ya feel better!"

Finally, he let me answer. "I don't want to turn you in."

He calmed down a bit. "Then I don't know what to tell you." He was determined to get off the phone, but I was too quick for him.

For one desperate moment, I got real with him. "What about the money?"

His tone softened. The money was important, and he probably felt like I'd earned it. His demeanor turned from anger to empathy. He almost sounded a little teary-eyed. I suppose it *had* been an emotional day. "You'll have to come to the New York office and file a claim."

This was hopeful. I guess there was a process. He clearly thought there could be a claim to be filed. Why else would he tell me to do that?

"I can't come to New York. It's too far." Maybe he didn't realize I was in Texas.

He went back from empathetic to harsh. "Then I can't help you!"

At that point, I was done. There was no more information to be had. I still wasn't sure what to do next. I just knew that I wanted to get off the phone.

I told him "thank you" and "take care," and that was it.

I would never call the New York FBI office again.

I sat there for a couple of minutes, stunned, quietly seething. The call had been brief and rushed, but it represented some of the most meaningful minutes of my life. This was the closest I would ever get to a confession that the FBI Terrorism Task Force had arrested Osama bin Laden, acting on my tip. Yet the moment was bittersweet as I began to give into the idea that there would be no announcement.

A few minutes later, I picked up the phone and rage-called the Houston office. But before the screener answered, I slammed down the handset. I knew what the outcome would be. I was done with these people.

I wheeled around in my chair and faced Nicki, pausing for a moment to catch my breath.

She gazed back. She knew what was happening. She had been listening in on my end of the conversations, and I had been filling her in on some of the details between calls. She knew they were shutting me out.

"What?"

My words came out more excited than disappointed. Mostly, I felt vindicated. "I told him I knew they got Osama!"

I stammered, unable to get the syllables out fast enough, so Nicki kept prodding.

"And?"

"He told me to prove it!"

Nicki was visibly stunned. *"Wow!"*

We immediately began analyzing the scenario.

"I mean, why would he tell me to 'prove it' if there

was nothing to prove?"

We went on for the next hour or so, going over every detail of that call and all the others from the past. This was one of the dozens of such conversations we would have over the next several years. And we would always come to the same conclusion: Osama bin Laden was, in fact, arrested on the morning of August 16, 2006 by the New York FBI Terrorism Task Force, which was acting on my tip.

Yet despite the apparent coverup, I couldn't give up. My financial situation was still just as desperate as before. Of course, I was glad the FBI had caught him. Even if I never received a dime, there would always be the satisfaction of knowing that it was because of my efforts.

But I really needed the money—the $25 million. I wouldn't give up, not that easily.

I started thinking hard. All I had was a worthless pseudo-confession. What next? I turned back to my old friend, Google. Maybe Google would help me figure out how to attain the $25 million. A few minutes later, I stumbled on the answer: I needed to go to an office— any FBI office—and file a claim.

Houston was no longer an option, so I started checking to see if there were any other branches in my area. I would tell them what happened and see if I could get some answers. I saw online that there was a Texas City office that was actually closer to our home than Houston. Maybe I'd try them.

But for some weird reason, I had trouble finding their contact information. Maybe this was another missing car keys situation. Maybe like the many times I'd lost my keys, I was panicking. Maybe that's why I couldn't find the number. Eventually, I lost patience and started frantically calling 411, but the operators kept giving me wrong numbers. Finally, after a whopping half-dozen tries, I had the correct number. I would call the Texas City office. *But later...* I needed to take a break. Nature was calling.

About a fifteen minutes later, my phone rang, but I was still on the toilet. *Damn! ...* It was in the other room. I finished my business and sprinted out of the bathroom and headed for my desk. There it was: my phone. I picked it up and flipped it open. I had a missed call from a blocked number. *Strange...* I didn't usually get calls from blocked numbers. *I wonder who that was? ... I hope they call back...*

Not even a minute later, they called again. Whoever it was must have *really* wanted to speak with me. I cautiously flipped open the phone.

"Hello."

There was a familiar voice on the other end: It was Agent Miles, the Houston agent I knew best and trusted most. *I wonder what she wanted.*

I replied suspiciously, "How can I help you?"

She sounded stern and tense. "You're going to have to stop calling."

It was evident that this was important to Agent Miles.

I understood why they picked her. They knew I trusted Agent Miles and would listen to her. But I had already made the decision, on my own, not to call Houston anymore.

I felt as tense as Agent Miles sounded. My words had an edge of anger. "*I know.* I'm actually switching to the Texas City office. I'm going to be talking to them from now on."

Agent Miles seemed relieved. She thanked me and then it was over. No more calls to or from Houston.

What made this conversation almost laughable was that just two hours before, Houston FBI agents had been claiming they didn't know who I was or why I was calling. And then, suddenly, a familiar Houston agent took the time to call me personally? This was not the behavior of an organization that didn't know me. *No...* This was the opposite.

My thoughts quickly wandered back to the Texas City office. Maybe I would have better luck with them. Maybe they would be amicable. I was still clinging to a tinge of hope.

37

TEXAS CITY

That night, I called the Texas City FBI and left a message for the duty agent. I briefly explained to the screener why I was calling. I needed to file a claim for some reward money. I avoided mentioning bin Laden. A little before 7 p.m., a mild-mannered Texas gentleman called me back.

The agent was friendly, polite, and chatty—more like the FBI I was used to. We spoke for around a half hour while I described my dilemma and gave some of the backstory, careful not to disclose too much. I explained that I had found a major terrorist and was looking to claim the reward money. He didn't seem at all surprised, which led me to believe he'd heard the news. The fact that I'd found Osama bin Laden would have to wait. I knew how crazy it sounded.

Eventually, the agent explained that I would have to come into the office and file the claim in person. I agreed to set an appointment. But as luck would have it, he had an immediate opening. The thought occurred to me that maybe he was anxious to meet the person who found bin Laden. This would explain why he was willing to see me so soon. *Maybe...*

Nicki and I quickly got ready, then took off. Fifteen minutes later, not long before sunset, we arrived at a drab, light-brown brick building that looked like a typical government structure. Why did federal agencies always have such boring architecture? It reminded me a lot of the Social Security Administration in Angleton. It's like the government takes itself too seriously—or perhaps they buy the bricks in bulk to share across agencies. Why were they always drab brown?

But that aside, I was finally at the FBI satellite office in Texas City, moments away from filing my claim for $25 million.

Walking into the building that day was my first real attempt to "prove it." If they paid me the reward, then they'd be admitting it happened—that I'd found bin Laden. This made my chance of collecting the bounty very unlikely. But still, I was hopeful. At least the Texas City agent was willing to talk to me.

A few minutes later, I stepped into a sparsely-furnished room. Even though it was an unadorned, ordinary space, I was intimidated. I'd never been inside an FBI office before. My head rushed to a rather benign image of *The X-Files'* Fox Mulder sitting in his basement office at headquarters. I could see his cluttered desk and his corkboard, crammed full of pinned maps and photographs.

Then my mind quickly turned to a darker, more sinister version of FBI offices—one that was often portrayed in the movies. They could be a place for brutal interviews with criminals. A sense of panic rushed over me. What if I was detained for questioning? What if

I was taken into custody for the sake of keeping this secret? What if something worse happened? I mean, what if I was silenced *permanently?* For a moment, I wanted to run. But instead, I took a deep breath. Up to this point, the FBI had been nothing but nice to me—at least until Houston and New York started snubbing me.

I tried to calm myself by thinking of all the agents I'd encountered over the past couple of weeks. I thought about the excitement in Agent Miles' voice when I called in my first terrorist tip: *"I'll pass it on!"* I recalled the calm, professional demeanor of the man who took the bin Laden tip, and the agent I spoke to the next day, who called me a "gifted researcher" and a "true patriot." Then there was the female agent who, after I introduced myself, had vocally snapped to attention and proudly declared, *"I have been briefed!"*

Next, I remembered the cheerful New Yorkers celebrating bin Laden's arrest and the man who promised me that evening that *"absolutely"* there would be an announcement. As I entered the Texas City office, I relived the teary words of the gratitude from the Houston agents. Finally, I bristled at the memory of the New York agent's defiant words, posed as a challenge the day the story was crushed: *"Prove it!"*

Would the Texas City agent be any different? Any less human? No, it seemed impossible that this agent or this branch would harm me. The agents had always been so accommodating and professional. They were not a shady branch of government. They were an autonomous wing of the federal government responsible solely for law enforcement. I took a deep breath. It was going to be okay.

Despite my fears, the office itself was benign. It

looked more like the waiting room to a doctor's office than the entrance to a law enforcement agency. It was actually dull, with nothing on the light-colored walls or carpet. Maybe a half-dozen lightly-padded chairs lined the walls. Across the room was a second door that presumably led to the interior of the suite. Nicki sat down as I walked up to the glass-paneled reception office and lightly tapped on the window. But it was late, the window was dark, and no one was there. There was no sign-in sheet and no bell.

I was waiting by the window for several seconds when I was startled by the sound of a door opening behind me. I spun around. Someone was standing just inside the entrance: a man in a suit. He stepped out and extended his hand toward mine.

"Barbara Janik?"

I stepped toward him, briskly extended my arm, and greeted him with a firm handshake. "Yes, I'm Barbara Janik. Pleased to meet you." He matched me with an equally firm handshake. *Confidence... Good...*

He let out a small smile. "Same. Pleasure to meet you."

The man who stood before me had an appearance that fit precisely with how I imagined an FBI agent would look. He was a mild-mannered, attractive man in his mid-thirties with dark-brown hair, sporting a navy suit and tie. If I didn't know where I was, I would think he was straight out of corporate America—perhaps in middle management.

We bantered briefly before heading back to his office. The agent seemed like a normal, peace-loving human being. He had the calm, professional manner that was typical of the FBI agents I'd spoken to so many times over the phone. I breathed a slight sigh of relief.

He then directed me to follow him through the door and, at a rather brisk pace, led me through a small twist of hallways. The inner part of the suite was dark and devoid of people. I assumed the day-staff had already gone home.

Moments later, the agent and I were sitting alone in a relatively large office which had a décor that was much friendlier than the reception area. In contrast, unlike the entry, there were paintings on the wall, and the furniture was inviting. Even the carpet was less oppressive. The room was *almost* comfortable. I was seated in a small, black, faux-leather office chair, and he was behind his desk in a bigger one with a full back. The space between us was empty, a chasm.

The chair under me was soft, but not too soft. I think the environment was supposed to make people feel at ease.

It wasn't working.

The agent looked at me from across the abyss. "So, what brings you here today?"

"I'm sorry. Just let me take a moment. I'm really nervous."

I took a couple of deep breaths. Talking on the phone was one thing, but sitting in a chair across from one of them was different. *Really different.*

The agent tried to calm me, to reassure me that there was nothing to be nervous about. I balked, telling him I was afraid he would think I was crazy. But he continued his efforts to assuage my fears. He told me that as an FBI agent, he had seen and heard all kinds of crazy stuff that happened to be true. Then, in a soothing voice, he told me that he wasn't going to judge me. He was just going to do his job.

After a while, I finally gave in.

"I don't know if you know it or not, but Osama bin Laden was arrested by the FBI in Brooklyn yesterday."

Silence... He maintained a straight, serious face.

"And I'm the one who turned in the tip. I'm here to claim the $25 million reward."

The agent's face was dead-pan—no snark, no nods of approval, completely unreadable—a true poker face. Yet he didn't seem the least bit surprised by what I'd said. He was quiet and emotionless as he wrote down bin Laden's current alias and address, which I offered as proof of my claims. Perhaps the agent already knew what had happened. Word of big events might have had a way of spreading within the rank-and-file agents in the FBI. And maybe he hadn't caught wind of the coverup yet. Still, I couldn't know for sure.

Next, the agent explained the process: He would take my information and fax the claim to Washington. Once it was verified, he'd call me with the results.

I was worried the process could drag on for a while. "How long will it take?"

His response was short and confident. "It should be only a day or so."

Then he paused for a moment, thinking. "Do you have any other questions?"

"Actually, yeah. I'm really worried they aren't going public with this. What if they refuse to pay me the money as part of a coverup? I mean, I'm willing to sign a nondisclosure agreement."

Unconcerned, the agent gave me a pep talk. "The government would have no reason to keep the reward money from you, if you indeed turned in Osama bin

Laden. I will verify your claims and put in a request for payment."

We went in circles for several minutes as he tried in vain to assuage my doubts. Finally, he grabbed his notes, got up, and started heading toward the door. "I have to go file the claim. I'll be back in a min—"

But as he started to turn the nob, I cut him off mid-sentence. *"Wait..."*

He stopped and turned toward me, seeming harried. "Yes?"

"Don't forget to tell them I'm willing to sign a nondisclosure agreement."

He looked at me quizzically. "I'm sure that won't be necessary..." He fell silent for a few seconds as he assessed the situation. "But I'll let them know."

A few minutes later, he returned and led me back to the reception area. And that was it: my first face-to-face meeting with an FBI agent. I didn't know it at the time, but the next one would be just a few months later—in my very own home.

***

The following day, I called the Texas City office to check on the claim. However, I found myself stone-walled once again. The agent who had been so accessible just the day before, was suddenly unavailable. I tried throughout the morning and couldn't get a hold of him. The screener just kept saying he was busy. And I knew...I just *knew*...I was being ignored.

The assumption I made was that Texas City had finally gotten the word that news of bin Laden's arrest was being suppressed. I was growing impatient. I needed to know something. Because the minute I knew for sure that I wasn't getting the reward, I was going to call the press. *I needed to know.* I needed to know if it was time to inform the public.

So instead of being patient and waiting for a call-back from the agent—a call that was probably never going to happen—I made a radical decision: I would call repeatedly until I finally got an answer. In other words, I would harass the FBI Texas City office. Looking back, this was an embarrassing decision. But somehow, it worked. After numerous calls, I wore down the screener. Tense and annoyed, she told me that there would be no reward. My claim had been denied. The friendly man who had promised to phone me with news would never even bother to return my call. I never spoke to him again.

It was official. There would be no money, no recognition. I had found the most wanted man on the planet, and it looked like no one would ever know about it. My efforts may have saved lives, but bin Laden would still be out there as the "boogie man" fanning the fires of war. Meanwhile, I was left trying to prove he was no longer out there. I had nothing but the angry words of a New York agent echoing in my brain: *"Prove it!"*

Little did I know that I would be trying to "prove it" for the next sixteen years.

38

ON THE RUN!

The moment I got the word that I wasn't getting the reward, I went into action mode. The first thing I did was try to alert the media. There was going to be a government coverup, and I knew something I wasn't supposed to know. And there was safety in numbers. If I could somehow notify the public, everyone would know about bin Laden's arrest. It would no longer be a secret, and I could collect the reward money.

I called Brandy first. *Of course!* ... My sister. She was a journalist. I'd give *her* the story. It would be a huge break for her. I just knew she'd help me.

Unfortunately, I was wrong.

It was an awkward conversation (more later), and Brandy turned me down cold. She rebuffed me without much thought and acted like I'd lost my mind.

After talking to Brandy, I was annoyed, sad, and discouraged, but not ready to give up. I frantically called CNN and a few other outlets. But there was a process, and no journalists called me back. In the end, I was left feeling angry and frustrated.

And when the press wouldn't take me seriously, that's when I started to get really scared, paranoid even. If no one knew about bin Laden's arrest but me and my family, I was a liability, a potential security breach. Maybe I'd seen too many movies, but I was afraid for my family's safety as well as my own—anyone close to me who knew the truth.

Minimally, I was worried that our home would be raided and my laptop seized. They might want to examine it to figure out how I found Osama bin Laden or perhaps erase any evidence of the coverup that existed on my hard drive.

And like I said, I was also deeply worried about being "disappeared." Would I be taken into custody and dumped in a dungeon to rot? Would they cross-examine me to find out how I did it? Would I be taken out permanently?

I wasn't worried about the FBI as much as the CIA and worse, *secret* organizations. Did the government *actually* hire professional assassins, like in the movies? Flashes of James Bond flew before my eyes.

Then there was Al Qaeda. What if they found out I had taken out their beloved leader? What if they wanted revenge? Was I going to wake up to the sound of bombs and a burning house?

No... I couldn't take any chances. I had to believe we were safe—not that there was anywhere I could really hide. Even if it didn't really help, leaving would make me feel better, like I was doing something proactive. Staying at home would make me feel like a target, a sitting duck.

At this point, I knew exactly what to do. I'd taken all of the psychology classes. When presented with extreme danger or fear, there were two possible choices: fight or flight. I knew I couldn't fight the government nor the dark forces of Al Qaeda. This left only one option: I had to run.

But *where*?

I thought about it for a moment. I didn't have enough money to find a random hotel room in the area, and even if I did, it wouldn't be far enough away from home to give me a sense of security. *But wait...* Austin! Nicki's apartment in Austin: As a PhD candidate at UT, Nicki had a place in Austin where she stayed on weekdays during Fall and Spring semesters. We could go *there!* We'd run to Austin. Maybe the Feds didn't know about the apartment. Hell, maybe they didn't even know about Nicki. It's not like I discussed my personal life with them. And there was no evidence that they were spying on me up to this point.

I left the bedroom, where I'd been hiding out, and headed to the living room to talk to Nicki. We needed a plan.

***

After going over my fears at length with Nicki, she agreed that we should go to Austin. Then I took the next logical step: I called my father. If we were going to do this, we would need help. That meant family involvement.

I flipped open my phone and entered Dad's number. Like all the other important people in my life, I had his number memorized. I punched it in absently, calling upon my muscle memory to get the job done.

Dad answered his phone in his usual manner, with

a Texas drawl. "Hello."

"Hey, old man!" I liked to call him that, and I was the only one who could get away with it. He was in his seventies, and he was fun to tease.

The greeting always elicited a laugh. But what I was about to tell Dad was no joke.

He gave me his usual greeting: "Hey. What's goin' on?" He was always happy to get a call from me. I could hear it in his voice.

My normal response would have been "Nothin' much."

But this time, "Nothin' much" came out as "Way too much." This was probably the most emotionally honest thing I'd said to my dad in a while.

There was a unique quality to my voice: My small-town Texas accent was always exaggerated when I spoke to my dad. I couldn't help it. I just sort of automatically "hicked" it up around him and other country folk.

Before he could respond, I quickly added, "And no, I'm not callin' about money this time."

I stumbled over my words. I couldn't tell my father about bin Laden over the phone. I was too paranoid. Was the FBI listening in? I couldn't risk it. They didn't need to know he was involved.

I continued addressing my dad. "It's hard to explain. Can I just come over? There's somethin' I need to give you. I'll explain it all when I get there." I was going to give him a flash drive with relevant evidence that I had pulled off my computer—mostly links to important websites and copies of the results of paid searches.

Nicki and I hopped in the Hyundai Santa Fe and headed for Dad's house–the place where I had grown up. About ten minutes later, we pulled up to Dad's small, quiet, country brick home. As we parked behind his beat-up old pickup truck, I noticed maybe a half-dozen of his cows standing idly by in the fenced field to the right. They were mooing and nodding as if to greet us. I had spent many happy hours along that fence line, picking dewberries in the spring.

As I headed toward the screen door with Nicki behind me, I smiled at the covered 1954 Ford Convertible parked on the right side of his carport. He'd probably never drive it, but it made him happy.

My dad had a bad habit of collecting classic cars he intended to fix up later. Some of them were scattered along the shell-covered dirt road that led to the barn, while others were collecting rust in the muddy field next to it. We'd tease Dad that his property looked like a junkyard. It wasn't quite that bad, but it was close.

However, the 1954 Ford convertible had a special meaning for Dad. I think it reminded him of younger, happier times—times when he and Mom were first dating. My mind wandered for a moment as I remembered Dad's bittersweet plans to get a vanity plate for the car that read "JER BET"–Mom and Dad's nicknames. But my folks had been divorced not long after he obtained the car. Visiting my Dad's house—my childhood home— was both happy and sad for me. Memories would sometimes flash through my mind—mostly positive ones, but some were crushingly negative. I lost that home to my parents' divorce, and a part of me would always resent what had happened.

Deep breath... This was now. And Dad, when I could catch him alone, always made me feel happy.

I carefully pulled back the screen door and knocked on the solid wooden one behind it. A few seconds later,

I heard the loud squeak of old hinges as Dad swung it open. "Hey. Glad ya made it."

I reached out for a tight hug. "Glad I made it too, Dad."

Pulling back, Dad invited me inside. Why don't ya come on in?"

I looked at him suspiciously and let out a low whisper, "Is Nina here?" His wife and I didn't get along. She didn't need to hear this. She would never understand. She'd only judge.

"No. She's up in Old Conroe with Lesa (her daughter)." I let out an audible sigh of relief. Nina's love of shopping was working in my favor.

Dad directed his eyes toward me and then panned to Nicki, who was standing next to me. "Hey, maybe we should just sit out here and enjoy the fresh air." Dad, always the country boy, preferred being out on the front porch more than just about anywhere else in the world.

He directed me toward two scuffed-up plastic chairs where he and Nina would sit outside in the mornings reading the newspaper. I sat down in Nina's spot as Dad pulled a third chair from the cubby between the wall and the convertible. I noticed a small bin next to the car that had a little bit of cat food in it. Dad had left it out there for feral cats and raccoons.

Even though it was August, it didn't seem that hot. We were sitting under the shade of his carport, and there was a bit of a breeze. Dad reached into the cooler that lived in a spot next to his chair and popped open a can of Lonestar. "Ya want one?"

He always bought the cheap beer. When I was a kid, it was Old Milwaukee. I used to take sips of it occasionally. It tasted so good—like Daddy was sharing a part of himself with me, something that was important to him.

But then I felt myself getting a little nervous. Dad could become a bit cantankerous when he was drinking. I knew better than to talk to him after 6 p.m., when he'd be drunk and unreasonable... But what if he'd started early today?

"Hey. How many of those have you had?" I *had* to know if he was drunk. I couldn't always tell at first.

Dad got a little defensive. "This is my first one. And you don't hafta worry about me. I'm in perfect health. Believe it or not, the doctor said I have better numbers and blood pressure than most thirty-year-olds."

It was true. Dad had always enjoyed perfect health and perfect teeth. He very rarely got sick, and during the entire thirty years he worked for the local chemical plant, Union Carbide, he never called in once. He used to save all his sick leave for summer vacations. That's how we could afford six weeks in California every year.

I was relieved this was only Dad's first beer—that is, *if* he was telling the truth. That was a big *if* because Dad had a bad habit of lying unnecessarily. I hoped this wasn't one of those times.

Then I thought about his offer again. I was under a lot of stress with all this bin Laden stuff. Maybe I could use a beer. But wouldn't that just *encourage* him? Fuck it! I knew I wasn't going to change him. He was too old.

"Hey, ya know what? I think I *will* have one of those beers."

Dad reached into the cooler, popped one open, and handed it to me. Then he turned to my partner. "You want one too, Nicki?"

Nicki wasn't much of a drinker, and she was always really responsible. So her answer was unsurprising.

"No thanks. I have to drive."

Finally, Dad attempted to strike up a conversation. "How're the kids?"

I replied almost automatically. "They're doin' great. School just started. No problems so far." But I didn't feel like I could talk too much about the kids right now. I was too preoccupied with the bin Laden stuff. I decided to change the subject.

I took a long gulp of beer, took a deep breath, and looked over at Dad.

"You still feedin' the raccoons?"

"Yep. They come out here every evenin'. The momma's real friendly. She'll walk right up to ya and take food out o' your hands. Sometimes I'll give 'er some of our leftovers."

He then began telling all of his favorite stories about raccoons, most of which I'd never heard before. I was always amazed at how he could usually come up with new material. I guess there's an advantage to living a long life. Besides, I loved raccoons. They were so cool. I was a little envious that he got to see the little bandits every night. I'd never seen his raccoons because I was never over late.

A few minutes later, I had to interrupt my father. Dad liked to talk, and he could go on with his stories for hours. I glanced nervously toward Nicki, who gave me a half-grin and a nod. *I had to do this...* I had to tell him. It was time.

"Dad, can I stop you for a second?"

"Sure..." Dad paused and waited for me to speak.

"There's somethin' we need to talk about. Somethin' I need to tell you."

Although my nerves had calmed a bit from the beer

and small-talk, my heart started to race. I was about to tell my father the unthinkable: that I had found Osama bin Laden, that he'd been arrested, and that the government owed me $25 million. I was still under the impression that I would someday get the money. I was still hopeful. But my heart sank at the thought of what Dad might say.

In many ways, his response was more receptive than I had been expecting. But it also included an air of negativity. "You might be onto somethin'." In other words, he believed my story was possible. Of all people, Dad had faith in me, as did my mother. He used to brag about my mechanical abilities. He would tell stories about when I was a kid—how I would get under the car with him and try to give him advice when he was stuck on a repair project, and how I would put together all the bikes and toys at Christmas.

But Dad's voice got stern as he added something. "You might be onto somethin', but..."

Here was where his mood shifted:

"They're not gonna give you any money."

In that moment, all my focus was on Dad. I was oblivious of Nicki, who was still sitting right next to me. What he had said blew me away. *What if he was right? What if I never got the money?*

I had a sick feeling, but I tried to fight it off. Pausing, I considered the source—my Dad. After all, this was *him* speaking. He was a cynic and a bit paranoid about the federal government. Mostly, he believed politicians were all a bunch of crooks. He often didn't even bother to vote because he didn't like either party.

Yet I worried that Dad's skepticism toward the reward was on the mark this time. But I wasn't quite ready to give up hope of ever collecting it.

Not yet...

I brushed his comment aside.

Nicki and I talked to Dad for a few minutes, and he agreed to our plan. I would give him a flash drive that contained links to relevant websites. Then, Nicki and I would drop off my laptop and our phones at Dad's run-down rental property that we affectionately called the "Old Green House" (named for it's weathered, mint-green siding). We would leave our devices there for safekeeping. I couldn't risk my data being lost forever.

Besides, we were going incognito. We would replace our normal phones with prepaid versions for anonymity. I needed to make sure no one was listening.

Dad and Jerry would take turns watching the kids while we were gone. Jerry lived across the street from Dad. He had purchased Jim Henry's old house—complete with its swimming pool—after Jim's passing.

If Jerry agreed to help watch the kids, we would call the "bus barn," where the school district's buses were stored, and tell them to pick up the kids at his address.

Honestly, the kids would probably spend most of their time at Jerry's place. They were more familiar with him and his home. They'd be more comfortable there. After all, it's where we had most of the family parties. Dad would serve as a backup if Jerry had to leave town.

I told Dad we were going to Nicki's apartment in Austin and would be gone for about a week while things settled down.

That was it. We had a plan. *And* I had told my dad the truth and survived.

He had even been helpful, which left me feeling both grateful and relieved.

Finally, Dad and I exchanged hugs and I-love-yous, and Nicki and I took off for Walmart to buy cheap Tracfones. For the sake of further anonymity, I chose the new phone numbers by using an out-of-state zip: Beverly Hills, 90210, the only zip code I remembered from California, which was my second-favorite state. Before leaving for Austin, we'd give our new, albeit temporary, numbers to Dad, Jerry, and the kids.

When we finally arrived home, I wanted to immediately pack up the car, shuttle Peter and Daun to my Dad's house, and leave. I was terrified for my life and the lives of Nicki and our children. We needed to go, and we needed to go now.

But Nicki had different plans.

"We're not leaving tonight. I'm exhausted."

We argued for a while—something we didn't do often. "I'm scared. I don't want to stay here another minute. We have to go—*now!*"

But in a rare act of determination, Nicki held her ground. As we debated the issue for several minutes, her anger began to rise, and I could tell this was going to turn into a full-blown meltdown if I didn't back off.

I tried to relent. "*Fine!* We'll stay tonight, but I don't like it. I'm terrified, and I probably won't even sleep."

I was panicked, but determined. I kept going. "I still don't understand why you won't just let me drive."

"Because you're a terrible driver."

She was right... Recall, that I had been in numerous wrecks. I had also been getting tickets once a year ever since I'd gotten my license at age twenty-one. One time, I totaled my Saturn when I was trying to drive my kids to school. Daun had nearly lost an eye when she was pelted with spraying glass.

But Nicki not letting me drive still hurt. It felt like she didn't trust me.

"I know, but there isn't even going to be that much traffic. It's the middle of the night."

We kept arguing. "You really want to drive on those hilly, dark roads outside of Austin in the middle of the night? Not to mention all the drunks that come out at two in the morning."

It was true. Texas had a huge drunk driving problem that started at dusk and got considerably worse after 2 a.m., when the bars closed. It was dangerous out there, and visibility could be poor. I thought about the time I had driven for over three hours in dense fog on my way to Austin for a weekend visit with Nicki. It had been awful.

I gave a shrug. Nicki had defeated me with logic, and I was afraid if I kept going, her anger would turn to rage. I didn't know who I was more scared of at this point—the government or Nicki. Ultimately, I knew I needed to keep the peace. Besides, I wasn't going to win this one.

I took a deep breath. "Okay, you win. We'll leave in the morning, first thing. But you know I'm probably not going to sleep."

Nicki calmed down a bit. "Well, it's more important that I sleep since I'm driving."

She had made another good point.

I decided to try to go to bed early after we finished packing. At midnight, I took my sleeping pills. They wouldn't work if I took them too soon, and I doubted even midnight would be late enough.

It felt like the longest six hours of my life. The sleeping pills barely helped, and I tossed and turned all night. My head wouldn't stop catastrophizing as it played through every imaginable worse-case scenario. There were times when I was absolutely shaking with fear.

At least three or four times, I woke up and binged on sweets: honey buns, Blue Bell Pralines and Cream—my favorite ice cream—and some plain M&Ms Nicki had stashed in her area of the kitchen. I hoped she would forgive me for eating her chocolate. I was desperate and had completely lost control.

And even then, the binging didn't really help with my stress, and it certainly didn't help me get any more sleep.

Finally, at 6 a.m., after my last snack, I went back to the bedroom to wake up Nicki. I was envious. I could tell from her heavy breathing and light snoring, that she'd gotten better sleep than I had. But it didn't matter. We would both be equally miserable from sleep deprivation. I gave her a slight shove, and she growled at me. Moments later, she reluctantly crawled out of bed. Next, I woke up the kids. It was time to start the day.

After what felt like an eternity and way too much hassle, we dropped Peter and Daun off at school and headed to Austin. Ordinarily, I loved to travel. But this trip wouldn't be fun. It would be horrible.

39

CAVE TIME

About four hours later, the wheels of our car made crumpling noises on the gravel as we pulled up to the familiar sight of Nicki's apartment complex. The kids and I had spent many happy weekends there, visiting Nicki while she was completing the coursework for her PhD. She wouldn't move in with us full time until she was "All but Dissertation (ABD)." When the kids and I weren't traveling to Austin, she came to our house. We saw each other every weekend and all summer, as well as every holiday. In other words, we spent every spare moment together. Our relationship felt just as committed to me as if we lived together full-time.

Regardless, the weekends at Nicki's Austin apartment when the kids weren't with us usually meant one thing: lots of intimacy. The experience was generally pretty great. But not this time. There was too much fear, too much anticipation. *No...* This wouldn't be a fun trip. This was business. This was hiding.

A few minutes later, we climbed the outdoor steps to her second-story apartment. Nicki unlocked the door and swung it open. I stepped into the hot apartment and plunked down on the lumpy rainbow tie-dye futon. Not only was it lumpy, but it was hard—horribly uncomfortable. Sitting or lying on it too long aggravated my back. But Nicki kept it because it could be conveniently flattened out for the kids to sleep on when they were visiting. I envied how they could sleep literally anywhere.

Nicki bumped up the a/c a bit and slumped down next to me. "Hungry?"

"Yeah. But I don't want to go anywhere." I was tired from the trip, and my eyes were burning and watering from prolonged exposure to bright sunlight.

Nicki glanced over at me. "Let's just order a pizza."

I didn't resist. I was starving. "Wanna try Papa John's? I've never had them before."

Nicki agreed. "Sure. It'll be something different, at least."

But I needed to rest. "Do you mind ordering? I wanna take some Cave Time."

"Cave Time" was a ritual I had been engaging in since I was nineteen and working on my bachelor's at UST. I had only been getting about four hours of sleep at night, so by mid-day, I would become exhausted, tense, sullen, and foggy-headed. To help myself get through the day, I would initiate "emotional reset," something other people called a "power nap."

Sometimes when I was working my shift at the campus print shop (General Office), I'd go into the bathroom and turn off the light. There were no windows, so it would be mercifully pitch dark. I would lie flat on my back on the carpeted floor and close my eyes for about five minutes. Afterward, I would inevitably feel better mentally and emotionally, which made it possible for me to continue my work shift without feeling as miserable. No one ever suspected a thing. My coworkers and I used to joke that we needed a cot in the back office for naps.

On other occasions, when I was home and had the time and inclination, I would strip down to a T-shirt and underwear and lay on my bed or the couch for about an hour. Darkness was essential, along with cool air and water–always ice water. No other drink would do. It was all about resting and meeting basic needs: hydration, comfort, relaxation. It almost never involved sleep. I might drift a bit, as if I were meditating, but that was normally as far as it went.

When Nicki and I got together, she started affectionately calling these longer rests "Cave Time" because they happened in cool, dark places. You know, like caves.

As I prepared for Cave Time, I headed to the small kitchen alcove and plucked some ice from the freezer. I dumped it in a glass, adding some Austin tap water. It was even worse than the mineral-laden well water at home. At least the well water had nostalgic value. After all, I had grown up drinking that type of water. But Austin water was barely tolerable, even with ice.

Then I sauntered off to the bedroom, turned off the overhead light, and cranked the ceiling fan on high. I lay down on my back on top of the single-bed mattress and box springs that sat frameless on the floor. Next, I curled a pillow under my neck and covered myself with a soft, rainbow-colored sheet. A cover, albeit thin, was essential for comfort because it made me feel more secure.

Any other cover would have been too hot, especially since Nicki had been running the a/c at 85 degrees to save money during her long absence. Fortunately, she ran it a little colder than usual when I was there. After all, I was the "Air Conditioner Queen."

I had a vague thought about how small the mattress was. It was designed for one person, but we would share that mattress at night, with me crammed against the wall. It was way too small for two adults. I made a note to myself as I entered into Cave Time: Convince Nicki to buy a bigger mattress.

As soon as I lay down, I started breathing heavily, hyperventilating a bit. My head was throbbing. I reached over and took a huge swig of water and promptly spilled some on my bosom. Drinking from a glass while lying on my back was always challenging.

Mmmmm... water.

Finally, I set the water down next to me and closed my eyes to try to relax, to meditate. I felt my mind was too preoccupied for sleep, but I hoped Cave Time would help. Unfortunately, I was unsuccessful at quieting my brain. It began swimming with thoughts of everything that was happening. Was anyone really after me? Was I in danger? Was my *family* in danger?

Then I started thinking about the announcement. Was Bush going to eventually make one? Was he planning an October surprise in anticipation of the midterm elections? The polls were predicting the Democrats would take both branches of Congress by a landslide. Would Bush make the announcement days before the election and kill their chances? If this was true, I needed to warn them. I desperately wanted them to win. I was very concerned about the wars in Iraq and

Afghanistan, and I believed, for sure, the Democrats would tell the truth about Osama bin Laden and bring our troops home. I especially trusted and admired Senator Hillary Clinton.

But was there anything I could do to warn them? To help?

At this point, I stopped myself.

No...later... I would would think about that later. I was exhausted and desperately needed to rest.

Then I remembered the portable CD player in the backpack next to me. I pulled it out and plugged in my earbuds. I needed music, something soothing. *Yes...* KD Lang. I was a big fan. I loved that she sang so passionately about women. I loaded up *Ingénue* and put it on the loudest setting. I needed to drown out my thoughts.

A few seconds later, I let out a sigh of relief. My breathing began to slow to deep, involuntary waves of air. *Sweet...* I felt a little better already.

KD Lang's *lyrics* flowed through me:

> *Drink, drink from my spell*
> *Quench, love's drying well*
> *Wash, wash me clean*
>
> *Mend my wounded seams*
> *Cleanse my tarnished dreams*

Slowly, her words relaxed my mind, as the cozy bed, cool air, and water relaxed my body.

40

HAMMER OUT WARNING

After what seemed like only a few moments, my body convulsed as a yell came from the other room.

"Pizza's here!"

I glanced at my watch. *Wow...* I had been out for thirty minutes, but it felt like only thirty seconds.

I lurched forward and got up quickly. *Oof! ... Too* quickly. I was light-headed. *Easy, Barbara...* Don't fall over.

I stumbled into the living room and sat down next to Nicki, who was on the futon, next to a Papa John's box. A couple of Coke Zero bottles sat on a nearby tray table.

I grabbed a piece of pizza and hastily crammed it into a napkin. I took a few bites, eating quickly. "Wow... This pizza isn't very good."

Nicki looked up from her food. "Yeah. The sauce is way too sweet."

"I think this is some of the worst pizza I've ever had."

We agreed to never order Papa John's again and

gobbled it down quickly in silence, taking long swigs of coke. Nicki always said that she ate fast because of her experience in the army. The soldiers were given something like five minutes to eat their food during basic training and were told, "Eat it now, taste it later, soldier." I guess that time in her life had made an impression on her. I also usually took in sustenance too fast, but for completely different reasons: I had always struggled with food issues. I was only rarely aware of what food tasted like. I often would just sort of dissociate and eat quickly. But I had never tried this brand before, and it was too bad not to notice.

Poor flavor or not, within a few minutes I was miserably full, having eaten five large slices. I wiped my hands and mouth on a napkin and grinned at Nicki.

"Well... That was food."

Nicki grinned back. "Yes. It certainly was."

We shared a little giggle as she shoved all the trash in the pizza box and tossed it over toward the trash can in the kitchen.

"*Oops...* Missed!" I don't know how she was expecting that big pizza box to fit in that little can, but she managed to knock over the garbage with her toss. She didn't bother to get up. I knew she would get it later.

The pizza behind us, Nicki and I begin to really talk. We went over everything.

"Why do you think they never made an announcement?"

The food had made me a little sleepy. I glanced over at Nicki. "Hang on. I can tell this is going to be an intense conversation. I need to stretch out."

I lay back on the futon, curled a rainbow-themed pillow under my neck, and stretched my legs over

Nicki's lap. "Is this okay?"

"Yes. But I asked you a question."

"Sorry. My back was starting to hurt. What were you saying?"

Nicki seemed a little annoyed, her words tense. She hated repeating herself. "I *said*, 'Why do you think there wasn't an announcement?'"

I took a deep breath. "I was thinking about it earlier. Maybe they're going to make the announcement later. Maybe in a couple of months."

"But why? Why would they put it off?" Like me, Nicki was struggling to put the pieces together.

Pausing, I got ready to lay out my theory. "You ever heard of an October surprise?'"

"No. What's that?"

I tried to lay it out for her as clearly as possible: "Well, I mean, the Democrats are set to sweep the next election and take over both the House and the Senate. All the polls are in their favor. And the Republicans are scared. They know they have to do something really big to swing things in their favor."

"Makes sense."

I kept going: "So, what if they say they've captured Osama bin Laden in October, a couple of weeks before the election, instead of now? It would make Bush look like a big hero, just in time for the election. There would be a wave of patriotism kind of like after 9/11. And it would look like the Republicans had kept them safe. Everyone would run to the polls to show their gratitude."

"But why wait until October? Why not announce it *now*?" This was a good question. Its answer was the entire basis for an October surprise.

"Because the American public has a short memory.

The wave of patriotism and gratitude won't last long. They would want to strike while the iron was hot. So they would wait until right before the election to make the announcement."

"Oh... So, they'd get a 'bin Laden bump?'" We both started giggling. Nicki had just invented a new phrase.

"Exactly!"

Nicki looked down for a moment, her gears appearing to shift. "But there's something I don't get... I mean, if they were planning an announcement later, why didn't they just tell you?"

"Yeah... You're right. That is weird. If they were just putting off the announcement, they wouldn't have to keep the twenty-five million from me. It wouldn't matter if I knew. They could just give it to me and tell me to hold off on talking about it."

I kept trying to work things out in my head. There had to be more—more than just plans for a delayed announcement. There *had to* be something else in the works.

I came up with an idea: "Maybe they can't tell me we found him because they aren't planning on telling the whole truth."

"Oh... So, a half-truth?"

"Yeah. What if they don't want to admit he was in Brooklyn? What if that's the real problem?"

"Brooklyn? True... It'd look bad for them if bin Laden turned up in America and so close to Ground Zero."

"Yeah."

Nicki kept going. "So, you think they'll lie about where they got him?"

"Well, yeah. Probably. Seems logical... Lie about the

date and place."

But before she could respond, my thoughts shifted as I made a new connection. "Hey, I just thought of something. Trust me, it's related. Bear with me. You remember the ad on CNN for the documentary? It was a couple of days ago, before we came out here."

"No. What documentary?" I guess she hadn't been watching the news as closely as I had.

"Yeah, they've been advertising it on CNN. It's called *In the Footsteps of bin Laden*. It's supposed to air in a few days..." Quickly rolling my eyes, I continued. "Not suspicious *at all*..."

Nicki picked up on my sarcasm. "A documentary about bin Laden? *Now*? That *is* suspicious!"

I kept going, laying out the theory I'd mentally developed the first time I saw the trailer. "Yeah. I mean, why would there be a documentary about bin Laden *now*? Why at this point in history? He's barely been mentioned in the news the last few years and all of a sudden, the day of his arrest, CNN announces that they're airing a frickin' documentary about him–about his life?"

Nicki was stunned. "Yeah. They probably know something. Like, maybe they've heard about the arrest."

I nodded. "*Exactly.*"

"So, you think CNN could be ramping up for an announcement?"

I mostly agreed with her line of thinking. "Yeah, but get this. The trailer for the documentary said they were tracing his life throughout the Middle East and Pakistan. There wasn't even a mention of the US or New York."

Nicki continued my line of logic, as we bounced ideas off of each other. "Well, of course. No one was expecting him to be in the US."

I was persistent. "Yeah. But don't you get it?"

"Get what?"

I kept going, "What if Bush *is* ramping up to make an announcement, but he's going to say they caught him in the Middle East or something? Maybe Afghanistan or Pakistan?"

"Yeah. Maybe they'll say they got him in the Middle East somewhere... Makes sense. Like you said, they wouldn't want people to know they got him in Brooklyn. Better if they just 'found' (she put up air quotes) him somewhere else. The Middle East. That makes sense."

I was working on my reasoning out loud at this point, refining it as I presented my thoughts to Nicki. "Think about it. We went to Afghanistan, specifically, to look for bin Laden. And for the past five years, the public was led to believe he was hiding in a cave somewhere. Then finding him in Brooklyn... It would be an embarrassment."

"Yeah... True... Bush has already started two wars looking for him."

When she mentioned the wars, I was triggered, enraged. "Yeah! ... Thousands of lives lost—all those soldiers. They had families!" I wanted to cry. "Not to mention all the guys who come back maimed or fucked in the head—I mean PTSD. And fucking bin Laden was here all along! How are people going to feel about that? Don't you think they'll feel betrayed? Pissed? Bush... the Republicans...all of them. They'd be screwed. No one would want to vote for them... But you know what? Fuck them! Fuck Bush. Fuck the Republicans. They can all just burn in hell!"

The funny thing is that despite being a lesbian, I

had always voted Republican. I was a loyal pro-lifer, a former activist. I had voted for Bush twice, and I felt betrayed. In that moment, I realized that I would never vote Republican again. I kept going back to the thought that maybe the Democrats would tell the truth. Maybe if we put a Democrat in the White House—maybe Hillary Clinton—this would all be over. The truth would come out, we could end the wars, and I could collect my $25 million. Unfortunately, I would find out in two years how wrong I was.

But Nicki wasn't as quick to jump on the "they'd all hate Bush" bandwagon. "I don't personally think people would care where they got bin Laden... Afghanistan, Pakistan, Brooklyn, Disneyland. I just think they'd be happy that we got 'em."

I calmed down a little and took a deep breath. "Yeah. You might be right. But it doesn't matter. That's what Bush probably thinks. He probably thinks finding bin Laden in Brooklyn would make him look bad...hurt their chances of reelection."

Then I thought about something else, another possible motive for lying about the location: "But there's another thing. Something we haven't thought of. What if finding bin Laden here caused a public panic? Remember how it was after 9/11, how everyone hated Muslims? All the hate crimes? It was awful. Maybe they're worried about that happening."

But Nicki shot down my ideas. "No. I doubt they're worried about that. They're Muslims. I don't think Republicans give a fuck about Muslims."

I stammered a little. "Do you really think they're that callous?"

"I don't know. They didn't do much about it the

first time it happened. I mean Bush spoke out against it. But they really didn't do much to stop—"

I interrupted her. Bush was a lot of things, but I didn't think he was racist. I really didn't want to get into it. I didn't like where this was going. I acknowledged her comment but decided to move the conversation forward. "Yeah... But there's one other thing I don't get..."

"What's that?" Nicki didn't resist the topic change. Sometimes we would argue about politics, and it made her uncomfortable, especially when the topic of abortion came up. She was staunchly pro-choice. Sometimes we would just have to agree to disagree. I hated that topic. It almost always ended in screaming.

But during *this* discussion, when Nicki asked me what other thing I didn't understand, I stumbled. "I don't get why..." Then nothing... My mind went blank. I think I was overwhelmed. I was shutting down.

"...Never mind. I lost my train of thought... Where were we?"

Nicki gave me a quick reminder. "We were debating about whether or not Bush cares about Muslims."

Ugh... that topic!

"No. That's not it. I was going to say something else. What else were we talking about?"

She tried again. "You were saying finding him in Brooklyn could cause a public panic."

"No, that's not it either..."

She kept going. "And you basically started screaming about how they never should have started the wars."

"Nope."

By now, Nicki was getting frustrated. "I don't know. I give up!"

But I pressed her harder. "*Come on*. It's right on the tip of my tongue. One more try!"

Nicki shrugged. "One more, but this is the last try. *I'm done...* Before your rant about the wars, you said that finding bin Laden in Brooklyn would be an embarrassment."

"Oh yeah. That's it! It'd also be embarrassing to admit that a normal person—a person like me—found him."

Nicki giggled. *"Normal?"*

I let out a sardonic laugh. "Yeah. Ha! I guess I'm not really normal, but you know what I mean!"

She waved her hands in a forward motion. *"Yes... go on..."*

As I processed my idea, I became increasingly animated. "I mean, all of our greatest minds–half the intelligence community—and a big chunk of the military was working on it. Wouldn't it be embarrassing if people knew that a regular person found bin Laden using the internet? I mean, how would that look for them? ... I can tell you! It'd make them look really bad! Like they didn't know what the fuck they were doing!"

Despite my clear agitation, Nicki remained calm. "You know, all this makes sense. They could change the story enough to make themselves look better."

I continued to theorize. "Yeah. They could announce that because of superior intelligence, bin Laden had been arrested in the Middle East."

In that moment, a dark thought crossed my mind: If they did this—if they told this lie—I was never going to get the $25 million. They could never admit to anyone, not even me, that Osama bin Laden had been arrested in Brooklyn on August 16, 2006. After all, I wasn't an intelligence agent and was under no obligation to keep their secret.

Nicki added to my conclusion: "So, they get the glory for finding bin Laden, but without the humiliation of *where* they found him or *who* found him."

I added disparagingly, "Yeah, and they could do it right before the election, so the Republicans could keep their seats—maybe even gain a few."

My head began to spin. If this were really what they were planning, we had to somehow warn the Democrats. They needed to know what was happening. Did they even know bin Laden had been captured? Probably not. I mean, why would the Republicans reveal their biggest ace-in-the-hole to their competition? That would be a bad strategy.

Maybe if the Democrats got the information before October, they could leak it. Bush would look bad for keeping it secret, the Democrats would win the elections, and I would collect my money. *Win-win...*

I immediately went into troubleshooting mode. I needed a plan. How could I help the Democrats? How could I warn them? I couldn't just call them. Maybe I could just—

But before I could finish my thought, I noticed a hand waving in front of my face. I looked up. It was Nicki. "*Hey!* I thought we were having a conversation!"

"Sorry. I got lost in thought. Why don't you do your own thing for a while? I need to sort this out in my head."

Nicki sounded a little disgusted. "Sure. *Whatever...* I was getting tired of talking, anyhow." She hopped off the futon and headed over to her old, refurbished eMachines PC that was set up on the other side of the room. At this point, I stopped paying attention to her altogether. Maybe she would just play some *Neopets*. But it hardly mattered. I needed to plan my next move.

***

For a frantic moment, I considered taking a trip to DC to reach out to members of Congress in person. But after a quick Google search, I discovered that Congress was in recess... Apparently, they traditionally took off during the entire month of August.[72] Then I had another thought: *Maybe*...maybe we could take a trip to New York and try to gain audience with Hillary Clinton. I would have to mention that idea to Nicki, but later. I needed a faster way to reach the Democrats. I needed to act sooner.

I took a deep breath... *Think, Barbara, think...* That's it... I got it! A fax... I'll send a fax. I could send a fax to some of their home-state offices!

I let out an audible sigh. There was hope. It was only mid-August, so the election was still more than two months away. But I couldn't rely on that. There was too much at risk. I began to worry. Would the fax be enough? What if they didn't read it?

Still on the futon, I borrowed Nicki's laptop (her other computer). Recall, I had left mine at the Old Green House in a fit of paranoia. Then I opened the laptop and cracked my knuckles. *This could take a while...* I began typing, carefully, but feverishly crafting my words. After a couple of hours I was done. I rushed over to Nicki and proudly showed her my finished work. I needed her to read over it to make sure my words came across as credible. She waved it on as acceptable, so I decided to send it. I picked high-ranking Democratic senators, members of the Intelligence Committee. Maybe if they had high-level clearance they could look into this for me, verify my claims, and do something about this situation.

I pulled up my eFax subscription software and attached the message, sending it on to one of the senators. A few minutes later, I called his office and spoke to a youthful-sounding woman who was probably an intern. I asked her if she'd received the fax. She put down the phone and took a moment to search for it. She came back and said it was in her hands. I asked her to make sure it got to the right person. She sounded kind of excited. Perhaps she'd scanned its contents. The young woman gave me an enthusiastic, figurative click of her heels. "I'll make sure they get it!"

Later that evening, I mentioned the idea of a New York trip to Nicki. She thought it could be a fun adventure. Neither of us had ever been to New York. But ultimately, our travel dreams were dashed when I called Dad. "I'm not watchin' your kids for another two weeks while y'all run off to New York. That's the dumbest idea I ever heard." The conversation ended abruptly, and I realized he was right. It had been a pipe dream, a fantasy. It's unlikely Hillary would have granted us an audience, anyhow.

Instead, we took a much shorter trip: a twenty-minute drive to the local Democratic Party office in Austin. Maybe they'd have the means of contacting the powers that be.

I called them and introduced myself, explaining the situation. We headed to the office with a flash drive loaded with any evidence I could find to prove my case. Like the one I gave my Dad, there wasn't much on it. it was mostly just a few links to some websites about recent terror attacks and information about the pending documentary.

But when we got there, it was obvious that the local Democrats weren't really interested in hearing what I had to say. I can only imagine what they must have been thinking when they talked to me. Perhaps to them, I came off as crazed and paranoid. I probably seemed exhausted and disheveled, with the wild-eyed look of a zealot.

However, they courteously, albeit reluctantly, copied the contents of the flash drive and said they'd look it over later. Unsurprisingly, I never heard back from them. Even if they had believed my story, which they clearly did not, they probably couldn't have done anything about it anyhow. Looking back, these people likely had about as many ties to Washington as I did— that is, none.

Yet I wasn't ready to give up. I was determined to keep trying. Perhaps I needed a different approach. Soon, I would come up with some fresh ideas. But not today.

41

A BRIEF ENCOUNTER WITH CNN

Despite my efforts to warn the Democrats about a possible October surprise, I never stopped watching the news. When I wasn't on a project, I was glued to CNN. I kept hoping upon hope that something would come up—something that would prove that bin Laden had been arrested. Mostly, I was still desperately hoping there would be a late announcement.

However, in Austin there was a problem. Nicki didn't have cable or satellite TV, so there was no convenient way to watch CNN or any other national news channel. And getting all of my news from reading online articles didn't seem like enough for me. *No...* I needed CNN. I needed their thoroughness, their nitty-gritty obsession with detail, their over-the-top reporting. I was addicted.

But how would I get my fix without cable? I thought briefly about online streaming. It was something I'd only recently discovered when we finally made the switch from dial-up to broadband, albeit flaky DSL.

Fortunately, what Nicki's apartment lacked in cable TV was counterbalanced by her superior internet. She had Time Warner's Roadrunner, which was cable-based, and it was awesome! This meant I could easily stream video. And at the time, there was a new subscription service I could join that would give me online access to CNN. It was called CNN Pipeline, and it was fabulous.

I quickly set up my subscription, which included a fourteen-day free trial. *Perfect!* ... I probably wouldn't even need it longer than two weeks because by then I'd be home. And even if I continued past the trial, it was worth the money. For $2.95 a month, I would get live, unlimited access to all CNN feeds. This meant that I would see everything from the perspective of the CNN camera, even when the network wasn't broadcasting to the general public.

There were four feeds: the first one constantly broadcast the main news, two and three were reserved for raw footage, while the fourth showed the weather. The two raw feeds were always live and often featured minutia when there wasn't any news breaking. It was not uncommon to see an empty set, some scenery, or maybe people milling around preparing for a story.

From Nicki's apartment, I spent hours toggling between the different feeds. Mostly, I would watch the news as it came in. But occasionally, I would stare for several minutes at images of people doing random things on an inactive set. I kept hoping I could catch them doing something interesting. Maybe I would see someone picking their nose or cleaning their ears.

On the second day of persistently watching CNN Pipeline, I finally got my wish: I saw something interesting on a raw feed. Well, I mean, it was broadcasting on the Pipeline, but that was it. The majority of the public wouldn't see what I saw. Around 4 p.m., I turned on the third feed and noticed a huge group of CNN staff and journalists camped outside the White House. There were chairs and cameras and dozens of people. Some of them were milling around, but most of them were sitting there as if waiting for something. With that amount of media staff camped out on the lawn, I could only assume that the president was about to make an announcement—maybe *the* announcement.

Here's where it got even more interesting: After several minutes of watching a large crowd of people sitting around doing nothing, CNN switched it up and started placing patriotic images over the feed. First, there was a waving flag. Then, there were images of the Statue of Liberty. And playing in the background was "The Star-Spangled Banner."

This was fascinating, especially considering the flagrant display of patriotism was only viewable through a paid subscription to CNN Pipeline. I was gaining unique insights into what CNN was waiting on, and it looked promising. The images of the Statue of Liberty seemed especially symbolic to me. After all, 9/11 had happened in New York, and bin Laden had been captured in Brooklyn.

My mind flashed back to the surge of extreme pro-USA sentiment after September 11, 2001. Everyone had waved flags from their cars and homes and wore red-white-and-blue clothing. It became almost ludicrous, to the point where *SNL* did a skit with Will Farrell wearing what looked like a flag-colored Speedo in an office meeting. But no one could complain because he was showing his "patriotism."

It made sense that capturing bin Laden could lead to another wave of extreme patriotism. Minimally, such an announcement would explain CNN's display of American pride that was being broadcast over the air that evening.

I hollered over to Nicki, who was sitting on the opposite side of the futon. "Hey... Scoot over here... You've gotta see this!"

Nicki looked up from her television, which was playing an awful commercial through her antenna. A local legal firm was trying to encourage lawsuits. *"Let the Hammer work for you!"*

Nicki looked over in my direction "What?"

I repeated myself. "You have to come over and see this."

She seemed annoyed. "Why? ... *Now?* ... I'm comfortable." It was true. She was snuggled up with a pillow and blanket. She looked pretty cozy.

"I'm sorry, honey. This is important. Can you please just come over?"

Nicki reluctantly moved over next to me and leaned toward the laptop. It didn't even occur to me that *I* could have moved over to *her*.

Regardless, I explained to Nicki what I'd been witnessing and showed her the patriotic music and symbols.

Her green eyes widened a bit. "Do you think this means they're going to make an announcement?"

"Yeah... I mean, I hope so. It sure seems suspicious."

I kept monitoring the feed for several hours, noting every time CNN switched between the deluge of journalists and the patriotic symbolism. The change of scenes happened about every fifteen or twenty minutes.

As the hours passed, I became increasingly impatient. I had to know why they were out there. I mean, were they expecting an announcement from the president or what? And was it about bin Laden's capture? Every fiber of my being was telling me that my instincts were correct. There was going to be an announcement—and *soon*.

I finally decided to do something logical. I would call CNN and ask them why they were out there. My heart was pounding as I punched in the number. It all just felt so important... Although I was nervous, the question I asked was short and to the point: "Do you know why y'all are out there?"

The answer came as a bit of a surprise. The man on the other end of the line gave a flat, "No."

I thanked him quickly and ended the call. That was it.

Nothing to see here... *So I thought...*

But not even five minutes later, I received an unexpected phone call.

The woman articulated in loud, clear words.

A woman introduced herself using a loud, clear voice. I can't remember her name, but she said she was with CNN. Then she asked me if I'd called a few minutes ago.

She sounded like she could be in her mid-thirties and had a neutral accent that could not easily be pinned to any particular region. She spoke with the confidence of a seasoned reporter.

CNN? Why would *they* call *me*? But there was no more time to think or to even breathe. She was moving quickly, apparently conducting an interview–an interview with *me*.

"Yes, that was me."

There was an edge of excitement to her voice. "Do

you know why we're waiting outside of the White House?"

This threw me a bit. The woman, who was most likely a reporter, was asking me the question that I'd asked *them*. At this point, I assumed she, in fact, had no clue why she was out there. I thought perhaps I knew more than they did. Maybe she was fishing for new information, which her reporter instincts made her guess I possessed.

I replied with what little information I had. "I think I know why y'all are out there, but I'm not 100 percent certain."

She kept going, raising her voice another notch. She seemed exhilarated. "Well, why do you think we're out there?"

I was cagey when I should have been honest. "I would tell you, but I don't want to steal the president's thunder." Looking back, my words were foolish. This was the perfect opportunity to get the truth out, and I blew it.

I still regret not being honest with the woman. If I had told her everything I knew, we could have commiserated and had a proper interview. But I guess at this point, I was so used to being cagey with the FBI that I was still in that mode. I wasn't used to getting or receiving information without speaking in code. My experiences with the Bureau were just too fresh.

She was persistent. "Can't you at least give me a hint?"

That's when I gave out as much information as I was comfortable with. "It's going to be huge. It's gonna be the biggest thing since 9/11, but it's going to be positive and really good for this country. It's good news, really good news."

This satisfied the reporter.

Moving forward, she took a deep breath and asked me an unexpected question. Although she was using her best reporter voice, her words were loud and ecstatic. "Are you psychic?"

I replied flatly, "No."

Whatever she had been hoping to hear, that must not have been it, because her next words were abrupt and flat. "Well, that's all I need. Thanks."

And that was it. The conversation was over. The reporter had sounded disappointed, and I was left more confused than before the call started.

Then I began to think about it. Why would a CNN reporter try to get me to tell them what the announcement was going to be? More importantly, why would she ask me if I was psychic?

Before I could even begin to fully process what had just happened, I heard a voice from behind me. Nicki had just come out of the bathroom. "Who was that?"

"You're not gonna believe this. It was CNN!"

She sat down next to me, and we started discussing what just happened. After several minutes, we drew a few conclusions.

First, we concluded that after I initially reached out to CNN to ask why they were waiting outside on the White House grounds, the reporter must have suspected that I knew something. Just as I had found Osama bin Laden using investigator instincts, she had used her reporter instincts to find *me*. This must have been why she called back.

The reporter must have known—or at least heard rumors—about bin Laden's arrest and a pending announcement from the president. She'd probably also heard whispers that the person responsible for locating him was psychic.

If there were rumors about a psychic leading the FBI to bin Laden, then she thought I might be that person.

So, when she asked if I knew why they were out there, she was fishing to see how much I knew. She wanted to verify whether the rumors were true and if we were on the same page. But she didn't want to put words in my mouth. Her job was to report the news.

When I said the news was very "positive" and the "biggest thing since 9/11," she became convinced that I knew what the president was going to announce.

Once she realized that we were, in fact, on the same page, she seemed thrilled. She must have been nearly convinced she was talking to the person who had found bin Laden. This would be a huge break for her, as a reporter, and for CNN.

Then, there was the mysterious question: "Are you psychic?" This was the third time someone suspected me of using psychic abilities to lead the FBI to Osama bin Laden. The first time was when the Houston agent had questioned me the morning after I reported bin Laden's alias and location. The second time was when the celebrating New York agent asked, "Ya got the lotto pics?" And now, number three: The CNN reporter had just asked me the direct, blunt question, "Are you psychic?"

But why did people keep thinking I was psychic? Like I said, at this point, I could only conclude that the prominent rumor was that bin Laden had been found by a psychic. What else could possibly explain an average citizen with ordinary resources finding him?

The reporter most likely believed that I'd been

claiming to be psychic.

So, there it was: Again, like I said, when I didn't claim to be psychic, the reporter was probably disappointed because she thought she had the wrong person. At that point, her voice had dropped and fallen flat, as she told me, "That's all I need." She must have been really disappointed. It's a pity that she hadn't been open to the possibility of hearing a different explanation for what I'd accomplished. It's too bad her reporter instincts had failed her at that important juncture.

However, after speaking to CNN, I became convinced that the president had experienced a change of heart and was going to make an announcement that night. I stayed up late watching CNN Pipeline. But once again, I was disappointed. Figuratively, the ice melted, the champagne grew warm, and the announcement never came. The president had changed his mind.

Once again, it was just over.

42

PHONE A FRIEND

Not long after my encounter with CNN, I began to realize that being in Austin wasn't actually making us any safer. I knew in my heart that if the government wanted to find me, I'd be found. Being there and using a prepaid phone made me feel slightly better, but it wasn't really enough. Nothing but time was going to help at this point.

So, about a week after we fled to Austin, we returned home. I was broken, but not defeated. Enough days had passed that it was starting to sink in that nothing terrible was going to happen to my family or me. But I was still worried that I was being monitored. What if they were waiting, watching to see how things played out on my end? Regardless, I couldn't hide indefinitely. I needed to go home. My kids needed me.

Even before we pulled into our driveway, I knew that my efforts were far from over. For the next few weeks, I would continue to try to get the word out to the Democrats about the possibility of an October surprise. I would call CNN repeatedly, but my story wasn't taken seriously. My words must have seemed crazy to the person answering the phone—that I had found Osama bin Laden, and the government was covering it up. I even tried mentioning that one of their reporters had called me to ask questions. I explained that I was trying to follow up. But nothing I said made any difference. They were no longer interested. I'd blown my window of opportunity to speak to CNN.

Frustrated, I tried to think of another way to reach out to the press. I immediately thought about Brandy. Maybe I could try again, make her see reason. Maybe if I gave her all the details, she would listen. And if that didn't work, I'd try my mother's tactic: I'd use guilt.

***

After flipping open my phone, I absently keyed in my sister's number. Like most people in 2006, she still had a landline.

It rang seven times before I gave up. Mom had taught me that it was rude to let it ring longer than that. I always counted. I tried again, in case she just hadn't made it to the phone in time. *No luck...* She was probably still at work... So, I called her cell phone, which I also had memorized. After several rings, it went to voicemail. I rang it again. Same thing. There was only one other option: her work phone. Brandy wasn't supposed to get personal calls on it, but we'd occasionally sneak one by. I input her number and said a little prayer that she'd answer.

Finally, my sister picked up, sounding exasperated. "*What?!* I'm in a big hurry. I have to get this out in an hour!" I could tell from her tone that she'd seen my number come up twice on her other phone and was annoyed by my repeated calls.

At that point, I felt a little guilty about calling Brandy at work. I knew I had to be quick.

"Brandy, I need your help with something important."

"Really? What is it?"

I hesitated. I knew if I admitted it was about bin Laden, she'd be resistant. "I can't talk about it right now."

But Brandy was suspicious. "Does it have to do with that Osama bin Laden stuff?"

I dodged the question. "Look. It's important. I can't talk about it right now. Can we just meet up?"

Fortunately, Brandy didn't put up much of a fight. "*Fine.* I don't have time to talk right now, anyhow." She sounded a bit panicked, but being in a rush didn't usually stop her from taking a few minutes for her little sister, especially when I needed help. Brandy was a kind, caring individual, albeit a worrier.

Still, she needed to get off the phone. "Can I just call you when I get off work?"

I pressed a little. I wanted to make sure I heard back from her. "When do you get off work?"

"After nine. I'll call you when I get home."

A couple of hours later, she called me, and we agreed to meet at her place at 4 p.m. the next day. I was relieved we weren't meeting at my place. What if my house was bugged?

The evening passed, and I woke up the next day, nervous about meeting with my sister. A couple of hours after waking, Nicki and I gathered up the kids. Sometimes when I was particularly anxious, I would take them with me everywhere, no matter how mundane. It was like the severe anxiety attack I'd had in Walmart. I felt like I needed to know where everyone was, that they were safe. It was instinct. If they were with me, I didn't have to worry. If they were with me, I knew nothing bad would happen to them without my knowledge. I was like a mother duck lining up her ducklings. They would follow close.

About forty-five minutes after leaving home, we knocked on Brandy's door. It was time to get down to business. She and I settled in on her reclining couch. Nicki leaned back in the easy chair that was positioned near the couch. I doubted she would participate in the conversation. She was mostly there for moral support. But when push came to shove, I knew that she could back up my story. After all, Nicki had been with me during most of my calls to the FBI and had heard my half of the conversations. She had often extrapolated the words of the agents based on my responses. She knew what was up. She knew the truth. But primarily, the conversation would be between me and my sister, whose help I desperately needed.

Meanwhile, Peter and Daun ran off with Stella. (Recall, this was Brandy's five-year-old—my niece—who I usually only saw at family parties.) She and the kids were going to play Super-Nintendo together in the sunroom. Stella was always happy when she had kids to play with, especially Daun. She didn't mind that my kids were older than she was. And, no doubt, Brandy was glad they were around to entertain her.

Before we got started, Brandy got up and grabbed us some glasses of ice water. I took a long sip, grimacing a bit at the flavor. Her water, like at Nicki's Austin apartment, was disgusting city water, made only slightly better by adding ice.

"I wish you had some diet soda or something." But I knew what the response would be before she opened her mouth.

"I don't believe in artificial sweeteners. They're worse for you than the real stuff." She kept on for a few minutes about why aspartame was so awful. It was supposedly a derivative of ant poison. And according to her, it caused cancer and mental confusion and had all kinds of horrible side-effects. As she continued her tirade, I became increasingly frustrated. I wasn't here to be lectured to about the evils of diet soda.

"Okay! ... *I get it!* ... I don't like it, but I get it. But honestly, I'm not supposed to have real coke because I have diabetes. And I'm not giving up soda."

Despite my protests, she wouldn't stop. "But diet soda has *so* much sodium in it. It makes you retain fluids. It increases blood pressure—"

"Oh, my God! *I give up.* We have more important things to talk about."

Brandy finally stopped her polemic. "Okay. What is it? What's so important that you couldn't talk about it on the phone?"

I stared at her for a few seconds and took a deep breath, unsure of what words were going to come out of my mouth. "Okay... Yes... I hate to say it, but you were right. It *is* about the bin Laden stuff."

Her jaw dropped. "*I knew it!*"

Brandy had a very strong intuition. I should have known I couldn't hide my motives from her. She kept going. "I already told you... I can't help you. I need evidence. I can't just report that stuff based on your word."

But I brushed it off. "I know. I know what you said... But you haven't heard everything. You don't know all the details."

After a few minutes of negotiations, Brandy agreed to hear my story. She didn't promise she'd help, but at least it was a start.

I began with the early cases. I told her about the serial killer, the missing pregnant woman, and a few others. During my recount, I meticulously laid out the evidence I had gathered to find them, followed by the responses from law enforcement. I told her that I wasn't sure of the results of some of them because I hadn't followed up yet.

Finally, I told her about my progression to hunting terrorists, starting with Boussora. I tried to choose my words carefully, but found myself stumbling.

I emphasized that my research had been solid. I told her about the suspicious MySpace page and the pattern I'd discovered. I gave her all the details of my system. I told her about how I called the FBI with his contact information and how, the next day, the FBI had asked me for my Social Security number.

Then I excitedly told her about the take-down of the transatlantic aircraft plot, and explained that I thought it had happened because I found Boussora.

She was incredulous. "But how do you know your tip had anything to do with it?"

I was annoyed. "Weren't you listening? Didn't you hear everything I said?"

But clearly my word wasn't good enough. "That doesn't prove anything. You need hard evidence. You're just guessing."

She was right, of course. I was just guessing. But I was convinced I was correct—mostly. I wasn't as sure about Boussora, but I was 100 percent certain I was right about bin Laden.

I continued down a linear path, describing every detail of the events leading up to bin Laden's arrest. I included quotes from several federal agents. I told her about one of them asking me how I found The Big Guy. I recounted how the same agent had concluded that I was a "gifted researcher" and "true patriot."

Finally, I told her about the unusual occurrence, when the agents had been celebrating loudly in the New York office—even putting me on speakerphone. I explained how they had a nickname for me: The Green Lady. Then, I described how one of them asked me for the lotto picks, presumably because they thought I was either psychic or really lucky. Finally, I went into details about their laughter and how happy they all were.

Then I shared my conclusion with her—my sister, the journalist.

"That's when I realized that they got 'em."

Brandy paused for a moment... "Got *who*?"

My sister was frustrating me. I mean, was she even paying attention?

"Got bin Laden."

"*Bin Laden?* What makes you think that? You don't know why they were acting that way. It could have been anything!"

I tried to explain my intuition. "They were celebrating something really huge, and it was only a few days after I turned in my tip. My tip led them to bin Laden."

My gut lurched as she shifted forward in her seat a

bit before dismissing my words. "*No...* There's no way. Barbara, you didn't find bin Laden. Those guys were joking around with you."

I tried to break down my reasoning, carefully going back over the facts. "What do you mean, joking? They sounded like they were celebrating. They were all really happy. They put me on speakerphone. I know in my gut that they were celebrating something really big, and it involved me. I know they found bin Laden."

But this wasn't enough. And looking back, it shouldn't have been enough. The New York agents hadn't actually said *what* they were celebrating. But there was so much more—so much more evidence to come. There was no refuting the truth.

I went on to explain the conversation I'd had with an agent later on the same night of the celebration. "Brandy, I was promised an announcement from the president. The agent said there would 'absolutely' be an announcement."

But she replied with deeper skepticism, "I don't think he was being serious. More like sarcastic."

I got defensive. "Brandy, I can tell when someone is being sarcastic. He was dead serious and calm. His words were sincere."

Brandy was being unreasonable. "Even if he meant it—that there was going to be an announcement from the president—he could have been talking about something else. You didn't find bin Laden. Maybe it was a different terrorist. Someone less import—"

I cut her short. "Why would it be someone less important? The president doesn't make special announcements for every little thing. Besides, there was the celebration. Like I said, what had happened was huge. The announcement *had* to have been about bin Laden."

Brandy continued with her negativity. "I don't think so. No way." At this point, she stopped making logical arguments and resorted to simple, emotional appeals.

Despite this, I attempted to push past her cynicism, moving forward to disclose how I'd been treated like a hero the day after Osama bin Laden's arrest—how the Houston agents had thanked me profusely for my tips. They wouldn't have done this if I found any other terrorist. They would only have done this for bin Laden. Then I went on to recount how, after hours of being treated like a hero, the FBI suddenly and abruptly cut me off.

"You see? They cut you off because they didn't want to talk to you. You didn't find anyone."

I continued my defense. "*No!* They had been thanking me and treating me like a hero. In fact, some of them even sounded like they wanted to cry... They were so sentimental. Then they suddenly switched and wouldn't even acknowledge my exis—"

She abruptly stopped me. "See?"

"No! They quit talking to me because they were planning a coverup. It had happened, but there wasn't going to be an announcement!"

Brandy persisted. "Barbara, if they *had* gotten bin Laden, why *wasn't* there an announcement? Why on Earth would they cover it up?"

I stumbled a bit. I didn't know why. I grasped for straws. "I don't know. Maybe because he was in Brooklyn. We went to Afghanistan to find bin Laden, and here he was in the United States. We started a war for no reason. Or maybe they wanted to avoid a public panic."

"*Get real!* It'd be to Bush's advantage to announce such a thing."

I took her cue. "Exactly why I think they're planning to announce it in October, closer to the midterms. I think they're planning an October surprise to stop the Democrats from taking over Congress. And I think they're going to lie about where they found him. There are recent so-called leaks all over the news that he was spotted near Pakistan."

But talking to her was like talking to a brick wall. It was like she couldn't even process my words, or draw logical conclusions. "Barbara, you're not making any sense. If this had really happened, the president would've just announced it."

In that moment, I realized we were going in circles. I had to do something to get through to my sister. Something... *Anything...* I was desperate.

Brandy probably didn't want to believe that her sister, of all people, had found Osama bin Laden. To her, the scenario must have seemed ridiculous.

Desperate to convince Brandy of the truth, I threw out the final punch—what I saw as the clincher, the smoking gun. I told her about the agent who challenged me to "prove it" when I said, "You know you guys arrested Osama."

But Brandy was persistent. "'Prove it' could have meant anything. *Prove what?*"

I kept going. "Were you even listening? What did I just say?" I repeated myself for emphasis, "He said, 'prove it' right after I said, 'You know you guys arrested Osama.' That means he wanted me to prove they'd gotten bin Laden. I mean, why would he say that if there was nothing to prove? What else could he have possibly meant?"

But Brandy didn't budge an inch. "Maybe he was jerking your chain. Like, yes, you know so much. Why don't you prove it? How dare you accuse me?"

"But, Brandy, you didn't hear his tone. He wasn't jerking my chain. I could tell he was being honest. And he was really angry. And when I told him they'd been celebrating something really big the other day, and that's when they found him, he replied, 'You got me. Now turn me in. It'll make ya feel better.' Just like that: 'You got me. Now turn me in. It'll make ya feel better.' He repeated it like three times."

But Brandy wouldn't stop. "Don't you see? He was messing with you. 'You got me. Now turn me in.' He knew you didn't have any proof. No proof of something that never happened."

I found myself repeating the same arguments, as if saying it enough times would change her mind. I felt like a very noisy, frustrated, broken record. I was begging for my sister's support and not getting it, so my temper kept rising. "You don't get it! The FBI doesn't joke around! He would have no reason to pull my chain! He was angry. He didn't get credit for what he'd done, and I didn't get credit for my part!"

"But he told you to turn him in. Why would he say that? He was being a smart-ass." Well, this could have been true. The "evidence" I presented to him to try to "prove it" was no evidence. I had nothing on him. I relented to my sister's claim that he probably didn't literally mean that I should turn him in.

My sister brandished a look of satisfaction. She must have thought I'd given in.

But I hadn't...

I kept going. "But he wasn't joking when he told me to prove it! He was really mad!"

As the argument escalated, I was getting louder and angrier, and so was she.

Brandy shook her head hard and lit into me. "Barbara, you're *crazy*! There's no, no, *no* way you found Osama bin Laden!"

I hollered back furiously, letting every ounce of my frustration out on my sister.

"Why would he say 'prove it' if there was nothing to prove?!"

I was only vaguely aware that I was screaming at the top of my lungs. I was running on rage and adrenaline.

"And why was I promised there would be an announcement from the president?!"

"And why would an agent ask me if I found The Big Guy?! Why would he ask me how I did it?!" I kept going, unable to control myself. "And why would he call me a 'gifted researcher' and a 'true patriot' if I *hadn't* found The Big Guy?"

I started hyperventilating as tears poured from my red, hot face.

"Why? Why?! *Why?!*"

It was useless. I was on a merry-go-round, spinning completely out of control. Clearly, this conversation— argument—was going nowhere. Brandy saw it, too.

She snapped back at me loudly and emphatically. "Barbara, you need to *calm down*! I'm not your enemy here. I'm just saying that no one is gonna believe your story. The FBI was joking with you. I'm sorry for what you've gone through. You have been horribly, horribly misled. Those guys weren't celebrating. They were being assholes. They were jerking your chain."

I took a couple of deep breaths. Brandy was right. I needed to calm down. This was my sister, not an enemy. I clenched my fists tightly on the arms of the sofa chair. I drew in another deep breath, tightened my neck and shoulders, and released the energy all at once as I breathed out. This was the best I could do for stress relief. I had to get myself under control. In that moment, I realized I was crying—no, I was wailing.

More deep breaths.

Finally, I took a huge swig of water, set down the glass, and began talking through loud sobs, gasping for air. "Brandy, I'm sorry. I didn't mean to blow up at you. I'm just really frustrated. I can't get anyone to believe my story, and I'm really desperate to get the word out. I didn't mean to take it out on you."

Brandy softened, although she fell short of crying. "I know. I'm sorry if I pushed you too hard. Obviously, we have a difference of opinion."

Neither of us had budged. We agreed to disagree. And I was no closer to getting the truth out to the public than before I'd met with my sister.

***

Over the next several days, I would continue to plead with Brandy, seeking her help as a journalist—sometimes over the phone, other times through email. But she still wouldn't budge.

Brandy summed up the problem well in one particularly heated phone conversation: "Barbara, I keep trying to tell you...I can't just take your word for it. I can't, I *cannot* present your story with no real evidence."

I was desperate. "But there *is* evidence! There's my word! I'm a witness."

But she stood her ground, frustrating me more and more with each utterance coming from her lips. "No. I need more than just your word. I need hard-core evidence—facts—something in writing. A recording... *anything*."

This was going nowhere. We each stubbornly dug our heels in, neither of us moving an inch. I knew what I knew, and Brandy thought she knew best.

For the first time, I regretted not recording my conversations with the FBI. Brandy said she needed hard-core proof. Hell, the *world* needed hard-core proof. They needed to hear the tone in the agents' voices. They needed to believe that my account of the facts was accurate because, according to my sister, my eyewitness testimony wasn't powerful enough evidence. She was a journalist, and she required more. It was disheartening. Brandy—my own sister—clearly didn't see me as a credible witness. *No...* She needed more than just my word to report the news.

However, there were very good reasons why I never recorded my conversations with the FBI. Mostly, never in a million years did I think I would get screwed over. Plus, recording the calls would have been awkward. It would have ruined the flow and made me anxious and paranoid. What if they knew I was recording them? Surely, they'd be able to tell. Then I would have gotten zero information out of them.

But none of that mattered anymore. The opportunity had been lost. I had no proof, just the words of numerous federal agents and the CNN reporter echoing through my brain. And who knows what Brandy was thinking. For some reason, instead of accepting the truth, it was easier for her to believe there was an agency-wide conspiracy to make fun of me—that the FBI agents from both the Houston and New York offices had made a coordinated effort to jeer at the person who claimed she'd found Osama bin Laden.

In fact, the theory that the FBI was playing a joke on me was laughable—much more so than the idea that I'd found bin Laden. Her thoughts didn't hold water, especially because they were espoused by a person who had never really dealt with the Bureau. Sure, she'd spoken to individual agents casually while on a story. But she'd never spoken to them in an official capacity. What she didn't seem to realize is that the FBI does not joke around while on the job. They're trained professionals who follow protocol to the best of their abilities.

That being said, federal agents are human beings, not robots. They celebrate, like the rowdy New Yorkers at the beginning of the story; they are curious, like the agent who asked if I was psychic and how I'd found The Big Guy; and sometimes they're even openly enthusiastic, like Agent Miles, when she responded to my first terrorist tip by emphatically exclaiming, *"I'll pass it on!"*

But these agents would never, for any reason, conspire to concoct a huge, ridiculous prank that spanned multiple offices and multiple agents, in order to screw with someone who was clearly trying to help them.

No... If the FBI were tired of me, or they thought I was crazy, they wouldn't have pranked me. They simply wouldn't have taken my calls. I never would have made it past the screener. I never would have spoken to a single duty agent, and I certainly wouldn't have been asked by the Houston office to call New York directly and ask for the Terrorism Task Force. If my tips had been worthless, the Bureau wouldn't have wanted me to waste the Task Force's time. Their job was too important to take trivial tips or pull pranks.

On my end, I was convinced it all added up. There was only one conclusion, and I didn't understand why my sister couldn't see it. I had led the FBI to bin Laden, and he'd been taken into custody in Brooklyn by the New York branch. There was no refuting it, and like I said before, Nicki was there to back me up. She'd heard my end of almost all the conversations with the FBI. She knew what was going on. Her brain had often filled in the gaps of what must have been said on the other end. She was my witness.

But the pain of the conversations I had with Brandy went far beyond her refusal to cover the news. It felt personal, like she was refusing *me*, refusing her sister. No matter what I said, she wouldn't believe the truth. And if my own sister wouldn't believe it, what chance did I have with everyone else?

Plus, Brandy had taken things a step further. She didn't think I could tell the difference between an agency-wide conspiracy to jerk my chain and a sincere outpouring of information. I knew there was only one conclusion that she could be drawing.

My sister thought I was delusional.

43

THE STORY OF MY LIFE

In the end, after leaving Brandy's house, I felt like a failure. I had failed to get the word out to the press or the public and failed to warn the Democrats of a possible October surprise. I had failed on all fronts.

But I wasn't ready to give up. I wanted to be believed, even if it wasn't by the press or the general public. Maybe I could try someone I wasn't related to, someone less skeptical, someone who would listen. *But who? ...* I thought about it for a moment: *Adam...* I would tell Adam! Surely, *he*, above everyone I knew, would be happy for me. I mean, this was all so exciting, and I had no one to share it with but Nicki and the kids. *Yes...* I would go to work, and I would talk about it. Maybe, just maybe, he would be supportive.

So, a few days later, I tried to brush off my sister's cynicism and headed into the shop. I turned the key and walked into the dusty room, hoping Adam would be there. But there was no Adam. However, he had told me on the phone earlier that he'd left me some work. I checked the usual spot along the wall, and there were three dusty computer towers laid out with a little yellow Post-It note on each. As I approached them, the scent of stale cigarette smoke, heavy dust, and cobwebs filled my nose. *Typical...* You could always tell when the PC owners were smokers.

The first sticky was attached to the side of the source of the smell: a large black, older-looking Dell. The note simply read, *"Viruses."*

I let out a deep sigh. I worried it was going to be boring. I didn't want to get stuck watching the screen again, like so many times before. But maybe I'd get lucky and the computer would require some challenging tweaks.

The next assignment was a dust-covered, white Hewlett Packard (HP). The note read, *"BSOD."* I shuttered a bit. *Those were the worst!* Adam was referring to the dreaded "blue screen of death," which was the mysterious blue splash screen that appeared right after *Windows* crashed. If it popped up, that meant there would be codes at the bottom to look up. Their meanings were often redundant, so could be difficult to decipher. The fix might be as simple as replacing the RAM or as complicated as figuring out which software driver was causing the issue. Whatever the cause, BSODs could be a nightmare, and sometimes indicated a problem that could only be fixed with a new motherboard. Those were the cases where machines were usually added to the junk pile in the center of the office.

The note on the third computer, a gray eMachines, simply said, "Won't boot." My thoughts turned to sarcasm. *That's specific, Adam.* Did he mean it was dead, or did he mean the screen was black? Did it whir? Did the motherboard beep? I took a deep breath. I guess I'd find out.

I carefully lifted the "virus" system. I was going

to run the scans while I worked on the other more demanding projects. I heaved the heavy tower onto the table and connected all the necessary peripherals. I did the VGA video port first, and then the PS2 mouse and keyboard. Finally, I plugged in the machine and pressed the "on" button. It whirred on and slowly began to boot. After several seconds, it seemed to be stuck on the black *Windows XP* title screen. I stared at it for a full minute, quickly losing patience. *Argh!* ... Should I shut it down and try again? Should I start over and go into Safe Mode? But, in that moment, I hated my brain. I never knew when to give up. How long would it take just to get a frickin' desktop?

I didn't know if I should force a shutdown and restart, or wait. This was the story of my life.

Wasn't that exactly what was happening to me in the real world, the world outside this office? I was pushing and pushing and pushing, waiting for something to happen, waiting for the news of Osama bin Laden's arrest to take off. Waiting to make some money so I could pay off my debt. I was waiting for uncertain results, not knowing if I should quit and do something else or keep hoping that the desktop would pop up.

So many times, I would give up and long-press the power button to force a shutdown. Or worse, I would just unplug the cord. But this "solution" would sometimes only serve to further the PC's complications by causing file corruption.

Other times, I would get to the desktop, and it would be too slow and broken for me to even run a scan. That's when I would go into Safe Mode and tackle the problem. This barebones, diagnostic version of *Windows* usually boots, even if normal mode fails.

Maybe that's what my life needed: a Safe Mode–an easier, less complicated version from which to work out the kinks.

If only life were as simple as running a virus scan...

But this time, I did something that I didn't normally do: After a full three minutes of gawking at the title screen, I walked away. Maybe I would do something else and come back later. Staring at it would do no good. As I stepped back, I thought perhaps this was what it would take with the bin Laden news. Maybe if I walked away from it, some years down the line, it would resolve. The challenge was that in the case of bin Laden, I couldn't stop staring. It would be several months before I could pull away.

After moving on from the "virus" computer, I headed toward the next project. But before I could reach it, I heard a noise—something coming from the door—the sound of rattling keys. I walked over to the entrance and hollered, "It's unlocked!"

Adam came in the door, exasperated. "You really shouldn't leave it unlocked. It's not safe."

I shrugged. It wasn't actually that bad of a neighborhood, but I knew where my friend was coming from. I was a woman alone in a shop full of valuable equipment. Of course, we never locked it when we were both there. There was safety in numbers.

Adam walked over toward the jobs he'd left me. "Did you get my notes?"

"Yeah. I already started setting them up. The Dell is being really stupid. Stuck at the *Windows* splash screen."

"Yeah, I noticed that when I tried to boot it earlier. How long has it been stuck there?"

I glanced over at it. "Wait! I see some icons! I think

it's coming up."

If only my life were *that* simple...

My thoughts turned glum. I felt like the bin Laden "icons" were never going to appear.

Adam and I bantered about computers for a while, discussing recent projects. But although I enjoyed the tech talk, I needed to take the conversation in a different, heavier, direction.

Regardless, we kept up the banter for a while. And around the time Adam began complaining about the server job he was stuck on, I interrupted him.

"Hey, can I change the topic for a minute?"

Adam had been a little worked up by the previous topic, but when I moved to change the subject, his features softened. "Sure. What's up?"

"Do you remember how I said I was searching online for missing people and killers to try to get the reward money?"

Recall that I had filled him in on the details a few weeks prior.

"Yes. What ever happened with that?"

I hesitated for a moment. "Well, actually ... I started looking for terrorists."

Adam seemed surprised, but intrigued. *"Really?"*

I kept going. "Yeah. Some of them are worth $5 million."

I definitely had his interest at that point.

"Wow... That's a lot of money! How's that going?"

I paused again, thinking of how to tell him about bin Laden. "Well, actually, I found a really big one. This one's worth twenty-five million."

"Wait. *What?* Isn't that *bin Laden?*" I guess he'd heard about the extravagant reward.

"Yeah... And guess what?"

"What?"

"I found him, and I'm gonna be rich!"

Despite everything that had happened over the last few weeks, I was still convinced that I could get the truth out and collect the money. I wasn't ready to stop staring at the screen. I was going to beat this. I was *going* to get the money. I wasn't ready to walk away.

Adam's face dropped. I watched his eyes shift from intrigue and amusement to concern. His face flushed red, and he shook his head slightly as if shaking off a dream. *"No!* Sorry, but it didn't happen."

I was frustrated. *Great!* ... Another skeptic.

But he didn't know the details, so I was determined to fill him in.

"No, wait. Let me explain." Then I went through the entire story chronologically, telling Adam about everything the FBI had said to me. To name a few, I told him how I had been called a "gifted researcher" and a "true patriot" and how I'd been promised an announcement. I even explained the teary-eyed accolades by grateful agents and the bitter challenge of the New York agent who told me to "prove it!"

But nothing worked. Adam couldn't be happy for me. He couldn't accept that his friend had found the most notorious terrorist in the world. Maybe Adam was too smart, or maybe he didn't have enough faith in me. All I knew was that it hurt.

When Adam left the office, I tried to avoid falling into a pit of despair and self-pity. It felt like no one would ever believe my story—not the media, not my family, not even my closest friends. I was stuck, and the computer just kept whirring. I wondered if I would ever see the desktop.

44

WAPO

But my self-pity didn't last long. Even with Adam's disbelief and my sister's cynicism, I wasn't deterred. I *would* get the word out. I *would* collect the money. And maybe by doing so, I could help get the Democrats elected or even help stop the wars in Iraq and Afghanistan.

My next, more long-term effort to warn the Democrats of the possibility of an October surprise would come a few weeks later. I would join a *Washington Post (WAPO)* political forum, where I would spend nearly a month communicating with members, many of whom I suspected held positions of power.

So, two weeks after I found bin Laden, I joined the forum using my real name and sharing "rumors" about bin Laden's arrest. However, after a couple of days, I got nervous, deleted most of my posts, and went incognito. I chose the pseudonym "Leslie Powers." The name was meant to be a play on words for "powerful lesbian." I crossed my fingers that the meaning was subtle. I didn't really want to be super out, the name was just supposed to be my own little inside joke.

When I first started reading the board, I found the posts to be kind of difficult to comprehend. The participants were intellectual, often using long sentences and big words. Even worse, they used a lot of slang terms and acronyms—many of them obscure. For example, instead of Osama bin Laden, they always used the initials "UBL," while President Bush was called "W," "Junior," or "Chimpie." So, because of members' wordiness and frequent use of slang, the threads were difficult to decode. But eventually I caught on. After hours of scrutiny, I mastered the forum's unique lexicon and used it to infiltrate the threads.

The site was inundated with avid Democrats debating with staunch Republicans. And there was a quality to their posts that made the forum unique. Trolling and flaming were rare. I mean, as with most message boards, there were unfair jabs, sarcasm, and things of that ilk, but they were mostly harmless attempts at humor. One moment, the participants would seem to be shouting at each other; the next, they'd be conceding points or congratulating people for good arguments. In other words, most of the discussions were civil, but perhaps unpredictable.

So, this wasn't an ordinary message board. Unlike other forums I'd encountered, the participants often disagreed, but mostly got along with, and even liked, each other. By today's standards, the level of civility in the *WAPO* interactions was most comparable to that of Quora.

Among the group members, I found open-minded, politically-active people from both parties. But most importantly, the members were classy. It was clear from the content that the majority of them were highly educated and that some were wealthy. One Republican even confided that his family had made its money in oil.

To earn the trust of participants, I became deeply involved in the forum's intense discussions, covering a wide range of political topics and current events—some of which included Osama bin Laden.

Once, I even initiated a rather formal debate about abortion with a woman who was a fan of Hillary Clinton. Although there was no clear winner, the discourse had been respectful. This result was highly unusual for a topic that normally ended in screaming under other circumstances.

Eventually, once I'd proven that I could hold my own in civil debates, I started posting about bin Laden's arrest and warned the readers about the threat of an October surprise. Despite how impossible my story must have sounded, they treated me with respect and never judged nor called me crazy or a liar. Many seemed to consider the possibility that my intel was correct.

Because of their hyper-awareness of the intricacies of American politics, I suspected that a lot of the forum participants were DC insiders or even members of Congress. I also got the impression that some of them knew each other in real life and were perhaps even friends. Plus, I thought it was logical that politicians would frequent the *Washington Post* forum because it was based in DC, and the most likely to cover even the most minuscule events in Washington.

A few weeks into my message board experiment, I created a rather lengthy post in which I asked for help from people "in the know." I mentioned thinking that some of them were people of influence with access to insider knowledge. One of the participants replied to this comment, *"You're not wrong."*

Days later, a member who I believe had some access to intelligence agreed to help me. He was a Democrat, going by a screen name that parodied "William Jefferson Clinton." After a lengthy discussion with him, he agreed to look into my claims. Of course, I had no way of knowing whether or not he could obtain such information. However, a few days later, he indicated that he'd found something. He told me I should watch the news over the next few weeks, and suggested it was time to pull out the champagne

So on September 23, 2006, I felt like I was being taken seriously by my new friends and that I had successfully infiltrated this tight-knit community. More importantly, I had a sense that I was making progress toward my goals of getting the word out about bin Laden's arrest and verifying the truth.

But then there was a sudden shift in attitude on the board. There was a disturbing rumor circulating in the news that Osama bin Laden had died of natural causes as a result of a severe case of typhoid.[73] I was shocked and dismayed, and some other members seemed equally stunned by the news. I asked the William Jefferson Clinton clone—the man I was certain had verified my claims—if he thought the word of bin Laden's arrest would ever be released, in light of the death rumors. We both agreed that this was probably the end of the line and the truth would not be revealed any time soon.

My thinking was that the news of bin Laden's death by natural causes was a clever cover story for what I suspected had really happened: Osama bin Laden had died in custody and news of his arrest had been buried along with his body.

**

Within a day of their release, the rumors of Osama bin Laden's death were quickly refuted by US intelligence.[74] However, my mind wasn't changed. I continued to believe that he had, in fact, passed away by either natural or nefarious causes. His death was the only thing I could think of that would explain why there had been no delayed announcement about the arrest—no October surprise. Years later, after attaining new information, my opinion of what happened to bin Laden after his incarceration would change. I would consider the eerie possibility that he could still be alive and in hiding under house arrest. (More on this later.)

However, in 2006, the thought of bin Laden's death made my imagination run wild. Had he been summarily executed? Was he beaten to death during an interrogation? Did he commit suicide? Was he denied healthcare?

There had been credible rumors as far back as March, 2000, that bin Laden was suffering from kidney and liver failure and required regular dialysis.[75] Maybe he didn't get his dialysis treatment. Or perhaps he refused it. A few weeks could be more than enough time for someone with end-stage kidney failure to die without treatment.[76]

Yet regardless of whether or not bin Laden had died, the idea of it was a game-changer for me. At this point, I believed there was not going to be an announcement from the president, even in the form of an October surprise about a so-called arrest in or near Pakistan. (Like I indicated earlier, recent rumors from the intelligence community had placed him in the area.) *No...* If any semblance of the truth was to ever be released, it was on me.

At that point, I abandoned my efforts on the *WAPO* forum. After nearly a month of intense infiltration, I stopped leaving messages. I dropped the site like a hot potato. I was going to stop trying to get the word out and get some rest. I was done for the moment.

45

NO EXIT

Exhausted by more than a month of tireless effort on the *WAPO* boards, I felt lost and defeated. And two months later, my hopes of getting the truth out about Osama bin Laden's arrest seemed like a distant memory. Plus, it was late November, and the 2006 mid-term elections had sailed by with no October surprise and an easy Democratic sweep. In my mind, it was all over. I didn't want anything more do with the bin Laden stuff. I just wanted to forget about it all and move on with my life.

Determined to wash my hands of it, I decided to drop everything, throw myself deeper into PC repair work, and apply to graduate school at Sam Houston State University (SHSU). I needed a distraction. I needed to do something that didn't involve bin Laden or amateur detective work. I needed to focus on fixing computers for a while and get my mind off my troubles. Grad school would help bring in money via financial aid. In that moment, I was planning on getting a master's in education and a certification to teach high school computer science.

So I happily worked for Adam, making about $300 a week and having lots of fun solving problems. But about six weeks in, something started gnawing at me. There was a case that I had never reported to the FBI. It had been one of my early ones. But before I could call in the results, I had become knee-deep in terrorists, including bin Laden. In fact, I had nearly forgotten about it until now. The target had been the writers of the MyDoom virus.

As of 2004, MyDoom, also known as Novarg, was the fastest-spreading virus in history,[77] still holding the record for the fastest-spreading mass mailer worm to this day. It infected millions of machines,[78] spreading through email attachments and utilizing victims' contact lists.[79] It tied up the web and operated as a denial of service code, mostly against SCO, the company that had threatened to sue Linux users in an intellectual property complaint.[80] Eventually, MyDoom would cost SCO and other companies at least $38 billion in damages, presumably because of slowdowns, removal efforts, and system repairs.[81]

Fairly soon after the initial attack, SCO offered a $250,000 reward for information leading to the arrest of the MyDoom authors. Subsequently, Microsoft added an additional $250,000 incentive for finding the perpetrators.[82] I'd conducted research in an attempt to root them out and collect the bounty, but I was side-tracked by my bin Laden efforts and failed to report my findings to the FBI. So two months later, after giving up on getting the word out about bin Laden's arrest, I decided to take a shot at the reward and disclose my MyDoom data. It had the potential to end my financial problems without dredging up too many memories of my hunt for the notorious terrorist.

I walked into the living room and found Nicki, grabbed her attention, and explained that I was thinking about pursuing my MyDoom case. I was actually afraid she would be against getting involved with the FBI again. After all, she and the kids were enjoying the end of my investigative work and were especially happy to have me back in their lives full-time.

Despite my fears, Nicki didn't balk at the idea. "Yes, I remember the MyDoom stuff. It seemed like you'd gathered some pretty credible evidence."

I took a few minutes to jog her memory about my work on the case. It had been one of my best efforts. I used *PrimoPDF* to create digital prints of dozens of forum threads that were based in the Ukraine. Copies of most of them were both in Russian and English. I used *SYSTRAN Translate,* one of the same tools I'd used during my hunt for bin Laden.

Forum members had been discussing the virus prior to its release and talking about what it would do. They referred to the upcoming virus as Novarg and were suspiciously and unapologetically excited about its release. There was also lots of speculation about the fate of Linux. These communications were consistent with what authorities suspected about the authors of MyDoom: They had written and executed the virus as retaliation against SCO for its attacks against Linux.[83]

After digging further, I found a man who might have been the ringleader. He was an activist and programmer who was extremely pivotal on the forum. The other members seemed to look up to him. I even had a name and a photograph of the man. He was my chief suspect, although it's likely that more than one person was involved in the MyDoom execution—perhaps even other members of the message board in question.

Finally, after my recap, I made a closing argument: "...and there's a $250,000 reward."

Nicki was mildly enthusiastic. "Yes. You could pay off your debt."

I kept going, needing more reassurance. "So, I should do it? I should call the FBI?"

She was positive. "Yes. This seems legit. I think you have a better shot at collecting the money for this than for bin Laden."

Part of me wanted her to be opposed. I didn't necessarily want to get involved. I didn't want to be sucked back into the hell I'd been living in during my weeks of communication with the FBI. I had been so exhausted, barely sleeping, and suffering from near-daily anxiety attacks. Looking back on those days made me feel jittery inside. *No...* I didn't want to think about it! And I definitely didn't want to relive it.

Stepping away had been such a relief. I was finally sleeping better. I was finally not obsessed. I could finally rest my mind and focus on the mundane, but intellectually stimulating world of computer repairs. Did I really want to stir it all up again and trigger my obsession?

But I listened to Nicki's advice. She thought that pursuing the MyDoom case was worthwhile, and I knew in my heart that I wanted to at least give it a chance. I would do it. I had to try. So I braced myself to do something I'd promised myself I would never do again: I would call the FBI.

46

MEN IN SUITS

My first thought was that the FBI wouldn't take my call, that I wouldn't make it past the screener. After all, Agent Miles had expressly told me to stop calling. This had been after weeks of almost constant communication with the FBI and always getting past the screener.

As I flipped open my phone, a rush of adrenaline washed over me. I was nervous and a little shaky. My stomach was turning with the feeling of butterflies. I really didn't want to do this. What would be the screener's response? Was I still being shut out?

I flipped the phone closed.

Then I sat in my chair for a couple of minutes, shaking.

Finally, I drew a deep breath... I had to...*had to* do this. I typed in the number of the Houston office and paused a few moments with my finger hovering over the "call" button. Mustering all my courage, I pushed it.

It felt like an eternity since I'd spoken to a federal agent. *Here I go again...*

I heard the familiar businesslike voice of a male

agent as he greeted me.

I responded confidently, "Hello. This is Barbara Janik. How's it going?"

The man was cordial. "Pretty good. How are you?"

After the initial exchange, I explained that I'd been working with them on other cases a few weeks earlier but wanted to discuss a different issue. I told the agent that I had information about the writers of the MyDoom virus.

"Okay. I'll transfer you to the Cyber Crimes Unit."

It was that easy.

Once transferred, I introduced myself and told the agent about my research. There were a lot of brief pauses, during which I could hear the sound of typing, so I assumed he was taking notes.

I offered to email the data to him, but he had a different idea—an idea that caught me off guard.

"No. We'll come to your house and collect it."

Come to my house? *Wow!* ... They *did* that? I mean, I didn't know the FBI would travel to people's homes to collect data. And if he was coming to *my* house, in particular, he must have had confidence that my tip could be a legitimate lead. Perhaps he knew who I was, or perhaps—*all that typing.* Maybe he was looking at my file.

The agent then proceeded to schedule an appointment for the day after next.

And that was it. The FBI was coming to our home.

Fortunately, the two-day warning gave the kids and me time to clean the place. I wanted to make a good impression.

Cleaning ordinarily involved me sitting in the middle of the living room floor, picking things up off the carpet, couch, coffee table, and end tables, and handing items to Peter and Daun. They'd fight over who got to use the old red-and-blue plastic wagon to make the trips around the house more streamlined. They played *Rock, Paper, Scissors*, and Peter won. But it wasn't a fair fight. Peter almost always won that particular game, even when they did best two out of three.

I picked up a few socks and handed them to Peter. "Put these in the white laundry basket in my room." After all these years, I hadn't gotten used to referring to the master bedroom as "our" room—mine and Nicki's. Of course, she still only lived with us full-time during the summer, so I guess it was a forgivable offense.

Peter added the socks to the wagon, where he already had a small stash of things I had handed him. Then he wheeled off down the hallway toward the master bedroom. He nearly ran over Midnight as he shoved the wagon along.

I picked up a screwdriver and commanded Daun, "Put this in the 'junk drawer.'"

Midnight, who'd somehow avoided being bludgeoned by the wagon, was running up and down the hallway like a crazy cat. He wasn't used to seeing so much activity in his home—that's right, *his* home. We were just sort of here with him, co-occupants of *his* place. He stopped for a moment and looked at me quizzically as if to say, "*What on earth are you doing, human?*" Then he scurried back down the hall, his claws digging into the carpet as he ran off.

Midnight wasn't the only one confused. Daun had a fleeting moment of amnesia.

"Mom, why'd you say we're cleaning the house?"

We hadn't really cleaned in months, and she knew

that we usually didn't do it unless someone was coming over. We used to tidy up when Nicki came home from UT-Austin on the weekends, but we hadn't even done *that* in a while. I was too preoccupied and, frankly, a little more self-assured that Nicki would stick around, with or without a messy home.

I paused, letting out a loud sigh. I didn't understand how Daun could so quickly forget why were cleaning. I reminded her, "Because the FBI is coming to our house, and I want it to look nice."

As Daun grabbed the large screwdriver from my hand, she accepted my words. "Oh. Okay."

I wasn't sure if she completely appreciated who the FBI was. I would explain it to her later before they came over.

Once the living room was picked up, Daun ran the vacuum cleaner—her favorite part. But it was so clogged that it did a poor job. When she finished, I looked down at the dark-purple carpet, which still bore some annoying specks of white. Oh well, good enough.

Next, we moved to the kitchen. Peter loaded the dishes. He was terrible at it. He would put in all large items and barely fill it. Still, we would all take turns until they were done. At least he didn't overload. When I loaded, about a third of the stuff didn't even come clean.

I scowled at the remaining dishes. This would probably require about three or four loads, plus some hand washing. It would take a couple of days. We would barely have enough time to finish them before the FBI got here. It never occurred to me that they most likely wouldn't even see the kitchen. When it came to cleaning, I often had an all-or-nothing mentality. The house was either filthy or spotless. There was no in-between.

While Peter loaded, Daun and I started clearing everything off the kitchen table and counters. We removed spices, small appliances, pots and pans, banana peelings, and empty mac-and-cheese boxes. Satisfied, Daun wiped down the table while I tackled the counters.

Then I swept all the yogurt cups, coke cans, napkins, plastic grocery bags, and other trash and dirt off the kitchen floor. Finally, I gave each kid a wet rag and pointed to spots on the floor that needed to be wiped up. They wouldn't notice these spots on their own. I called this procedure "spot mopping" because none of us wanted to tackle a full mopping job.

A few hours into the daunting task at hand, I handed each kid a dollar and released them from further obligation.

Peter snatched the dollar out of my hand. "Cool."

He headed off to his room. I knew he was going to add it to his hoard of birthday money the family had given him over the years. He had nearly $100 saved up, and each dollar counted.

Daun also took off with her dollar and headed to her room. No doubt, she was going to pick up the landline and call Alicia, her best friend. Recall, she didn't have the luxury of a cell phone.

I was left to face the bathroom, alone...

***

The next day, maybe twenty minutes before the FBI was supposed to arrive, I looked over at Daun, who was sitting next to me on the living room couch watching Animal Planet.

"The FBI agent is fixin' to be here. I want you to be on your best behavior."

Daun was curious. "Why?"

"This is one of the same people I spoke to about Osama bin Laden. And I'm giving them tips about a different case. I'm *telling* you: I need you to behave yourself."

Daun's words were quick and enthusiastic. "I know all about the FBI. I've seen them in the movies!"

She was wiggling around and jumping up and down a bit. She seemed so excited. "Can I meet them? I've never seen a real live FBI agent!"

I thought about it for a moment and imagined her embarrassing me by coming out and asking the agents a million questions. I also imagined her showing off by doing her perfect cartwheel and proving her physical flexibility by doing the splits. *No...* I didn't want *that*.

I looked at Daun, unsympathetically. "No. I think it'd be better if you just stayed in your room."

"Really? *Why?*" She looked like she wanted to cry. But no, she was doing what kids do best: She was whining.

"I can't explain it. I just want you to go to your room and play video games or read or something. This is too important."

"But–"

"No buts. Go to your room. He's gonna be here any moment." It took a while to convince her, but she finally, reluctantly, went back to her room. *Done...*

A few minutes later, there was a heavy knock on the door. A distorted image of a face peered through the glass part of the entrance and I saw what appeared to be the moving pattern of a dark suit and tie.

I cautiously swung open the door...

Wait...

What was this?

There were two of them. I was caught off-guard because I was only expecting one. *Wow...* Two agents just for me. They must have *really* wanted my intel.

The men standing in front of me shared similar looks. If not for the fact that one had blond hair and the other dark brown, they could have been brothers. They were both around six feet tall, with the dark-haired one being slightly taller. Both wore what looked like identical dark-navy pinstriped suits.

The one with the light hair took the lead as they introduced themselves, speaking with a dry, flat tone, apparently trying to remain as professional as possible.

"Hello. We're with the Cyber Division of the Houston FBI. We had an appointment?"

I stretched out my right arm and gave them each a firm handshake. "Yes. Very pleased to meet you. Do you mind if I see your badges before you come in?"

Unfortunately, paranoia was playing a factor in this precaution.

The dark-haired agent looked at me with kind eyes. "Of course." They reached in their coats and flashed their badges, which was really cool. I imagined Mulder and Scully from *The X-Files* doing the same.

A few seconds later, the men walked through the door. I sat down on the couch and opened my laptop. In that moment, I began to realize just how incredibly nervous I was. There were FBI agents in my house! What had I gotten myself into? My hands were shaking a little.

I glanced over at the men who were standing

awkwardly in the center of our living room.

"Would y'all like to sit down?"

The blond spoke again. "No thanks... This shouldn't take long."

I took a deep breath and started talking.

"How're we gonna do this?"

The blond stared at me blankly. "What do you mean?"

"I mean, are you going to copy the data onto a flash drive or what?"

"Sorry, we don't keep them on us. Do you have any disks?"

This was a shocker. In my rush to clean the house, I hadn't considered logistics. I had assumed that one of the agents would whip a flash drive out of his pocket and take the data off my laptop.

I thought vaguely of the time a philosophy professor at St. Thomas taught us, his students, a valuable lesson: Someone had made an assumption. His irritation was palpable. Quickly, he snatched up some chalk and scrawled the word "assume" on the chalkboard. He then dramatically underlined the "ass" and "me" in the text. Finally, while punctuating the letter chunks with the tip of his chalk, he articulated the syllables in an agitated tone. "Ass-u-me makes an 'ass' out of 'u' and 'me.'" *It was kind of perfect!*

I'd never forgotten that lesson. No, I shouldn't have *ass*-u-med that the FBI agents would bring a flash drive.

Finally, I replied, "Yes, I have some CD-Rs, but it'll take *forever* to burn all those."

I imagined the difficulty of breaking a gig of data onto several 737-megabyte disks. It would be hard to break the files up in a logical manner.

"The folder is pretty large. It'd be a lot quicker if I could use a flash drive."

They glanced at each other for a moment, thinking. Finally, the blond spoke up.

"If you have one we can borrow, we'll mail it back to you when we're done."

"Sure. I have about a million of 'em. I repair computers for a living. Techs always keep them around. Let me go get one."

I was always using flash drives to rescue people's photos and music off dying hard drives. I also loaded some of them with useful software tools and anti-malware programs for easy access when repairing systems.

In that moment, I suddenly felt uncomfortable with the fact that the agents were still standing. Their hovering was making me anxious.

"Are you sure you don't want to sit down? This might take a little while."

They exchanged nods, and this time the dark-haired one interjected. "Sure. Where should we sit?"

I gestured toward the easy chair. "One of you can sit over there and the other can sit next to me on the couch. I'll just scoot my laptop over."

As I left to go to my room, the blond man took a seat on the sofa while the dark-haired agent gingerly eased himself into the recliner.

I spent what seemed like an eternity rummaging through my drawers to find the perfect flash drive. Even though I owned quite a few of them, they were hiding; mixed with all the other junk in my nightstand.

Eureka! I found it! ... I scooped up my blue-and-black PNY Attaché flash drive—one of my favorites at the time. I held it in the air and walked toward the living room with a huge triumphant grin on my face.

But before I could get a response, my face dropped as my arms collapsed to my side; I noticed something disconcerting: Daun was standing in the center of the living room facing the two men on the couch and chair, and asking them questions. She had seized the opportunity to greet the agents. Her curiosity had gotten the better of her.

I walked up behind Daun and addressed the agents.

"Oh. I'm sorry about that. This is my daughter, Daun." I shot her a menacing look, gritting my teeth "She was *supposed* to stay in her room."

The dark-haired man spoke up. "It's okay. She's not bothering us. She seems like a nice kid."

Luckily, on that day, Daun hadn't had a chance to show off by demonstrating her physical prowess. In other words, no cartwheels or splits. I manage to shoo her off before the circus started.

Daun told me years later that she couldn't resist coming out because she'd never met a real FBI agent and thought that their being there was really awesome. She especially remembered how nice they were and how cool they looked in their dark suits. She would remember that moment for her entire life: the day the FBI came to our house.

With Daun back in her room, I finally faced the two agents. Once again, I held up the flash drive triumphantly, letting loose a broad smile. "*Ta-dah!*" In that moment, I was a magician who had simultaneously pulled a flash drive out of thin air while causing my daughter to disappear.

The federal agents smiled back, giving slight applause.

Then I approached the couch and asked the agents if I could sit back down.

The blond looked up at me. "Of course." He then scooted over to make sure I had plenty of room.

So there I was, sitting on the right side of our sofa, hunched over my laptop, with an FBI agent sitting next to me and another one in our recliner.

I flipped the laptop back open and inserted the flash drive. Fortunately, it was plug-n-play. My latest laptop was advanced enough to automatically recognize a flash drive. *Hallelujah!* ...

I stuck it in a rear slot... No familiar ding. No whirring. No signs of the system "thinking." Nothing. Several seconds later, my PC still didn't recognize the drive.

I began to worry. How would I get the data to them if my laptop didn't recognize the drive? I looked at them. "It's okay. Let me just try a different slot. If it doesn't work, there are always disks." I was panicked. *What if I couldn't find the CD-Rs?* I tried to calm down and redirect my thoughts. *Breathe, Barbara...* You know exactly where the disks are. They're on the metal shelf next to the garage door with all your other computer junk. You just used one last week. *Stop this!* ...

For a brief moment, I had to resist the impulse to check for them.

I pulled out the flash drive and plugged it into a different port—one on the side of the machine. As I waited for it to load, I tried to make small talk. "It's going to be fine. I've got this."

The blond gave me a slightly suspicious, toothy grin. "Didn't you mention that you're a computer repair tech?"

"Yes."

He appeared to start moving into a light interrogation mode. "What kind of computer work do you do?" My stomach sank. *Did I just become* a suspect? We were discussing the authors of a virus, and I just admitted to being tech-savvy.

I felt my body convulse. Was I really going to admit to a federal agent that I had a job? What if they looked into it and discovered that it was "cash under the table?" I mean, I didn't pay taxes on that money. I had to backtrack.

"I help out a friend's shop. We mostly just replace hardware and clean up viruses and fix *Windows* glitches. I don't get paid. It's strictly voluntary."

This seemed to satisfy the agent. He backed off just as the flash drive finally finished installing on my laptop. I heard the familiar "ding" as the port connected to the drive. No more troubleshooting or worrying—well, at least no more worrying about data transfer.

Thank goodness...

I looked at the men and explained what I was doing. "Okay, I'm going to have to back up my data first. Then, I'm going to wipe the drive."

I began copying the data into a folder on my desktop, but *Windows Explorer* stopped and crashed before completing the job. *Great!* ... Okay, I'd have to use Roadkil's *Unstoppable Copier* for this. I went to my computer's desktop and clicked on the software's familiar black-and-white icon: an image of a cat.

The entire time I found myself meticulously explaining to them exactly what I was doing.

"I'm sorry. This should fix the issue."

*God...*this was taking forever. It took more than

fifteen minutes to copy my files and another minute to wipe the flash drive. In the meantime, I found myself awkwardly trying to make small talk with the two FBI agents sitting in our living room.

I felt myself beginning to sweat. *This was awful.*

Then, there was an uncomfortably long pause. I looked over to the men, not sure what else to say. Thankfully, after several seconds, I noticed their "matching" suits, which were both dark-navy with light pinstriping.

"So. Are those suits standard issue?"

The dark-haired agent tugged at his coat, giving me a slight crooked smile. "No. They're actually different."

Then they started gesturing at each other's suits, describing subtle variances. The blond pointed at the stripes on both jackets, touching them lightly. "Actually, the pinstriping on mine is a little thicker."

The dark-haired agent then chimed in, "And look, our buttons are slightly different."

They both seemed amused,but fell short of laughing out loud. Even in this moment, the men were trying to remain dry and professional.

But although they had just pointed out the differences, to me the suits looked identical. And, for sure, they shared the exact same shade of navy.

Finally, after my files were backed up and wiped off the flash drive, I used the same software to initiate copying of the MyDoom folder from my desktop to my Attaché.

Unfortunately, like before, the copying process was crawling. I wasn't sure why. I'd never had this issue before. Normally, the process was rather quick. I figured out later that some of the ports on my computer were the older, slower USB 1.1 rather than the faster

2.0 versions. I must have using one of the older-model ports. *Bummer...*

Once again, I found myself shaking a little from nerves as I fell all over myself apologizing for how long the copying was taking. It was embarrassing. *Oh well...*

I decided to try to take advantage of this situation by fishing for information.

I looked over to the left, toward the agents. "Do y'all know who I am?"

The men quickly looked at each other and then back at me. The dark-haired one responded, "I'm not sure what you mean."

I was blunt. "If you were in the office a few months ago, you would know. But something really huge happened, and I was part of it."

"Yeah?"

"Well, I'm not sure if you know this, but I'm the one who found Osama bin Laden."

I carefully gauged their responses. *Nothing...* No look of shock or disgust, nothing.

But soon after, the men started shooting subtle glances at each other. Finally, the blond took the reins and spoke up, glancing at me sheepishly. "We don't know anything about that." He did his best poker face. Maybe I was reading too much into it, but I thought I noticed a slight guilty smirk, as if he was hiding something.

I could smell guilt like a shark smells blood. One word: Catholicism.

After an uneasy pause, the dark-haired agent interjected an interesting comment in a dead-pan voice. "But I wouldn't be surprised."

The blond nodded in agreement. "You'd be amazed at some of the stuff we've seen and heard."

I replied, tantalized, "I'm assuming y'all can't talk about it."

The blond gave a quick, blunt response.

"Nope."

The dark-haired agent nodded in agreement and gave me a vague hint of a smile.

Even though I knew they wouldn't discuss bin Laden with me, I kept fishing a bit. "Well, y'all must have known I gave good tips or something. I mean, y'all came all the way to my house."

The blond replied, trying to sound matter-of-fact. "Actually, we would've come anyhow."

But, to me, his words seemed disingenuous. And I found the use of the word "anyhow" to be very telling. In other words, there was a reason they came to my place in particular. The unintended implication was that they knew something about me, perhaps that I'd found Osama bin Laden. But who knows? They *were* with the Cyber Crimes Unit. Maybe word hadn't made it to that department.

Regardless, even with the unlikely chance that they didn't know I found Osama bin Laden, something in my file, which they probably read, might have told them I had given reliable tips in the past. After all, past behavior is the best predictor of future behavior. And if my file had said I was a crackpot and unreliable, they never would have bothered with coming to my house. In other words, they came there precisely because of my track record. After all, I *had* found bin Laden.

At that point, I began to think of how far out of their way they had to go to get to my place.

"Was it a long drive?"

The dark-haired agent answered, "Not too bad.

About forty-five minutes."

In other words, it was a typical trip from Houston to my place—a trip I'd made countless times. Still, the drive took a lot of time out of their busy schedules. They must have *really* wanted my files to put forth that type of effort.

A few seconds later, I heard a car pull up, not even stopping to consider who it could be. Next, there was a light knock on the door.

I thought about it for a moment. The knock was familiar. "Oh, that must be my son. He's probably back from his friend's house."

I got up and unlocked the door for Peter.

"Hey, Peter. Come on in. We have guests."

Peter looked at me. "I know. I saw the car out there."

Then I introduced my son to the federal agents, and he politely but enthusiastically, replied, "Nice to meet y'all!" Before he could ask too many questions, I shuttled him off to his room. He confessed to me years later that seeing the FBI in our home was "kind of badass."

With both kids in their rooms, I needed to keep the conversation going while the flash drive sluggishly copied my files. I started describing what was in the folder and how they could process it.

Then I said something kind of dumb: "You'll need to get an actual person to translate this stuff, though." Later, I would think back on my words and cringe, because they were *so* unnecessary. *Of course* the agents would know that they needed a human translator. Computerized translations would be too literal and could only get them so far. But in retrospect, I guess I was, indeed, just trying to keep the conversation going.

Despite my stating the obvious, I didn't feel judged,

thank goodness.

After about a half hour of anxiety-provoking inter-actions—both small and serious—the copying was finally complete. I did a software eject of the flash drive, pulled it out, and handed it to the blond agent.

"Here you go. Sorry that took so long."

He gently took the drive from my hand. "That's okay. We'll mail it back to you as soon as we've finished copying the data."

With that, they thanked me, and once again, we exchanged firm handshakes. After we said our good-byes, I let them out the door. That was it: the first and only time the FBI would come into my house.

Within a couple days of their visit, I slowly began to realize that I never wanted to see or talk to the FBI again. I was done with all that. I couldn't deal with the stress anymore and wanted to move on. At that point, I felt like sacrificing my sanity wasn't worth the reward money. Besides, I didn't want to know if I was wrong. I couldn't bear the thought of it. I would never call to find out if my tips were helpful. Regardless, fourteen years after I presented my intel, the authors of the virus still haven't been arrested.

A week after the FBI came to my place, I received a small package in the mail.

It was my flash drive. They had kept their promise.

47

MYSPACE

Unfortunately for me, my recent encounter with the FBI had triggered a renewed personal interest in spreading the word about Osama bin Laden's arrest. This meant a renewed obsession. This meant anxiety. This meant exhaustion. But despite it all, I was ready for another try at getting the word out about bin Laden's arrest and my part in it.

But if I was going to succeed, I would have to take things in a new direction: From that moment forward, my mission moved beyond warning the Democrats to appealing directly to the public and alerting them to what happened.

Even if I failed, ultimately, I believed history would prove my case. But how long would it take? According to federal law, nothing can remain classified beyond 75 years.[84] Then maybe some centenarian former FBI agent would step forward. But it would be 2081, and I would be long dead. I mean, my children and grandchildren would be vindicated on my behalf. Maybe they could even sue for the $25 million... *No!!!* ... I found myself screaming inside. I wanted justice in my lifetime. I wanted the truth to be honored, and I was going to do my best to see that it happened.

Thus, even three months after Osama bin Laden's arrest, I was still holding on to a tinge of hope. I was unaware that I would still be trying to prove my case fourteen years later. Regardless, my mind had gone to a dark place as I had a disturbing thought. Something was gnawing at me and wouldn't go away.

What about the war? *What about the war?!*

What *about* it? I continued to ruminate. This concern had been with me from the beginning—from those early weeks after I found Osama bin Laden. I thought back on my tirade when Nicki and I were hiding out in her Austin apartment. My thoughts were the same: The government had sent troops into Afghanistan, touting the express purpose of killing or capturing bin Laden. The implied promise was that the war would be over once he was captured. I felt myself roll my eyes slightly. *Obviously*, that never happened.

So, at this point, my worries went beyond honor, truth, or even the reward money. Getting the word out about bin Laden was about stopping a war that never should have happened. I mean, he hadn't been in Afghanistan, so why did we go there? Our government probably knew better. The sleeper cells—the attackers on 9/11—were in America. And I would find out later that Al Qaeda itself was partially founded in Brooklyn. So, why did they invade Afghanistan? Iraq? Was it just a show? Proof that we were doing something by putting boots on the ground? ... I felt like the weight of the world was on my shoulders. It was my prayer that if the story of the arrest came out, there would be a public outcry to finally bring our troops—all of them—home.

But I was quickly running out of options as I failed all attempts to promote the truth. I needed a new tactic, one that would reach a wider audience. And since there were no more worries about a looming October surprise, there was no need to target the people in power. It was time to reach out to the general public. *But how? ...*

Social media was still in its infancy. Twitter had not yet gained traction, and Facebook was only for college students. Tumblr, Instagram, Pinterest, and Snapchat hadn't even been invented yet. Blogging and podcasts were still relatively hip and new, as was MySpace.

I decided to take a stab at blogging first. But after a brief, vain attempt to make it on Blogger.com, I began to realize how hard it was to gain a following. I quickly turned to the familiar: MySpace. I would spend the last month-and-a-half of 2006 there, trying to make the news of bin Laden's arrest go viral. Unfortunately, I had no clue what I was doing.

Although I was familiar with MySpace from my efforts to locate missing people, criminals, and terrorists, I had only scratched the surface of its potential. I had set up an account for the express purpose of accessing MySpace's vast search engine, not for socialization. But at this point, the solution seemed simple: I would have to become active.

I created a new MySpace account using the same pseudonym from the *WAPO* boards: Leslie Powers. Then I uploaded a swanky image of The Queen of Rock—Janis Joplin—for my profile pic. (There are still remnants of my old MySpace posted online, complete with some of the original uploads. Note the picture of Sharon Stone. At one point I briefly used her image instead of Joplin's.)[85]

I even created a fake profile because I knew, from experience, how easily people could discover my whereabouts if I put in any real information. I admitted to being a lesbian, but everything else was fabricated. I placed myself in New York City and (embarrassingly) set my birthdate as July 4.

My first task on MySpace was to find a target audience. There were more than 298 million people in the US in 2006,[86] and I had no idea where to begin. I considered just closing my eyes and pointing at a random place on the map. But after some thought, I decided to start with the geographical center of the US: Lebanon, Kansas, the place I started with when looking for Boussora. Unfortunately, Lebanon had a population of less than two hundred, so I opted to use Kansas City instead.

Conveniently, MySpace was searchable by areas of interest, so I looked for people in that city who were into politics. I would especially target them if they identified strongly as Democrats because they were unlikely to care about Bush or his secrets. I would sometimes throw in "lesbian" as a criterion, because why not? I appreciated people who could relate to my home life.

Headway was tedious, mostly because I wasn't using a bot. Even if I had known how to use one to make friend requests, they were against MySpace's terms of service and could have gotten me banned. So I was manually putting out hundreds of requests a day and following up by sending instant messages to people who accepted. In other words, like an old-school politician, I was figuratively going door to door, shaking hands, and kissing babies. But without help, the task in front of me was frustrating, if not impossible.

Despite this, I was determined to win people over, one at a time. But telling each person individually about bin Laden quickly became unrealistic, so I thought of another popular feature on MySpace: blogs. I started one for all my friends and anyone who happened by. I would tell them my story, then point them to my entries for more details and answers to common questions. On the site, I also uploaded a couple of redacted screen-shots of some of my emails to the FBI, a picture of the rainbow, and a few other things.

A week after I began my fresh effort to get the word out, I was exhausted and had managed to gain only a half-dozen believers. However, some of them were so enthusiastic about my story that they displayed a link to my profile prominently on their homepage as part of their Top Ten Friends list. This felt amazing, because it made me think they believed my story and were somewhat willing to help me promote it. I would return the favor and put them on my own Top Friends list. Yet these few supportive people weren't enough. I needed news about bin Laden's arrest to go viral.

But regardless of my inability to get the word out, I managed to have some interesting encounters with people. One of the better ones was with a lesbian in Kansas who invited me to come to a huge party she was throwing at her home. She thought I was interesting and "eccentric." Looking back, I think her opinion of me might have been influenced by my profile pic. And maybe she didn't realize that it was Janis Joplin, and not an actual photo of me. I mean, what is more eccentric than the wild-haired, hippie extravagance of Janis?

I briefly fantasized about making a road trip to

Kansas. It sounded like fun, and I was growing increasingly tired of almost exclusively communicating with people online. And I thought it would be nice to have some face-to-face friends.

My thinking was that we could go to Oklahoma to visit Peter and Daun's grandparents on Jimmy's side. The kids had only seen them a handful of times, and they were past due for a visit to the aging couple. We could then extend the trip and head up to Kansas City in time for the party.

A split second later, I snapped back to reality. Kansas was a long way from home, the kids couldn't take off from school, and I considered how awkward the entire situation would be. I mean, I barely knew the Kansas woman, and what would she think of me once she realized I didn't look anything like Janis Joplin? *No...* Such a trip would be impractical at best, crazy at worst. I wasn't going to run off to Kansas. *Thank goodness...*

***

Not long after, I was back on MySpace trying to meet new people and get the word out about Osama bin Laden. Each day was both a fresh beginning and a fresh disappointment.

But despite a slow start, a few people began following my blog, and I was fostering relationships with them and others through private chat. One such person—a believer—sent me an instant message one day. She made a friendly suggestion that I try contacting Michael Moore. This seemed logical. Michael Moore loved to fly in the face of the status quo and was good at revealing conspiracies. I sent him a nice instant message and waited. A few days later, I concluded that he wasn't going to respond.

While hoping for a reply, I began reading his blog and friending people who followed it. I specifically tried to connect with those who were using obnoxious political symbols for their profile pics. There were red-white-and-blue donkeys, bloated elephants, cartoonish Statues of Liberty, and many other wild images. These people turned out to be the most radical. However, for some mysterious reason, most of these radicals were no more likely to believe the truth than anyone else.

Finally, after weeks of following Michael Moore and his friends, I unwittingly expanded my outreach to a new group of people: conspiracy theorists. I contacted a man with an obnoxious profile pic: an image of the smoking Twin Towers. This was someone who obviously felt deeply about 9/11, even five years after it happened. Maybe he would have an open mind.

Unlike so many others, this person thought my story came across as credible and was concerned about helping me get the word out. He started making suggestions, most of which I had already tried. Finally, he suggested that I contact Alex Jones. I'd never heard of him, but my Twin Towers friend believed Alex would be open-minded and that he was in a unique position to help. The man indicated that Alex was leading some sort of movement and had lots of connections. My heart rushed with hope. Maybe I was finally making headway.

I shot off a quick message to Alex Jones, having no earthly idea of what to expect. But he never replied. It seemed even this man, who I would find out later was the king of conspiracy theorists, considered me crazy. I had reached a new low.

Even though Alex never responded, I did speak to some of his followers. I found them confusing and had no idea what their agenda was. Many were willing to consider that I was telling the truth, while others were vehemently opposed to my story.

And for reasons I didn't understand at the time, people kept sending me links to videos that tried to prove that 9/11 was an inside job. I would soon find out that these people—most of whom were the early followers of Alex Jones and InfoWars—were known as "Truthers". They had a mission to reveal what they thought was a government conspiracy. They were convinced that September 11th had been a "false flag." In other words, they thought they had "proof" that the government had planned and executed 9/11 in an attempt to rile up the public and start a war. The motives? Supposedly, the war was started to promote oil and big business interests. Plus, the government wanted to draw on 9/11 to restrict civil liberties and create a New World Order—a "*world government run by the elites who will enslave the masses.*"[87]

I had no idea what I'd gotten myself into and what kind of world these people were living in. Although it was true that a lot of them were open-minded, others were so convinced that they were right about 9/11 that I couldn't even talk to them about Osama bin Laden. They were convinced that he was not guilty because he wasn't behind the attacks, our government was.

After a couple of weeks of infiltrating the followers of Alex Jones–the Truthers–something happened. A pissed off person posted on my wall, "Fuck you and what you are doing to the Truth Movement!"

This man appeared to think I was making headway.

Enough people believed my story that some of the Truthers felt I was causing a rift in their movement. This was never my intention. Before he used the words "Truth Movement," I had no idea that there even was such a thing. I had been clueless. But apparently, I was causing quite a stir.

Eventually, over a month into my MySpace efforts, an extremely open-minded German hippie, going by the screen name Akareyon, was introduced to my blog by one of his friends. He read my posts with great interest and was intrigued. Most importantly, he wasn't a Truther and had no motive to discredit me. And he must have seen how much I was struggling. Finally, he reached out to me via instant message.

We communicated back and forth for a while. Soon, Akareyon asked me if he could introduce me and my claims to a website: AboveTopSecret.com. He said I would find friendly, open-minded people there who would be willing to listen.

I'm not sure why, but it didn't really sink in that AboveTopSecret.com was a conspiracy theory website. I just thought that meeting open-minded, friendly people sounded nice. I had not found many of those types on MySpace. Besides, I was desperate to be heard.

I agreed to let Akareyon introduce me to the site. I created an account a few days later, once again going by Leslie Powers. I was hopeful that I would get a positive reception. What I didn't realize was that I was about to go to war.

48

ABOVE TOP SECRET

December 28, 2006: More than four-and-a-half months had passed since bin Laden's arrest. And as big as day, on the front page of AboveTopSecret.com was the header of a new thread: "Osama Bin Laden arrested by FBI in Brooklyn?"[88]

Akareyon had copied and pasted a portion of my MySpace blog that summarized the story. Then, he added an introduction:

> *The story Leslie tells in her blog sounds sensible, however: sure, "truth is stranger than fiction," but I remain skeptical as always. Why did she not come forward earlier, why didn't she contact some independent networks, or Alex Jones? Because she's alone? Bunk or not?*[89]

Recently, I showed these lines to a friend. She thought they seemed harsh. But to me, his words seemed friendly and inviting, especially compared to the reception I'd received from most people on MySpace. My favorite line was, "*Because she's alone?*" It seemed so sympathetic and kind. It gave me a warm feeling.

From the moment Akareyon's post appeared on the main page, the questions started streaming in. And from the beginning, I was met with distrust, disbelief, and ridicule. Still, I trusted Akareyon's words that these people were open-minded, and I believed that I could reason with them.

Mostly, I was wrong.

The first questions were about MySpace. No one wanted to think that bin Laden was on the site. They saw it as a place for fun, not to be taken seriously. Many people also thought of MySpace as a place for hookups and booty calls, which was often the case. They refused to see the site's potential for bringing terrorists and other criminal organizations together. They also failed to see its potential for anonymous conversations and recruiting.

There were a lot more questions, of course. I calmly answered my peers, giving them the highlights of my story and linking them to my blog. Most of the questions are also addressed in this book. However, the responses were often ugly and even abusive, far from the open-mindedness I had been promised by Akareyon. And many of the comments were just classic bullying and humiliation. My heart sunk when I read the following lines by Bob2000. Here they are, raw and unedited:

> *Leslie is goofing us, her story is a lie. there's plenty of evidence that proves it a lie (symbols for myspace pics provide us with no infomation if someone is a terrorist or*

*not, theres no correlation. I caught you in
your lie leslie).*

*Shes doing this for kicks, or shes F'd up in
the head, and truly beleives she somehow
found UBL and reported him to the FBI and
they thanked her etc. Dellusional could be
one explanation why shes doing this.[90]*

I could hardly take it. In the same breath, I was
being called both crazy and a liar!

Here's another particularly rancid comment by the
same guy, this time calling me a "sicko:"

*On the other hand, the probability of
someone who needs psychiatric help who
did some research and planned out a well
organized lie just for kicks (you sicko) is
definitely a million times more probable
than the one where someone actually
experienced this UBL capture the way you
described it happened to you.[91]*

Then there was Kickoutthejams. This guy got under
my skin more than anyone else in the forum because
he knew how to push my emotional buttons. He kept
telling me that the FBI had been joking with me and that
I was delusional. These comments were so eerily similar
to my sister Brandy's words that they hit me particularly
hard. And the more I protested, the more he pushed.
What's worse is that he stuck around for months—the
entire span of the thread—and never gave an inch. What
bothered me most was that he was smart—smart enough

to know better. But he wouldn't listen; he never listened. In retrospect, maybe he was fucking with me, maybe he was a typical internet troll.

Regardless, I would figure out later that he was an expert at gaslighting. He was effectively mentally manipulating me into thinking I was crazy. And he nearly succeeded.

Reading back over Kickoutthejam's words today still gives me a sick feeling:

> *From reading through all this I'm pretty convinced Lesley is a spoofer, it's just too funny and too bizarre to possibly be true and I'm sure Lesley is having a good laugh getting a rise out of the members here.*
> *If by chance what you say you have done Lesley is true then I'm afraid those agents were humoring you and getting a good laugh out of it at your expense such as when they asked you for the lotto numbers is pretty close to ridiculing you. Again if you did do all that then I do hope you didn't bring any unnecessary misfortune down onto those you 'reported' on. There's enough necessary misfortune going round for everyone than to have that hit you like a thunderbolt from the blue just for having a seahorse on your 'mysterious' myspace account.*
>
> *You need to own up one way or the other. Either to all of us for having a good laugh at our expense. Or . . .more seriously to*

*yourself that you have become obsessive to
the point of delusion and may have, in your
obsession, made yourself a target and put
others peoples lives under suspicion with
little or no evidence or qualification on your
own part.*[92]

Oh, and I found out later that apparently Kickout-thejams was an "expert" in OCD because he had family members with it. I mean, he gave me an armchair diagnosis and even feigned concern. What a joke. The guy was an asshole! I mean, even if he were right and I had OCD like my sister Anne, that didn't mean I was crazy, just anxious and obsessed!

And the idea Kickoutthejams placed in my head that I had hurt an innocent Middle Eastern man made my stomach churn. It forced me to take a look at myself, to go back over all the facts in my mind—everything that happened. And, as usual, it sucked. No matter how many times I told the story or thought about it, recalling the details stung. And as usual, I came to the same conclusion: I mean, the Middle Eastern man I turned in was far from innocent. Ali Hussain was, in fact, Osama bin Laden.

Then there were the Truthers, the same type of conspiracy theorists I'd met on MySpace who were proponents of the idea that 9/11 was an inside job. Like some of the people on MySpace, a few of the Above-TopsSecret thread participants thought I was trying to create a rift in the Truth movement. One guy, Talisman, was worried because he heard the story mentioned on *Coast to Coast*, a then-obscure late-night radio show that focuses on the paranormal, conspiracy theories, and hidden histories. Here are his words:

> *I am personally leaning toward you being*
> *a disinfo person, I already heard this Bin*
> *Laden thing mentioned on coast to coast,*
> *so it has already got some media attention,*
> *if it gets any more media I can see where*
> *this will lead, it will discredit anything to do*
> *with 9/11.*[93]

Discredit them? Disinfo agent? ? The first time I saw the term "disinfo agent" in the thread, I had to Google it. Apparently, this is a so-called government agent who goes online and spreads false information to hide and discredit truths.[94] *A disinfo agent? Me? ... Really? ...* I had to laugh. People on the board threw around this term when they wanted to try to dismiss someone's comments. It was lot like screaming "bot" today.

But not everyone on AboveTopSecret bullied me. Some defended me, while others appeared to believe my story. One of my first advocates created an avatar for me that replaced my default one. When I mentioned that Storm was my favorite X-Men, he created a graphic for me. Storm was the white-haired, dark-skinned mutant who could control the weather. She was once worshipped as a goddess in her home country in Africa. The avatar depicted her floating in the air, arms outstretched with balls of lightning crackling from her fingertips. My screen name—Leslie Powers—was superimposed on the bottom.

Maybe his small act of kindness kept me going during the entire two-and-a-half months and 349 printed pages of torture. And it's a good thing, because some of the stuff coming out of it would help build my case.

Darklight12 made perhaps the most important post. It seemed to corroborate my story:

> *I'm not going to uncover anything but my cosin called me the day they arrested him its true but i dont know if he is alive or dead but i do know is that he was sent to a top secret base in texas thats all i know ill keep you in on it*[95]

Four days later, he added:

> *yes he called me he is a millitary genral he got back from iraq a few days ago and was doing some work in charlotte and his friend called him and told him then he called me*[96]

Was this for real? He was claiming his cousin, a military general, had told him about the arrest and that Osama bin Laden was moved to a Top Secret base in Texas. This was new information, and it confirmed my story.

Unfortunately, Darklight12's words fell on deaf ears. They were quickly dismissed by skeptics because he was only thirteen. They said he was lying to get attention. I thought about Peter, my own son. He had turned thirteen in November. I knew for a fact that he'd never do that! But none of this mattered. Many adults have zero respect for teenagers.

I tried sending Darklight12 a U2U direct message but got no response. I had a lot of questions for him. However, after only having posted twice, he disappeared from the conversation. He probably didn't like being called a liar.

Yet this boy wasn't the only one who tried to back me up. One member went out of his way to look up bin Laden's old address in Brooklyn. He actually went so far as to drive there and observe the area.

From the start, Airtrax007 presented himself as an advocate. This was evident when he introduced himself to the thread:

> *Hello all, im very dissapointed in the way everyone here is down playing this post. After all this is a board that does discuss this very sort of information. The info provided is very plausible—NYC is in my opinion is the best place for OBL to lye in wait for the next attack—and a perfect place to hide. Maybe OBL was here when the attacks took place— say as to oversee the plan of attack, by the way most leaders of an attack are sitting on the sidelines very close to the actual battle. Who know's—the pictures that we have seen of OBL walking down a mountain with boulders all around him could have been taken here in the tri-state area keep up the good work—leslie.[97]*

In a separate post, he also gave me strong words of encouragement that touched my heart:

> *Don't give up leslie, your doing great—stick to your guns. I think if we all put our minds together we can help put some parts of this*

puzzle together.[98]

Eventually, Airtrax007 asked me for bin Laden's address so he could investigate the area for me. However, I hesitated to give it to him because I was afraid of the location being made public and putting residents in area at risk of harassment. So instead of giving Airtrax007 all the details, I revealed bin Laden's neighborhood: the Brighton Beach area of Brooklyn. Airtrax007 took that information and conducted some research:

> *Well now , i had just started searching and*
> *this area is a good place for him to hide ,*
> *it would have been nice to have an actual*
> *adress--but , i will post some info on this*
> *area Brighton Beach was redeveloped as*
> *a fairly dense residential community with*
> *the final rebuilding of the Brighton Beach*
> *railway into a modern rapid transit line of*
> *the New York City Subway system c. 1920.*

Then he gave a brief synopsis of the history and demographics of the area. He concluded with the following paragraph:

> *Brighton Beach is also home to many other*
> *ethnic groups such as immigrants from*
> *Pakistan. On Brighton 7th Street, there is a*
> *mosque where Muslims (mostly Pakistani)*
> *go to pray. There is another mosque located*
> *between Brighton 8th Street and Banner*
> *Avenue. Brighton Beach is also home*
> *to people of Mexican and other Latino*

*descent. There are some Polish and a
sizeable community of Georgian residents,
but relatively few Italian-Americans or
African-Americans remaining. There are
some Korean markets also, but for the most
part their owners do not reside in the neighborhood.*[99]

I was grateful for Airtrax007's hard work because
what he said was really relevant. *"A good place for [bin
Laden] to hide"*? Two mosques in the neighborhood?
This was great news! Airtrax007 seemed to be backing
me up here. And the level of detail he found about the
neighborhood was incredible. This guy was quite an
advocate. I would find out later that he was willing to go
to extraordinary measures to get at the truth.

After summarizing his research, Airtrax007 posted
a link to a Google bird's eye view of the area[100] and
promised to look for webcams of the neighborhood.
This was before the days of Google cars driving around,
taking panoramic images of every road and alleyway in
the world.

But even back then, cameras—specifically,
webcams—were commonly placed near buildings and
could be found almost everywhere. And these images
were live-streamed onto the internet. In 2006, it was a
popular pastime to spy on these locations by watching
the streams. You could watch almost anywhere, at any
time. Yet, when Airtrax007 searched this area—bin
Laden's neighborhood—he couldn't find any webcams,
which seemed weird for what should have been a
crowded part of Brooklyn.

After failing to find the webcams, Airtrax007 asked

me, once again, for bin Laden's address. After all his hard work, I finally trusted him enough to send it to him in a U2U message. And he shocked me when he did the unthinkable: He made a two-hour drive to Brighton Beach and hit the pavement. As he walked down bin Laden's street, he was alone and scared, but determined. Here is what he observed:

> Hello all, over the weekend i decided to take a trip to the suspected hideout of OBL . To start with --i searched all web cams in area and found none on the street of hideout, I checked on the net and by actually walking up and down the street(very scarey). So finding any info by web cams is out of the question.---next step is to actually KNOCK on the suspected hideouts door and see what happends.

> My plan was to see if anyone still lives there and if so ask how long they have been at this adress --and then ask if on the said date of arrest there was any police activity. The street in front of the apartment was full of parked cars so i thought i would ask the others who lived in the area if they had noticed any unusual activity on the date in question.

> I had knocked on apartment #14 (obl hideout) no answer--so i decided to ask the neighbor in #12 --no answer. I went across the street to ask apartment #3 --no

answer. Getting frustrated i knocked on all doors--24 in all and there was no answer on all of them.

Standing there frustrated at myself in taking the 2hr trip, i had noticed that all the doors in the complex were the exact same doors except for #14 it was different and had tinted window's .

Standing in front of #14 and looking left --1 block over i saw a POLICE station--kind of silly to have a hideout in the backyard of the police. So i went to ask the obvious question at the station--after waiting 35 min i had a responce from a patrolman-- He informed me on that said date on that street there was NO activity.
So i end my quest with no real answer's ---WHAT A WAIST OF MY TIME.[101]

No answers? ... He knocked on twenty-four doors! Now, this was weird and suspicious. I had conducted a PeopleLookup search of the entire property where bin Laden had been living before I turned him in. It had been teaming with people with confirmed current addresses and phone numbers! Where had they all gone? Were the residents arrested? Were they driven out later, after the FBI got bin Laden? Were the owners arrested and the complex closed? It was clear that something had happened here. These apartments would be prime property with high rent, why would they be abandoned?

But this information proved hollow. Unfortunately for me, the moderators of AboveTopSecret interpreted the patrolman's claim that there was "no activity" on that street as proof that bin Laden had not been arrested at that address. So, not long after Airtrax007's visit, my thread was moved into "Skunk Works," a section of the site where "debunked" claims go to die. However, "no activity" probably meant no police activity. But bin Laden wasn't arrested by local cops, he was arrested by the FBI. Also, federal agents might have shown up in unmarked cars and plain clothes. They also might have arrested him in relative silence, at 4 a.m., when bin Laden was asleep and the officer in question was not on duty.

Regardless, Airtrax007's venture to Brighton Beach hadn't been a waste of time, especially in light of the details he added later:

> ...the house in question is a group of row homes --apartments that look all the same.
>
> I did find it interesting that the door of #14 was different then the rest--maybe it was replaced after the FBI had broke it down when entering.
>
> When i was there the street was filled with parked cars on both sides--but there was nobody around--no walking couples or people no dogs no noise.
>
> But the next block down the place was bustling with activity.

By the way the whole place was filled with middle eastern people--no whites --blacks-- hispanic--mexican.

Mostly the population was made up of people wearing funny (big) hats--veils over faces--robes and the likeness of the pictures that we see of mid eastern decent.[102]

The door was different than the others? *Interesting...* I mean, he mentioned the tinted windows before, but it hadn't occurred to me that maybe it had to be replaced after federal agents kicked it in.

Also, the fact that the streets were packed with cars, but no one was on the sidewalks, says a lot. First, we found out the apartments were abandoned. Now this? The whole block was abandoned? No one on the sidewalks? Really? This was incredibly odd, not at all how I picture the crowded neighborhoods of New York, where most people walk wherever they need to go.

And then the most important fact of all: One block over was a bustling community, typical of the area. Plus, they were *all* Middle Eastern! Osama bin Laden would have been difficult to spot walking around in such a neighborhood. Even if he kept his "funny hat" and robe, he'd fit right in.

Then there was Akareyon, the guy who introduced me to AboveTopSecret: After initial skepticism, he really went to bat for me. This was mostly because once I trusted him, I forwarded him copies of my emails to the FBI and sent him copies of all my phone records. Most of these are currently available on my website for anyone interested in taking a peek. His main contribution was to put together all the evidence I presented in the thread and on MySpace. Here's one significant example:

> *She's now presenting the scans of her telephone logs, so it's not about whether she talked to the FBI, but what the conversations were about. Let us use common logic. You see a flash, and you hear a thunder a few seconds after that. Could flash and thunder be related? Maybe. The same thing happens one or two days later. It's becoming likely that the two belong to each other.*

> *Do you think that the emails, which were sent to the same office she talked with, could have anything to do with the calls she made before and/or after? I think so, and that's why I believe her story so far.[103]*

I really liked the lightning flash followed by thunder analogy. Basically, Akareyon compared the phone records of my communications with the emails. He concluded that I always sent an email and followed up with a call a few minutes later, or vice versa. Anyone visiting my website can see the records and make the same observation. I was so incredibly grateful that he noticed this. It pretty much proved what I had been talking about with the FBI—the contents of the emails, of course.

In another post, Akareyon explained why he thought the records were legit. I mean, the phone records were obvious scans of a paper document, and the emails were forwarded to him rather than mere screenshots or PDF prints.

Then Akareyon took some time to flat out defend my honor:

> *I have a hard time imagining a pathological liar or professional hoaxer spending so much of his free time making up a story that nobody believes anyways.*

Later, in the same post, he added:

> *So she's suffering from a mental disease and has been annoying the FBI offices in Houston and NY with her mails and calls right from the beginning. But then, I wonder, would any FBI agent bother to chat 14 minutes away with her, and the next day another agent even 20 minutes?*

Wow... I was being defended in a huge way. This almost made up for the bullies that had been calling me crazy and a liar for weeks. Plus, he made some good points. What on Earth would be my motivation for taking the kind of punishment I was suffering during that thread? I mean, why would the FBI spend as much as twenty minutes talking to a lunatic? These were great points.

And Akareyon took things a step further: He attempted to prove my case for me by putting together all the information I had given him. He meticulously went through my forum posts and MySpace blogs and compared them to the phone records and emails. He then posted a layout of his work on page 24 of the thread. His post goes on for seven printed pages. He finally wrapped it up, concluding, *"I choose to believe her..."*[104] Anyone who wants to follow his logic can download the records from ChasingBinLaden.com/records.[105]

But Akareyon's greatest contribution, by far, was asking me for my telephone history. I hadn't even considered requesting them from my landline and cell phone companies until he suggested it. And even more importantly, the act of emailing the records to Akareyon had an unintentional effect: They were saved to my email server. In other words, like my emails, the phone records were stored indefinitely on the Cloud. Without that happening, they would have been lost a long time ago.

So, all in all, the AboveTopSecret thread had been useful and productive. But it didn't feel like it at the time. The story never went viral or made it to the press. And I was left battered and bruised by the bullies and skeptics. In other words, in that moment, it felt like the forum hurt more than it helped. It had left me damaged and silent. Once I finally left the thread in March, I was reluctant to ever talk about the bin Laden stuff again. I was defeated, and I didn't even want to think about it. *Ever...*

Here are some of my final remarks on the forum:

> *I'm tired of fighting it. No matter what I say people will believe what they want to believe.*

Then later:

*I saw a news show today about a guy
claiming to be Jesus reincarnated. He has
way more people believing him that I do. It
is amazing to me that people will believe any
bs it seems but my story. I also noticed that
the teleporting lizard men on this site are
taken more seriously. I give up. I will never
win you people over. I have to be at peace
with myself and my family first. I also have
to take care of my physical health, because
it is not doing well. If you have any more
questions, I may or may not answer them
right away. ATS and Myspace is low on my
priority list right now. Maybe someday when
we have a new president the truth will come
out. For now I have given up on trying to get
it out to the ungrateful, cynical, masses that
have chose to make a mockery out of me.*[106]

And here's what amounted to my final goodbye on
AboveTopSecret.com, as I replied to Kickoutthejams'
latest attempt to discredit me:

*I've just about given up all hope of getting
the truth out. Ya'll should be happy. The
government wins. I lose. The end.*[107]

49

--- ▸ ---

REGRETS

The shame and discouragement I felt after my months on AboveTopSecret.com would stay with me for years. I tried really hard to forget any of it had ever happened. I tried to convince myself that they were right, that I had been crazy. *No...* Reality was too hard. I had to push it down, to forget. I wanted nothing to do with it—any of it. A huge part of me regretted ever finding Osama bin Laden. I just wanted to wish it all away.

But I couldn't forget, not completely. There were triggers—maybe a snippet about bin Laden in the news. Any time I saw his face on TV or heard his name mentioned, the cynical words of my sister and the cruel taunts of strangers would return to haunt me.

September 7, 2007, was no exception. It was nearly a year after bin Laden's arrest, and I was watching CNN. My heart began to race. There it was, staring at me from the screen for the first time in months: the eerie face of Osama bin Laden.

Al Qaeda had released a so-called "new" video of

bin Laden.[108] It was the first release since a June 30, 2006 audiotape that had circulated a couple of weeks before his arrest. So, a year later, the release of a new video was particularly troubling.

My mind slid into disbelief. *Nooo!* ... This wasn't happening.

People on AboveTopSecret had asked me whether I would believe my story was false if there was a new video. My heart started racing as I began to shake. *It can't be bin Laden.* Bin Laden is dead. That's what I'd told them, that's what I believed, so a new video could discredit me.

It didn't even occur to me until years later that bin Laden might have been kept in hiding somewhere after his arrest and occasionally propped up like a scarecrow to keep the threat of terrorism alive.

Then, I began to struggle with myself. *No!* ... It had to be—the video had to be a fake.

But instead of refuting the video in my mind, I tried to hold in the memories—everything. I clenched my fists and squeezed my eyes closed, trying to wish it all away. *No!* ... It didn't happen! ... *None of it happened!* ... I was crazy. Those people were right. The FBI had been joking with me!

I couldn't face the truth. As always, it was easier to believe that I had been out of my mind than to deal with the reality that I'd been betrayed by our government and the general public.

But now, here I was, forced to confront the issue because of the new video.

At this point, I was in a full-blown panic. I felt like I couldn't breathe. The memories—all of it, including my sister's disbelief and the ridiculing by AboveTopSecret members—came crashing down on me. I couldn't stop the thought, no matter how hard I tried. My mind kept cycling the same sentiment: *No! ... I don't want to think about this. Any of this!*

But the news of the new video left me little choice. I had to deal with it.

Finally, I forced myself to watch it and noticed something odd about bin Laden's image. His normally long, white beard was black, and shorter. And his cheeks were more filled out. Was this even him? Was the tape real? I *had* to know. Maybe it had been concocted by the federal government as part of the coverup. I could only hope.

I wasn't the only one questioning the authenticity of the tape. And although I had an ulterior motive to believe it was a fake, the media did not. As I recall, CNN anchors seemed skeptical, questioning the length and color of his beard, and whether or not bin Laden would trim and dye it.

But more important was the analysis by CNET's Robert Vamosi that would be released in the coming days. As a professional audio/video editor, Vamosi possessed the technical skills needed to conduct a thorough investigation into the video's authenticity or lack thereof. CNET published his results not long after the tape's release. He had come to a conclusion: The video was a fake. It had been heavily doctored, most likely using an old video from 2004. The clothing, backdrop, and desk in both videos were the same. It also appeared that the contrast had been adjusted, creating the image of a black, shorter beard.

There were six splices in the video and numerous audio edits, with large portions of the production consisting of only a still frame. References to current events came from audio splices that had been placed with the unmoving pictures. There were so many splices that Vamosi speculated the words were spliced together to form new sentences. He also didn't discount the possibility of a vocal imitator.[109]

This was the last bin Laden video ever put out. There would be eighteen audiotapes released over the next four years. But, of course, audio can be more easily faked than video.

The media's disbelief surrounding the 2007 videotape calmed me a bit. My story was safe and unrefuted, at least by credible means. But it was too late to stop the memories. They wouldn't go away so easily. I had to assuage my doubts. Had I found bin Laden, or had I been crazy?

***

I lay on my back in bed next to Nicki, my neck propped on a pillow. I was still shaken. I couldn't stop obsessing on the past, the bin Laden stuff. I was stuck in my head, mulling over all the details.

Nicki must have thought that I was peculiarly quiet and that I seemed disturbed, because she expressed concern. "Are you okay?"

Tears were flowing softly from my eyes. "Not really."

In that moment, she began to piece together what was bothering me. After all, she had been watching the news with me and had seen the video. "Is it all the Osama bin Laden stuff?"

"Yeah. I can't stop thinking about it."

I briefly paused before I kept going. "The tape's got

to be a fake." Unfortunately, the analyses that would prove the tape was doctored had not yet been released. There was little to comfort me but my own perception of the images.

Then Nicki made an apt observation: "I know. I mean, it didn't even look like him. Why would he dye his beard?"

I speculated. "I know. Wouldn't that be against Sharia law or something? And what would be his motivation. Vanity? To look younger?"

Nicki reinforced my doubt. "Yeah. Bin Laden wouldn't care about any of that."

I began to discuss motives. "I mean, the government probably created the tape as part of the coverup. They'd want to make it look like he's still at large."

"Yes. Makes sense. Besides, we know you found him."

That's when it happened: We spent an hour retracing all the facts. And it all came flooding back to me in vivid, overwhelming detail: everything the FBI said to me, the call with the excited reporter from CNN, my sister's cynicism, MySpace, AboveTopSecret–all of it. I could no longer forget. It was back, and I didn't want it to be. But there it was, dragging me down.

Then somehow, after multiple days of struggle, I shoved it all back down again. Forget.

But it was futile. Over the next several years, the same thing happened every time bin Laden's face appeared in the news. I would have a panic attack. The memories would come flooding back. I would cringe and try to convince myself I had been crazy. Then, Nicki and I would have the same conversation, reminiscing about all the details. We would repeat the words and events together, almost like a mantra.

If I hadn't found bin Laden, why was I told to call the New York office directly? Why was I instructed to ask for the Terrorism Task Force? If I were crazy or wasting their time, they wouldn't have bothered with me. I would have never made it past the screener.

If I hadn't found bin Laden, why did the agent talk to me for twenty minutes the morning after I called in my tip? Why did he ask all those questions? Why was he so curious about me?

And if I hadn't found bin Laden, why did the agent ask if I thought I'd found The Big Guy. I had been turning in Al Qaeda operatives. There was only one *Big Guy*— the leader of the pack—*Osama bin Laden*.

If I hadn't found bin Laden, why did the agent go on to ask me if I thought he was in Brooklyn? Why did he ask me if I was psychic? He was clearly fishing for an explanation.

After I denied being psychic, why did he ask me how I found The Big Guy?

Why would he ask me that if I hadn't found bin Laden?

Why did he go on to call me a "gifted researcher" and a "true patriot"?

And why was the New York FBI Terrorism Task Force so rowdy and happy on the morning of August 16?

Why did they call me "The Green Lady"? Because they thought I was going to see green? Were they expecting me to get the $25 million?

If I hadn't found bin Laden, why did one of the agents ask me for the lotto picks? Did he think I was psychic, like the agent I'd spoken to a few days earlier?

And why was I promised there would "absolutely" be an announcement from Washington if there was nothing to announce?

Why was I being treated like a hero the next morning?

And why did the FBI suddenly stop speaking to me after weeks of welcoming my calls?

And then, when I confronted the New York agent by stating, "You know you guys arrested Osama." why did he angrily retort, "Prove it!" if there was nothing to prove?

And when I scrambled to prove it, why did he respond with, "You got me. Now turn me in. It'll make ya feel better." It was obvious I couldn't prove it, but this was close to a direct admission that they'd arrested him.

And ultimately, if I hadn't found Osama bin Laden, why would CNN call me a week later, when I believed Bush was close to making an announcement? Why did the reporter ask me if I was psychic?

So many questions...

Why? Why?! *Why?!*

Every time Nicki and I went over the facts, we always came to the same conclusion: I had found Osama bin Laden, and he'd been arrested on the morning of August 16, 2006. There was no refuting it. These were the facts.

But like I said, over the years so-called audiotapes of bin Laden would pop up on the news, or the topic of Osama bin Laden would come up in some other context.

I had no doubt that these tapes were faked. There was never a release of new video footage of a moving, breathing bin Laden. But the release of the footage made me continue to think that our government wanted to keep the Osama bin Laden bogeyman alive, to maintain a state of fear amongst the general population. I speculated that they wanted to keep us afraid so we would support the war. The motives for keeping the fighting going were unclear, although there was a plethora of theories available online.

Regardless of the reasons for bin Laden's appearance, every time I saw him on the screen, which was mercifully rare, I would relive the same trauma. Cringing. Panicking. Believing that I had been crazy—that I was wrong, and that the FBI had been joking with me. Reminiscing with Nicki and, ultimately, concluding that I had *actually* found Osama bin Laden. Then I would push the memories out of my mind again and try to forget any of it ever happened.

Lather. Rinse. Repeat.

This cycle happened for years. Every time the topic of bin Laden came up, it was excruciating. Every time, I was full of regrets. It always ended with my mind returning to the single, selfish thought—the one that had tortured me since my AboveTopSecret days: I would wish it had never happened, that I'd never found Osama bin Laden. My life would be so much easier.

But then, as usual, I would feel horrible. I would cry hard, overwhelmed with remorse. *How could I even think that?* So many lives were probably saved. And the madman behind 9/11 was off the streets for good. How could I regret it? Why? *How?*

The bullying had done me in. I couldn't talk about bin Laden with anyone. My greatest hour had become my darkest secret.

***

And I wasn't the only one holding on to the secret.

Nicki was shy around most people and didn't care to tell anyone about bin Laden, which allowed her to avoid being bullied or experiencing the pain of being called a liar or told she had a crazy partner. When it was all said and done, she was mostly unharmed. But regardless, events had left her bitter.

Nicki was frustrated with the government. She was incredulous that they would cover up Osama bin Laden's arrest. And she was livid about being ripped off financially—even more than I was.

After all, we were supposed to be rich. We were supposed to receive a $25 million reward. To Nicki, this was the biggest betrayal. She would often say, "What's the point of offering a reward if you have no intention of ever paying it?" Her argument was that this situation could discourage people in the future from giving out tips. She thought that the government could have had me sign a nondisclosure agreement in exchange for the money–an option I'd offered the Texas City agent when I tried to collect.

At that point, my attitude was different from hers. I tried hard to convince myself that maybe God didn't want me to have the money at that moment because it would ruin me. It wasn't meant to be. I mean, I was upset, but I had come to peace with it—mostly. Nicki never did.

But we could both agree on one thing: We were relieved it was finally over. Nicki had been incredibly anxious, especially during the paranoia that had ensued immediately after I was denied the money. Because I was so scared, a part of her wondered if her life was *actually* at risk. Her fear didn't subside much until a couple of weeks after the bin Laden coverup began. She felt better after we returned home from hiding out in her Austin apartment. Things were much calmer from that point on.

But my own fears, although they eventually diminished, would stretch out for years, decreasing bit by bit as time passed. For a really long time, there would be some small part of me that would wonder if the feds were keeping an eye on me.

In addition to the pervasive fear, Nicki had missed me. I had been so preoccupied for so long that I had spent little time with my family. It had been difficult to be in a relationship with me during those days. After my detective work was over, our lives had gone back to normal. And like me, Nicki mostly stopped thinking about it all unless bin Laden was mentioned in the news.

After me, Peter was hit the hardest. For years, when the topic of bin Laden came up, my son refused to discuss it with me. He would get nervous and try to change the subject. When I finally asked him why the topic bothered him so much, he told me.

My original thought was that maybe Peter didn't believe my story. But it was the opposite. He believed it too much. After I found Osama bin Laden, Peter needed more than anything to process what was happening with his peers. He told a few people, mostly online "friends," but no one would take him seriously. Like me, but to a lesser extent, my son was mocked and cyberbullied. No matter how many details Peter provided, he was perceived as either lying or defending an insane mom— things no one wants to hear, especially a sensitive kid like Peter.

Even years later, the bullying had such a profound effect on Peter that he never wanted to talk about the bin Laden stuff with me or anyone else. It was all an unpleasant memory that he was trying to put behind him.

Daun also tried to tell "friends" about what happened.

One day, while at school, the topic of bin Laden came up. She was wiser than Peter and didn't outright say that her mom had found him. Instead, she quipped, "What if he has already been arrested?"

She was laughed at. They didn't even want to consider that possibility.

Daun never told anyone again until high school, when she had more open-minded friends who knew me well. I had kind of adopted them all. We often played games like *Dungeons & Dragons* together, and they all called me "Momma Barbara" or "Momma B" for short. They also often turned to me for advice.

They knew I wasn't crazy or a liar. They all affirmed that they believe my story, which I've shared with several of them in detail.

Yet even today, Daun doesn't like to discuss or even think about what happened in 2006. She says it embarrasses her and worries that releasing my book will not end well, and she'll have to watch me fail. Daun doesn't like to see me suffer. Just the thought of it causes her anxiety. Her stress about my manuscript is so severe that she won't let me read any of the bin Laden stuff out loud to her. I can only read her parts about family, etc. In other words, the bulk of the story is too much for her to take emotionally.

Even though Daun's current friends are supportive

of her and the stories she tells about how I found bin Laden, this doesn't erase the past. For many years, she'd been stuck with the burden of a huge secret she couldn't talk about.

It was a burden we all shared.

50

THE BROOKLYN CONNECTION

Of all the criticism I endured on AboveTopSecret. com, one point stands out as particularly ridiculous: Some members found it impossible to believe that Osama bin Laden had been living in Brooklyn.

But I wouldn't have the means to properly confront their doubts about his location and other aspects of the bin Laden saga until years later.

Facing financial failure and an uncertain future, I returned to school five months after finding bin Laden. After years of working in the computer industry, I was determined to take my life in a new direction as I began my graduate studies at at Sam Houston State University (SHSU).

Recall that my initial intent was to attain a master's in education so I could teach computer science to eager young high school students. But a few semesters later, I took a few history courses and fell in love. I found my new home in the history master's program, and in December 2011, after passing my grueling comprehensive exams, I graduated with an M.A.

After graduation, I worked for a couple of years as an adjunct professor at Alvin Community College. But the real benefit of my degree wouldn't come until October 2014, when I started laying the foundation for my book. My education had brought my research skills to a new high, so that I finally had what it took to back up my statements about bin Laden. I would try to put the criticisms to rest by gathering historical evidence.

The original plan was to incorporate my research into a paper for submission to the press. But when I failed to get their attention, I decided to combine my work with my personal testimony to paint a comprehensive picture of what happened in 2006 and beyond.

To begin my research, I spent countless hours utilizing SHSU's database access that had continued beyond graduation. But eventually, my efforts evolved as I became increasingly frustrated by the crawl of our home internet connection. I realized that scrolling through microfilm reels would be way faster and more efficient than waiting for individual web pages to load. So I did something that every historian loves: I headed to the library.

With Nicki by my side as my research assistant, we would drive long distances to Houston-area public and university libraries and spend countless hours in their dusty basements and quiet cubicles, sifting through dozens of reels of microfilm from major newspapers. We were meticulously searching for—hoping for—any clues that would help me expose the Bush/Obama conspiracy to hide bin Laden's arrest.

The following section and the entire next chapter are the result of my research. They contain some really important background information.

***

In 1998, long before Osama bin Laden was arrested, Jack Cloonan, a now-retired New York FBI agent, had been hand-picked to be the one to slap the handcuffs on Osama bin Laden. According to Cloonan, the US had discovered bin Laden's location, and there was a secret plan for agents to fly into Afghanistan from New York.[110] But the mission was canceled, and Cloonan retired before he could fulfill his duty. He wouldn't be the lucky New York agent who got to arrest Osama bin Laden. Still, on September 10, 2006, only a few weeks after bin Laden's arrest, Brian Ross interviewed Cloonan:

> *BRIAN ROSS (ABC NEWS) The FBI agent assigned to put the handcuffs on Osama bin Laden had practiced what he would say.*

> *JACK CLOONAN (FORMER FBI AGENT) I would have said, "Mr. bin Laden, my name is Jack Cloonan, I'm from the FBI in New York. You are under arrest." Then he would have been handcuffed.[111]*

This snippet struck me as particularly appropriate. I mean, Cloonan, a former *New York* FBI agent, was recalling this imaginary scenario only a few weeks after Osama bin Laden's very real, albeit secret, arrest by a *New York* agent. This made it seem like Cloonan knew something about bin Laden's incarceration. After all, he still had ties to the intelligence community, and perhaps even clearance. Plus, his words made it seem like he was living vicariously through the New York agent who made the actual arrest on August 16, 2006.

Regardless, I can understand why people would have trouble believing bin Laden had been in Brooklyn. It is shocking, unexpected news. The US government led us to believe that he had been hiding in a cave in Afghanistan. We'd even sent troops there and started a war under the pretext of finding him.

However, would a cave be a logical site from which to run a huge global terror network? *No...* The best place would be somewhere with easy access to technology—a place like New York City.

But there were other advantages to living in a big, modern city. Around 2004, bin Laden, who used to look gaunt and sickly, perhaps from kidney failure, appeared full-cheeked and healthy in a newly released video.[112] The question is, what changed? Why the improved health? Maybe living long-term in Brooklyn, where he had access to excellent healthcare, could explain the improvement in his vitality. Ironically, the country that he hated the most might have been providing him with the means to survive. And with his wealth, he could afford to pay cash for the services.

But how long did bin Laden live in Brooklyn? And why?

Recall, after I discovered Osama bin Laden's alias, I found evidence that he might have been living there a few months *prior* to September 11, 2001. In other words, if this were true, bin Laden didn't have to hop on an airplane and wriggle through the clutches of post-9/11 security. *No...* Like I said, he was likely already in New York on that horrible day, overseeing his troops and observing the whole scene from a safe distance in Brooklyn.

And, as I mentioned earlier, Brooklyn is really close to Ground Zero. In fact, Brooklyn Bridge Park is a mere 1.7 miles from the site—a thirty-minute trip by foot and ferry, or twelve minutes by car.[113] And Brighton Beach, where bin Laden was living when he was arrested, is only 13.7 miles away from where the Twin Towers once stood.[114]

Maybe Osama bin Laden remained close to Ground Zero because, like some military generals of the past, he wanted to oversee his troops in person. Being near the attack zone would allow him to exert the most control. This might have been considered honorable under different circumstances.

Still, why had bin Laden been living in Brooklyn, in particular? Why not the Bronx or Manhattan? Why not any other part of New York City? It could be because Brooklyn was conveniently located a mere hop, skip, and a jump across the bridge from The World Trade Center.[115] This alone would have made Brooklyn a convenient hideout. But there's so much more.

Brooklyn was intimately connected to the founding of Al Qaeda and the men who executed the 9/11 plot. Here I'll offer some more history. Let me begin with an excerpt from John Miller, Michael Stone, and Chris Mitchell's, *The Cell*. In this book the authors describe the importance of Brooklyn to Al Qaeda:

> *Located in a remodeled tenement in a dingy section of downtown Brooklyn's Atlantic Avenue, the al-Kifah Refugee Services Center was the main US branch*

*of the Pakistan-based Office of Services,
the organization that would later become
al Qaeda. Throughout the 1980s, al-Kifah
functioned chiefly as a recruiting post,
propaganda office and fund-raising center
for the mujahideen fighting the Soviet army
in Afghanistan. But the office, located in
a suite of rooms on the ground floor of
the al-Farooq Mosque, was also a hotbed
of radicalism, a place where Muslim men
from the area came together with militant
religious leaders to exchange ideas and rally
to Islamic fundamentalist causes.[116]*

The first time I read that I had to do a double-take. Did I read that right? The Al Kifah Refugee Services Center in *Brooklyn* was "*the main US branch of...the organization that would become al Qaeda.*"

And here's something from a 1998 *New York Times* article. According to the authors, the government had recently released this information:

...the roots of Mr. bin Laden's organization could be traced, in part, to a sparsely furnished office on Atlantic Avenue in Brooklyn that was called Alkifah Refugee Center and had for many years been a gathering place for that same fringe group of terrorists.[117]

So this was it, the bottom line: Al Qaeda was founded, in part, in Brooklyn. This was astonishing! In fact, the Al Kifah Refugee Center was cofounded in 1987 under direct order of Osama bin Laden and Abdullah Azzam. Azzam was bin Laden's mentor and the man who convinced him to join the jihadist movement. While bin Laden provided the money for the new Brooklyn office, Azzam brought fiery inspiration.[118]

Let me reiterate: The Al Kifah Center was primarily a recruitment office that used propaganda to get young men to join the jihadist movement. And hundreds joined.[119] Many were American Muslims of both Middle Eastern and African descent. The Brooklyn center also served as a way station for new fighters and veterans coming in and out of the US. As a "charity" front, it was used by bin Laden and other wealthy individuals to funnel money to support jihadists in Afghanistan and Pakistan. Initially, the CIA itself contributed millions through the Brooklyn office to fund the mujahideen.[120] These were the rebels who fought against the Russian troops sent from the USSR to help the communist regime that had taken hold in Afghanistan.[121]

Meanwhile, London's *Independent* described the Brooklyn office as *a "place of pivotal importance to Operation Cyclone, the clandestine American training effort to support the mujahideen."*[122]

Through Operation Cyclone, the CIA was not only funding the rebels, but also providing them with weapons, logistics, and training—all funneled to the mujahideen in Afghanistan through the Al Kifah Refugee Center.[123]

The relationship between the CIA and the Brooklyn office continued even after Russia pulled out of Afghanistan in 1989. At the time, the mujahideen rushed in and occupied most—but not all—of Afghanistan. They wouldn't completely drive the communist government from all regions until 1992.[124] In the meantime, in 1989, the organization running the Al Kifah Refugee Center in Brooklyn was rebranded as Al Qaeda. It was formed to fight future holy wars. But bin Laden and Azzam, the aforementioned founders of the Brooklyn office, disagreed on the direction to take Al Qaeda. Bin Laden wanted to expand the cause and turn it into a global effort. But Azzam wanted to keep the focus on Afghanistan and fight to create an Islamist government there.[125]

Not long after the disagreement, Azzam was mysteriously murdered via car bomb, and bin Laden inherited total control of Al Qaeda. And a little over a year after that, Mustafa Shalabi, Azzam's right-hand man, who had set up the Refugee Center and was running it, was also murdered. This left Osama bin Laden and his followers in complete control of the Brooklyn office. Peter Lance spelled it out in his bestseller, *Triple Cross*: "...*with their takeover of the Alkifah, bin Laden, al-Zawahiri, and the blind Sheikh had a brick-and-mortar al Qaeda office in New York.*"[126]

Unbeknownst to the United States, once bin Laden took over, the mission of Al Qaeda and the Brooklyn office began to turn against the US. But the US was still helping bin Laden by funding Al Qaeda and training his operatives in the hopes of using them to drive the remaining communists out of Afghanistan. And get this: They were still working through the Al Kifah Refugee Center in Brooklyn. This relationship continued until 1991, when the CIA pulled its funding. Around the same time, the US started the Gulf War.[127] These two events likely aggravated Osama bin Laden's turn against America.[128] [129] [130]

The result of his fury was seen in the first World Trade Center bombing: On February 26, 1993, Ramzi

Yousef and Eyad Ismoil, drove a rented yellow Ryder van loaded with twelve-hundred pounds of homemade explosives into the level B-2 underground parking lot and ignited their four twenty-foot fuses. They then got in a car and sped from the scene. The terror attack caused six deaths and 1,042 injuries. However, the men fell short of their goal of destroying both towers.[131]

Yousef, Ismoil, and others—recruits from the Brooklyn office who had trained in Afghanistan—were later convicted of the plot. Osama bin Laden himself was in direct communication with Yousef via telephone and was believed to be both funding and aiding him.[132] The Al Kifah Refugee Center had drawn so much attention to itself and the al-Farooq mosque, which it had inhabited, that it soon closed down. It immediately reopened in Boston under a different name.

Regardless, this didn't end the connection between Al Qaeda and Brooklyn. Operatives remained in the area. In fact, not long before September 11, 2001, a US Army intelligence program called Able Danger had been investigating five Al Qaeda cells in the US. This included a group of men labeled the "Brooklyn Cell" because of their ties to Brooklyn. Four of the 9/11 hijackers were identified as members of the Brooklyn Cell: the now-infamous Mohamed Atta, along with Marwan Alshehhi, Khalid Almihdhar, and Nawaf Alhazmi.[133]

Atta, an Egyptian, was considered the mastermind behind 9/11. He was also the hijacker-pilot who took over American Airlines Flight 11 during the attacks. He flew the plane into the North Tower, ultimately destroying the entire structure, and killing everyone on the flight, as well as multitudes of people in the building and on the ground.[134]

Unfortunately, the information about the Brooklyn Cell never made it to the FBI. At the time, the different intelligence agencies didn't always communicate. Three planned meetings for intelligence sharing between Able Danger and the Bureau had been canceled by the Department of Defense' Special Operations Command (SOCOM).[135]

And before a fourth meeting could be scheduled, the Pentagon caught wind of something embarrassing in Able Danger's data: Former US Army sergeant Ali Mohamed, who had been an important US spy was shown to be part of Al Qaeda's inner circle. In other words, he had been a double agent.[136]

So in early 2000, a little over a year before September 11th, the Pentagon ordered the intelligence gathered by Able Danger destroyed. Along with it were records about the Brooklyn Cell, including some of aforementioned major players who plotted and executed 9/11. As a direct result, the FBI was unable to combine information about the Brooklyn Cell with its own intelligence. This information could have enabled the agency to connect the dots and unravel the 9/11 plot before it happened.[137] In other words, if the intel from Able Danger hadn't been crushed, 9/11 might have been prevented.

Of course, blaming the entirety of 9/11 on the Brooklyn Cell is an oversimplification. The information on Al Qaeda in the US prior to September 11, 2001 was quite robust, and the Brooklyn Cell was merely one piece of the puzzle. The FBI actually missed *multiple* opportunities to stop 9/11 by failing to properly piece together data. For anyone who is interested, these failed opportunities to stop the attacks are carefully laid out in

Triple Cross.[138]

Regardless, the Brooklyn branch of Al Qaeda was extremely important to Osama bin Laden and his followers. It was the hub of their American operations and had been under close scrutiny by US intelligence. Knowing this, it's not surprising that bin Laden would turn up there sometime before 9/11 and stay until August 16, 2006, when he was arrested.

So when the FBI Terrorism Task Force in New York received my tip that bin Laden was in Brooklyn, they probably weren't surprised by his purported location. Minimally, the Terrorism Task Force in New York was probably aware of the history between Brooklyn and Al Qaeda. They also had likely been keeping their sights on Brooklyn for years.

However, the sheer size of the Brooklyn population would have made it hard to root out all the terrorists, even Osama bin Laden. And trying to target one individual in a population of nearly 2.5 million[139] would be like the worst game of *Where's Waldo?* ever. It would have been nearly impossible, although bin Laden was hiding in plain sight. Plus, it didn't appear that the FBI was even looking in Brooklyn. But with my unexpected tip, the Bureau was able to find and arrest bin Laden, despite the neighborhood's burgeoning population.

Most Americans, like the participants in my Above-TopSecret thread, are unaware that the roots of Al Qaeda are firmly grounded in Brooklyn. If my critics had known this, discovering Osama bin Laden there might not have seemed as unlikely. Instead, they laughed at the idea that bin Laden had been hiding in Brooklyn.

I was determined to change their minds some day.

51

WHATEVER HAPPENED
TO OSAMA BIN LADEN?

But to change minds, I needed more evidence. More than the connection between Al Qaeda and Brooklyn. More that can be seen through the eyes of a historian.

Three months after my 2014 research began, I put together my sources and wrote a paper that presented all the data I'd gathered. The sole purpose of the piece was to create a case for my claim about bin Laden's arrest. Here are the results:

First, the buzz: During the weeks after Osama bin Laden's secret arrest, there were a number of so-called "leaks" to the press that he'd been spotted in Pakistan near the Afghanistan–Pakistan border. According to their sources, an arrest was imminent. This created a lot of media hype about bin Laden, leading to a torrent of stories about him. This news flooded the press for a full three months after bin Laden's *actual* August 16, 2006 arrest. This seemed to indicate that Bush had been planning to eventually make an announcement. I believed back then that Bush was going to present bin

Laden's secret arrest as though it had just happened. Major media outlets like CNN,[140] ABC,[141] and *The Australian*[142] were reporting the rumors of bin Laden's location and imminent capture in Pakistan.

Then there was George W. Bush: It is well documented that for several years before Osama bin Laden's secret arrest, Bush seemed to be avoiding the topic of bin Laden altogether, only rarely mentioning him during public appearances. In fact, as early as May 2, 2002, less than a year after 9/11, Bush's attitude reflected that he had completely given up hope of finding Osama bin Laden.

During a press conference, a reporter asked him,

> *Mr. President, in your speeches now you rarely mention Osama bin Laden. Why is that? Also, can you tell the American people if you have any more information, if you know if he is dead or alive? Final part— deep in your heart, don't you truly believe that until you find out if he is dead or alive, you won't really eliminate the threat of (Bush cuts him off)—*

Bush then rambled for a while about the US anti-terrorism efforts and why locating bin Laden wasn't a priority in their strategy. Then he said something that appeared to take the reporter off guard.

> *So I don't know where he [bin Laden] is. You know, I just don't spend that much time on him...*

Then the reporter asked a pointed follow-up question:

> But don't you believe that the threat that bin Laden posed won't truly be eliminated until he is found either dead or alive?

The president's response, again, seemed to take the reporter off guard:

> Well, as I say, we haven't heard much from him. And I wouldn't necessarily say he's at the center of any command structure. And, again, I don't know where he is. I—I'll repeat what I said. I truly am not that concerned about him.[143]

These were not the words of a man who was actively pursuing the world's most wanted terrorist. I mean, it looked like Bush had given up all hope of ever finding bin Laden.

But after Osama bin Laden's secret arrest, Bush did a complete and very public 180. During the months immediately after bin Laden's capture, Bush seemed publicly obsessed with him. One small example was Bush's September 5, 2006, "Remarks to the Military Officers Association of America." During this speech, Bush quoted bin Laden frequently and invoked his name *seventeen* times.[144] Let me reiterate: That's *seventeen* times in *one* speech!

And during the months after bin Laden's arrest, Bush mentioned him more often than after 9/11. Let me clarify using data from University of California-Santa

Barbara's *American Presidency Project:* During the three months after 9/11, Bush mentioned Osama bin laden in *thirty-eight* separate public appearances.[145] In contrast, in the three months following bin Laden's secret arrest, Bush mentioned Osama bin Laden on *fifty-three* separate occasions.[146] That's a huge difference. And that doesn't even include television interviews. If these numbers don't stink of obsession, nothing does!

And then there were the promises: During those public appearances, Bush frequently promised we would "get" Osama bin Laden or bring him "to justice." And often Bush implied that an arrest was imminent. Like I've said before, unlike most people, I knew that he was merely "predicting" the secret arrest that had already happened. Again, I think he was originally planning on making an announcement. He was just waiting for the most strategic, convenient time.

Regardless, here is my favorite example of one of Bush's many promises to "get" bin Laden. In this snippet from September 6, 2006, CBS' Katie Couric interviews the president:

> COURIC: Why hasn't he been caught five years later?
>
> BUSH: Yeah, no, that's a good question. I mean, he's hiding. And—we're on the hunt, obviously. We—
>
> COURIC: Does it matter?
>
> BUSH: Yeah, it does matter. Of course. It matters. He's—he's the head of Al

Qaeda. And—but one thing is for certain, though, he's—he's not moving like he used to. Another thing is—he's, you know, not communicating like he used to. And— and we'll get him. It's just a matter of time. We've got a unit in the CIA who is spending a lot of time thinking about these high-value targets.[147]

This interview was conducted only a few weeks after the CIA task force responsible for finding bin Laden had been shut down. Yet suddenly, according to the Couric interview, we were not only going to *"get him,"* but it was imminent, *"just a matter of time."*

In summary, within weeks of bin Laden's arrest: 1) There were rumors that Osama bin Laden had been spotted near the Afghanistan-Pakistan border. 2) There was a lot of media-hype that bin Laden was going to be arrested soon. 3) Bush became obsessed with getting bin Laden and promised we would "get" him soon.

This research seemed to confirm my 2006 theory that Bush had been planning to announce a past event— bin Laden's arrest—as though it had just happened. He would do this using "alternative facts" (lies) about the arrest date and location. Instead of August 16, 2006, he would say the arrest was in October. And instead of in Brooklyn, he would say bin Laden was captured in Pakistan. This would have been the October surprise I mentioned earlier—his plan to announce this fantasy days before the 2006 midterm election to give the Republicans the "bin Laden bump."

In fact, the last time in 2006 that Bush mentioned Osama bin Laden in a public appearance was November

6, the day before the midterm election.[148] He wouldn't invoke bin Laden's name in public again until the following year. This seems to lend credence to the idea that Bush was pushing hype about him in order to bolster the Republicans' chances. However, in the absence of a late announcement about bin Laden's arrest, in the form of an October surprise, the hype didn't help. The Democrats took control of both the House and the Senate.[149]

***

Confident that I had enough data to elicit interest, I presented my paper—my evidence—to several independent news outlets. But I was wrong. I was given the cold shoulder. None of them even bothered to respond to my calls or emails.

The sad truth is that my hard work wasn't enough. Although my research definitely demonstrated the media and the president's renewed interest in Osama bin Laden after August 16, 2006, it fell short of proving a conspiracy to hide a secret arrest. And in the end, there had been no announcement of bin Laden's capture in Brooklyn, in Pakistan, or anywhere else. As far as the public knew, he was still at large until the alleged raid of his bunker on May 2, 2011.

Once again, I had failed to alert the media. This left me frustrated, but not defeated. I eventually abandoned my effort to reason with the press and decided to write a book about my experience instead. I would incorporate some of my research into the manuscript.

My work would continue for another six years. And five years in, I finally asked the right question—the one

I should have been asking from the start: I mean, what happened to Osama bin Laden after he was arrested? Why was there never an announcement? And how did he turn up later, in Pakistan? Or was his placement there just another lie?

A viable answer wouldn't come to me until I stumbled upon an article by Dr. Nafeez Ahmed, the renowned British investigative journalist who serves as chief editor of *Insurge Intelligence*. His news organization, which is independent and completely crowdfunded, prides itself on digging deep into the bowels of hidden US and world government secrets.

The article, aptly titled, "The bin Laden Death Mythology,"[150] immediately caught my eye. Here was a respected journalist calling the raid "mythology–" something that I already knew to be true. I was interested in hearing his perspective.

Ahmed drew from several sources, one of which was Seymour M. Hersh, the renowned journalist and author of *The Killing of Osama Bin Laden*. Hersh's book contradicted conventional wisdom regarding bin Laden's fate. According to his sources in the intelligence community, *"bin Laden had been a prisoner of the ISI (Pakistani Intelligence) at the Abbottabad compound since 2006,"* the site of the eventual raid.[151]

This was exciting stuff! Hersh had used the magic number—the magic year: *2006*. And he used a magic word: *prisoner*. If bin Laden had been a prisoner since 2006, this meant he was arrested in 2006! This was the best evidence I'd seen in print to back up my claims! Of course, he was arrested in Brooklyn. But maybe he was *moved* to the bunker in Pakistan shortly afterward.

And Hersh's story was backed by another renowned

journalist—Dr. Raelynn Hillhouse. Hillhouse is a former political science professor, Fulbright Fellow, and national security and intelligence community analyst. Her blog, "The Spy Who Billed Me,"[152] has broken multiple national security stories and is often cited by global media.

According to Hillhouse's sources, *"bin Laden was essentially being kept under house arrest. His contact with the outside world was controlled and he was not allowed to leave the compound without Pakistani approval."* [153]

So these two esteemed journalists are essentially telling the same story: Osama bin Laden was under house *arrest* in Abbottabad around the time of the raid. And this idea jives well with my claim that bin Laden was *arrested* on August 16, 2006.

But what about bin Laden's "handling" by ISI? Why would they be holding him and controlling him if the US had arrested him? I think I can reasonably assume that the real force behind bin Laden's handling was the CIA, perhaps aided by ISI because he was on Pakistani soil.

Then there were the Saudis: Hersh and Hillhouse both claim that the bin Laden operation was funded by the Saudis.[154] [155] But based on what I know, it seems more likely that funding was actually coming from the US. After all, they made the arrest, and they set the scene for bin Laden's incarceration.

This idea is backed up in "The bin Laden Death Mythology." In his article, Ahmed, citing various sources, drew the conclusion that *"if bin Laden had a dedicated ISI handler, by definition he was operating as an agent on behalf of the ISI. And at least some senior US officials were aware of this."*[156] So, if you believe Ahmed, you could deduce that the US was running the show, and ISI was working on its behalf to handle Osama bin Laden and his imprisonment.

But bin Laden's house arrest in the Abbottabad compound begs a crucial question: If Osama bin Laden was arrested in Brooklyn and subsequently transferred to Abbottabad, what would the US hope to gain from it? In other words, how on Earth could his cooperation help the CIA? And why would bin Laden agree to work with them?

Ahmed may have already spelled out a rationale: According to his research, the US takes a very controversial approach in its counter-terrorism efforts. They have moles within Al Qaeda and ISIS who hold leadership positions and help plan and execute terror attacks. The beauty is, if the US controls when and where the attacks happen, then they have all the information they need to swoop in, stop it, and kill or arrest the terror agents.[157]

Maybe they could use bin Laden in the same way. They could monitor him and get him to command his troops from the bunker. In this way, they would always know what Al Qaeda was up to, and they could stop them at every corner. Perhaps this is why Al Qaeda became so weakened during the years following August 16, 2006. Al Qaeda could have continued to thrive without bin Laden. But if their precious leader was working against them, they didn't stand a chance.

And there's another crucial question: How would the CIA get Osama bin Laden to cooperate? Why would he turn on his own people? The answer is simple: He was a coward. Bin Laden was never the one getting in a plane and crashing it into a building. He was never the one strapping explosives to his chest and blowing himself up in a crowd full of people. *No...* He valued his life above others and above all. He was the ideas guy, the money source, the cult leader. And I think he would do anything to save his own skin, including lead his own devoted followers to their futile deaths.

I imagine Osama bin Laden panicking and begging for his life and freedom, negotiating with the CIA. He might have even offered some of his billions as a bribe. Conversely, I could imagine his powerful, wealthy family swooping in with their money in an attempt to rescue their prodigal son. Regardless, I can see him pleading with the agents: "I can make myself useful."

Then, the CIA takes the negotiation to the White House after realizing it can, in fact, use bin Laden to cripple Al Qaeda. *Boom!* ... No announcement. No nothing. Bin Laden is left alive and transferred to a bunker in Pakistan. Although he would be monitored closely and likely could never leave his home, he got what he wanted—his life and his freedom. He would get no humiliation, no prison time. All he had to do was betray everything he believed in and nearly everyone he knew.

And what about the raid? If, in fact, Osama bin Laden was under house arrest in the bunker in Pakistan, working for the CIA, why would there suddenly be a raid? Here's my best guess: According to Hillhouse, an ISI informant seeking the $25 million reward leaked bin Laden's position.[158] This seems to indicate that the CIA's operation to house and handle bin Laden had been compromised, and minimally, they had to pretend they were moving on the tip. At that point, it is reasonable to assume that the CIA was pressured to either kill bin

Laden or move him to a new location. So, it is likely they ordered the raid as part of the coverup. Whether or not bin Laden was killed during it is a matter of debate. My personal thought is that his death was faked, and he was relocated and is still working as a CIA asset. Here's my rationale.

First of all, there are numerous, well-documented contradictions in the official US accounts of the bin Laden raid, which means it was likely cloaked in untruths. As with any pathological liar, the government couldn't keep its story straight.

There were many exposés immediately after the raid, but one stands out as particularly well researched: *The Guardian's* Robert Booth concisely laid out some of the contradictions in the government line in his article, "The Killing of Osama Bin Laden: How the White House Changed Its Story."[159] It is an excellent, detailed example of investigative journalism, and I like to recommend it to anyone who wants to see how ludicrous the government claims were after the raid. Other notable reports covering the discrepancies in the government's account are available from such mainstream organizations as *The Atlantic, The New York Times*, and more.[160] [161]

The fact is, that if the government was lying about the details of the raid—and it seems they were—what other things could they be lying about?

Of course! ... They could be lying about bin Laden's fate. He might not be dead. He might not have even been in the bunker at the time of the raid.

And other damning clues indicate a coverup: One particularly dubious assertion is the ridiculous claim that bin Laden's body was "shot out to sea." If this doesn't stink of a coverup, nothing does. Why would the US give one of the most despised criminals in the world a burial at sea? Why such a permanent solution? Why such dignity? Why no real paper trail?

More importantly, the public has never been presented with any photographic nor DNA proof of bin Laden's death. The so-called photo that was being shared around the internet in 2011 was proven to be a fake that had been circulating for two years prior to the raid.[162]

Regardless, the media has made numerous Freedom of Information Act (FOIA) requests for such evidence, only to be denied repeatedly.[163] FOIA is the federal law that allows the press and general public to ask for full or partial disclosure of previously unreleased information and documents controlled by the US. However, there is a loophole: The government doesn't have to disclose anything it deems to be a security risk. In other words, *the fox is guarding the henhouse.*

Nevertheless, according to the AP's Richard Lardner, access to the alleged photos and DNA test results was denied because they were supposedly *"purged from Defense Department computers and sent to the CIA, where they could be more easily shielded from ever being made public."*[164]

So there's no evidence–absolutely nothing empirical—presented to the public that proves Osama bin Laden died during the raid. There have only been anecdotal stories told by so-called eyewitnesses as well as dubious, convenient intelligence "leaks."

***

I realize my ideas are complex, so I've put them

together in a timeline. Hopefully, this will make them easier to digest. It illustrates a logical alternative to the official government version of bin Laden's fate— an alternative that easily includes his 2006 arrest in Brooklyn. It starts with his incarceration on August 16, 2006, and ends in 2011 with what I think happened after the alleged raid of his bunker. But, of course, much of this is guess work. In the end, I only know what I know, and that should be enough.

Timeline of My Theory: Bin Laden After the Arrest

AUG. 16, 2006

FACT: Osama bin Laden is arrested in Brooklyn by the New York FBI Terrorism Task Force, acting on my tip.

SEPT. 2006

FACT: Weeks after the arrest, there is a lot of media hype surrounding bin Laden as numerous "leaks" to the press indicate that he had been spotted in Pakistan and that his arrest seems imminent.[166][167][168]

SEPT. > OCT. 2006

THEORY: Bush's frequent promises that we would "get" Osama bin Laden soon,[171] indicate that he was planning an "October surprise." He would announce the arrest ahead of the November mid-term election to give Republicans the "bin Laden bump."

2006

THEORY: The US decides bin Laden is more useful as a CIA asset than as a trophy. His family's power and their billions might have influenced this decision.

AFTER AUG. 16, 2006

FACT: According to Darklight12's post on AboveTopSecret.com, bin Laden was moved to a Top Secret base in Texas. Darklight12 claimed he attained the intel from his cousin, who was a military general.[165]

ALSO SEPT. 2006

FACT: Bush starts obsessively mentioning Osama bin Laden during public appearances and repeatedly promises that we would "get" him, often implying that this would happen soon.[169][170]

NOV. 6, 2006

FACT: The last day in 2006 that Bush mentions bin Laden in a public appearance is the day before the midterm election.[172] This seems to lend credence to the idea that Bush was using promises to arrest bin Laden in order to bolster the Republicans' chances.

ALSO 2006

FACT: According to Hersh's sources, bin Laden is detained in Pakistan sometime in 2006.[173]

SHORTLY BEFORE MAY 2, 2011

FACT: According to Hillhouse, an anonymous Pakistani intelligence agent leaked bin Laden's whereabouts, hoping to get the $25 million reward.[175]

MAY 2, 2011

FACT: According to US authorities, Seal Team Six storms bin Laden's compound in Pakistan and claims they killed bin Laden during the raid.
QUESTIONS: Was he ever living in Abbottabad? Did the US relocate Osama bin Laden from the bunker in Pakistan to a secret location, or was he killed as part of the cover-up?

SOMETIME, PERHAPS YEARS, BEFORE MAY 2011

FACT: According to Hillhouse's sources, bin Laden is placed under house arrest in theAbbottabad bunker in Pakistan.[174]

ALSO SHORTLY BEFORE MAY 2, 2011

THEORY: After the leak, the US realized that bin Laden's position had been compromised and scrambles for a plan to cover its tracks.

PRESENT

FACT: No photographic nor DNA evidence proving bin Laden's death has been presented to the public. The US claims his body was "shot out to sea."
THEORY: Bin Laden might be alive, but relocated from the Abbottabad bunker in Pakistan. He is possibly still under house arrest at his new home. He may or may not still be working as a CIA asset. I have created this theory because of the lack of hard evidence that bin Laden is dead. Plus, the circumstances surrounding his so-called burial are suspect.

52

A GREAT STORY

But despite my hard work, for many people—perhaps, most people—neither my research nor my word would ever be enough to prove my case. They would never believe that I found Osama bin Laden and my tip led to his arrest by the New York FBI.

Regardless, even though I was terrified of criticism by doubters and mockers, I would sometimes, albeit infrequently, gather up the courage to talk to people about what happened.

***

It was July 2007: Nearly a year after Osama bin Laden's arrest, I found myself seated at the little glass kitchen table in Mom and Tim's small, pristine home in League City, staring at the tiny pink-and-blue flowers on their wallpaper. I was surrounded by family at yet another party.

We'd all convened to see Grandpa, who was in town on a rare visit from California. He was in his nineties and had finally given up his stubborn avoidance of Texas—a place where he thought he'd surely die from an asthma attack. He'd had a bad experience during a visit thirty years prior. This was the reason I hadn't seen him since The Monster Trip, which had been the previous summer.

Naturally, my attention turned to Grandpa, who was sitting across the table from me, smiling. We quietly started discussing politics—his second-favorite topic, just behind telling stories about the Great Depression.

Grandpa was one of the most liberal people I knew. He was even pro-choice, despite Mom and Grandma's protests. But when it came to political parties, he was aloof. He would sometimes wave his hand dismissively, stating, "Republicans. Democrats. It doesn't matter. They're all a bunch of crooks."

Despite this, he came from the generation that staunchly supported the progressive, democratic socialist leanings of FDR. And he would never be caught dead voting Republican. In other words, despite his misgivings, he was a Democrat.

Somehow, during our casual conversation, the topic of George W. Bush came up. Like seeing pictures of Osama bin Laden, the mention of Bush's name provoked immediate ire in me. After everything that had happened, I wasn't a fan of the president.

I began to talk about Bush disparagingly.

Brandy, who was standing close by, overheard my comments. "*Gawd.* I thought you liked Bush. Didn't you vote for him?"

It's true. I had voted for Bush *twice.* Although I had been mostly liberal, at the time I had been a single-issue voter. As you know, I was Catholic and staunchly pro-life. Bush could be the president to end abortion, and although he wasn't too smart, I believed that deep down, he was a good person. But my opinion changed when Bush decided to cover up bin Laden's capture and keep the war going. In my mind, this made him a war criminal, especially after his defense of waterboarding and other forms of "enhanced interrogation" (i.e., torture).[176] [177]

But that's not what filled me with ire at that moment. Hearing Brandy's words—"I thought you liked Bush"—made my blood boil. I felt my emotions go from zero to a hundred in a few seconds. Before I knew it, I was screaming at the top of my lungs.

"That's before he ripped me off for $25 million!"

I was so angry that I was practically in tears. The best way to describe it was rage.

Grandpa seemed stunned. He clearly had no clue about what just happened. Brandy tried to change the subject.

"Let's not talk about that right now." To her, there was never a good time to get into it. She wanted to pretend August 2006 never happened. She didn't want to think about the time her little sister had lost her mind and believed she'd found Osama bin Laden.

It was too late. I had piqued Grandpa's curiosity, and he had already started asking questions. "That sounds like a good story. Why don't you tell me about it?"

Brandy tried to shut it down. "Grandpa doesn't need to hear this."

I pleaded with her, "But I want to tell him. He needs to know."

It had been a while since I'd shared the bin Laden stuff with anyone, and I wanted to know how he'd respond. I trusted his intelligence and his opinion. Brandy and I went back and forth for several minutes before Grandpa finally spoke up.

He gazed directly at Brandy and waved his hand toward her, dismissively. "You go away. Us adults are gonna talk."

She left in a huff.

Grandpa looked over at me, still curious. "Tell me all about it."

He stared at me with rapt attention.

As I told him every detail, from beginning to end, he nodded and smiled. Mostly, he came across amused. Above all, Grandpa loved a great story, and this was a truly great one—maybe the best he'd ever heard.

Most importantly, Grandpa didn't judge or criticize. I had never really confided in him before, and he turned out to be a pretty good listener. And at the time, I thought he might even believe my story, which made me happy. But looking back, who knows? He might have been placating me. But it hardly mattered. At a time when nearly everyone in my life was judging me as crazy or a liar, Grandpa's attitude and demeanor was a breath of fresh air. His positivity would help propel me forward when I finally started telling more people about my experiences.

53

A TALE OF TWO THERAPISTS

Flash forward to December 2013. Kylie's long dark ponytail flew backward as she reared her head and let out a loud horse-like belly laugh. My gut wrenched. This was horrible. I'd just told her my darkest secret, and this was her response? She was laughing at me? *My therapist was laughing at me!*

My face dropped...

I looked across the room at Kylie. "What's so funny?"

She looked back at me with a wild smile. "Nothing. I just think it's such a great story!"

"But you don't believe it?"

I was expecting a typical response.

"*No!* I can't believe that no one would believe this. It's so obvious you're telling the truth. And it's awesome!"

I was relieved. This was the first person in years who'd trusted me without question, and her response had been precious.

Kylie had been my first eating disorder therapist.

My food issues had gone from compulsive overeating to a full-blown case of binge eating disorder in the years after I found Osama bin Laden. Over those years, I had lost 150 pounds and gained most of them back. I was obsessed with body image and weight, and was on a long roller coaster ride of feast and famine. I'd been numbing out with food, using it as a means to repress and forget about the bin Laden stuff. Food was both my best friend and worst enemy. Either way, I was miserable.

The day before, Kylie had told me that whatever my darkest secrets were, I needed to write them down and tell her about them to help me stop binge eating. I needed to stop burying my feelings with food.

When Kylie asked me to self-disclose, I struggled to know what to say. But then something ominous crept up from the back of my mind—something that I didn't even want to think about, much less talk about. I looked Kylie directly in the eyes, trying to decide if I should tell her about what had happened in 2006. "There *is* something. But I don't want to talk about it."

She gave me a nod. "Well, that's exactly what you need to talk about!"

"But you won't believe me. No one believes me. You'll think I'm *crazy*!"

Tears welled in my eyes as I began to panic.

Kylie was compassionate. We argued back and forth for a few minutes before she finally convinced me to write it all down.

A few hours later, I sat in my room with a small Mead composition book she'd given me. I opened it and stared down at the page. It had been years since I'd written anything significant by hand. I was used to typing everything. Finally, I picked up the only pencil around—a stubby, dull one. *Sigh*... Sobbing the entire time, I angrily pushed hard on the lead and felt my hand cramping as I scrawled out all the details surrounding bin Laden's arrest. Something about handwriting the experience made reliving it seem more real, cathartic.

In the end, my journal entry—the first draft of what would become this book—was six barely-legible, cursive pages. I showed them to Kylie the next day. As she read it, she laughed out loud at times. This didn't really bother me. Sometimes when I wrote, I was unintentionally funny.

But at the end of her reading, when she'd let out the belly laugh, I had been offended.

After she'd reassured me that she believed me and thought it was a great story, I had a lot of questions. We needed to piece this together. Why was the truth so hard to trust? And more importantly, why did *she* have faith in it when my own sister, who wasn't a therapist, considered me crazy?

I gazed at Kylie with wonder. "So, if you think it's so easy to believe, why do you think my sister doesn't believe me?"

Kylie took me through some simple logic. "Well, if you found bin Laden, who would that make *her*?"

I considered her words for a moment and understood. "*Oh!* ... It would make her the *sister* of the person who found Osama bin Laden."

Kylie nodded. "Yup."

I contemplated her words for a moment. She must have thought Brandy's attitude was a reflection of envy, a subconscious sibling rivalry. If I had done something so special, where would that leave her in the family's specialness hierarchy? In other words, she would have diminished feelings of self-worth.

But there was more: The story was so unusual and spectacular that, even when people believed it, they were often left with a strong sense of unreality. It was like something Amy, one of Daun's friends, once told me after I gave her all the details. "It's not the kind of thing you would expect to hear from someone you *actually* know." The comment made it seem like Amy looked toward my accomplishment with a certain level of awe. I mean, even *I* had difficulty believing what I'd accomplished—finding bin Laden. My mental process was often reflective of the way I felt immediately after the hunt was over: dumbfounded. *What made me so special?* ... I would figuratively pinch myself. Maybe it had all been a dream. I couldn't have possibly found Osama bin Laden. After all, this was *me*, Barbara Janik. I was just a normal person living a normal life. How could I have done something so great? It blew my mind.

So maybe my sister couldn't deal with that mind-blowing aspect of everything that happened. It was too much to imagine. But it's like the sage lyrics of "What to Do" by OK Go:

> *Sweetheart, you'll find mediocre people*
> *do exceptional things all the time.*

When I was breaking through my denial about the bin Laden stuff, I would play that song loudly and scream that line at the top of my lungs, sometimes hard-crying. Maybe in this infinite world, I was just one of those "mediocre" people. *Yes...* That would explain it—how I, of all people, found Osama bin Laden.

As I sang, I was shouting at all the naysayers. *"I'm*

telling the truth! He was arrested and it was because of me!"

On day three, Kylie came back with more news: She'd gone home and rented *Zero Dark Thirty* because she wanted to see how the official 2011 government account of events played out in the movie. After watching it, Kylie seemed even more convinced that I was telling the truth because she felt certain aspects of the film were reflective of my claims.

Kylie's eyes lit up as she described the movie that I had never dared to watch. I didn't want to see Hollywood's rendition of false events. "You've *got* to go home and watch it! You're gonna love it!"

I was skeptical. "What do you mean? Why would I like that? It's all based on lies."

Kylie smiled so hard that I thought she was going to start giggling. "I think they designed the main character after you. She fits so perfectly with your story!"

I looked over at her. "Wow... *Really?*"

"Yes!"

Kylie went on to describe the movie, making comparisons between the protagonist of *Zero Dark Thirty* and me. Maya, the main character, was credited as being the person who found Osama bin Laden. Like me, she went on a one-woman crusade to put an end to his tyranny. She was essentially the only one in the movie working on the case and appeared to be the only one with any hope of ever finding him. Like me, Maya located bin Laden through extreme persistence and an overwhelming obsession with the task at hand. She was very intense and driven throughout the entire movie, what I would call hyper-focused. Also, like me, she used the internet and computers to discover bin Laden's whereabouts, although our particular methods were dissimilar.

Then there was the ending: After bin Laden was killed, Maya was sitting in the cargo bay of an airplane. The pilot looked at her and stated warmly, "You must be pretty important, you got the whole plane to yourself!"

The fact is that he and the rest of the world would never know what she'd done. They'd never know what an important person she was. Perhaps the point of that scene was that, like me, she never got any credit for her accomplishment. It was just over.

But it didn't end there. Not for me. During the last of our brief series of sessions, Kylie gave me a final commission.

"I think you should write a book about this! This story is too amazing to keep to yourself!"

I left that session determined to write a book.

But that was the last time I would see Kylie. For reasons beyond our control, I had to switch therapists.

***

Dr. Simmons was a nervous, cantankerous older lady with a bitchy edge. She was one of the quirkiest women I'd ever known, especially for a therapist. But she was also wicked-smart, and I trusted her opinion. Unfortunately, she wasn't as enthusiastic about my project.

I took a deep breath, and braced myself for severe anxiety. My body didn't disappoint, as I felt my breathing and heart rate speed up a bit, and I found myself shaking slightly. I was going to tell Dr. Simmons everything that had happened in 2006. More importantly, I needed to talk about the book.

I prefaced the dialogue in my usual fashion. "You're probably going to think I'm crazy, and you probably won't believe me. But I have to tell you this."

Dr. Simmons sat behind her neatly arranged desk. She was more formal than most therapists, insisting on being called "Doctor." She was proud of her PhD, and seemed to believe it made her an expert in literally everything. She didn't like anyone questioning her opinion, she would never admit to being wrong, and she was always blunt. Sometimes I would leave her office in tears because we had spent half the session arguing a point.

I knew if she didn't trust my story, she would tell me flat-out, with complete honesty. I was prepared for the worst.

After a few moments of angst, I let loose and told her everything. When I finished, she was silent at first. I think she was taking it all in. I kept working on her, summarizing the details, still trying to convince her. "I mean, why would the agent call me a 'gifted researcher' and a—"

Her hand flew up, her words abrupt.

"*Stop right there!*" Dr. Simmons, above all, lacked patience.

Then she did something unexpected: With a dismissive wave of her hand, her voice softened, and she said casually, "You can stop trying to convince me. I believe you."

Such a relief... If Dr. Simmons said she believed me, she did. She never lied, and blunt didn't even begin to describe her. She was more like brutally honest.

One time, I told her that I had worked out at the

gym and hadn't taken a shower afterward. Her face had dropped, and she had wrinkled her nose, agitated.

"That's *disgusting!*"

My thoughts rebelled. *Tell me how you really feel.*

The bottom line was that I could trust Dr. Simmons' opinion.

After our angst-filled talk about bin Laden, I finally mustered up the courage to tell her I was thinking about writing a book.

She tilted her head to the side in a jerky motion. "I don't think you can handle writing a book right now. You have too much going on."

It was true. Like I said, I had been newly diagnosed with a condition now known as binge eating disorder and was dealing with a lot of issues. I was also having panic attacks nearly daily—almost as often as in August 2006. However, I wasn't ready to drop the topic. "But my last therapist told me to write it. She said I need to deal with this stuff to get over my eating disorder."

Dr. Simmons was characteristically persistent. "Look, I don't think you can handle the publicity." She kept going. "The one thing you keep saying is that you're scared of being considered crazy. And the minute this story goes public, they're going to try to discredit you."

However, I didn't want to give in to fear. "But I'm going to use a pseudonym. I've already thought of a name." (I'd chosen my old screen name, Leslie Powers.)

She seemed incredulous and annoyed. "They will find you. The media has resources. They have a way."

A wave of anxiety washed over me. I knew Dr. Simmons was right. If someone like me could locate Osama bin Laden using MySpace, the press, which had infinitely more resources, would have no problem figuring out who I was. And it's not like I would even be hiding that carefully.

The idea of being discovered bothered me. The press would put me under a microscope, and people who support Bush or Obama might threaten me. If I was successful, neighbors and people I barely knew would come out of the woodwork asking for money. This was presuming my book was a success.

The more Dr. Simmons spoke, the more she insisted, and the more she pushed, the more anxious I became. Maybe that was her plan: exposure therapy. To be honest, I never thought her techniques would work. But somehow, over the months, with her help, I got better at managing my anxiety. As I slowly improved, I was able to more easily place myself in uncomfortable situations–even trips to Walmart.

However, it would be nearly a year before I was ready to face my demons and write the book. Like I said, I respected Dr. Simmons' opinion. I knew she was right. At that point in my life, I wasn't ready to write the book. The very thought of public exposure and the world thinking I was crazy made my heart race. I couldn't let it happen again. I had to keep my secret. I was going to shove this story deep back in the closet and hide it under a thick pile of clothing.

The evening that Dr. Simmons told me I wasn't ready to write my book, I went home and shoved my handwritten journal in the "junk drawer"—the place where random objects are left to die.

I was done.

There would be no book.

54

OUT OF THE BIN LADEN CLOSET

The year 2014 passed slowly. As usual, winter turned into spring, spring turned into summer, and summer turned into fall. *Blah blah blah...*

But something in my mundane, unimpressive life was gnawing at my subconscious: What if I died and the story of Osama bin Laden's arrest—*my story*—was never told? Yet at the same time, how could I preserve my experience short of writing a book? I knew that I didn't want to write one. After all, nearly a year prior, Dr. Simmons had advised me that it was a bad idea, and I agreed. Writing one sounded emotionally excruciating, and I wasn't ready to face the pain or possible public humiliation.

Then, one day in mid-October, the thoughts of my part in bin Laden's arrest flew off the back-burner of my mind and landed front and center. I decided that if I couldn't write it all down in a single cohesive manuscript, I could at least make an audio recording. I would get some of the grief and anger off my chest while simultaneously preserving my voice and my lore for posterity.

Although making a recording would be a lot less work than writing a book, creating it still wouldn't be easy. I decided the best way to tackle it would be for Nicki to conduct an interview with me. I knew she'd have trouble coming up with relevant questions, so instead, I wrote it all out as a script.

A day later, we sat down in front of my bulky Asus gaming laptop—which, incidentally, I never used for gaming—and read into the microphone. We then spent hours editing with Audacity, the popular, free, open-source audio editing software. We recorded over bumbles, corrected errors, and cut blank space. (Well, I say "we," but Nicki did all of the actual editing. I mostly just sat there and looked pretty, occasionally spoke into the microphone, and shouted orders.)

By the time we finished, Nicki was done with me. But I felt it was perfect.

I was proud of our efforts—so much so that I was worried about what would happen if we lost the recording. Files get lost or deleted all the time. Hard drives crash. Flash drives get misplaced. *No...* I need assurance. I also wanted to make sure I could share it with people.

So, Nicki created a catchy thumbnail for our presentation: a corny Photoshop of Osama bin Laden behind bars. Then she stuck an image of the Twin Towers over the audio to give people something to look at while listening to my story. Finally, we posted it to YouTube and forwarded the link to a few friends. I briefly put it on Facebook before chickening out. I wasn't ready for my friends and family to know that I had found bin Laden. I wasn't ready for their reaction and, perhaps, their mockery.

Nevertheless, something was bothering me. In the audio, I had said that during the weeks after bin Laden's arrest in 2006, President Bush promised multiple times that we'd "capture" him. But were those his exact words? I began to doubt myself.

I remembered that he never said we were going to "kill" Osama bin Laden. However, I had only seen the speeches once, eight years prior, and I needed to be sure he said the exact word, *"capture."* This would serve as compelling circumstantial evidence. It would show that Bush somehow knew in advance we were going to "capture" bin Laden rather than kill him. How would he know this unless bin Laden had *already* been captured, and Bush had been planning a delayed announcement?

This train of thought led me to start the research project I mentioned earlier. I quickly took down the presentation, had Nicki edit out the claim that Bush said "capture," and resubmitted it. I would try to find proof that he used that word and add it back in later.

But the project and its subsequent research had the unfortunate effect of forcing me once again to recall everything that had happened in 2006 in excruciating detail. And this came with an intense emotional price. During the process, a segment of Johnny Cash's cover of "Hurt" played continually in my mind:

> *I hurt myself today*
> *To see if I still feel*
> *I focus on the pain*
> *The only thing that's real*
>
> *The needle tears a hole*

The old familiar sting
Try to kill it all away
But I remember everything

This somber last line had become my mantra. When I could no longer stand the repetition in my head, I would crank it up on my PC speakers, sing aloud, and bawl my eyes out. Although I had never hurt myself physically, I could relate to Cash's raw emotion and sense of numbness and unreality. I didn't want to remember the bin Laden stuff. But here it was, screaming at me. It wouldn't go away, no matter how hard I tried to push it down into my subconscious.

And for the first time in eight years, I was finally allowing myself to fully remember in vivid detail. So I would shout it out. There was no more hiding. The truth, no matter how uncomfortable, was real. It was like I was screaming at the FBI, my sister, the media, the public, all my mockers—anyone who'd listen, *"I'm not crazy! I've awoken from my slumber. I tried to 'kill it all away, but I remember everything'!!!"*

In the end, the process of going back through the pain of it all again was freeing. I had been stuck for years in the cold, dark bin Laden closet. I was finally prepared to bust open the door and escape.

***

When I was ready, the first thing I did was call my sister. I was proud of my early efforts. I thought that if she would listen, she'd finally see reason and believe my story. But I knew it would take some convincing to get her to give it a chance. The ordeal was probably a painful memory for her, too.

When I called her, I had a difficult time getting her to talk to me about the bin Laden stuff. And when I finally told her about the YouTube audio, she said she was "too busy" to listen to it. But I knew this was total BS. Frustrated and annoyed, we said our goodbyes and I hung up the phone...

A few minutes later, I called her back and tried to reason with her. "Come on, can't you at least give it a shot? It's not like you have to *read* it. Just listen to it on your way home from work. All you have to do is plug your phone into your car stereo and listen to the YouTube audio while you're driving."

She had no more excuses. "Okay. I'll do it."

"Do it today after work?"

"Yes!"

"Promise?"

Brandy seemed exasperated. "Yes, I promise!"

I knew she'd do it. She never broke a promise. The next day, I called her and asked for an opinion.

"So, did you listen to it?"

"Yes."

I was a little surprised, but happy I would finally be getting some feedback.

"What'd you think?"

Brandy's response wasn't as enthusiastic as I'd been hoping for.

"It was pretty good."

"Well, did it change your mind about anything?"

She sounded slightly whiny and a bit concerned, but not at all flippant. "Did the FBI *really* come to your house?"

"Yes. Peter and Daun were there. We all saw the

FBI. You can ask them if you don't believe me."

"No, I believe you. It's just surprising. And why didn't you tell me before?"

I wasn't sure why I hadn't told her. "I guess I just didn't think of it. Sorry."

I repeated the question. "But did it change your opinion?"

"Well, I still don't think you found Osama bin Laden. But they came to your house, so there's probably something to your story." She paused, apparently thinking. "Maybe you found someone else."

I couldn't believe my ears. *How dense could Brandy be?*

I started arguing my point. "But what about the celebration? Why would they be so excited about a different terrorist?"

But she continued to resist. "I don't know. It'd still be a big deal."

"But I was promised an announcement from the president! He wouldn't make an announcement for just any-old terrorist. It had to be bin Laden. No one else would be important enough. What you're saying doesn't make any sense."

We kept on like this for a while, going in circles like every time before. Brandy wasn't going to give in. She still wasn't able to grasp the truth, even though I reminded her of all the details. I even mentioned the agent asking me how I found "The Big Guy" and calling me a "gifted researcher" and a "true patriot."

This was clearly about Osama bin Laden, not someone else. I repeated the same old tired argument. Who else could The Big Guy be? He wasn't some underling. He was the man at the top: bin Laden. But no matter what I said, Brandy wouldn't admit I'd found him. A few minutes later, I gave up. I would have to try again later.

Although I was frustrated, I still felt like I had made some headway. The fact that Brandy was willing to believe I might have accomplished something important was, at least, progress. I would just have to keep chiseling away at her. But not now. *Later...* I was done for the night.

***

Later would come in a few weeks...

At the next family party, which was at Lee's house, Brandy approached me at our spot on Lee's white leather sofa. Even at Lee's place, Nicki and I had an established spot—a comfort zone not unlike The Cave at Jerry's house.

When Brandy walked up, we chatted for a bit, and I brought up the bin Laden topic.

Brandy was resistant. "Do we really have to talk about this *now*?"

But I kept pressing her.

"When are we supposed to talk about it?"

"I dunno. We're supposed to be having fun and relaxing."

But I was determined. I continued to present the evidence, repeating myself *ad nauseam*. I should have learned from previous discussions that this was a futile tactic.

After some time, Brandy looked rattled. "Why do you keep trying to convince me?"

This was when things got real. I felt anger and tears

rising in me. "Because you were my biggest critic. You kept telling me I was crazy." Well, she might have only done it once or twice eight years ago, but it had cut me to the core.

But she denied it. "I *never* said you were crazy."

"Yes, you did, I remember it!" My face was burning hot, and I could feel tears streaming from my eyes.

I couldn't believe it. How could Brandy deny the awful things she said? But I suppose it had been a long time, and I guess she had a selective memory.

"No. I didn't think you were crazy. I thought you were misled. Those guys were being assholes. They were yanking your chain."

However, I wasn't convinced. "Well, I actually thought you thought I was delusional. Like I was imagining everything they said."

"*No!* I just thought you were misinterpreting it."

That made me feel slightly better. My sister hadn't believed I was batshit crazy—just a *little* crazy. But I was still amazed that she kept going back to the same tired argument. What could I possibly say to get through to her? *Damn it!*

We kept going for a while. But when things got too tense, I decided to diffuse the situation.

"I'm thinking about writing a book. If I do, will you read it?"

She was emphatic. "*Of course*, I will!"

"Okay, because you'll be in it."

The mood suddenly shifted as Brandy's face dropped. She seemed a little panicked. "I don't want to be in it."

"You *have* to be. You're too important a character. Sorry, but you're in it."

Brandy shrugged it off. "Well, just don't use my real name."

"I won't. I'm not using *any* real names. Hell. I might not even use *my* real name." (Recently, I had been fluctuating on the topic.)

Finally, I finished the conversation and decided to move on to my next victim: Lee.

I walked into the dining room and greeted him. I never liked his table set. The chairs were way too high. Regardless, I sat down next to my brother. I hadn't actually planned on talking to him about bin Laden, but after my conversation with Brandy, I was busting at the seams. After chatting with Lee for a few seconds, I brought up the awkward topic.

"I have a YouTube audio recording I want you to listen to."

He sounded intrigued. *"Really? ... What is it?"*

I took a deep breath. Despite my excitement, I still hated this topic.

"Remember in 2006 when I told you I found Osama bin Laden?"

Lee shrugged. "Barely... It was a long time ago."

I directed him to the audio, trying to convince him to listen to it. It was clear that the topic disturbed him, so he wouldn't even consider it.

"I don't have time."

Then I proceeded to ambush him with the details of the bin Laden stuff. I reminded him of everything that happened back then.

First, he called it a conspiracy theory.

So I fervently tried to reason with him. "No, Lee. It's *not* a theory. It's my own eyewitness testimony. It's not like I was sitting around like..."—I pinched my fingers and pretended to be inhaling a doobie— "...smoking pot, speculating about a second gunman. This isn't speculation. I *heard* what the FBI said to me. I'm not guessing."

Then Lee said something unexpected: "I believe it's possible you found Osama bin Laden."

My heart leapt. *He was considering it!* Maybe someone in the family would finally accept my story.

But then, he kept going. "But I also believe in the possible existence of aliens."

I was pissed. Was my brother really comparing my experience to the existence of aliens? *My God...* He had some nerve! I got up and walked away in a huff. I would have to take this up with him another time.

Several weeks later, at a different family gathering, I showed up prepared. I *would force* him to read the transcript of the YouTube audio. I *would* be heard!

When Lee approached my couch, I cornered him. "Sit down. I have something for you to read."

He sat down, but when he found out what it was, he refused to even look at it. "It's too long. I don't really like to read that much."

After I begged him, he reluctantly read it. Then he finally made a comment. "Hey. There could be something to this."

We discussed its contents for a bit, going in circles. Still, Lee fell short of believing my story.

Finally, close to tears, I addressed him honestly. "Lee, I know you don't believe it. You compared it to the existence of aliens."

"No. I never said that." *Ha!* ... First, Brandy had denied calling me crazy and then Lee denied comparing my claims to his belief in aliens, although he had just said it a few weeks prior. Like our older sister, he seemed to have a selective memory. They were true siblings, carved from the same stone.

I gave up on Brandy and Lee and decided to email Allen. Hopefully, he would be more reasonable. After all, he was my smartest sibling, or at least the most educated. For God's sake, he had been valedictorian of his class and held a master's in computer science. Maybe he, of all people, could follow my logic.

I sent Allen a copy of a very early draft of my story—the one I had put on Tumblr during yet another recent, but lame, attempt at going public. I was hoping Allen and his extensive network of friends could help me get the word out about bin Laden's 2006 arrest. But Allen's response was not to respond. After what I'd just disclosed, I could only assume he didn't believe me.

But after a while, I grew impatient. I needed to... *needed to* know Allen's opinion of what I had sent him. I shot him a follow-up letter and told him that I was the woman in the story. In the earlier drafts, I had still been using a pseudonym. And even though I considered Allen smart enough to figure it out, I wanted to be sure he understood that Leslie Powers was me.

The next day, he finally wrote me back with a disappointingly brief response: *"I got it. Thanks for sharing it with me."*

Nothing more. *Dead...* It was evident that, like my other siblings, Allen didn't want to hear about the bin Laden stuff. He must have thought his sister had lost her mind. It was years before we'd speak of it again, years before I could bring myself to confront him with more details.

At that point, I gave up talking to my family about the truth. I wouldn't even bother telling Anne or Jerry because I was afraid I'd get the same response from them that I had gotten from the others. And although I'd already told Mom, Tim, and Dad about bin Laden back in 2006, nine years later, in 2014, I stopped short of reminding them about what happened. I was frustrated and humiliated, and didn't want to continue stirring the pot.

***

Despite my lack of family support, I decided to keep adding details to my draft. I turned to a couple of my former professors for advice.

One of them, my favorite history instructor from SHSU, advised me on my research and made suggestions about where to publish. At the time, the draft still read more like a journal article than a memoir.

Later, as I began to incorporate more details of my life into the manuscript, I contacted another one of my favorite instructors, an English professor from UST. At her urging, I joined a critique circle—a writers' group where authors meet regularly and share feedback on each other's work. The next year, I would even attend a writers conference that our organization was sponsoring.

Over the years, I was making slow and steady progress, and my writing style was improving. And what had started as a short paper with a focus on historical evidence had turned into a detailed memoir. I was hopeful for the future and confident that I would eventually wind up with a full-length manuscript. The experience of writing it was freeing, life was getting easier for me, and I felt happy for a change.

But then, my world was torn apart...

55

SHIT HAPPENS

It was January 2015, about a year into my writing process. Peter, who was then twenty-one, had dropped out of Texas State University after a bout of depression and moved home temporarily. He was delivering pizza for Domino's.

Now that he had a job, I began to talk to him about signing up for Obamacare. I had always worried about the fact that he didn't have health insurance. Fortunately, the deadline had been extended that year.

I had been nagging him for weeks, but this was the last day to sign up. So I ambushed him in the kitchen after dinner. "Peter, this is your last chance. You *have* to sign up for Obamacare."

"Mom, I looked into it. It's too expensive."

I knew something was wrong with this picture. I went onto the website and filled out the form as if I were someone with Peter's income. Then I approached him. "Peter, it's only twenty-one bucks a month."

"It's still too much."

He could be really stubborn. He was constantly

trying to maintain his independence.

I begged him to sign up. "No, you *can* afford it. For health insurance, twenty-one dollars is cheap. It's nothing. And what if you get sick? You *need* this!"

"Okay. I'll do it! But I don't see why this is so important." He had finally relented. But I hated his tone. He was doing it again, the thing he'd been doing since he was little: emulating his Dad's "man-whine." As usual, I cringed.

Unconvinced that he was going to follow through with his promise, I gazed directly into Peter's eyes. "Just humor me. You're not invincible, even though you think you are."

"*Mom... I said*, I'll *do* it!"

He was becoming increasingly annoyed.

"Okay, well, do it *now* before you forget."

He dug his heels in. "*Mom*, I *said* I was going to do it. Now leave me alone!"

Peter stomped off to his room. A few minutes later, I quietly cracked his door open and peeked in on him. He was hunched over his laptop.

Unfortunately, he heard me open the door. But at least he was calmer. "I'm working on it right now."

***

A week after his new insurance kicked in, Peter approached me, looking sad. "Mom, I'm tired all the time. I'm having trouble keeping up with my job."

Another week passed.

"Mom, I'm having trouble sleeping. My back hurts. I can't find a comfortable position. I took some ibuprofen, but it isn't helping."

Peter never complained when he was sick, so the pain must have been excruciating. Even when he was a little boy, it had been difficult to tell when he had a fever.

I took Peter to urgent care. They ordered imaging that was to be performed at a separate facility. We went back and got the results a few days later. They blamed the pain on what they claimed was a hairline fracture showing up on his scan. It was weird. He had never injured his back—at least not that I was aware of. He'd never even had any hard falls on that part of his body. Still, I accepted the diagnosis and moved on. They sent him home with some light pain medication.

But by the following week, the problem had grown worse. "Mom, my gut hurts really bad. I don't think I can take this."

That's when I got worried. I was afraid Peter might be having an appendicitis attack like the one Allen had in high school. I knew they were life-threatening, so I tried to rule out the possibility. I pushed where I thought his appendix was supposed to be and jabbed other parts of his belly, trying to find the source of the pain. He said the pain kept moving around and that I was hurting him. I had to stop.

My next idea was that he was having a gallbladder attack like Nicki had experienced a few years earlier. Either way, he'd need surgery.

We rushed him to the ER, leaving the house at 3 a.m. When we got there, Peter went into triage without me. In typical Peter fashion, he underplayed his symptoms.

Hours later, he was shown into a room so he could get a blood test. We waited two hours to see the doctor, but when he finally came by, he didn't give Peter a physical exam. Instead, he simply stated that the blood tests had come back normal.

But his answer wasn't good enough for me. "What about his gut pain? It's horrible!"

The doctor looked at me matter-of-factly. "The blood tests came back normal. There is nothing *medically* wrong with him."

I was livid. The diagnosis was total bullshit. I knew the pain wasn't in Peter's head. But maybe he was just constipated or something. Besides, we had been in the ER all night, and I was exhausted. With our concerns unresolved, we headed home.

Later, I would closely examine the documents from the ER. They said something vague about a viral infection. I tried not to worry. Maybe they were right. Maybe it was nothing. After all, the blood tests had come back normal.

A few days later, Nicki and I left for a trip to Phoenix. We'd been planning the getaway for weeks. We were going to visit Nicki's elderly father.

A few days into our trip, I got a phone call from Peter.

"Mom, the gut pain's not going away. It's getting so bad I can hardly eat. My back still hurts, and now I think I have a cold. I can't stop coughing. And this is all keeping me up. I'm taking some time off work."

I began to panic. Most moms, especially me, worry when their kids don't eat. But this was worse. He had so much going on at once that there must have been something really wrong. I started freaking out internally but tried to maintain a slightly calmer front for Peter. I didn't want to add to his anxiety.

Still, I begged Peter to go to the ER. But as usual, he

was stubborn. "I got some DayQuil and some NyQuil. I'll be fine. It's just a cold. Don't worry, Mom."

That night, I came close to getting on a plane and heading home early. I was hysterical and crying. What if he *died* while I was gone? He needed to go to the ER! But then I thought about the response he got from the ER doctor. Surely, he'd be okay for a couple of days.

When I finally made it home, Peter was in horrible shape. His coughing was so severe that it sounded like a dog barking. He'd barely eaten anything in days, and he looked like he'd lost some weight. But even with all that, I still couldn't convince him to go to the ER. We went back to urgent care instead.

The nurse at urgent care had trouble drawing his blood. "I think you're a little dehydrated." This was a common thing for nurses to say when they couldn't find a vein. It had nothing to do with test results.

When he finally saw the physician's assistant, she was baffled. His lungs sounded clean, yet he kept coughing. She suggested to him that he go to the ER, but he refused. For the *nth* time in his life, he was being stubborn. He was definitely *my* son.

She was going to prescribe cough syrup and antibiotics, and send him home. But something told me to mention the dehydration.

"Well, if he's dehydrated, you definitely need to go to the ER."

This time, I went into triage with him. I wasn't going to let him downplay his condition again. I helped him emphasize how awful the pain was. He wasn't going to slip through the cracks. I was a momma bear.

This time, he was put on the fast track and moved to a room right away. This time, he was taken seriously.

But when I spoke to the tech, he said they were going to do standard blood tests and a series of X-rays. He said that if it were an appendicitis attack, it would show up in the labs. However, I was worried about gallstones, so I insisted on a CT scan. The tech looked at me and nodded. "Sure, we can do that."

A few hours later, after an examination and lots of questions, I heard the doctor utter a word that chilled me to the bone: lymphoma.

What?! I felt like I'd been socked in the gut. Wasn't that *cancer?* I found myself shaking. Was my son going to *die?*

But cancer wasn't always a death sentence. It was more like a roll of the dice.

I spent the two hardest months of my life living in the hospital with Peter. I never went home. I never left the room during the day. Nicki would bring me food and clothing, or whatever else I needed, because I wasn't going anywhere. I didn't want to miss a single doctor's visit, regardless of whether they were a generalist or a specialist.

Nicki and Daun, who was nineteen and living at home while attending College of the Mainland, would stay as often as possible and keep me company. At night, I would sleep on a foldout chair/bed. Before Peter was moved to the cancer ward, Nicki would often spend the night on a cot that the nurses brought in, and Daun would frequently camp out on a sleeping bag on the floor. I took muscle relaxers every night before turning in. My back was unforgiving of the accommodations.

Peter's father would sometimes come to visit. Jimmy and I would try—often unsuccessfully—not to argue. Mom, Brandy, and the rest of the family would also visit from time to time. And a few of Peter's friends would come around to see how he was doing. But most of the time, I was alone with Peter. This was Peter's journey, but it seemed like mine, too. It was almost as if we had cancer together.

I was on a one-woman mission to save Petie. In that respect, I felt utterly alone. When I cried, I cried alone. I wouldn't let Peter see how devastated I was, how worried. He needed to keep a positive attitude, to have zero doubt he would survive. I had to stay strong—or at least put on a good front. I was fighting for my son with everything I had. Fighting for his life.

I never gave up, and I never gave in. Peter would get through this, even if it killed me. My son *would* get all his needs met. All the appropriate tests *would* be run. And if he needed a nurse, I would encourage Peter to call—or call them myself if I had to.

Nearly two months later, Peter was in the cancer ward of Methodist Hospital in Houston. He had been there for almost a month. Before that, he'd been in St. John's for just as long. Despite all the turmoil, we still didn't have a final detailed diagnosis. Chemo couldn't start until we had that information.

At that point, Peter had so much stomach pain that he couldn't even tolerate ice water. He was dying before my eyes, and there was little I could do but wait.

Finally, the doctor walked into the room for the millionth time. Dr. Roger Finch was a tall, lanky elderly gentleman with smoke-gray hair. He had an awesome sense of humor and an infectious smile. Even though he was American, he kind of reminded me of Peter O'Toole.

But he wasn't smiling. The news was grim.

Peter had a very aggressive form of non-Hodgkin's lymphoma.

Very aggressive? *No shit!* He was disintegrating before my eyes. In two months, he'd gone from a vibrant, young working man, to sick, exhausted, and agonized by excruciating pain. Keeping Peter alive was like trying to hold water in my hands. He kept slipping through my fingers. I was so afraid I was going to lose him.

However, as I'd hoped, Peter never lost spirit. If he had any doubts about making it, he wasn't showing it. He even joked around a lot, often saying, "It's just lymphoma. It's the *easy* cancer."

And when things got so bad that he could only eat Jell-O, he would say, "I know I have cancer. But hey, I can have all the Jell-O I want... *Worth it!*"

But Peter's illness wasn't just aggressive. Dr. Finch described it as *Stage 4*.

When I heard the words "Stage 4," my worrying escalated exponentially. Wasn't that the final stage of cancer? *Oh my God!* Was Petie...was my son going to die? As much as I wanted to scream and cry, I tried to keep a cool exterior. I had to put on a good show. I had to remain strong for Peter. If he saw how terrified I was, he might lose hope. And hope was what was keeping him alive–hope–and faith in his future.

We needed to keep things positive.

The doctor kept going, describing the situation in detail: There were tumors all throughout his body, and they had even spread outside of his lymphatic system. The excruciating gut pain and inability to eat were the results of tumors blocking his pancreas, leading to severe pancreatitis. The coughing was caused by more of the same pressing against his lungs. The back pain was also caused by pressure from tumors.

I was shaken. This was bad...*really bad*... I imagined all these little white golf balls everywhere in my son's body, pressed up against most of his vital organs. I imagined a large area on his bottom filled with the white stuff that had spilled beyond his lymph nodes.

It was all so horrible. My poor boy. My poor son. My poor Petie. Trying to hold back tears, I addressed Dr. Finch. "What's his prognosis?"

"This is an unusual case. Typically, this type of lymphoma has a lower survival rate." The doctor furrowed his brow and continued, explaining that there was a silver lining: A factor in his particular case (that I can't recall) would increase his prognosis. Smiling gently, Dr. Finch concluded, "I would give him about an 85 percent chance of survival."

Eighty-five percent? That sounded good. But what he said next made my heart sink.

"Now, survival is not the same as being cured. Those are two separate things. Normally, you have to wait five years and be completely cancer-free for the entire time, before you can call him cured."

Five years? *Wow...* That was an *eternity*.

He kept going. "However, in cases of very aggressive lymphomas, the cure can be declared sooner. This is because the quicker it comes on, the quicker it goes away with treatment. And if it's going to come back, it will also come back quickly. So we can say he's cured after only two years cancer-free."

Two years was better than five, but it still felt like a long time.

When the doctor left the room, I turned to Peter. "When those two years are up, we're going to throw a huge party. *I can't wait...* So be thinking about what you want to do for it."

Although I initially found the high survival rate to be a comfort, my attitude changed quickly when Dr. Finch kept changing his story. Every time we saw him, he threw out different numbers, and Peter's chances would seem to go down. I think the lowest I heard the doctor say was 45 percent. In other words, he didn't really know the exact prognosis. He was guessing.

Not being certain of Peter's odds increased my anxiety, but I decided to believe Dr. Finch's original assessment: 85 percent. After all, he had given it not long after he'd looked at the PET scan and biopsy results.

But here was the most terrifying part: Peter had a tumor pressed against his carotid artery. Like Dr. Finch had explained, the more aggressive the lymphoma, the quicker it goes away. The first treatment was designed to quickly shrink the tumors. The cancer needed to be treated aggressively because it was so advanced. The implication was that Peter was close to dying. But there was significant risk involved in this strategy.

"If I give him too little chemo, he might not survive," the doctor explained. "But if I give him too much, the tumor on his carotid artery might disappear too quickly, and he could bleed internally and die."

I felt my gut wrench. The staff was about to start chemo, and Peter could die during the night. I prayed really hard that evening, begging God for mercy. I found myself wailing in my pillow from grief and worry. What if he *did* begin bleeding internally? What if they couldn't save him? Would this be the last night I spent with Petie alive?

I stayed up all night, keeping a vigil. If anything

went wrong, I would be the first to know. I would alert the nurse.

But nothing bad happened. Peter slept through most of the next day, but he was alive. Fortunately, on the second day after chemo, he was awake and alert.

Peter pressed the buzzer to order food. He asked for a burger and fries.

I looked at him: the boy who'd gotten sick from a few Skittles a few days ago, the boy who couldn't drink ice water.

"Are you sure that isn't a little ambitious?"

Peter grinned at me. "I don't care. I'm going to try it. I'm *hungry.*"

I begged him to go with something easier to digest, less greasy. Fatty foods were particularly hard on the pancreas.

But he was stubborn. "I got this."

And you know what? He ate his food and it hardly caused him any pain. *What a miracle!* ... My son was getting better. My son was getting better! *Little Petie was getting better!*

A few days later, we left the hospital and headed home.

He would go to chemo treatments every few weeks for six months. He opted to not go back to work. He mostly played video games all day, which was fine. It was better that he not be exposed to other people's illnesses. Getting sick at this point in his life could have killed him. He had almost no immune system because of the chemo.

He would lose all his hair and become completely infertile. And he wouldn't even be able to qualify for Make-a-Wish. He was twenty-one and too old, I guess.

Each time he was treated, he'd be sick for a day or two, followed by weeks of feeling better. He only threw up once the whole time, that I knew of. His worse side effect was numbness in his finger-tips. He quickly gained all of his weight back.

After the third chemo treatment, he was asymptomatic. No more coughing. No more abdominal pain. No more stomach pain. No more back pain. No more of any of that.

At this point, I wasn't sure what the future held. Would the cancer come back? Was he cured? It would be years before we knew for sure.

My book wasn't even an afterthought. With all my focus on Peter, I wasn't sure if I would ever go back to it.

56

A NEW BEGINNING

About a month after Peter finished chemo, on a cool December night, I lay in bed worrying. Would the chemo stick? Would my son live to see twenty-three years old? How long would it be until he had another bout of cancer, maybe something worse?

Before passing out from sheer mental exhaustion, I uttered a desperate prayer. *"God, please let everything be okay."*

The next day, I got out of bed at about 2 p.m., as usual. I didn't spring up. I just sort of sauntered off into the living room, where Nicki and Peter were hanging out.

Peter was sitting up in front of our rather large plasma TV, which he was using as a computer monitor. Well, it wasn't really *that* large, but it was the biggest one we'd ever had. I had bought it online a while back for $300 using a Dell instant rebate.

Regardless, Peter seemed to be having fun. Chemo was over, but he hadn't started back to work yet, although he had recently applied to Pizza Hut. He had been fired from Domino's after missing too many days.

I rubbed his head.

Yes!

Hair was beginning to grow back. Exciting stuff!

"God, Peter, your hair! It's so fuzzy. I just want to pet it!"

Peter turned around and flashed me a huge smile. "Yes, isn't it great? I can't wait to grow it back all the way." Peter had always prided himself on his long, blond, curly hair. He'd shaved it before it all fell out—a sad day for him. But each millimeter of new hair was a millimeter of new hope. *Yay, Peter!* ...

Nicki was lounging on the black leather couch, playing on her laptop. We had picked up the sofa for $200 on Craigslist a few years earlier. Always frugal, I never paid full price for furniture.

Nicki was laughing loudly. I looked up from petting Peter's hair. "Hey, what's so funny?"

She glanced back at me. "Oh nothing. I'm just down the YouTube rabbit hole."

Despite my enthusiasm for Peter's hair, I was in a bad mood. I could feel it. This wasn't going to be a good day. Maybe I was going to start my period. All I knew was that I felt overwhelmed. All the worrying had been interfering with my sleep.

No... I wouldn't follow Nicki down the YouTube rabbit hole. I didn't care about YouTube. I could only watch so many cat videos. And anyway, Nicki and I didn't always share the same sense of humor.

So I dodged and changed the subject. "Did you make any coffee?"

"*Of course.* I make it every morning. I saved you some."

I slunk off toward the kitchen and poured a cup. Then I added some powdered creamer. I was looking forward to this. Maybe it would improve my mood.

And...

History repeated itself.

Clump.

The creamer wouldn't dissolve!

I yelled toward the living room, *"It's cold!"*

Nicki yelled back so I could hear her from the kitchen. She sounded annoyed. *"Sorry!* Just make some more!"

I shrugged my shoulders, replying in a similar tone. I hated these long-distance conversations. So much screaming. "Never mind!" I felt a rush of emotion. I was too lazy to make myself another pot. What was the point, anyhow? Most of it would just go to waste.

I began heaving hard tears, struggling for air. I felt so horrible, and now there was no coffee. It seemed like my life was over.

After about thirty seconds of uncontrolled crying, I grabbed a paper towel and blew my nose. Then I tried to slow my breathing. *Man...* I needed to get a grip...

Next, I snatched a repurposed jelly jar from the cabinet and filled it with lukewarm tap water, taking a big swig. Ice was too much effort. Then I blew my nose again, took a few deep breaths, and tried to compose myself. I didn't want Nicki to know I was upset. Besides, it wasn't her fault I'd woken up at two in the afternoon. She'd probably been up for a long time. Of *course* the coffee was cold!

Mustering some energy, I reached in the Pepsi Max box and grabbed a can. I had switched to it when it came on the market because it had more caffeine than

Diet Mountain Dew. Regardless, I poured the Pepsi into a glass of ice. *Blah...* Coffee substitute... Not a morning drink.

I headed back to the living room and plopped down in our newish recliner—the one I'd recently co-opted from Nicki. It was supposed to be hers. After all, she'd paid for it. But I had claimed it because I felt it was easier on my back. She never forgave me for taking her chair. Instead, she just sort of stopped fighting for it, except for an occasional jab. *It was mine now.*

Finally, I calmed down and addressed Nicki. "Did you get the mail?"

Nicki didn't bother to look up from her video. "Nope."

"Alright, well, I'll go get it." I glanced toward the window. Based on the tint of the sky, it had been raining. I shrugged my shoulders. *Great!* ... I hoped the mail hadn't gotten wet, because holes had been starting to rust through the surface of our small mailbox.

I headed toward the door, dodging cardboard boxes full of product for my Amazon shop. I had spent the last several years cultivating a thriving reselling business that had quickly become our primary source of income. The boxes hadn't been opened yet, but I was pretty sure they contained the Plantronics headsets I'd ordered from one of my sources two weeks earlier.

Careful not to trip over the large clump of plastic packing bubbles that were blocking the exit, I made my way outside and quickly closed the door behind me. I didn't want to let Midnight out.

But before heading toward the mailbox, I looked up.

That's when I saw something...

Something...

Beautiful...

Stretched out before me in the field across the street were the arcs of a full double rainbow. I could see every inch of it, from beginning to end, without breaks. They were perfect.

The view was even more spectacular than the rainbow I'd seen nine years prior, in 2006, a mere two-and-a-half weeks before I found Osama bin Laden—the rainbow that had inspired me to continue my amateur detective work. *Yes...* It had been a sign from God to keep going, at a time when I had been ready to quit. If I hadn't been moved by it, I would have never found bin Laden.

And here I was again, looking at the same scene. It was the second time I'd been blessed by what should have been a once-in-a-lifetime miracle.

I ran in to grab my phone and get Nicki and the kids. I wanted to take pictures. This had to be documented, just like the first time it happened. I needed proof.

Moments later, we all basked in the rainbow's splendor for a while. With Peter and Daun on both sides of us, Nicki and I wrapped our arms around each other. My body relaxed a little as a wave of relief poured over me. Then tears welled in my eyes. They were tears of joy.

Averting my gaze briefly from the rainbow, my eyes scanned my grown children. *Survivors.* Both of them, especially Peter. I was so incredibly proud of the people they had become.

Peter caught me looking and grinned at me. "It's really beautiful, Mom."

Daun nodded. "Yeah. It's great. So perfect. And I can't believe there are two of them!"

But technology was calling. After only a few minutes, they headed back inside, leaving Nicki and me alone. I looked back up at the rainbow then back at her.

"Do you know what this means?"

"What?"

Soft tears began to flow.

"I think it means Peter is going to be okay."

Nicki agreed. "Yes. I think so, too."

"And I think I need to write my book."

"Makes sense."

It wasn't a coincidence that I was staring at this double version of the same rainbow, but nearly a decade after 2006, the year I found Osama bin Laden. Once again, God was telling me something: Peter was going to be okay. I was going to be okay. And the book was going to happen. It was *supposed* to happen. Something good was going to come from it. There was no room for doubt.

It was time to get to work...

EPILOGUE

A year later, a light had switched on inside of me. Energized, I bolted out of bed, ready to start a new day. The rainbow had changed me. I had a fresh zest for life, and it wasn't just about the book. It was about everything.

Of course, it helped that Peter was doing well. He had relocated to Austin—four hours away—where he was moving forward with his life. My little brother, Allen, was only a short drive away from Peter's residence, which made me feel better about him venturing off on his own after cancer.

But I wasn't thinking about Peter or cancer at that moment. It was time for spring cleaning—in December. I wanted everything to be in tip-top shape for Christmas. The living room, especially, had to be perfect. I wanted it to look nice, but more importantly, we needed a clear spot for the tree.

Weeks passed, and even after the holidays ended, my obsession with housework continued. Unfortunately for them, I had dragged Daun and Nicki along with me on my mission. Like Peter, I was also moving forward with my life.

The good news was that there were no more clumps of dirty clothes on the floor. The piles of coke cans and plastic cups had been cleared off the computer desk and coffee table. The dishes were caught up for the first time in months. And Daun even ran the vacuum cleaner, frequently stopping to clear clogs.

On one particular day, Nicki was working on the mounds of clutter on the bookshelf in the living room. There was no rhyme nor reason to the heaps of junk in the house, but we were slowly working our way through them.

Daun was catching up on her laundry while I began pulling everything out of the bottom cabinets in the kitchen and organizing them. When Nicki came into the room to get a Coke Zero, I pointed to a pile of pots, lids, glass pans, and other random cooking items sitting on the kitchen floor near the cabinets.

"Hey... When you get a chance, can you please look through those? I'm not sure what to keep."

Nicki seemed nervous. She didn't like letting go of things, and she sounded exasperated. "Have you *seen* how much stuff I've donated lately?"

It was true. During the process of cleaning, we had also donated what felt like truckloads of things to the local Disabled American Veterans Thrift Store. Most of the stuff was Nicki's.

"Yes. And that's awesome!"

"Well, *lay off!* I'm doing the best I can! Besides, I'm still working on the shelves in the living room. And I'm doing the shoe rack next!"

I knew I'd taken it too far and that I was being pushy, but once I started a project, I was all in. And like when the kids and I had been preparing for the FBI to come to our house, my housecleaning efforts tended to be all or nothing. In this case, our home had gone from piles of clutter and random trash to relative order. But I wanted the house to be perfect. There was no stopping me.

"I'm sorry, honey. I'll try to calm down. I just want everything to be nice."

Nicki grabbed her coke and lightly slammed the refrigerator door. "You do *your* job and I'll do *mine*. I'm going back to work."

I hollered at her as she exited the room, "That's fine. I'll just leave it out here. Look at it when you get a chance."

Nicki waved her arm behind her as she beelined for the living room. "Okay. I'll do it later."

In that moment, my new enthusiasm for life and spring cleaning had not spread to Nicki. But nonetheless, it felt good to feel good.

***

However, the next few years wouldn't be easy. Writing the book would be a long, arduous process. It was one of the hardest things I've ever done, confronting my bin Laden demons.

At first, the utter shock of reliving the memories was overwhelming. As I wrote my story in increasing detail, it would pierce the numbness I had been experiencing from closing off such a huge part of me. In some ways, my years in hiding had left me feeling dead inside.

But as months turned to years, I clawed and scratched my way through the book. Sometimes, the events were so painful to relive that I could only write one sentence a day. Sometimes, I would stop after a couple of paragraphs and cry. And sometimes, I would push the work away and write nothing for as long as a month. But I never gave up, and I never gave in. I was determined. I had a strong sense that my book was important, like it could make a difference to the world.

There were often times I would think about giving up, not writing for weeks at a time. But then encouragement would come from an unexpected source: Grandma.

She had passed on a long time ago. Yet somehow, she was still there for me.

Grandma appeared to me in a dream one morning. She was wearing her signature pink polyester pantsuit. I could see her clearly and hear her sweet voice.

I laid my head on her lap. I could feel the softness of her body and the roughness of the polyester. I could smell the combination of a clean body and laundry detergent that was unique to Grandma. As I rested my head there on her thighs, she gently stroked my hair with her right hand. She kept saying sweet, soft words to me. *"It's going to be okay, honey. You're really special. You can do this."*

When I woke up, I could still smell her, feel her, hear her sweet voice. I knew she'd actually been there. It had been much more than a mere dream.

Grandma's words made me believe that I was supposed to continue writing my book, and everything was going to be okay. The book was important. I already knew that, but her presence reaffirmed it. No matter what, I had to finish my work.

Over the next few weeks, Grandma appeared to me several times, giving me words of encouragement. During some of these encounters, I would ask her about heaven. One time, she even showed me where she was living in the afterlife.

It was a cute little mint-green cottage, not unlike the house she'd lived in with Grandpa for over fifty years. And white bunnies and brown squirrels were scurrying around their grassy yard. A wooden bench-swing sat on the front porch. A path on the other side of the yard separated the scene from a dense pine forest. It was all so perfect. Grandpa was there, too, although he didn't talk to me. They seemed really happy.

But I believe Grandma wanted me to write the book for more than one reason. First, I think she wanted me to write it so that God could use it for his purposes, whatever they might be. Perhaps it could be a catalyst for political reform. But for her, I think there might have been an equally important reason that she wanted me to write the book. The process was healing me, and she would have known that. Grandma would have wanted that for me.

In fact, as I worked my way through the story, the frequency of my anxiety attacks began to decrease. I only had them occasionally, rather than multiple times a week. And nearly four years after I scrawled my first draft—all six pages—into the small composition book, the biggest miracle of all happened. I woke up one day and realized I was no longer completely miserable. For the first time in my adult life, I was happy. I kept wanting to pinch myself. *This* wasn't real. I couldn't be happy. This wasn't me. I've *never* been happy.

But I was. And I owed it to writing this book. I had dealt with one of the hardest issues of my lifetime and pulled through it with grace. It felt like I had been stuck in the bin Laden closet for an eternity—a hellish place where memories go to die. But through doing the hard work of writing my story, I had finally been able to pull myself up out of the mire.

I had burst through the flames of Purgatory and found my way to the cooling pools on the edge of paradise. I was finally at peace.

Mostly...

ACKNOWLEDGMENTS

To all the incredible people who have supported me and my efforts from August 2006 and beyond: A few of you meticulously read and critiqued my early drafts. Others served as sounding boards or offered shoulders to cry on. But mostly, y'all believed my story and counter-balanced a cacophony of ridicule and hate. Thank you from the bottom of my heart. You know who you are.

NOTES

PREFACE

1. Barbara Janik. "Chasing Bin Laden: Research." Chasing bin Laden, n.d. http://www.chasingbinladen.com/research.

RESOURCES

2. Ibid

CHAPTER 1—AN UNUSUAL CELEBRATION

3. "CNN Presents: In the Footsteps of Bin Laden." Transcripts. CNN, August 23, 2006.http://transcripts.cnn.com/TRANSCRIPTS/0608/23/cp.01.html.

CHAPTER 2—THE MONSTER TRIP

4. "Circumstances and Dialogue of the 1917 Apparitions." The Fatima Center. Accessed February 29, 2020. https://fatima.org/about/fatima-the-facts/circumstances-and-dialogue-ofthe-1917-apparitions/

CHAPTER 4—DIAL M FOR MURDER

5. Scott Allen and Christina Silva. "Murder-Sui-

cide Stuns Peabody." The Boston Globe, June 25,2006. https://groups.google.com/forum/#!topic/alt.true-crime/IJ0BNk5ND0M.http://archive.boston.com/news/local/massachusetts/articles/2006/06/25/murder_suicide_stuns_peabody/.

6. O'Ryan Johnson. "Triple Shooting in Peabody Home Leaves 3 Dead." The Boston Herald, June 24, 2006. https://infoweb-newsbank-com.ezproxy.shsu.edu/apps/news/documentview?p=AWNB&docref=news/1305EDE144ED9CA8.

7. Allen and Silva. "Murder-Suicide Stun Peabody."

8. Jill Casey. "Blood Bath in Peabody - Man Shoots, Kills Sister." The Daily Item (Lynne, MA), June 24, 2006. https://infoweb-newsbank-com.ezproxy.shsu.edu/apps/news/document-view?p=AWNB&docref=news/1198174C2164C460.

9. Johnson, "Triple Shooting..."

10. Allen and Silva, "Murder-Suicide Stun Peabody."

11. Casey, "Blood Bath..."

12. Allen and Silva, "Murder-Suicide Stun Peapody."

13. Johnson, "Triple Shooting..."

14. Allen and Silva. "Murder-Suicide Stun Peabody."

15. Casey, "Blood Bath..."

16. Allen and Silva, "Murder-Suicide Stun Peabody."

17. John Philip Jenkins. "Jeffrey Dahmer." Encycloedia Britannica, March 12, 2020. https://www.britannica.com/biography/Jeffrey-Dahmer.

18. John Philip Jenkins. "John Wayne Gacy." Encyclopedia Britannica, March 13, 2020. https://www.britannica.com/biography/John-Wayne-Gacy.

19. Juan Ignacio Blanco. "Edward Gein." Edward Gein. Murderpedia. Accessed May 7, 2020. https://murderpedia.org/male.G/g/gein-edward.htm.

20. Alison Eldridge. "Jonestown." Encyclopedia Britannica, November 11, 2029. https://www.britannica.com/event/Jonestown.

21. J. Gordon Melton. "Heaven's Gate." Encyclopædia Britannica, October 7, 2013. https://www.britannica.com/topic/Heavens-Gate-religious-group.

22. Leslie Wagner-Wilson.. Slavery of Faith. New York: iUniverse, Inc., 2009.

23. Eudie Pak. "O.J. Simpson Murder Case: A Timeline of the 'Trial of the Century'." Biography.com. A&E Networks Television, June 25, 2019. https://www.biography.com/news/oj-simpson-trial-timeline.

CHAPTER 7—THE ACRES HOMES KILLER

24. Leslie Casimir. "Acres Homes Slayings Leave Indelible Marks." The Houston Chronicle, November 18, 2007. https://www.chron.com/news/houston-texas/article/Acres-Homes-slayings-leave-indelible-marks-1669871.php.

25. Monica Rhor. "Serial Killer Suspected in 7 Houston Deaths." Beautiful, Also, are the Souls of My Black Sisters. Associated Press, November 13, 2007. https://kathmanduk2.wordpress.com/2007/11/25/the-serial-killings-of-acres-homes/.

26. Elisabeth Wetsch. "Vigil Held for Victim of Possible Serial Killer." Beautiful, Also, are the Souls of My Black Sisters. Serial Killer News, July 23, 2006. https://kathmanduk2.wordpress.com/2007/11/25/the-serial-killings-of-acres-homes/.

27. Robert Crowe. "FBI Joins in Search for Killer - Agency Provides Investigators and DNA Lab Assistance to Houston Police." The Houston Chronicle, July 25, 2006. https://infoweb-newsbank-com.ezproxy.shsu.edu/apps/news/document-view?p=AWNB&docref=news/1131AF1F1E543C88.

28. Rhor, "Serial Killer Suspected..."

29. Casimir, "Acres Homes Slayings..."

30. Crowe, "FBI Joins in Search for Killer..."

31. Wetsch, "Vigil Held for Victim..."

32. Elisabeth Wetsch. "Victim's Sketch Could Lead To Serial Killer." Beautiful, Also, are the Souls of My Black Sisters. Serial Killer News, October 6, 2006. https://kathmanduk2.wordpress.com/2007/11/25/the-serial-killings-of-acres-homes/.

33. Wetsch, "Vigil Held for Victim..."

34. Crowe, "FBI Joins in Search for Killer..."

35. David Ellison and Roma Khanna. "One Site May Be Hot Spot for Serial Killer." Houston Chronicle, July 22, 2006. https://www.chron.com/news/houston-texas/article/One-site-may-be-hot-spot-for-serial-killer-1874884.php.

36. Skip Hollandsworth. "'If the Serial Killer Gets Us, He Gets Us.'" Texas Monthly, December 2011. https://www.texasmonthly.com/articles/if-the-serial-killer-gets-us-he-gets-us/.

37. Elisabeth Wetsch. "DNA samples taken from 24 in hunt for killer." Beautiful, Also, are the Souls of My Black Sisters. Serial Killer News, August 1, 2006. https://kathmanduk2.wordpress.com/2007/11/25/the-serial-killings-of-acres-homes/.

38. Paula McMahon and Brittany Wallman. "How the FBI Botched Tips about the Parkland School Shooter." Sun-Sentinel (South Florida), August 29, 2018. https://www.sun-sentinel.com/local/broward/parkland/florida-school-shooting/fl-florida-school-shooting-fbi-tips-problems-20180828-story.html.

39. Ibid.

40. Harold L. Hurtt. "Suspect Charged in Murder, Sexual Assaults in Acres Homes Area." Houston Police Department -- News Releases, September 24, 2009. https://www.houstontx.gov/police/nr/2009/sep/nr092409-1.htm.

41. "Arrest Made in Acres Homes Serial Murders." KHOU (Houston), October 26, 2009. https://www.khou.com/article/news/arrest-made-in-acres-homes-serial-murders/285-342822467.

42. Cindy George. "Man Sentenced to Life Term in Acres Homes Rape." The Houston Chronicle, August 1, 2011. https://www.chron.com/news/houston-texas/article/Man-sentenced-to-life-term-in-Acres-Homes-rape-1683044.php.

CHAPTER 8—OTHER EARLY CASES

43. Jessica Noll. "Tara Grinstead: The Beauty Queen Murder." 11 Alive (Atlanta), May 6, 2019. https://www.11alive.com/article/news/investigations/beauty-queen-murder/tara-grinstead-the-beauty-queen-murder/85-c2d33755-743b-476d-92e0-2c00965adb9c.

44. Steve Helling. "5 Things to Know About the Cold-Case Murder of a Georgia Teacher and Former Beauty Queen." People.com, February 28, 2017. https://people.com/crime/tara-grinstead-ryan-duke-murder-arrest-things-to-know/.

45. Samuel Chamberlain. "Tara Grinstead: Ex-Student Accused of Murdering Missing Georgia Teacher." Fox News, February 23, 2017. https://www.foxnews. com/us/tara-grinstead-ex-student-accused-of-murdering-missing-georgia-teacher.

46. Edie Magnus. "What Happened to Tara Grinstead?" NBC News, May 1, 2006. http://www. nbcnews.com/id/12583446/ns/dateline_nbc/t/what-happened-tara-grinstead/.

47. Samuel Chamberlain, "Tara Grinstead: Ex-Student Accused..."

48. Toney Thomas. "Tara Grinstead Case: Leaked Confession Reveals Motive behind Killing, Investigators Say." Dayton Daily News. WSBTV.com, December 10, 2018. https://www.daytondailynews.com/news/national/tara-grinstead-case-leaked-confession-reveals-motive-behind-killing-investigators-say/3caWUAc15P0r1R73HAYwuO/.

49. Andrea Reiher. "Why Tara Grinstead's Alleged Murderer Still Hasn't Been Tried in Her Death." Heavy. July 07, 2020. https://heavy.com/entertainment/2020/07/ryan-duke-bo-dukes-update-tara-grinstead/.

CHAPTER 12—JOINING THE WAR ON TERROR

50. Pete Cashmore. "MySpace, America's Number One." Mashable, July 11, 2006. https://mashable. com/2006/07/11/myspace-americas-number-one/.

51. Pete Cashmore. "MySpace Hits 100 Million Accounts." Mashable, August 10, 2006. https://mashable.com/2006/08/09/myspace-hits-100-million-accounts/.

52. Jarret M. Brachman. "High-Tech Terror: Al-Qaeda's Use of New Technology." Leeds, West Yorkshire, England, 2006. https://dl.tufts.edu/concern/pdfs/xd07h4667

53. Robert M. Cassidy. *Counterinsurgency and the Global War on Terror Military Culture and Irregular War.* Westport, CT.: Praeger Security International, 2008, 9.

54. Adam Augustyn, et al., eds. "Myspace." Encyclopedia Britannica. February 5, 2020. https://www.britannica.com/topic/Myspacecom.

CHAPTER 20—THE EYE OF THE HURRICANE

55. "Phone Tapping Number A Urban Legend?" ReversePhoneLookup.com. Accessed May 6, 2020. https://web.archive.org/web/20190706014445/https://www.reversephonelookup.com/articles/phone-tapping-number-a-urban-legend/

CHAPTER 21—THE TRANSATLANTIC AIRCRAFT PLOT

56. "UK US Airline Plot Fast Facts." CNN, September 4, 2019. https://www.cnn.com/2013/11/06/world/uk-us-airline-plot-fast-facts/index.html.

57. "Montreal, Toronto Flights Targeted in Alleged British Bomb Plot | CBC News." CBCnews (Canada), April 3, 2008. https://www.cbc.ca/news/world/montreal-toronto-flights-targeted-in-alleged-british-bomb-plot-1.747225.

58. "UK US Airline Plot..."

59. "Airline Terror Trial: The Bomb Plot to Kill 10,000 People." The Telegraph (London), September 7, 2009. https://www.telegraph.co.uk/news/uknews/terrorism-in-the-uk/6153243/Airline-terror-trial-The-bomb-plot-to-kill-10000-people.html.

60. "September 11 Terror Attacks Fast Facts." CNN, November 13, 2019. https://www.cnn.com/2013/07/27/us/september-11-anniversary-fast-facts/index.html.

61. "Police: Plot to Blow up Aircraft Foiled." CNN, August 10, 2006. https://www.cnn.com/2006/WORLD/europe/08/10/uk.terror/index.html

62. "UK US Airline Plot..."

63. Alan Cowell and Dexter Filkins. "British Authorities Say Plot to Blow Up Airliners Was Foiled." The New York Times, August 10, 2006. https://www.nytimes.com/2006/08/10/world/europe/11terrorcnd.html.

64. "Terror Plot: Internet Cafes Raided." CNN, August 13, 2006. https://www.cnn.com/2006/

WORLD/europe/08/12/terror.plot/index.html.

CHAPTER 26—BAHRAIN

65. "Bahrain May Build Sea Horse-Shaped Island." Associate Press. May 11, 2005. http://www.nbcnews.com/id/7819917/ns/us_news-environment/t/bahrain-may-build-sea-horse-shaped-island/.

66. Peter Bergen. "Bin Laden's Lonely Crusade." Vanity Fair. January 30, 2015. https://www.vanityfair.com/news/2011/01/osama-bin-laden-201101.

CHAPTER 27—THE DIRECTOR-Y

67. Michael Ray, et al., eds. "Donner Party." Encyclopædia Britannica, January 17, 2020. https://www.britannica.com/topic/Donner-party.

CHAPTER 29—INSPIRATION POINT

68. Shabablek.com. Archive.org, August 27, 2006. https://web.archive.org/web/20060827024208/http://www.shabablek.com/vb/index/.

69. Qatarfootball.com. Archive.org, August 24, 2006. https://web.archive.org/web/20060821230807/http://www.qatarfootball.com:80/vb/index.php.

CHAPTER 30—EYE OF THE TIGER

70. Serge F. Kovaleski and Fredrick Kunkle. "Northern New Jersey Draws Probers' Eyes." The Washington Post,

September 18, 2001. https://www.washingtonpost. com/archive/politics/2001/09/18/northern-new-jersey-draws-probers-eyes/40f82ea4-e015-4d6e-a87e-93aa433fafdc/?postshare=7281448290025183.

CHAPTER 31—CALLING IT IN

71. Christine Hauser. "Mastermind of U.S.S. Cole Attack Escapes Jail." The New York Times, February 5, 2006. https://www.nytimes.com/2006/02/05/international/middleeast/mastermind-of-uss-cole-attack-escapes-jail.html.

CHAPTER 40—HAMMER OUT WARNING

72. "The August Recess." U.S. Senate. The August Recess, January 12, 2017.http://www.senate.gov/ artandhistory/history/common/generic/News_ August_Recess.htm

CHAPTER 44—WAPO

73. Timothy Burger and Scott Macleod."Is Bin Laden Dead?" Time, September 23, 2006.http://content.time. com/time/world/article/0,8599,1538569,00.html.

74. Katie Turner, et al. "Officials, Friends Can't Confirm Bin Laden Death Report." CNN, September 24, 2006. https://www.cnn.com/2006/WORLD/ europe/09/23/france.binladen/index.html.

75. "Bin Laden Reportedly Suffering Kidney, Liver Failure." Chicago Tribune, March 20, 2000. https://

www.chicagotribune.com/news/ct-xpm-2000-03-25-0003250085-story.html.

76. "Dialysis: Deciding to Stop." National Kidney Foundation, February 3, 2017. https://www.kidney.org/atoz/content/dialysisstop.

CHAPTER 45—NO EXIT

77. Jeordan Legon. "Security Firm: MyDoom Worm Fastest Yet." CNN. Accessed May 30, 2020. https://edition.cnn.com/2004/TECH/internet/01/28/mydoom.spreadwed/.

78. "Mydoom Largest Virus Outbreak Ever." News | Al Jazeera, January 28, 2004. https://www.aljazeera.com/archive/2004/01/200841014125568492.html.

79. Loren Baker. "MyDoom Email Worm/Virus Spreading : VIRUS ALERT." Search Engine Journal. January 30, 2004. https://www.searchenginejournal.com/mydoom-email-wormvirus-spreading-virus-alert/215/

80. Matt Hines. "Hackers Deface SCO Site." CNET. CNET, November 29, 2004. https://www.cnet.com/news/hackers-deface-sco-site/.

81. Kalyan Yedakula. "Most Expensive Computer Viruses of All Time - List of Computer Viruses." Cyware. Accessed August 30, 2016. https://cyware.com/news/most-expensivecomputer-viruses-of-all-time-de0d5fae.

82. David Legard. "Microsoft Offers $250,000

Reward in Mydoom.B Attacks." Computerworld. IDG News Service, January 30, 2004. https://www.computerworld.com/article/2574948/microsoft-offers--250-000-reward-inmydoom-b-attacks.html

83. Hines, "Hackers Deface SCO Site."

CHAPTER 47—MYSPACE

84. "Declassification Frequently Asked Questions." The United States Department of Justice, September 13, 2016. https://www.justice.gov/open/declassification/declassification-faq.

85. "Leslie Powers Photos on Myspace." Myspace. Accessed January 24, 2020. https://myspace.com/leslie_powers/photos.

86. "US Population by Year." US Census Bureau. Multpl.com. Accessed January 10, 2021. https://www.multpl.com/united-states-population/table/by-year.

87. Stephanie L Singleton. "The Truth About 9/11 Truth Movement: A Folkloristic Study." Indiana University, October 1, 2017, 81. https://scholarworks.iu.edu/dspace/handle/2022/21803.

CHAPTER 48—ABOVE TOP SECRET

88. Akareyon. "Osama Bin Laden Arrested by FBI in Brooklyn?" AboveTopSecret.com, December 28, 2006. http://www.abovetopsecret.com/forum/thread256614/pg1.

89. Ibid.

90. Bob2000. "Osama Bin Laden Arrested by FBI in Brooklyn?, Page 4." AboveTopSecret.com, December 29, 2006. http://www.abovetopsecret.com/forum/thread256614/pg4.

91. Ibid.

92. Kickoutthejams. "Osama Bin Laden Arrested by FBI in Brooklyn?, Page 6." AboveTopSecret.com, January 1, 2007. http://www.abovetopsecret.com/forum/thread256614/pg6.

93. Talisman. "Osama Bin Laden Arrested by FBI in Brooklyn?, Page 14." AboveTopSecret.com, January 5, 2007. http://www.abovetopsecret.com/forum/thread256614/pg14.

94. "Disinformation Agents How Disinformation Agents Spread Their Web of Deception." WantToKnow. Info. Accessed March 29, 2020. https://www.wantto-know.info/g/disinformation-agents.

95. Darklight12. "Osama Bin Laden Arrested by FBI in Brooklyn?, Page 16." AboveTopSecret.com, January 6, 2007. http://www.abovetopsecret.com/forum/thread256614/pg16

96. Darklight12. "Osama Bin Laden Arrested by FBI in Brooklyn?, Page 18." AboveTopSecret.com, January 10, 2007. http://www.abovetopsecret.com/forum/

thread256614/pg18.

97. Airtrax007. "Osama Bin Laden Arrested by FBI in Brooklyn?, Page 13." AboveTopSecret.com, January 4, 2007. http://www.abovetopsecret.com/forum/thread256614/pg13.

98. Airtrax007. "Osama Bin Laden Arrested by FBI in Brooklyn?, Page 15." AboveTopSecret.com, January 5, 2007. http://www.abovetopsecret.com/forum/thread256614/pg15.

99. Airtrax007. "Osama Bin Laden Arrested by FBI in Brooklyn?, Page 18." AboveTopSecret.com, January 10, 2007. http://www.abovetopsecret.com/forum/thread256614/pg18.

100. Google Maps. Google. New York, NY. Accessed March 29, 2020. https://www.google.com/maps/place/New York, NY/@40.6971494,-74.2598655,10z/data=!3m1!4b1!4m5!3m4!1s0x89c24fa5d33f083b:0xc80b8f06e177fe62!8m2!3d40.7127753!4d-74.0059728?hl=en.

101. Airtrax007. "Osama Bin Laden Arrested by FBI in Brooklyn?, Page 20." AboveTopSecret.com, January 23, 2007. http://www.abovetopsecret.com/forum/thread256614/pg20.

102. Airtrax007. "Osama Bin Laden Arrested by FBI in Brooklyn?, Page 22." AboveTopSecret.com. Accessed January 25, 2020. http://www.abovetopsecret.com/forum/thread256614/pg22.

103. Akareyon. "Osama Bin Laden Arrested by FBI in Brooklyn?, Page 22." AboveTopSecret.com, January 25, 2007. http://www.abovetopsecret.com/forum/thread256614/pg22.

104. Akareyon. "Osama Bin Laden Arrested by FBI in Brooklyn?, Page .24." AboveTopSecret.com, January 28, 2007. http://www.abovetopsecret.com/forum/thread256614/pg24.

105. "Records." ChasingBinLaden.com, n.d. http://www.chasingbinladen.com/records

106. Barbara Janik (Leslie Powers). "Osama Bin Laden Arrested by FBI in Brooklyn?, Page 30." Above-TopSecret.com, March 7, 2007. http://www.abovetops-ecret.com/forum/thread256614/pg30.

107. Ibid.

CHAPTER 49—REGRETS
108. "US Warned in 'Bin Laden Video' - 07 Sep 07." YouTube.com. Al Jazeera English, September 7, 2007. https://www.youtube.com/watch?reload=9&v=CWH-KDASKChI.

109. Robert Vamosi. "Researcher: Bin Laden's Beard Is Real, Video Is Not." CNET, September 12, 2007. https://www.cnet.com/news/researcher-bin-ladens-beard-is-real-video-is-not.

CHAPTER 50 THE BROOKLYN CONNECTION

110. Brian Ross. "Plan to Catch Bin Laden Was Called Off." ABC News, October 1, 2004. https://abcnews.go.com/GMA/story?id=125150.

111. Brian Ross, anchor. "Hunt for Osama Bin Laden." Transcript. *Nightline.* ABC. September 10, 2006. http://search.ebscohost.com.ezproxy.shsu.edu/login.aspx?direct=true&db=bwh&AN=35078024&site=e-host-live&scope=site.

112. "Osama Bin Laden Video Message." ABC, October 29, 2004. https://abcnews.go.com/Archives/video/oct-29-2004-osama-bin-laden-video-message-11700438.

113. Google Maps. Google. Brooklyn, NY. Accessed April 3, 2020. https://www.google.com/maps/dir/Brooklyn Bridge, New York, NY 10038/9/11 Memorial, 180 Greenwich St, New York, NY 10007/@40.706748,-74.0209963,14z/data=!3m1!4b1!4m14!4m13!1m5!1m1!1s0x89c25a2343ce7b2b:0x2526ddba7abd465c!2m2!1d-73.9968643!2d40.7060855!1m5!1m1!1s0x-89c25a1a3be8cb45:0xf430ccc5401d1eed!2m2!1d-74.0135111!2d40.7115215!3e0.

114. Google Maps. Google. Brighton Beach to 911 Memorial. Accessed April 3, 2020. https://www.google.com/maps/dir/Brighton Beach, Brooklyn, NY/9/11 Memorial, 180 Greenwich St, New York, NY 10007/@40.6447749,-74.064923,12z/data=!3m1!4b1!4m14!4m13!1m5!1m1!1s0x89c244421f0faaf1:0xad-dcf4a47c4334fc!2m2!1d-73.9596565!2d40.5780706

!1m5!1m1!1s0x89c25a1a3be8cb45:0xf430ccc5401-d1eed!2m2!1d-74.0135111!2d40.7115215!3e0

115. Google Search. Google. Accessed April 3, 2020. https://www.google.com/search?client=firefox-b-1-d&q=distance+from+brighton+beach+to+wtc+memorial.

116. John Miller, Michael Stone, and Chris Mitchell. *The Cell: Inside the 9/11 Plot and Why the FBI and CIA Failed to Stop It*. New York, NY: Hyperion, 2002, 49.

117. Benjamin Weiser , and David Kocieniewski. "U.S. Sees Brooklyn Link to World Terror Network." The New York Times, October 22, 1998. https://www.nytimes.com/1998/10/22/world/us-sees-brooklyn-link-to-world-terror-network.html.

118. Miller, Stone, and Mitchell, *The Cell* ,156.

119. Thomas Hegghammer. "Why Jihadists Loved America in the 1980s." The Atlantic, March 6, 2020. https://www.theatlantic.com/politics/archive/2020/03/jihad-abdallah-azzam-america-osama-bin-laden/607498/.

120. Ibid.

121. Laura Etheredge, et al., eds. "Mujahideen." Encyclopedia Britannica, May 11, 2016. https://www.britannica.com/topic/mujahideen-Islam.

122. Andrew Marshall. "Terror 'Blowback' Burns

CIA." *Independent*. November 1, 1998. https://www.independent.co.uk/news/terror-blowback-burns-cia-1182087.html.

123. Alexander Rubinstein. "Trump's Taliban Talks Led by Neocon Operation Cyclone Agent & PNAC Member." MintPress News, September 27, 2019. https://www.mintpressnews.com/trump-taliban-talks-neocon-pnac-member-zalmay-khalilzad/261784/.

124. Adam Zeidan, et al., eds. "Afghan War." Encyclopedia Britannica, November 14, 2018. https://www.britannica.com/event/Afghan-War

125. "Al Qaeda." History.com. A&E Television Networks, September 9, 2019. https://www.history.com/topics/21st-century/al-qaeda.

126. Peter Lance. *Triple Cross: How Bin Laden's Master Spy Penetrated the CIA, the Green Berets, and the FBI*. New York: Harper, 2009, Chap.7, Kindle.

127. Marshall. "Terror 'Blowback' Burns CIA."

128. David Plotz. "What Does Osama Bin Laden Want?" Slate Magazine. Slate, September 14, 2001. https://slate.com/news-and-politics/2001/09/what-does-osama-bin-laden-want.html.

129. Barbara Maranzani. "How U.S. Intelligence Misjudged the Growing Threat Behind 9/11." History.com. A&E Television Networks, September 11, 2018. https://www.history.com/news/9-11-attacks-america-

missed-warning-signs.

130. Marshall. "Terror 'Blowback' Burns CIA."

131. Simon Reeve. *The New Jackels: Ramzi Yousef, Osama Bin Laden and the Future of Terrorism.* Boston: Northeastern University Press, 1999, 6-22.

132.   Ibid,   183,   241-243.

133. Lance, *Triple Cross.*

134. "Mohamed Atta." Biography.com. A&E Networks Television, September 4, 2019. https://www.biography.com/crime-figure/mohamed-atta.

135. Lance, *Triple Cross,* chap 31, Kindle.

136. Ibid, Timeline.

137. Ibid, chap. 32.

138. Ibid.

139. "Population - Decennial Census - Census 2000." NYC Department of City Planning. Accessed April 9, 2020. https://www1.nyc.gov/site/planning/planning-level/nyc-population/census-summary-2000.page.

CHAPTER 51—WHATEVER HAPPENED TO OSAMA BIN LADEN?

140. "Pakistan: No Bin Laden Arrest Deal." *CNN*, September 6, 2006. http://www.cnn.com/2006/ WORLD/asiapcf/09/06/pakistan.afghanistan/.

141. Ross, "Hunt for Osama Bin Laden."

142. Cameron Stewart. "US Will Step up Hunt for Osama." *The Australian*, September 9, 2006, 1st ed., Local sec. http://search.ebscohost.com. ezproxy.shsu.edu/login.aspx?direct=true&db=n-5h&AN=2006090901001413923&site=ehost-live&-scope=site.

143. George W. Bush. "President Bush Holds Press Conference." The White House: President George W. Bush, March 13, 2002. https://georgewbush-whitehouse. archives.gov/news/releases/2002/03/20020313-8. html.

144. George W. Bush. "Remarks to the Military Officers Association." The American Presidency Project. UC-Santa Barbara, September 5, 2006. https://www. presidency.ucsb.edu/documents/remarks-the-mili-tary-officers-association-america.

145. "Advanced Search, 2001." Documents Archive Search | The American Presidency Project. UC-Santa Barbara. Accessed April 11, 2020. https:// www.presidency.ucsb.edu/advanced-search?field-key-words=bin+Laden&field-keywords2=&field-key-words3=&from%5Bdate%5D=09-11-2001&to%5B-date%5D=12-11-2001&person2=200299&categ-ory2%5B%5D=&items_per_page=100.

146. "Advanced Search, 2006." Documents Archive Search | The American Presidency Project. UC-Santa Barbara. Accessed April 11, 2020. https://www.presidency.ucsb.edu/advanced-search?field-keywords=bin+Laden&field-keywords2=&field-keywords3=&from%5Bdate%5D=08-16-2006&to%5Bdate%5D=11-16-2006&person2=200299&category2%5B%5D=&items_per_page=100.

147. Katie W. Couric and George W Bush. "President Bush, Part 2." Transcript. CBS News, September 6, 2006. https://www.cbsnews.com/news/transcript-president-bush-part-2/.

148. "Advanced Search, 2006-2007." Documents Archive Search | The American Presidency Project. UC-Santa Barbara. Accessed April 11, 2020. https://www.presidency.ucsb.edu/advanced-search?field-keywords=bin+Laden&field-keywords2=&field-keywords3=&from%5Bdate%5D=11-06-2006&to%5Bdate%5D=12-31-2006&person2=200299&category2%5B%5D=&items_per_page=100

149. "Democrats Retake Congress." CNN. Accessed January 10, 2021. https://www.cnn.com/ELECTION/2006/.

150. Nafeez Ahmed. "The Bin Laden Death Mythology." *Insurge Intelligence*. July 3, 2015. https://medium.com/insurge-intelligence/the-bin-laden-death-mythology-9a3776a6e3c3.

151. Seymour M. Hersh. *The Killing of Osama Bin Laden*. London: Verso, 2017, chap 1, Kindle.

152. Raelynne Hillhouse. The Spy Who Billed Me. Accessed February 2, 2020. https://thespywhobilledme. typepad.com/.

153. Raelynne Hillhouse. "Questions Raised by Real Story of How US Found Bin Laden." The Spy Who Billed Me, August 11, 2011. https://thespywhobilledme. typepad.com/the_spy_who_billed_me/2011/08/ index.html.

154. Ibid.

155. Hersh, "The Killing of..."

156. Ahmed, "The bin Laden Death..."

157. Ibid

158. Raelynne Hillhouse. "Bin Laden Turned in by Informant -- Courier Was Cover Story." The Spy Who Billed Me, August 7, 2011. https://thespywhobilledme. typepad.com/the_spy_who_billed_me/2011/08/ index.html.

159. Robert Booth. "The Killing of Osama Bin Laden: How the White House Changed Its Story." *The Guardian*, May 4, 2011. https://www.theguardian.com/ world/2011/may/04/osama-bin-laden-killing-us-sto- ry-change.

160. John Hudson. "The Six Biggest Discrepancies in Accounts of the Bin Laden Raid." *The Atlantic*, November 11, 2011. https://www.theatlantic.com/international/archive/2011/11/six-biggest-discrepancies-accounts-bin-laden-raid/335825/ .

161. Mark Landler and Mark Mazzetti. "Account Tells of One-Sided Battle in bin Laden Raid." *The New York Times*, May 4, 2011. https://www.nytimes.com/2011/05/05/us/politics/05binladen.html?_r=0.

162. Amelia Hill. "Osama Bin Laden Corpse Photo Is Fake." *The Guardian*, May 2, 2011. https://www.theguardian.com/world/2011/may/02/osama-bin-laden-photo-fake.

163. "Judicial Watch Statement on Federal Court Decision Blocking Public Access to Bin Laden Death Photos and Videos." *Judicial Watch*, April 27, 2012. https://www.judicialwatch.org/press-releases/judicial-watch-statement-on-federal-court-decision-blocking-public-access-to-bin-laden-death-photos-and-videos/.

164. Richard Lardner. "'Adm. William McRaven Shields Files About Raid On Osama Bin Laden's Hideout From The Public." The Huffington Post. Associated Press. July 8, 2013. https://web.archive.org/web/20130709083819/http://www.huffingtonpost.com/2013/07/08/bin-laden-raid-files-hidden_n_3559948.html

TIMELINE

165. Darklight12, "Osama Bin Laden Arrested... Page 22"

166. "Pakistan: No Bin Laden Arrest Deal."

167. Ross, "Hunt for Osama Bin Laden."

168. Stewart, "US Will Step up Hunt for Osama."

169. Couric and Bush, President Bush, Part 2."

170. "Advanced Search, 2006."

171. Ibid.

172. "Advanced Search 2006-2007."

173. Hersh, "The Killing of..."

174. Hillhouse, "Questions Raised..."
175. Hillhouse, "Bin Laden Turned in by..."

CHAPTER 52—A GREAT STORY

176. George W. Bush. "Remarks on the War on Terror." Remarks on the War on Terror | The American Presidency Project. September 06, 2006. Accessed July 07, 2020. https://www.presidency.ucsb.edu/documents/remarks-the-war-terror.

177. Adam Aigner-Treworgy, John Helton, Ed Hornick, and Gabriella Schwarz. "Bush on Water-

boarding: 'Damn Right'." CNN. November 05, 2010. Accessed July 07, 2020. http://www.cnn.com/2010/ POLITICS/11/05/bush.book/index.html.

ABOUT THE AUTHOR

As of publication, Barbara Janik still lives in her rural home with her partner and black cat. Her children, who are now adults, are not far away. She spends her days writing, running a small Amazon reselling business, and obsessively Tweeting. In her spare time, she plays Dungeons and Dragons and other nerdy games.

Made in the USA
Middletown, DE
27 May 2021